IBM SPSS Modeler Cookbook

Over 60 practical recipes to achieve better results using the experts' methods for data mining

Keith McCormick

Dean Abbott

Meta S. Brown

Tom Khabaza

Scott R. Mutchler

BIRMINGHAM - MUMBAI

IBM SPSS Modeler Cookbook

First published: October 2013

Production Reference: 1211013

Published by Packt Publishing Ltd.

Livery Place
35 Livery Street
Birmingham B3 2PB, UK.

ISBN 978-1-84968-546-7

www.packtpub.com

Cover Image by Colin Shearer (shearer@uk.ibm.com)

Credits

Authors
Keith McCormick
Dean Abbott
Meta S. Brown
Tom Khabaza
Scott R. Mutchler

Reviewers
Matthew Brooks
Fabrice Leroy
Robert Nisbet
David Young Oh
Jesus Salcedo
Terry Taerum

Acquisition Editor
Edward Gordon

Lead Technical Editor
Arun Nadar

Copy Editor
Gladson Monteiro

Technical Editors
Tanvi Bhatt
Jalasha D'costa
Mrunmayee Patil
Shiny Poojary
Siddhi Rane

Project Coordinator
Shiksha Chaturvedi

Proofreader
Stephen Copestake

Indexer
Priya Subramani

Production Coordinator
Adonia Jones

Cover Work
Adonia Jones

Foreword

Our company, ISL was a provider of Artificial Intelligence tools and technology to organizations developing advanced software solutions. By 1992, what had started as a casual interest from our clients in applying some of our tools—the machine learning modules—to their historic data had evolved into a promising practice in what was to become known as data mining. This was developing into a nice line of business for us, but was frustrating in a couple of ways:

First, we'd always intended that ISL should be a software supplier. Yet here we were, because of the complexity of the technologies involved, providing data mining on a consulting services basis.

Secondly, we were finding that data mining projects involved a lot of hard work, and that most of that work was boring. Unearthing significant patterns and delivering accurate predictions... that part was fun. But most of our effort went on mundane tasks such as manipulating data into the formats required by the various modules and algorithms we applied.

So we built Clementine—to make our job easier and allow us to focus on the interesting parts of projects, and to give us a tool we could provide to our clients. When the first prototypes were ready, we tested them by using them to re-run projects we'd previously executed manually. We found work that had previously taken several weeks was now reduced to under an hour; we'd obviously got something right.

As the embryonic data mining market grew, so did our business. We saw other vendors, with deeper pockets and vastly more resources than little ISL, introduce data mining tools, some of which tried to emulate the visual style of the Clementine's user interface. We were relieved when, as the inevitable shoot-outs took place, we found time and time again evaluators reporting that our product had a clear edge, both in terms of productivity and the problem-solving power it gave to analysts.

On reflection, the main reasons for our success were that we got a number of crucial things right:

Clementine's design and implementation, from the ground up, was object-oriented. Our visual programming model was consistent and "pure"; learn the basics, and everything is done in the same way.

We stuck to a guiding principle of, wherever possible, insulating the user from technology details. This didn't mean we made it for dummies; rather, we ensured that default configurations were as sensible as possible (and in places, truly smart—we weren't AI specialists for nothing), and that expert options such as advanced parameter settings were accessible without having to drop below the visual programming level.

We made an important design decision that predictive models should have the same status within the visual workflow as other tools, and that their outputs should be treated as first-order data. This sounds like a simple point, but the repercussions are enormous. Want more than the basic analysis of your model's performance? No problem—run its output through any of the tools in the workbench. Curious to know what might be going on inside your neural network? Use rule induction to tell you how combinations of inputs map onto output values. Want to have multiple models vote? Easy. Want to combine them in more complex ways? Just feed their inputs, along with any data you like, into a supermodel that can decide how best to combine their predictions.

The first two give productivity, plus the ability to raise your eyes from the technical details, think about the process of analysis at a higher level, and stay focused on each project's business objectives. Add the third, and you can experiment with novel and creative approaches that previously just weren't feasible to attempt.

So, 20 years on, what do I feel about Clementine/Modeler? A certain pride, of course, that the product our small team built remains a market leader. But mainly, over the years, awe at what I've seen people achieve with it: not just organizations who have made millions (sometimes, even billions) in returns from their data mining projects, but those who've done things that genuinely make the world a better place; from hospitals and medical researchers discovering new ways to diagnose and treat pediatric cancer, to police forces dynamically anticipating levels of crime risk around their cities and deploying their forces accordingly, with the deterrent effect reducing rates of murder and violent crime by tens of percent. And also, a humble appreciation for what I've learned over the years from users who took what we'd created—a workbench and set of tools—and developed, refined, and applied powerful approaches and techniques we'd never thought of.

The authors of this book are among the very best of these exponents, gurus who, in their brilliant and imaginative use of the tool, have pushed back the boundaries of applied analytics. By reading this book, you are learning from practitioners who have helped define the state of the art.

When Keith McCormick approached me about writing this foreword, he suggested I might like to take a "then" and "now" perspective. This is certainly an interesting "now" in our industry. The advent of Big Data—huge volumes of data, of many varieties and varying veracity, available to support decision making at high velocity—presents unprecedented opportunities for organizations to use predictive analytics to gain value. There is a danger, though, that some of the hype around this will confuse potential adopters and confound their efforts to derive value for their business. One common misconception is that you just get all data you can together, and then poke around in the hope of finding something valuable. This approach—tell me something interesting in this data—was what we always considered "the data mining question from hell", and is very unlikely to result in real, quantifiable benefit. Data mining is first and foremost a business activity, and needs to be focused on clear business objectives and goals, hence the crucial business understanding phase in CRISP-DM that starts every data mining project.

Yet more disturbing is the positioning of Big Data analytics as something that can only be done by a new breed of specialist: the "data scientist". Having dedicated experts drive projects isn't in itself problematic—it has always been the case that the majority of predictive analytics projects are led by skilled analytical specialists—but what is worrying is the set of skills being portrayed as core to Big Data projects. There is a common misapprehension that analytics projects can only be executed by geeks who are expert in the technical details of algorithms and who do their job by writing screeds of R code (with this rare expertise, of course, justifying immense salaries).

By analogy, imagine you're looking to have a new opera house built for your city. Certainly, you have to be sure that it won't collapse, but does that mean you hand the project to whoever has the greatest knowledge of the mathematics and algorithms around material stress and load bearing? Of course not. You want an architect who will consider the project holistically, and deliver a building that is aesthetically stunning, has acoustic properties that fit its purpose, is built in an environmentally sound manner, and so on. Of course, you want it to stay up, but applying the specialist algorithms to establish its structural rigor is something you can assume will be done by the tools (or perhaps, specialist sub-contractors) the architect employs.

Back to analytics: 20 years ago, we moved on from manually, programmatically applying the technology, to using tools that boosted the analyst's productivity and kept their focus on how best to achieve the desired business results. With the technology to support Big Data now able to fit behind a workbench like Modeler, you can deliver first class results without having to revert to the analytical equivalent of chipping tools from lumps of flint. From this book, you can learn to be the right sort of data scientist!

Finally, for lovers of trivia: "Clementine" is not an acronym; it's the name of the miner's daughter with big feet immortalized in the eponymous American folk song. (It was my boss and mentor, Alan Montgomery, who started singing that one evening as we worked on the proposal for a yet-to-be-named data mining tool, and we decided it would do for the name of the prototype until we came up with something more sensible!) The first lines of code for Clementine were written on New Year's Eve 1992, at my parents' house, on a DECSstation 3100 I'd taken home for the holidays. (They were for the tabular display that originally provided the output for the Table node and Distribution node, as well as the editing dialogs for the Filter and Type nodes.) And yes, I was paged immediately before the press launch in June 1994 to be told my wife had just gone into labor, but she had already checked with the doctor that there was time for me to see the event through before hurrying to the hospital! (But the story that I then suggested the name "Clementine" for my daughter is a myth.)

Colin Shearer

Co-founder of Integral Solutions Ltd.,
Creator of Clementine/Modeler

About the Authors

Keith McCormick is the Vice President and General Manager of QueBIT Consulting's Advanced Analytics team. He brings a wealth of consulting/training experience in statistics, predictive modeling and analytics, and data mining. For many years, he has worked in the SPSS community, first as an External Trainer and Consultant for SPSS Inc., then in a similar role with IBM, and now in his role with an award winning IBM partner. He possesses a BS in Computer Science and Psychology from Worcester Polytechnic Institute.

He has been using Stats software tools since the early 90s, and has been training since 1997. He has been doing data mining and using IBM SPSS Modeler since its arrival in North America in the late 90s. He is an expert in IBM's SPSS software suite including IBM SPSS Statistics, IBM SPSS Modeler (formally Clementine), AMOS, Text Mining, and Classification Trees. He is active as a moderator and participant in statistics groups online including LinkedIn's Statistics and Analytics Consultants Group. He also blogs and reviews related books at `KeithMcCormick.com`. He enjoys hiking in out of the way places, finding unusual souvenirs while traveling overseas, exotic foods, and old books.

I would like to thank my coauthors for stealing time from their busy careers to meet a need that the SPSS community had for some time. It wouldn't have been the same without all five of us and our diverse experiences.

Thanks to *Colin* for his humor, unique perspective, and generous comments. Thanks also for our cover photo!

Thanks to *Jesus* and *Terry* for going above and beyond in their role as reviewers. Both were guest chefs, contributing last minute recipes after the initial reviews came back. Without Jesus' considerable editing skills this would not have been a 2013 release.

Thanks finally to *David Oh*, whose prior publication experience, persistence, and energy kept the project going even when no one else was able to keep other responsibilities at bay.

Dean Abbott is the President of Abbott Analytics, Inc. in San Diego, California. He has over two decades experience in applying advanced data mining, data preparation, and data visualization methods in real-world data intensive problems, including fraud detection, customer acquisition and retention, digital behavior for web applications and mobile, customer lifetime value, survey analysis, donation solicitation and planned giving. He has developed, coded, and evaluated algorithms for use in commercial data mining and pattern recognition products, including polynomial networks, neural networks, radial basis functions, and clustering algorithms for multiple software vendors.

He is a seasoned instructor, having taught a wide range of data mining tutorials and seminars to thousands of attendees, including PAW, KDD, INFORMS, DAMA, AAAI, and IEEE conferences. He is the instructor of well-regarded data mining courses, explaining concepts in language readily understood by a wide range of audiences, including analytics novices, data analysts, statisticians, and business professionals. He also has taught both applied and hands-on data mining courses for major software vendors, including IBM SPSS Modeler, Statsoft STATISTICA, Salford System SPM, SAS Enterprise Miner, IBM PredictiveInsight, Tibco Spotfire Miner, KNIME, RapidMiner, and Megaputer Polyanalyst.

Meta S. Brown helps organizations use practical data analysis to solve everyday business problems. A hands-on analyst who has tackled projects with up to $900 million at stake, she is a recognized expert in cutting-edge business analytics.

She is devoted to educating the business community on effective use of statistics, data mining, and text mining. A sought-after analytics speaker, she has conducted over 4000 hours of seminars, attracting audiences across North America, Europe, and South America. Her articles appear frequently on All Analytics, Smart Data Collective, and other publications. She is also co-author of *Big Data, Mining and Analytics: Key Components for Strategic Decisions* (forthcoming from CRC Press, Editor: Stephan Kudyba).

She holds a Master of Science in Nuclear Engineering from the Massachusetts Institute of Technology, a Bachelor of Science in Mathematics from Rutgers University, and professional certifications from the American Society for Quality and National Association for Healthcare Quality. She has served on the faculties of Roosevelt University and National-Louis University.

Many thanks to my patient and supportive family.

Tom Khabaza is an independent consultant in predictive analytics and data mining, and the Founding Chairman of the Society of Data Miners. He is a data mining veteran of over 20 years and many industries and applications. He has helped to create the IBM SPSS Modeler (Clementine) data mining workbench and the industry standard CRISP-DM methodology, and led the first integrations of data mining and text mining. His recent thought leadership includes the *9 Laws of Data Mining*.

I would like to thank *Colin Shearer*, *David Watkins*, *Alan Montgomery*, and *Aaron Sloman*, without all of whom there would have been nothing to write about.

Scott R. Mutchler is the Vice President of Advanced Analytics Services at QueBIT Consulting LLC. He had spent the first 17 years of his career building enterprise solutions as a DBA, software developer, and enterprise architect. When Scott discovered his true passion was for advanced analytics, he moved into advanced analytics leadership roles where he was able to drive millions of dollars in incremental revenues and cost savings through the application of advanced analytics to most challenging business problems. His strong IT background turned out to be a huge asset in building integrated advanced analytics solutions.

Recently, he was the Predictive Analytics Worldwide Industrial Sector Lead for IBM. In this role, he worked with IBM SPSS clients worldwide. He architected advanced analytic solutions for clients in some of the world's largest retailers and manufacturers.

He received his Masters from Virginia Tech in Geology. He stays in Colorado and enjoys an outdoor lifestyle, playing guitar, and travelling.

About the Reviewers

Matthew Brooks has spent 11 years in the Navy during which he became a SEAL. He left the Navy in 2003 and began working in the IT industry. He worked with the Center for SEAL and SWCC as the Operations Research Assistant, where he provided analytical support for many different career related issues for active duty SEALs and **Special Warfare Combatant Crewmen** (**SWCC**). He worked on different problems that range from simulating effects of policy on manpower distribution, assessment and selection of SEAL candidates, analyzing contributors to pressure on the force, and enlisted advancement by developing and maintaining the **Alternative Final Multiple Score** (**AFMS**) for SEALs and SWCCs.

Fabrice Leroy is a Principal Consultant in IBM Business Analytics Software Group. He has over 15 years of international experience applying advanced analytics to help organizations to solve their business problems.

He is a specialist in designing and implementing large scale data mining applications; he is also recognized as a world leading expert with IBM SPSS Modeler.

Robert Nisbet has a Ph.D. and is a consulting data scientist to IBM and Aviana Global, where he focuses on CRM modeling solution development. He recently built a churn model for a major bank in Texas, using the IBM Modeler package. He was trained initially in Ecology and Ecosystems Analysis. He has over 30 years of experience in analysis and modeling of complex ecosystems in Academia (UC, Santa Barbara) and in many large companies. He led the team at NCR Corporation in the development of the first commercial data mining solutions for telecommunications (Churn and Propensity to Buy). Currently, he is an instructor in the UC Irvine Predictive Analytics Certification Program.

He is the lead author of *Handbook of Statistical Analysis and Data Mining Applications* (Academic Press, 2009), and a co-author of *Practical Text Mining* (Academic Press, 2012). He serves as a general editor for a new book, *Predictive Analytics in Medicine and Healthcare*, under contract with Academic Press (Elsevier Publ.) for publication in 2014. His next book will cover the subject of Effective Data Preparation, coauthored with Keith McCormick.

David Young Oh is a practicing clinical mental health counselor with a continued interest in psychological research and statistics. His previous research on moral engagement and international perspectives on peace and war has resulted in several books and journal publications. Most recently, he has worked on *International Handbook of War, Torture and Terrorism* and *State Violence and the Right to Peace: An International Survey of the Views of Ordinary People*. He has completed his clinical internship and MS in Mental Health Counseling with the Johns Hopkins University and his BA and MA at Boston University. He currently lives and practices in Raleigh-Durham, North Carolina with his partner, dog, and chickens.

Jesus Salcedo is the QueBIT's Director of Advanced Analytics Training. Previously, he worked for IBM SPSS as the SPSS Curriculum Team Lead and as a Senior Education Specialist. Jesus was a college professor and worked at Montefiore Medical Center within the department of psychology. He has been using SPSS products for two decades. He has written numerous SPSS training courses and has trained thousands of users in both SPSS Statistics and SPSS Modeler. He received a Ph.D. in Psychometrics from Fordham University.

Terry Taerum is an analyst who has been fortunate to be in the Intel's data mining business for more than 25 years. The focus has to be on growing a profitable and sustainable network of information and idea exchange. To do this, we need good data, great analytical tools, a deep understanding of the subject matter, and a long-term commitment to continuously improve. No one can do this all on their own and it requires team effort and a partnership between all vested parties.

His college years at the University of Calgary, where he earned a doctorate, were spent primarily working on a timeshare PDP/8 and earning money as a Statistical Consultant. Inspite of changes in the speed of technology, the problems remain much the same except on a much grander scale. The problem continues to be finding better ways to maximize profit, whether measured as dollars, bushels of wheat, or happiness. The solutions are, however, much more interesting these days—pulling in resources from all around the world, using recording and digitizing processes rarely imagined in the past, and creating new and exciting means to increase all kinds of return on investment.

More recently, he has been part of larger teams prescribing actions intended to increase sales, identifying people most likely involved in fraud or transporting illegal property, providing post hoc analysis of merchandising efforts, and modeling early detection of faults in the manufacturing of electronic goods and other processes. He was one of the first users of IBM/SPSS Modeler in North America (13 years ago, previously called Clementine), when it was best known for its use of neural net. In all of these endeavors, the focus has been on growing the network of information in order to make the business processes sustainable and more profitable.

www.PacktPub.com

Support files, eBooks, discount offers, and more

You might want to visit www.PacktPub.com for support files and downloads related to your book.

Did you know that Packt offers eBook versions of every book published, with PDF and ePub files available? You can upgrade to the eBook version at www.PacktPub.com and as a print book customer, you are entitled to a discount on the eBook copy. Get in touch with us at service@packtpub.com for more details.

At www.PacktPub.com, you can also read a collection of free technical articles, sign up for a range of free newsletters and receive exclusive discounts and offers on Packt books and eBooks.

http://PacktLib.PacktPub.com

Do you need instant solutions to your IT questions? PacktLib is Packt's online digital book library. Here, you can access, read and search across Packt's entire library of books.

Why Subscribe?

- Fully searchable across every book published by Packt
- Copy and paste, print, and bookmark content
- On demand and accessible via web browser

Free Access for Packt account holders

If you have an account with Packt at www.PacktPub.com, you can use this to access PacktLib today and view nine entirely free books. Simply use your login credentials for immediate access.

Instant Updates on New Packt Books

Get notified! Find out when new books are published by following @PacktEnterprise on Twitter, or the *Packt Enterprise* Facebook page.

Table of Contents

Preface

IBM SPSS Modeler is the most comprehensive workbench-style data mining software package. Many of its individual modeling algorithms are available elsewhere, but Modeler has features that are helpful throughout all the phases of the independent, influential Cross Industry Standard Practice for Data Mining (CRISP-DM). Considered the de facto standard, it provides a skeleton structure for the IBM SPSS Modeler Cookbook and the recipes in this book will help you maximize your use of Modeler's tools for ETL, data preparation, modeling, and deployment.

In this book, we will emphasize the CRISP-DM phases that you are likely to address working with Modeler. Other phases, while mentioned, will not be the focus. For instance, the critical business understanding phase is primarily not a software phase. A rich discussion of this phase is included in the *Appendix, Business Understanding*. Also, the deployment and monitoring phases get a fraction of the attention that data preparation and modeling get because the former are phases whereas Modeler is the critical component.

These recipes will address:

- Nonobvious applications of the basics
- Tricky operations, work-arounds, and nondocumented shortcuts
- Best practices for key operations as done by power users
- Operations that are not available through standard approaches, using scripting, in a chapter dedicated to Modeler scripting recipes

While it assumes it will provide you with the level of knowledge one would gain from an introductory course or by working with user's guides, it will take you well beyond that. It will be valuable from the first time you are the lead on a Modeler project but will offer much wisdom even if you are a veteran user. Each of the authors has a decade (or two, or more) of experience; collectively they cover the gamut of data mining practice in general, and specifically knowledge of Modeler.

What is CRISP-DM?

CRISP-DM is a tool that is a neutral and industry-nonspecific process model for navigating a data mining project life cycle. It consists of six phases, and within those phases, a total of 24 generic tasks. In the given table, one can see the phases as column headings, and the generic tasks in bold. It is the most widely used process model of its kind. This is especially true of users of Modeler since the software has historically made explicit references to CRISP-DM in the default structure of the project files, but the polls have shown that its popularity extends to many data miners. It was written in the 90s by a consortium of data miners from numerous companies. Its lead authors were from NCR, Daimler Chrysler, and ISL (later bought by SPSS).

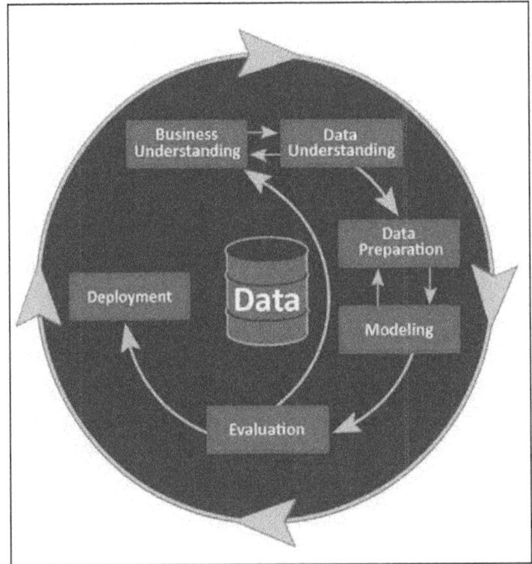

This book uses this process model to structure the book but does not address the CRISP-DM content directly. Since the CRISP-DM consortium is nonprofit, the original documents are widely available on the Web, and it would be helpful to read it entirely as part of one's data mining professional development. Naturally, as a cookbook written for users of Modeler, our focus will be on hands-on tasks.

Business understanding, while critical, is not conducive to a recipe-based format. It is such an important topic, which is why it is covered in *Appendix, Business Understanding*, in prose. Data preparation receives the most of our attention with four chapters. Modeling is covered, in depth, in its own chapter. Since evaluation and deployment often use Modeler in combination with other tools, we have included them in somewhat fewer recipes, but that does not diminish its importance. The final chapter, *Modeler Scripting*, is not named after a CRISP-DM phase or a task but is included at the end because it has the most advanced recipes.

Data mining is a business process

Data mining by discovery and interpretation of patterns in data is:

- The use of business knowledge
- To create new knowledge
- In natural or artificial form

The most important thing for you to know about data mining is that it is a way of using business knowledge.

The process of data mining uses business knowledge to create new knowledge, and this new knowledge may be in one of the two forms. The first form of new knowledge that data mining can create is "natural knowledge", that is, knowledge sometimes referred to as insight. The second form of new knowledge that data mining can create is "artificial knowledge", that is, knowledge in the form of a computer program, sometimes called a predictive model. It is widely recognized that data mining produces two kinds of results: insight and predictive models.

Both forms of new knowledge are created through a process of discovering and interpreting patterns in data. The most well-known type of data mining technology is called a data mining algorithm. This is a computer program that finds patterns in data and creates a generalized form of those patterns called a "predictive model". What makes these algorithms (and the models they create) useful is their interpretation in the light of business knowledge. The patterns that have been discovered may lead to new human knowledge, or insight, or they may be used to generate new information by using them as computer programs to make predictions. The new knowledge only makes sense in the context of business knowledge, and the predictions are only of value if they can be used (through business knowledge) to improve a business process.

Data mining is a business process, not a technical one. All data mining solutions start from business goals, find relevant data, and then proceed to find patterns in the data that can help to achieve the business goals. The data mining process is described well by the aforementioned CRISP-DM industry standard data mining methodology, but its character as a business process has been shaped by the data mining tools available. Specifically, the existence of data mining workbenches that can be used by business analysts means that data mining can be performed by someone with a great deal of business knowledge, rather than someone whose knowledge is mainly technical. This in turn means that the data mining process can take place within the context of ongoing business processes and need not be regarded as a separate technical development. This leads to a high degree of availability of business knowledge within the data mining process and magnifies the likely benefits to the business.

The IBM SPSS Modeler workbench

This book is about the data mining workbench variously known as Clementine, IBM SPSS Modeler. This and the other workbench-style data mining tools have played a crucial role in making data mining what it now is, that is, a business process (rather than a technical one). The importance of the workbench is twofold.

Firstly, the workbench plays down the technical side of data mining. It simplifies the use of technology through a user interface that allows the user almost always to ignore the deep technical details, whether this means the method of data access, the design of a graph, or the mechanism and tuning of data mining algorithms. Technical details are simplified, and where possible, universal default settings are used so that the users often need not see any options that reveal the underlying technology, let alone understand what they mean.

This is important because it allows business analysts to perform data mining—a business analyst is someone with expert business knowledge and general-purpose analytical knowledge. A business analyst need not have deep knowledge of data mining algorithms or mathematics, and it can even be a disadvantage to have this knowledge because technical details can distract from focusing on the business problem.

Secondly, the workbench records and highlights the way in which business knowledge has been used to analyze the data. This is why most data mining workbenches use a "visual workflow" approach; the workflow constitutes a record of the route from raw data to analysis, and it also makes it extremely easy to change this processing and re-use it in part or in full. Data mining is an interactive process of applying business and analytical knowledge to data, and the data mining workbench is designed to make this easy.

A brief history of the Clementine workbench

During the 1980s, the School of Cognitive and Computing Studies at the University of Sussex developed an Artificial Intelligence programming environment called Poplog. Used for teaching and research, Poplog was characterized by containing several different AI programming languages and many other AI-related packages, including machine-learning modules. From 1983, Poplog was marketed commercially by Systems Designers Limited (later SD-Scicon), and in 1989, a management buyout created a spin-off company called **Integral Solutions Ltd** (**ISL**) to market Poplog and related products. A stream of businesses developed within ISL, applying the machine-learning packages in Poplog to organizations' data, in order to understand and predict customer behavior.

In 1993, Colin Shearer (the then Development and Research Director at ISL) invented the Clementine data mining workbench, basing his designs around the data mining projects recently executed by the company and creating the first workbench modules using Poplog. ISL created a data mining division, led by Colin Shearer, to develop, productize, and market Clementine and its associated services; the initial members were Colin Shearer, Tom Khabaza, and David Watkins. This team used Poplog to develop the first version of Clementine, which was launched in June 1994.

Clementine Version 1 would be considered limited by today's standards; the only algorithms provided were decision trees and neural networks, and it had very limited access to databases. However, the fundamental design features of low technical burden on the user and a flexible visual record of the analysis were as much as they are today, and Clementine immediately attracted substantial commercial interest. New versions followed, approximately one major version per year, as shown in the table below. ISL was acquired by SPSS Inc. in December 1998, and SPSS Inc. was acquired by IBM in 2009.

Version	Major new features
1	Decision tree and neural network algorithms, limited database access, and Unix platforms only
2	New Kohonen network and linear regression algorithms, new web graph, improved data manipulation, and supernodes
3	ODBC database access, Unix, and Windows platforms
4	Association Rules and K-means clustering algorithms
5	Scripting, batch execution, external module interface, client-server architecture (Poplog client and C++ server), and the CRISP-DM project tool
6	Logistic regression algorithm, database pushback, and Clementine application templates
7	Java client including many new features, TwoStep clustering, and PCA/Factor analysis algorithms
8	Cluster browser and data audit
9	CHAID and Quest algorithms and interactive decision tree building
10	Anomaly detection and feature selection algorithms
11	Automated modeling, times series and decision list algorithms, and partial automation of data preparation
12	SVM, Bayesian and Cox regression algorithms, RFM, and variable importance charts
13	Automated clustering and data preparation, nearest neighbor algorithm, interactive rule building

Version	Major new features
14	Boosting and bagging, ensemble browsing, XML data
15	Entity analytics social network analysis, GLMM algorithm

Version 13 was renamed as PASW Modeler, and Version 14 as IBM SPSS Modeler. The selection of major new features described earlier is very subjective; every new version of Clementine included a large number of enhancements and new features. In particular, data manipulation, data access and export, visualization, and the user interface received a great deal of attention throughout. Perhaps the most significant new release was Version 7, where the Clementine client was completely rewritten in Java; this was designed by Sheri Gilley and Julian Clinton, and contained a large number of new features while retaining the essential character of the software. Another very important feature of Clementine from Version 6 onwards was *database pushback*, the ability to translate Clementine operations into SQL so that they could be executed directly by a database engine without extracting the data first; this was primarily the work of Niall McCarroll and Rob Duncan, and it gave Clementine an unusual degree of scalability compared to other data mining software.

In 1996, ISL collaborated with Daimler-Benz, NCR Teradata, and OHRA to form the "CRISP-DM" consortium, partly funded by a European Union R&D grant in order to create a new data mining methodology, CRISP-DM. The consortium consulted many organizations through its Special Interest Group and released CRISP-DM Version 1.0 in 1999. CRISP-DM has been integrated into the workbench since that time and has been very widely used, sufficiently to justify calling it the industry standard.

The core Clementine analytics are designed to handle structured data—numeric, coded, and string data of the sort typically found in relational databases. However, in Clementine Version 4, a prototype text mining module was produced in collaboration with Brighton University, although not released as a commercial product. In 2002, SPSS acquired LexiQuest, a text mining company, and integrated the LexiQuest text mining technology into a product called Text Mining for Clementine, an add-on module for Version 7. Text mining is accomplished in the workbench by extracting structured data from unstructured (free text) data, and then using the standard features of the workbench to analyze this.

Historical introduction to scripting

By the time Clementine Version 4 was released in 1997, the workbench had gained substantial market traction. Its revolutionary visual programming interface had enabled a more business-focused approach to analytics than ever before—all the major families of algorithms were represented in an easy-to-use form, ODBC had enabled integration with a comprehensive range of data, and commercial partners were busy rebadging Clementine to reach a wider audience through new market channels.

The workbench lacked one major kind of functionality, that of automation, to enable the embedding of data mining within other applications. It was therefore decided that automation would form the centre piece of Version 5, and it would be provided by two major features: batch mode and scripting. Batch mode enabled running the workbench without the user interface so that streams could be run in the background, could be scheduled to run at a given time or at regular intervals, and could be run as part of a larger application. Scripting enabled the user to gain automated control of stream execution, even without the user being present; this was also a prerequisite for any complex operation executed in batch mode.

The motivation behind scripting was to provide a number of capabilities:

- Gain control of the order of stream execution where this matters, that is, when using the Set Globals node
- Automate repetitive processes, for example, cross-validation or the exploration of many different sets of fields or options
- Remove the need for user intervention so that streams could run in the background
- Manipulate complex streams, for example, if the need arose to create 1000 different Derive nodes

These motives led to an underlying philosophy of scripting, that is, scripts replace the user, not the stream. This means that the operations of scripting should be at the same level as the actions of the user, that is, they would create nodes and link them, control their settings, execute streams, and save streams and models. Scripts would not be used to implement data manipulation or algorithms directly; these would remain in the domain of the stream itself. This reflects a fundamental fact about technologies—they are defined by what they cannot do as by what they can. These principles are not inflexible, for example, cross-validation might be considered as part of an algorithm but was one of the first scripts to be written; however, they guided the design of the scripting language. A consequence of this philosophy was that there could be no interaction between script and data; the restriction was lifted only later with the introduction of access to output objects.

A number of factors influenced the design of the scripting language in addition to the above philosophy:

- In line with the orientation towards nontechnical users, the language should be simple
- The timescale for implementation was short, so the language should be easy to implement
- The language should be familiar, and so should use existing programming concepts and constructs, and not attempt to introduce new ones

These philosophical and practical constraints led to a programming language influenced by BASIC, with structured features taken from POP-11 and an object-oriented approach to nodes taken from Smalltalk and its descendants.

What this book covers

Chapter 1, Data Understanding, provides recipes related to the second phase of CRISP-DM with a focus on exploring the data and data quality. These are recipes that you can apply to data as soon as you acquire the data. Naturally, some of these recipes are also among the more basic, but as always, we seek out the nonobvious tips and tricks that will make this initial assessment of your data efficient.

Chapter 2, Data Preparation – Select, covers just the first task of the data preparation phase. Data preparation is notoriously time-consuming and is incredibly rich in its potential for time-saving recipes. The cookbook will have a total of four chapters on data preparation. The selection of which data rows and which data columns to analyze can be tricky, but it sets the stage for everything that follows.

Chapter 3, Data Preparation – Clean, covers the challenges the data miners face and is dedicated to just the second generic task of the data preparation phase. Sometimes new data miners assume that if a data warehouse is being used, data cleaning has been largely done up front. Veteran data miners know that there is usually a great deal left to do since data has to be prepared for a particular use to answer a specific business question. A couple of the recipes will be basic, but the rest will be quite complex, designed to tackle some of the data miners' more difficult cleaning challenges.

Chapter 4, Data Preparation – Construct, covers the third generic task of the data preparation phase. Many data miners find that there are many more constructed variables in the final model than variables that were used in their original form, as found in the original data source. Common methods can be as straightforward as ratios of part to whole, or deltas of last month from average month, and so on. However, the chapter won't stop there. It will provide examples performing larger scale variable construction.

Chapter 5, Data Preparation – Integrate and Format, covers the fourth and fifth generic tasks of the data preparation phase. Integrating includes actions in Modeler, which further include the Merge, Append, and Aggregate nodes. Formatting is often simply defined as reconfiguring data to meet software needs, in this instance, Modeler.

Chapter 6, Selecting and Building a Model, explains what many novice data miners see as their greatest challenge, that is, mastering data mining algorithms. Data mining, however, is neither really all about that, nor is this chapter. A discussion of algorithms can easily fill a book, and a quick search will reveal that it has done so many times. Here we'll address nonobvious tricks to make your modeling time more effective and efficient.

Chapter 7, Modeling – Assessment, Evaluation, Deployment, and Monitoring, covers the terribly important topics, especially deployment, because they don't get as much attention as they deserve. Here too, deployment deserves more attention, but this cookbook's attention is clearly and fully focused on IBM SPSS Modeler and not on its sibling products such as IBM Decision Management or IBM Collaboration and Deployment Services. Their proper use, or some alternative, is part of the complete narrative but beyond the scope of this book. So, ultimately two CRISP-DM phases and a portion of a third phase are addressed in one chapter, albeit with a large number of powerful recipes.

Chapter 8, CLEM Scripting, departs from the CRISP-DM format and focuses instead on a particular aspect of the interface, scripting. This chapter is the final chapter with advanced concepts, but it is still written with the intermediate user in mind.

Appendix, Business Understanding, covers a special section and is an essay-format discussion of the first phase and arguably the most critical phrase of CRISP-DM. *Tom Khabaza*, *Meta Brown*, *Dean Abbott*, and *Keith McCormick* each contribute an essay, collectively discussing all four subtasks.

Who this book is for

This book envisions that you are a regular user of IBM SPSS Modeler, albeit perhaps on your first serious project. It assumes that you have taken an introductory course or have equivalent preparation. IBM's Modeler certification would be some indication of this, but the certification focuses on software operations alone and does not address the general data mining theory. Some familiarity with that would be of considerable assistance in putting these recipes into context. All the readers would benefit from a careful review of the CRISP-DM document, which is readily available on the Internet.

This book also assumes that you are using IBM SPSS Modeler for data mining and are interested in all of the software-related phases of CRISP-DM. This premise might seem strange, but since Modeler combines powerful ETL capability with advanced modeling algorithms, it is true that some Modeler uses the software primarily for ETL capabilities alone. This book roughly spends equal time on both. One of the advantages of the cookbook format, however, is that the reader is invited to skip around, reading out of order, reading some chapters and not others, reading only some of the recipes within chapters, gleaning only what is needed at the moment.

It does not assume that the reader possesses knowledge of SQL. Such knowledge will not be emphasized as Modeler considerably reduces the need for knowing SQL, although many data miners have this skill. This book does not assume knowledge of statistical theory. Such knowledge is always useful to the data miner, but the recipes in this book neither require this knowledge nor does the book assume prior knowledge of data mining algorithms. The recipes simply do not dive deep enough into this aspect of the topic to require it.

Conventions

In this book, you will find a number of styles of text that distinguish between different kinds of information. Here are some examples of these styles, and an explanation of their meaning.

Code words in text, database table names, folder names, filenames, file extensions, pathnames, dummy URLs, user input, and Twitter handles are shown as follows: " This recipe uses the `cup98lrn reduced vars2.txt` data set."

A block of code is set as follows:

```
if length(s) < 3 then '0'
elseif member(s(3),[B P F V]) and c2 /= '1' then '1'
elseif member(s(3),[C S K G J Q X Z]) and c2 /= '2' then '2'
elseif member(s(3),[D T]) and c2 /= '3' then '3'
elseif s(3) = 'L' and c2 /= '4' then '4'
elseif member(s(3),[M N]) and c2 /= '5' then '5'
elseif s(3) = 'R' and c2 /= '6' then '6'
else '' endif
```

New terms and **important words** are shown in bold. Words that you see on the screen, in menus or dialog boxes for example, appear in the text like this: "clicking the **Next** button moves you to the next screen".

Warnings or important notes appear in a box like this.

Tips and tricks appear like this.

Reader feedback

Feedback from our readers is always welcome. Let us know what you think about this book—what you liked or may have disliked. Reader feedback is important for us to develop titles that you really get the most out of.

To send us general feedback, simply send an e-mail to `feedback@packtpub.com`, and mention the book title via the subject of your message.

If there is a topic that you have expertise in and you are interested in either writing or contributing to a book, see our author guide on `www.packtpub.com/authors`.

Customer support

Now that you are the proud owner of a Packt book, we have a number of things to help you to get the most from your purchase.

Downloading the example code

You can download the example code files for all Packt books you have purchased from your account at `http://www.packtpub.com`. If you purchased this book elsewhere, you can visit `http://www.packtpub.com/support` and register to have the files e-mailed directly to you.

Errata

Although we have taken every care to ensure the accuracy of our content, mistakes do happen. If you find a mistake in one of our books—maybe a mistake in the text or the code—we would be grateful if you would report this to us. By doing so, you can save other readers from frustration and help us improve subsequent versions of this book. If you find any errata, please report them by visiting `http://www.packtpub.com/submit-errata`, selecting your book, clicking on the **errata submission form** link, and entering the details of your errata. Once your errata are verified, your submission will be accepted and the errata will be uploaded on our website, or added to any list of existing errata, under the Errata section of that title. Any existing errata can be viewed by selecting your title from `http://www.packtpub.com/support`.

Piracy

Piracy of copyright material on the Internet is an ongoing problem across all media. At Packt, we take the protection of our copyright and licenses very seriously. If you come across any illegal copies of our works, in any form, on the Internet, please provide us with the location address or website name immediately so that we can pursue a remedy.

Please contact us at `copyright@packtpub.com` with a link to the suspected pirated material.

We appreciate your help in protecting our authors, and our ability to bring you valuable content.

Questions

You can contact us at `questions@packtpub.com` if you are having a problem with any aspect of the book, and we will do our best to address it.

1

Data Understanding

In this chapter, we will cover:

- Using an empty aggregate to evaluate sample size
- Evaluating the need to sample from the initial data
- Using CHAID stumps when interviewing an SME
- Using a single cluster K-means as an alternative to anomaly detection
- Using an @NULL multiple Derive to explore missing data
- Creating an Outliers report to give to SMEs
- Detecting potential model instability early using the Partition node and Feature Selection node

Introduction

This opening chapter is regarding data understanding, but this phase is not the first phase of CRISP-DM. Business understanding is a critical phase. Some would argue, including the authors of this book, that business understanding is the phase in most need of more attention by new data miners. It is certainly a candidate for the phase that is most rushed, albeit rushed at the peril of the data mining project. However, since this book is focused on specific software tasks and recipes, and since business understanding is conducted in the meeting room, not alone at one's laptop, our discussion of this phase is placed in a special section of the book. If you are new to data mining please do read the business understanding section first (refer *Appendix*, *Business Understanding*), and consider reading the CRISP-DM document in its entirety as it will place our recipes in a broader context.

The CRISP-DM document covers the initial data collection and proceeds with activities in order to get familiar with the data, to identify data quality problems, to discover first insights into the data, or to detect interesting subsets to form hypotheses for hidden information.

CRISP-DM lists the following tasks as a part of the data understanding phase:

- Collect the data
- Describe the data
- Explore the data
- Data quality

In this chapter we will introduce some of the IBM SPSS Modeler nodes associated with these tasks as well as nodes that one might associate with other phases, but that can prove useful during data understanding. Since the recipes are orientated around software tasks, there is a particular focus on exploring and data quality. Many of these recipes could be done immediately after accessing your data for the first time. Some of the hard work that follows will be inspired by what you uncover using these recipes.

The very first task you will need to do when data mining is to determine the size and nature of the data subset that you will be working with. This might involve sampling or balancing (a special kind of sampling) or both, but should always be thoughtful. Why sample? When you have plentiful data, a powerful computer and equally powerful software, why not use every bit of that?

There was a time when one of the most popular concepts in data mining was to put an end to sampling. And this was not without reason. If the objective of data mining was to give business people the power to make discoveries from data independently, then it made sense to reduce the number of steps in any way possible. As computers and computer memory became less expensive, it seemed that sampling was a waste of time. And then, there was the idea of finding a valuable and elusive bit of information in a mass of data. This image was so powerful that it inspired the name for a whole field of study—data mining. To eliminate any data from the working dataset was to risk losing treasured insights.

Times change, and so have the attitudes of the data mining community. For one thing, many of today's data miners began in more traditional data analyst roles, and were familiar with classical statistics before they entered data mining. These data miners don't want to be without the full set of methods that they have used earlier in their careers. They expect their data mining tools to include statistical analysis capability, and sampling is central to classical statistical analysis. Business users may not have driven the shift toward sampling in data mining, but they have not stood in the way. Perhaps this is because many business people had some exposure to statistical analysis in school, or because the idea of sampling simply appeals to their common sense. Today, in stark contrast to some discussions of *Big Data*, sampling is a routine part of data mining. We will address related issues in our first two recipes.

Data understanding often involves close collaboration with others. This point might be forgotten in skimming this list of recipes since most of them could be done by a solitary analyst. The *Using CHAID stumps when interviewing an SME* recipe, underscores the importance of collaboration. Note that CHAID is used here to serve data exploration, not modeling. A primary goal of this phase is to uncover facts that need to be discussed with others, whether they be analyst colleagues, **Subject Matter Experts (SMEs)**, IT support, or management.

There is always the possibility (some veterans might suggest that it is a near certainty) that you will have to circle back to business understanding to address new discoveries that you make when you actively start looking at data. Many of the other recipes in this chapter might also yield discoveries of this kind. Some time ago, *Dean Abbott* wrote a blog post on this subject entitled *Doing Data Mining Out of Order*:

> *Data mining often requires more creativity and "art" to re-work the data than we would like, ... but unfortunately data doesn't always cooperate in this way, and we therefore need to adapt to the specific data problems so that the data is better prepared.*
>
> *In this project, we jumped from Business Understanding and the beginnings of Data Understanding straight to Modeling. I think in this case, I would call it "modeling" (small 'm') because we weren't building models to predict risk, but rather to understand the target variable better. We were not sure exactly how clean the data was to begin with, especially the definition of the target variable, because no one had ever looked at the data in aggregate before, only on a single customer -by-customer basis. By building models, and seeing some fields that predict the target variable 'too well', we have been able to identify historic data inconsistencies and miscoding.*

One could argue this modeling with a small "m" should always be part of data understanding. The *Using CHAID stumps when interviewing an SME* recipe, explores how to model efficiently. CHAID is a good method to explore data. It builds wide trees that are easy for most to read, and they treat missing data as a separate category that invites a lot of discussion about the missing values. The idea of a stump is simply a tree that has been grown only to the first branch. As we shall see, it is a good idea to grow a decision stump for the top 10 inputs as well as any SME variables of interest. It is a structured, powerful, and even enjoyable way to work through data understanding.

Dean also wrote:

> *Now that we have the target variable better defined, I'm going back to the data understanding and data prep stages to complete those stages properly, and this is changing how the data will be prepped in addition to modifying the definition of the target variable. It's also much more enjoyable to build models than do data prep.*

It is always wise to consider writing an interim report when you near completion of a phase. A data understanding report can be a great way to protect yourself against accusations that you failed to include variables of interest in a Model. It is in this phase that you will start to determine what we actually have at your disposal, and what information you might not be able to get. The Outliers (quirk) report, and the exact logic you used to choose your subset, are precisely the kind of information that you would want to include in such a report.

Using an empty aggregate to evaluate sample size

Having all the data made available is usually not a challenge to the data miner—the challenge is having enough of the right data. The data needs to be relevant to the business question, and be from an appropriate time period. Many users of Modeler might not realize that an Aggregate node can be useful even when all you have done is drag it into place, but have given no further instruction to Modeler.

At times data preparation requires the number of records in a dataset to be a data item that is to be used in further calculations. This recipe shows how to use the Aggregate node with no aggregation key and no aggregation operations to produce this count, and how to merge this count into every record using a Cartesian product so that it is available for further calculations.

Getting ready

This recipe uses the `cup98lrn reduced vars2 empty.txt` data set. Since this recipe produces a fairly simple stream, we will build the stream from scratch.

How to do it...

To use an empty Aggregate node to evaluate sample size:

1. Place a new Var. File source node on the canvas of a new stream. The file name is `cup98lrn reduced vars2.txt`. Confirm that the data is being accessed properly.
2. Add both an Aggregate node and a Table node downstream of the source. You do not need to edit either of the nodes.
3. Run the stream and confirm the result. Total sample size is **95412**.

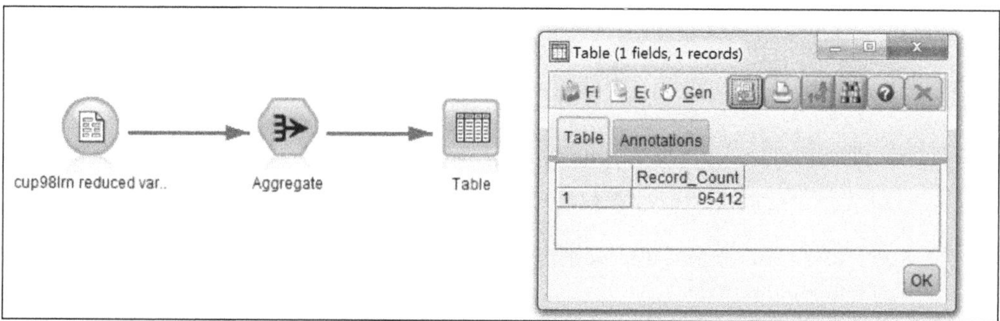

4. Now, add a Type node and a Distinct node in between the Source and Aggregate node. Move the variable `CUST_ID` into the **Key fields for grouping** box.

5. Select **Discard only the first record in each group**.

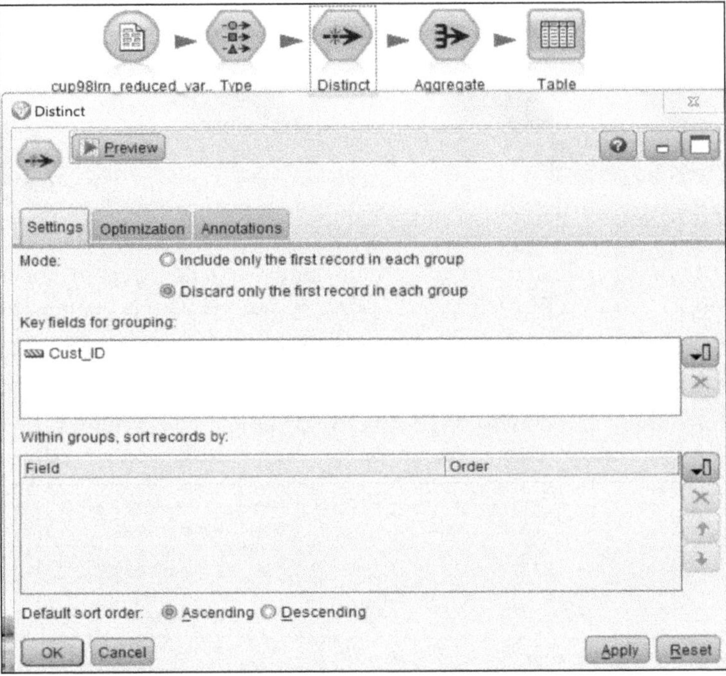

6. Run it and confirm that the result is **0**. You have learned that there are no duplicates at the customer level.
7. Place a Merge node so that it is combining the original source with the output of an empty Aggregate.
8. Within the Merge node choose **Full Outer Join**.

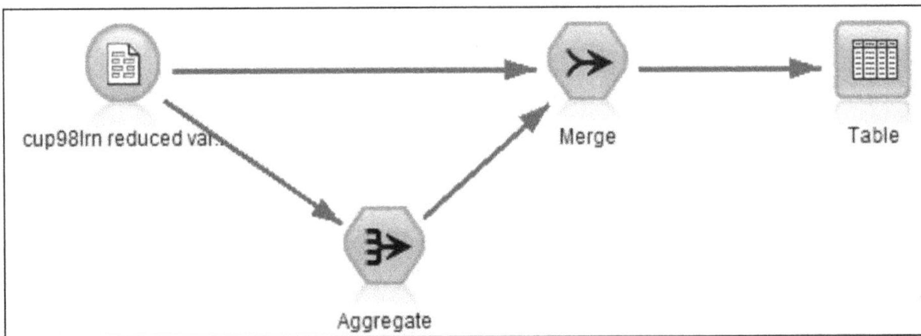

9. You have just successfully added the total sample size to the data set where it can be used for further calculation, as needed.

How it works...

What an Aggregate node typically does is use a categorical variable to define a new row—always a reduction in the number of rows. Scale variables can be in the Aggregate field's area and summary statistics are calculated. Average sales in columns arranged with regions in rows would be a typical example. Having given none of these instructions, the Aggregate node boils our data down to a single row. Having given it no summary statistics to report all, what it does is the default instructions, namely **Include record count in field**, which is checked off at the bottom of the Aggregate node's menu. While this recipe is quite easy, this default behavior is sometimes surprising to new users.

There's more...

Now let's talk about some other options, or possibly some pieces of general information that are relevant to this task.

If you are merging many sources of data, as will often be the case, you should check sample size for each source, and for the combined sources as well. If you obtained the data from a colleague, you should be able to confirm that the sample size and the absence (or presence) of duplicate IDs was consistent with expectations.

When duplicates are present, and you therefore get a non-zero count, you can remove the aggregate and export the duplicates. You will get the second row (or third, or even more) of each duplicate. You can look up those IDs and verify that they should (or should not) be in the data set.

A modified version

A modified version of this technique can be helpful when you have a nominal variable with lots of categories such as `STATE`. Simply make the variable your key field.

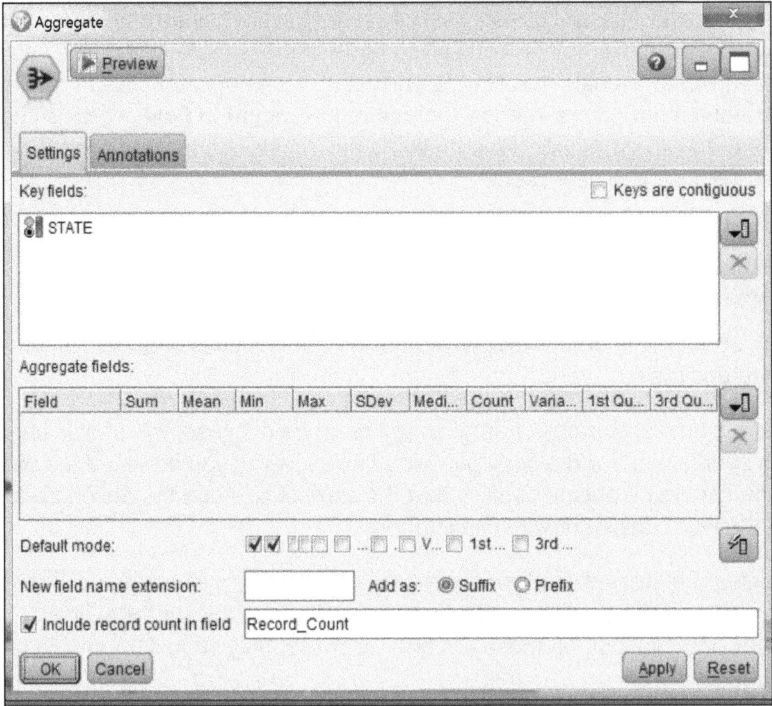

Additionally, it is wise to sort on `Record_Count` with a Sort node (not shown). The results show us that California has enough donors that we might be able to compare California to other states, but the data in New England is thin. Perhaps we need to group those states into a broader region variable.

STATE	Record_Count			
CA	17343	48	ME	11
FL	8376	49	NH	8
TX	7535	50	VT	7
IL	6420	51	RI	6
MI	5654	52	VI	5
NC	4160	53	GU	4
WA	3577	54	WV	4
GA	3403	55	DE	3
IN	2980	56	AS	1
WI	2795	57	DC	1

The same issue can arise in other data sets with any variable of this kind, such as product category, or sales district, etc. In some cases, you may conclude that certain categories are out of the scope of the analysis. That is not likely in this instance, but there are times when you conclude that certain categories are so poorly represented that they warrant a separate analysis. Only the business problem can guide you; this is merely a method for determining what raw material you have to work with.

See also

- *Chapter 4, Data Preparation – Construct*

Evaluating the need to sample from the initial data

One of the most compelling reasons to sample is that many data sources were never created with data analysis in mind. Many operational systems would suffer serious functional problems if a data miner extracted every bit of data from the system. Business intelligence systems are built for reporting purposes—typically a week's worth or a month's worth at a time. When a year's worth is requested, it is in summary form. When the data miner requests a year's worth (or more) of line item level transactions it is often unexpected, and can be disastrous if the IT unit is not forewarned.

Real life data mining rarely begins with perfectly clean data. It's not uncommon for 90 percent of a data miner's time to go to data preparation. This is a strong motivation to work with just enough data to fill a need and no more, because more data to analyze means more data to clean, more time spent cleaning data, and very little time left available for data exploration, modeling and other responsibilities. The question often is how large a time period to examine. Do we need 4 years to examine this? The answer would be yes if we are predicting university completion, but the answer would be no if we are predicting the next best offer for an online bookseller.

In this recipe we will run a series of calculations that will help us determine if we have: just enough data, too much data that we might want to consider random sampling, or so little data that we might have to go further back in our historical data to get enough.

Getting ready

We will be using the `EvaluateSampleNeed.str` file.

How to do it...

To evaluate the need to sample from the initial data, perform the following steps:

1. Force **TARGET_B** to be flag in the Type node.
2. Run a Distribution node for **TARGET_B**. Verify that there are 4,883 donors and 90,569 non-donors.
3. Run a Distribution node on the new derive field, `RFA3_FirstLetter`.
4. Examine the Select node and run a new Distribution node on **TARGET_B** downstream of the Select node. Confirm the numbers 88,290 and 4694 for the results.

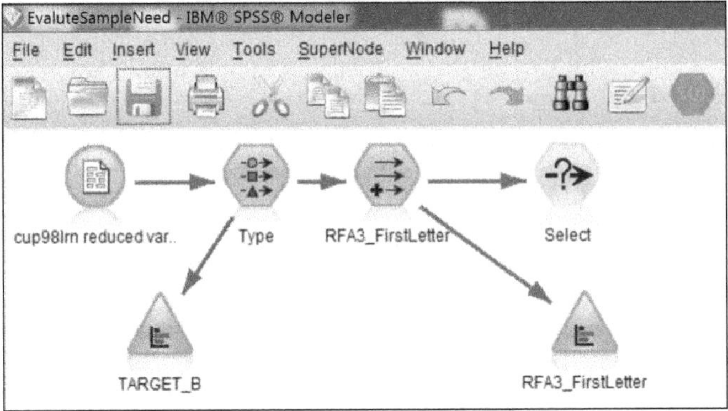

5. Generate using **Balance Node (reduce)**.

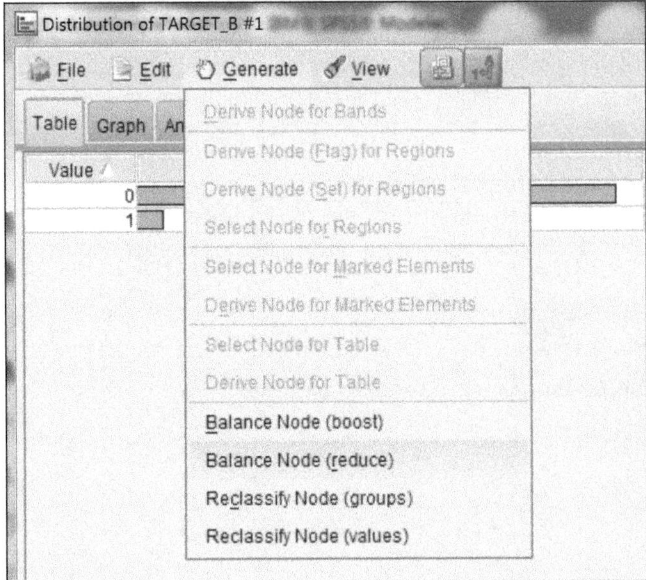

Insert it in sequence before the Distribution node and then run it.

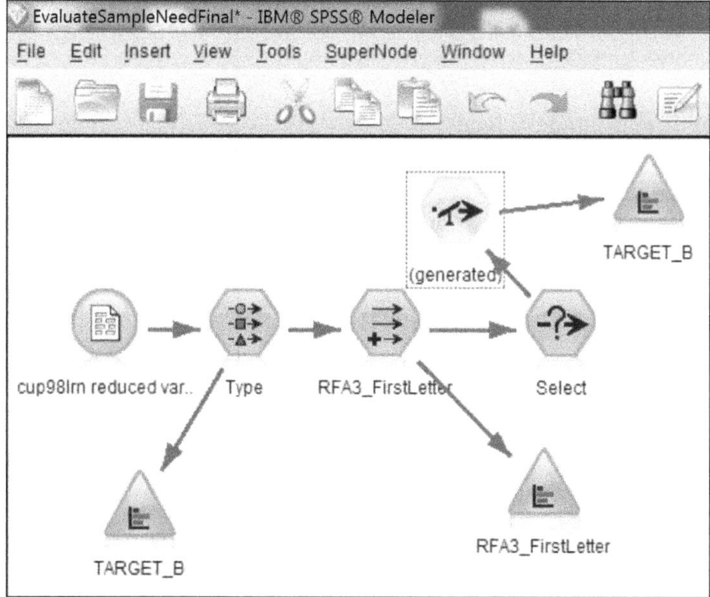

Confirm that the two groups are now roughly equal. This is a random process; your numbers will not match the screen exactly.

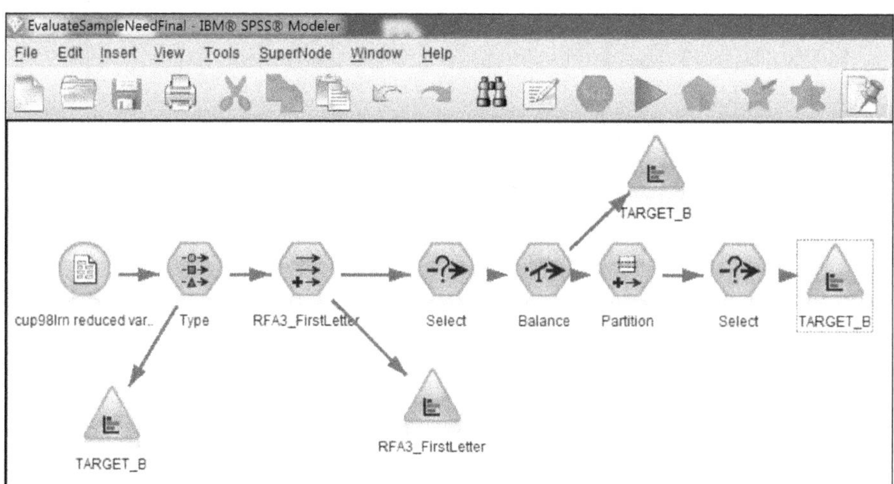

6. Add a Partition node after the Type node. Purely for illustration, add a Select node that allows only data from Train data set to flow to the Distribution node. We want to assess our sample size, but the Select node would be removed before modeling.

7. Do we have enough data if we remove Inactive or Lapsing donors? Add a Select node that removes the categories *I* or *L* from the field `RFA_3FirstLetter`. The downstream Distribution node of **TARGET_B** should result in approximately 2,300 in each group.

How it works...

Early in the process we determined that we have 4833 cases of the rarer of our two groups. It would seem, at first, that we have enough data and possibly we do. A good rule of thumb is that we would want at least 1,000 cases of the rarer group in our Train data set, and ideally the same amount in our Test data set. When you don't meet these requirements there are ways around it, but when you can meet them it is one less thing to worry about.

Train		**Test**	
Rare (donor)	Common (non-donor)	Rare (donor)	Common (non-donor)
1000+	1000+	1000+	1000+

When we explore the balanced results we meet the 1000+ rule of thumb, but are we out of the woods? There are numerous issues left to consider. Two are especially important: is all of the data relevant and is our time period appropriate?

Note that when we rerun the Distribution node downstream of the Partition node, at first it seems to give us odd results. Partition nodes tells Modeling nodes to ignore Test data, but Distribution nodes show all the data. In addition, Balance nodes only balance data in the Training data set, not the Testing data set. In this recipe, we add the select node to make this clear. In a real project one could just cut the number of cases into half to determine the number in the Train half.

The exercise in removing 1995 donors or lapsed donors cannot be taken as guidance in all cases. There are numerous reasons to restrict data. We might be interested in only major donors (as defined in the data set). We might be interested only in new donors. The point is to always return to your business case and ensure that you are determining sample size for the same group that will be your deployment population for the given business question.

In this example, we ultimately can conclude we have enough data to meet the rule of thumb, but we certainly don't have the amount of data that we appeared to have at the start.

	Codes for RFA3_FirstLetter
F	`First time donor`: Anyone who has made their first donation in the last 6 months and has made just one donation.
N	`New donor`: Anyone who has made their first donation in the last 12 months and is not a First time donor. This is everyone who made their first donation 7-12 months ago, or people who made their first donation between 0-6 months ago and have made two or more donations.
A	`Active donor`: Anyone who made their first donation more than 12 months ago and has made a donation in the last 12 months.
L	`Lapsing donor`: A previous donor who made their last donation between 13-24 months ago.
I	`Inactive donor`: A previous donor who has not made a donation in the last 24 months. People who made a donation more than 25 months ago.
S	`Star donor`: Star donors are individuals who have given to 3 consecutive card mailings.

There's more...

What do you do when you don't have enough data? One option is to go further back in time, but that option might not be available to you on all projects. Another option is to change the percentages in the Partition node. The Train data set needs its 1000s of records more than the Test data. If you are experiencing scarcity, increase the percentage of records going to the Train data.

You could also manipulate the Balance node. One need not fully boost or fully reduce. For example, if you are low on data, but have almost enough data, try doubling the numbers in the balance node. This way you are partially boosting the rare group (by a factor of 2), and you are only partially reducing the common group.

What do you do if you have *too much* data? As long as there is no seasonality you might look at only one campaign, or one month. If you had a lot of data, but you had seasonality, then having only one month's worth of data would not be a good idea. Better to do a random sample from each of 12 months, and then combine the data. Don't be too quick to embrace *too much* uncritically and simply analyze all of it. The proof will be in the ability to validate against new unbalanced data. A clever sampler will often produce the better model because they are not drowning the algorithm with noise.

See also

- The *Using an empty aggregate to evaluate sample size* recipe in this chapter

Using CHAID stumps when interviewing an SME

In this recipe we will learn how to use the interactive mode of the CHAID Modeling node to explore data. The name **stump** comes from the idea that we grow just one branch and stop. The exploration will have the goal of answering five questions:

1. What variables seem predictive of the target?
2. Do the most predictive variables make sense?
3. What questions are most useful to pose to the Subject Matter Experts (SMEs) about data quality?
4. What is the potential value of the favorite variables of the SMEs?
5. What missing data challenges are present in the data?

Getting ready

We will start with a blank stream.

How to do it...

To use CHAID stumps:

1. Add a Source node to the stream for the `cup98lrn reduced vars2.txt` file. Ensure that the field delimiter is **Tab** and that the **Strip lead and trail spaces** option is set to **Both**.
2. Add a Type node and declare **TARGET_B** as flag and as the target. Set **TARGET_D, RFA_2, RFA_2A**, and **RFA_2F, RFA_2R** to **None**.

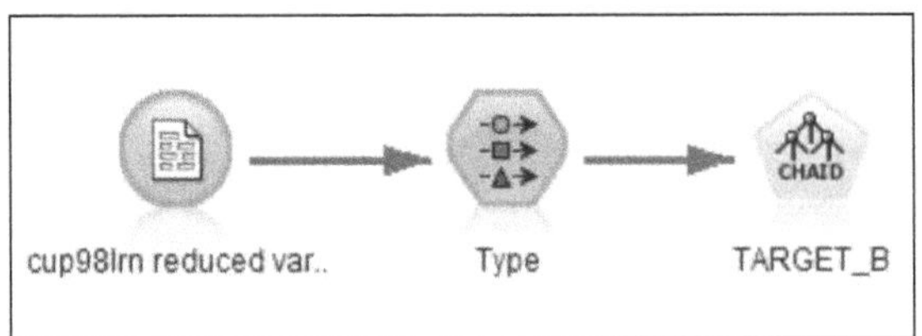

3. Add a CHAID Modeling node and make sure that it is in interactive mode.

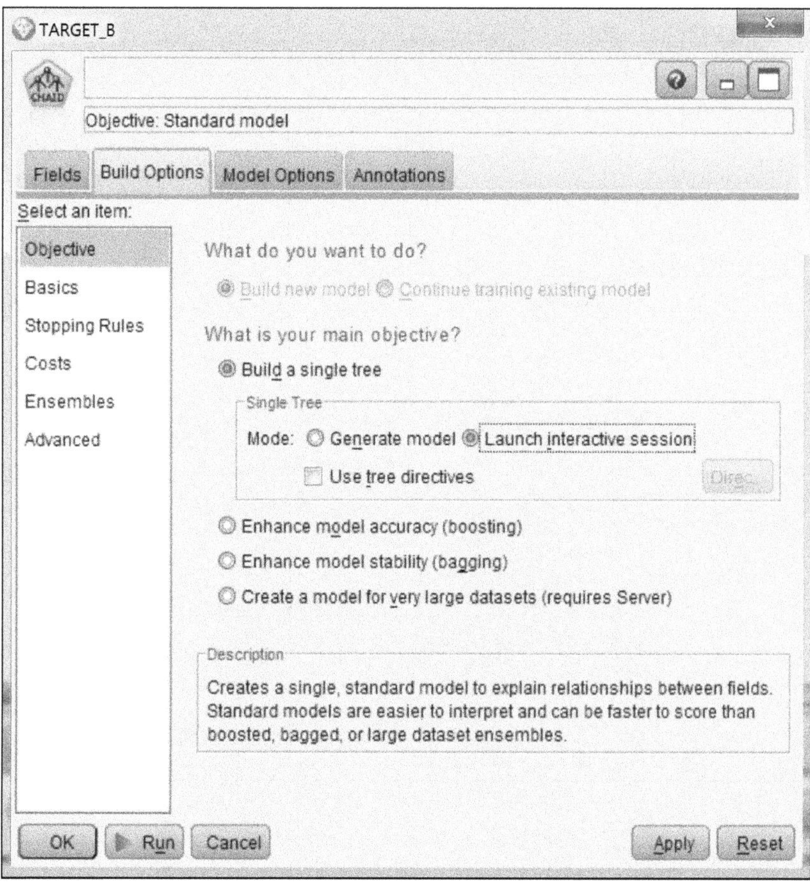

4. Click on the **Run** button. From the menus choose **Tree** | **Grow Branch with Custom Split**. Then click on the **Predictors** button.

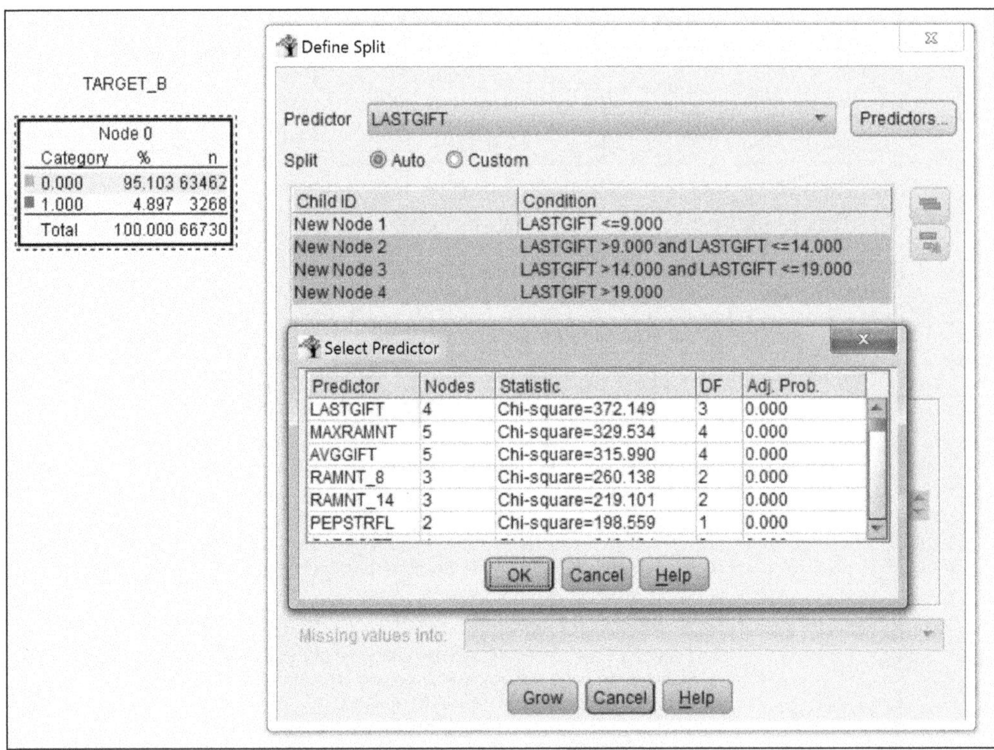

5. Allow the top variable, `LASTGIFT`, to form a branch. Note that `LASTGIFT` does not seem to have missing values.

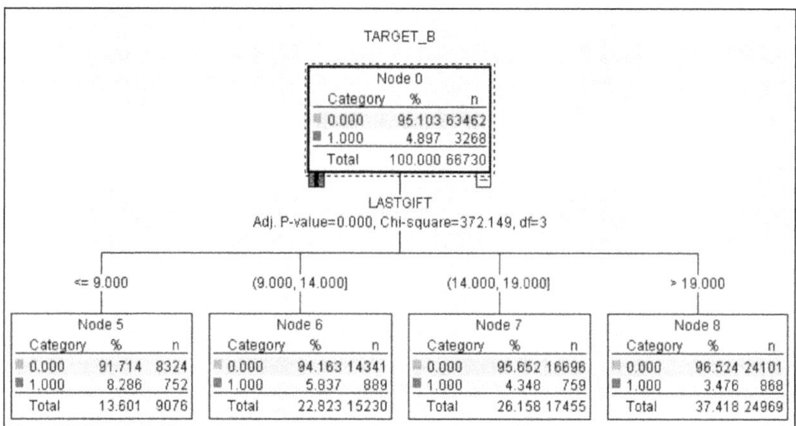

6. Further down the list, the `RAMNT_` series variables do have missing values. Placing the mouse on the root node (Node 0) choose **Tree** | **Grow Branch with Custom Split** again.

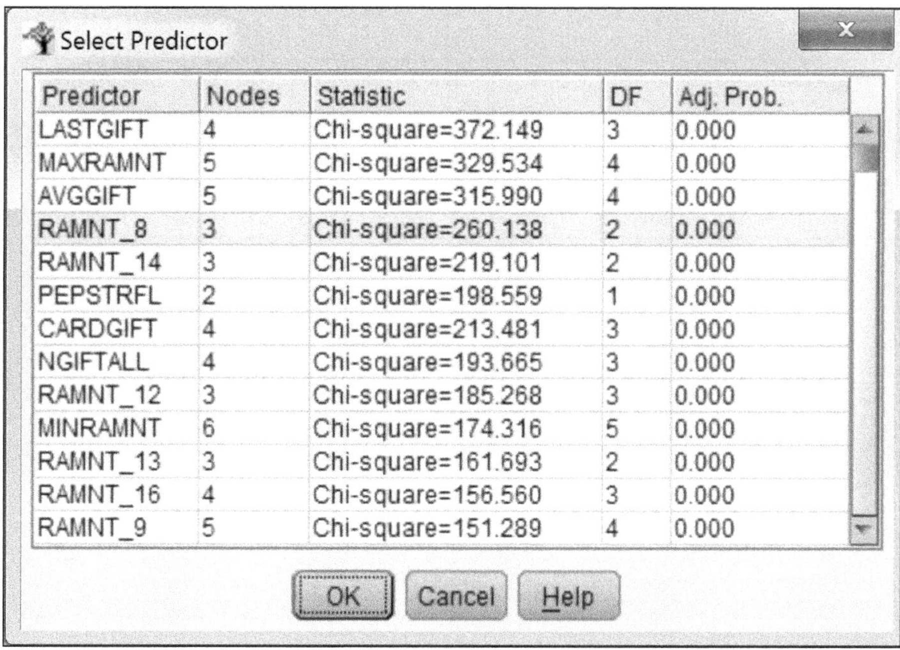

Predictor	Nodes	Statistic	DF	Adj. Prob.
LASTGIFT	4	Chi-square=372.149	3	0.000
MAXRAMNT	5	Chi-square=329.534	4	0.000
AVGGIFT	5	Chi-square=315.990	4	0.000
RAMNT_8	3	Chi-square=260.138	2	0.000
RAMNT_14	3	Chi-square=219.101	2	0.000
PEPSTRFL	2	Chi-square=198.559	1	0.000
CARDGIFT	4	Chi-square=213.481	3	0.000
NGIFTALL	4	Chi-square=193.665	3	0.000
RAMNT_12	3	Chi-square=185.268	3	0.000
MINRAMNT	6	Chi-square=174.316	5	0.000
RAMNT_13	3	Chi-square=161.693	2	0.000
RAMNT_16	4	Chi-square=156.560	3	0.000
RAMNT_9	5	Chi-square=151.289	4	0.000

7. The figure shows `RAMNT_8`, but your results may differ somewhat as CHAID takes an internal partition and therefore does not use all of the data. The slight differences can change the ranking of similar variables. Allow the branch to grow on your selected variable.

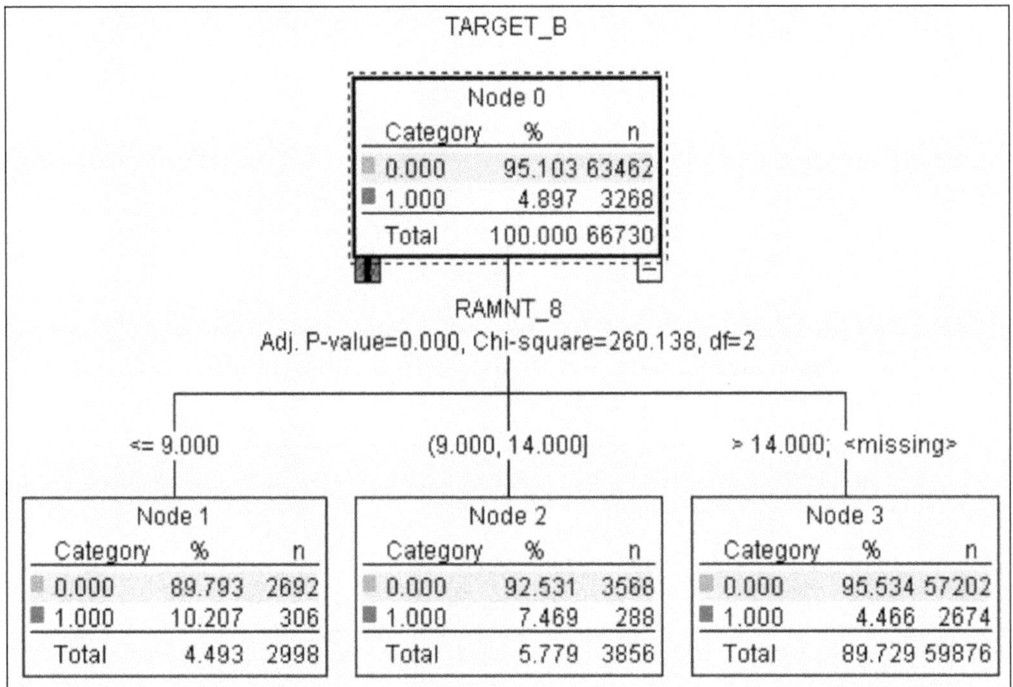

8. Now we will break away the missing data into its own category. Repeat the steps leading up to this branch, but before clicking on the **Grow** button, select **Custom** and at the bottom, set **Missing values into** as Separate Node.

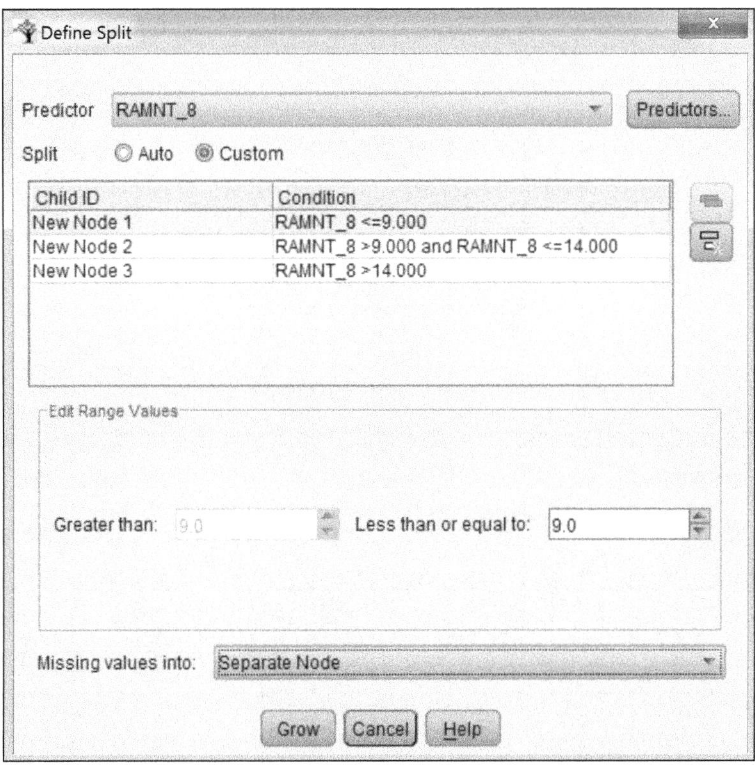

9. Sometimes SMEs will have a particular interest in a variable because it has been known to be valuable in the past, or they are invested in the variable in some way. Even though it is well down the list, choose the variable `Wealth2` and force it to branch while ensuring that missing values are placed into a Separate node.

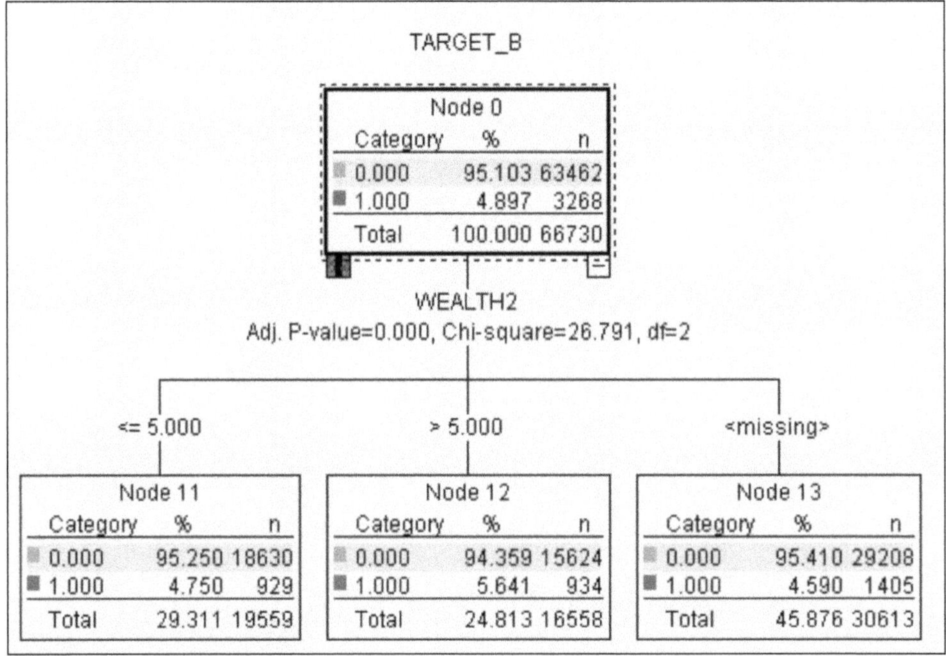

How it works...

There are several advantages to exploring data in this way with CHAID. If you have accidentally included *perfect predictors* it will become obvious in a hurry. This recipe is dedicated to this phenomenon. Another advantage is that most SMEs find CHAID rather intuitive. It is easy to see what the relationships are without extensive exposure to the technique. Meanwhile, as an added benefit, the SMEs are becoming acquainted with a technique that might also be used during the modeling phase. As we have seen, CHAID can show missing data as a Separate node. This feature is shown to be useful in the *Binning scale variables to address missing data* recipe in *Chapter 3, Data Preparation – Clean*. By staying in interactive mode, the trees are kept simple; also, we can force any variable to branch even if it is not near the top of the list. Often SMEs can be quite adamant that a variable is important, while the data shows them otherwise. There are countless reasons why this might be the case, and the conversation should be allowed to unfold. One is likely to learn a great deal trying to figure out why a variable that seemed promising is not performing well in the CHAID model.

Let's examine the CHAID tree a bit more closely. The root node shows the total sample size and the percentage in each of the two categories. In the figures in this recipe, the red group is the donors group. Notice that the more recent their `LASTGIFT` was, the more likely that they donated. Starting with 8.286 percent for the less than or equal to 9 group, dropping down to 3.476 percent for the less than 19 group. Note that when you add up the child nodes, you get the same number as the number in the root node.

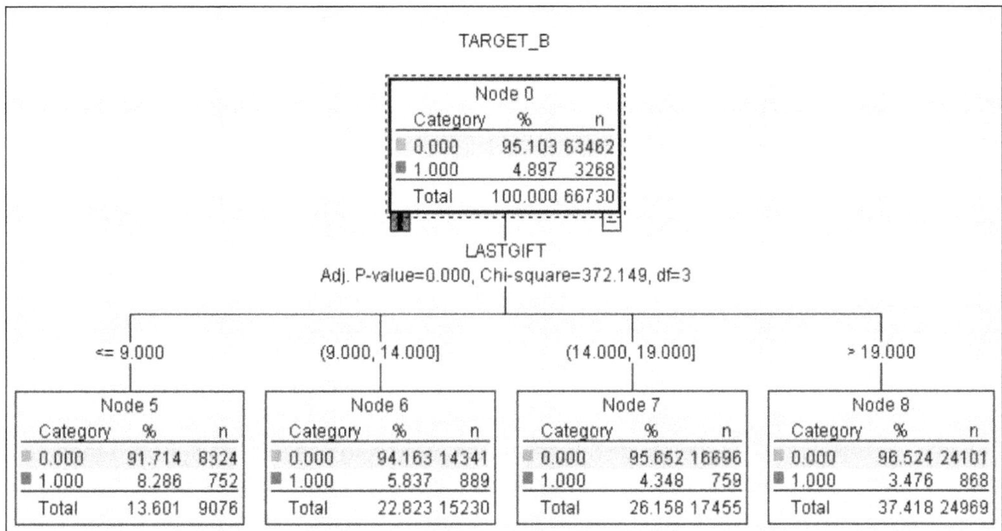

It is recommended that you take a screenshot of at least the top 10 or so variables of interest to management or SMEs. It is a good precaution to place the images on slides, since you will be able to review and discuss without waiting for Modeler to process. Having said that, it is an excellent idea to be ready to further explore the data using this technique on live data during the meeting.

See also

- The *Using the Feature Selection node creatively to remove or decapitate perfect predictors* recipe in *Chapter 2, Data Preparation – Select*
- The *Binning scale variables to address missing data* recipe in *Chapter 3, Data Preparation – Clean*

Using a single cluster K-means as an alternative to anomaly detection

Cleaning data includes detecting and eliminating outliers. When outliers are viewed as a property of individual variables, it is easy to examine a data set, one variable at a time, and identify which records fall outside the usual range for a given variable. However, from a multivariate point of view, the concept of an outlier is less obvious; individual values may fall within accepted bounds but a combination of values may still be unusual.

The concept of multivariate outliers is used a great deal in anomaly detection, and this can be used both for data cleaning and more directly for applications such as fraud detection. Clustering techniques are often used for this purpose; in effect a clustering model defines different kinds of *normal* (the different clusters) and items falling outside these definitions may be considered anomalous. Techniques of anomaly detection using clustering vary from sophisticated, perhaps using multiple clustering models and comparing the results, through single-model examples such as the use of TwoStep in Modeler's Anomaly algorithm, to the very simple.

The simplest kind of anomaly detection with clustering is to create a cluster model with only one cluster. The distance of a record from the cluster center can then be treated as a measure of anomaly, unusualness or outlierhood. This recipe shows how to use a single-cluster K-means model in this way, and how to analyze the reasons why certain records are outliers.

Getting ready

This recipe uses the following files:

- Data file: `cup98LRN.txt`
- Stream file: `Single_Cluster_Kmeans.str`
- Clementine output file: `Histogram.cou`

How to do it...

To use a single cluster K-means as an alternative to anomaly detection:

1. Open the stream `Single_Cluster_Kmeans.str` by clicking on **File** | **Open Stream**.
2. Edit the Type node near the top-left of the stream; note that the customer ID and zip code have been excluded from the model, and the other 5 fields have been included as inputs.
3. Run the Histogram node `$KMD-K-Means` to show the distribution of distances from the cluster center. Note that a few records are grouped towards the upper end of the range.

4. Open the output file `Histogram.cou` by selecting the **Outputs** tab at the top-right of the user interface, right-click in this pane to see the pop-up menu, select **Open Output** from this menu, then browse and select the file `Histogram.cou`. You will see the graph in the following figure, including a boundary (the red line) that was placed manually to identify the area of the graph that, visually, appears to contain outliers. The band to the right of this line was used to generate the Select node and Derive node included in the stream, both labeled `band2`.

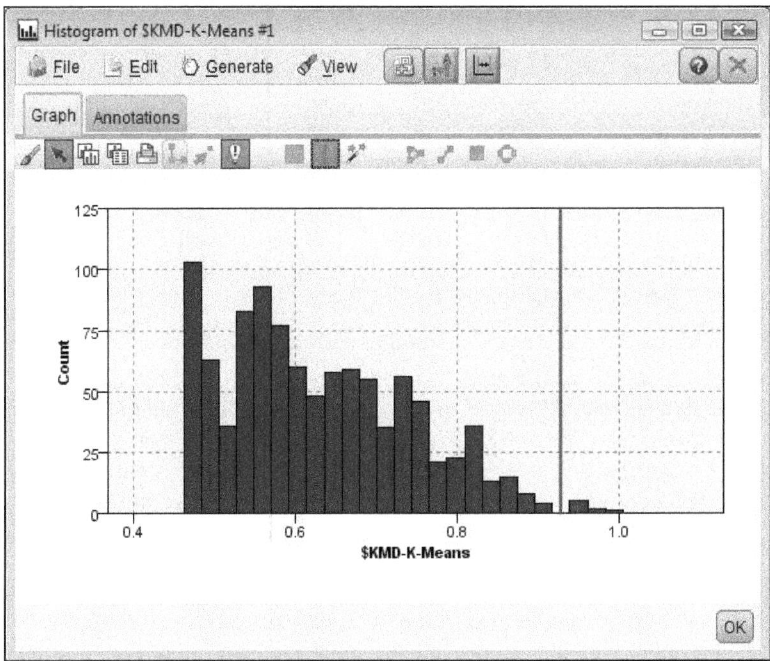

5. Run the Table node outliers; this displays the 8 records we have identified as outliers from the histogram, including their distance from the cluster center, as shown in the following screenshot. Note that they are all from the same cluster because there is only one cluster.

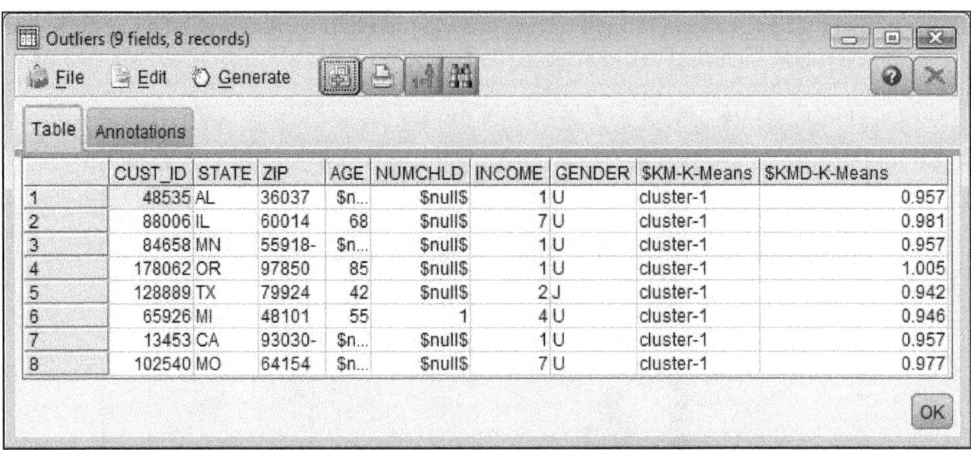
Outliers (9 fields, 8 records)

File Edit Generate

Table Annotations

	CUST_ID	STATE	ZIP	AGE	NUMCHLD	INCOME	GENDER	$KM-K-Means	$KMD-K-Means
1	48535	AL	36037	$n...	$null$	1	U	cluster-1	0.957
2	88006	IL	60014	68	$null$	7	U	cluster-1	0.981
3	84658	MN	55918-	$n...	$null$	1	U	cluster-1	0.957
4	178062	OR	97850	85	$null$	1	U	cluster-1	1.005
5	128889	TX	79924	42	$null$	2	J	cluster-1	0.942
6	65926	MI	48101	55	1	4	U	cluster-1	0.946
7	13453	CA	93030-	$n...	$null$	1	U	cluster-1	0.957
8	102540	MO	64154	$n...	$null$	7	U	cluster-1	0.977

OK

So far we have used the single-cluster K-means model to identify outliers, but why are they outliers? We can create a profile of these outliers to explain why they are outliers, by creating a rule-set model using the C5.0 algorithm to distinguish items that are in `band2` from those that are not. This is a common technique used in Modeler to find explanations for the behavior of clustering models that are difficult to interrogate directly. The following steps show how:

1. Edit the Type node near the lower-right of the stream, as shown in the following screenshot. This is used to create the C5.0 rule-set model; note that the inputs are the same as for the initial cluster model, both outputs of the cluster model have been excluded, and the target is the derived field `band2`, a Boolean that identifies the outliers.

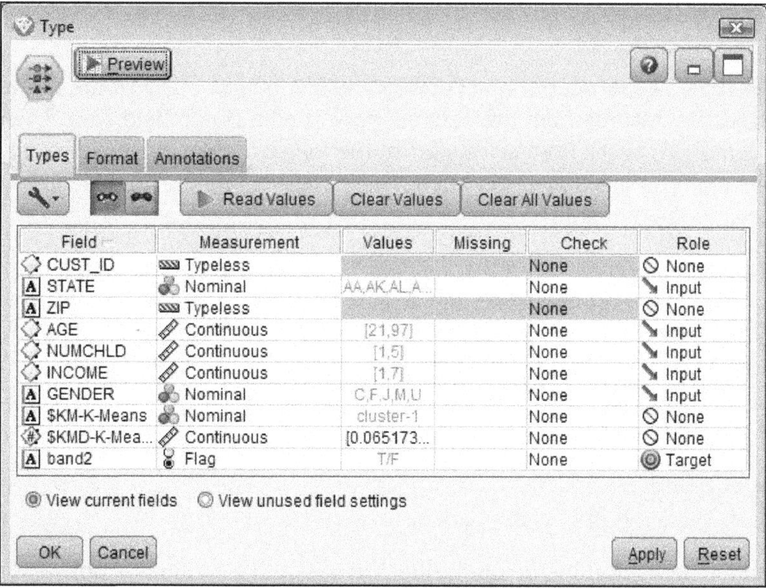

2. Browse the C5.0 model, `band2` and then use the **Model** pane to see all the rules and their statistics, as shown in the following screenshot. All the rules are highly accurate; even though they are not perfect, this is a successful profiling model in that it can distinguish reliably between outliers and others. This model shows how the cluster model has defined outliers: those records that have the *rare* values `U` and `J` for the `GENDER` field. The even more rare value `C` has not been identified, because its single occurrence was insufficient to have an impact on the model.

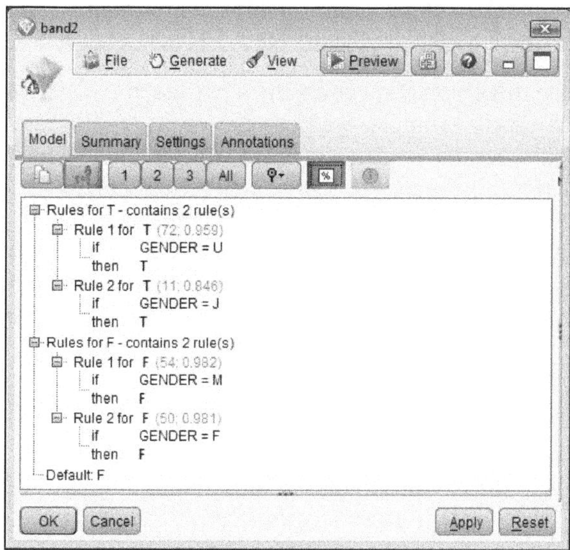

How it works...

Imagine a five-dimensional scatter-plot showing the 5 variables used for the cluster model and normalized. The records from the data set appear as a clump, and somewhere within that clump is its center of gravity. Some items fall at the edges of this clump; some may be visually outside it. The clump is the cluster discovered by K-means, and the items falling visually outside the clump are outliers.

Assuming the clump to be roughly spherical, the items outside the clump will be those at the greatest distance from its center, and have a gap between them and the edges of the clump. This corresponds to the gap in the histogram where we create a band of outliers from the histogram, which we have used manually to identify the band of outliers. The C5.0 rule-set is a convenient way to see a description of these outliers, more specifically how they differ from items inside the clump.

There's more...

The final step mentions that the unique value `C` in the `GENDER` field has not been discovered in this instance because it is too rare to have an impact on the model. In fact, it is only too rare to have an impact on the relatively simplistic single-cluster model. It is possible for a K-means model to discover this outlier, and it will do so if used with its default setting of 5 clusters. This illustrates that the technique of using the distance from the cluster center to find outliers is more general than the single-cluster technique and can be used with any K-means model, or any clustering model that can output this distance.

Using an @NULL multiple Derive to explore missing data

With great regularity the mere presence or absence of data in the input variable tells you a great deal. Dates are a classic example. Suppose `LastDateRented_HorrorCategory` is NULL. Does that mean that the value is unknown? Perhaps we should replace it with the average date of the horror movie renters? Please don't! Obviously, if the data is complete, the failure to find Jane Renter in the horror movie rental transactions much more likely means that she did not rent a horror movie. This is such a classic scenario you will want a series of simple tricks to deal with this type of missing data efficiently so that when the situation calls for it you can easily create NULL flag variables for dozens (or even all) of your variables.

Getting ready

We will start with the NULL `Flags.str` stream.

How to do it...

To use an `@NULL` multiple Derive node to explore missing data, perform the following steps:

1. Run the **Data Audit** and examine the resulting **Quality** tab. Note that a number of variables are complete but many have more than 5 percent NULL. The Filter node on the stream allows only the variables with a substantial number of NULL values to flow downstream.
2. Add a Derive node, and edit it, by selecting the **Multiple** option. Include all of the scale variables that are downstream of the Filter node. Use the suffix `_null`, and select **Flag** from the **Derive as** drop-down menu.

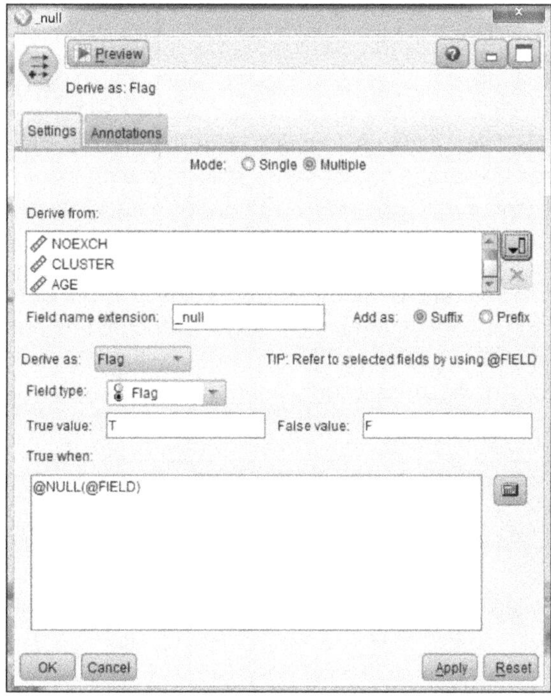

3. Add another Filter node and set it to allow only the new variables plus **TARGET_B** to flow downstream.
4. Add a Type node forcing **TARGET_B** to be the target. Ensure that it is a flag measurement type.
5. Add a Data Audit node. Note that some of the new NULL flag variables may be related to the target, but it is not easy to see which variables are the most related.

6. Add a Feature Selection Modeling node and run it. Edit the resulting generated model. Note that a number of variables are predictive of the target.

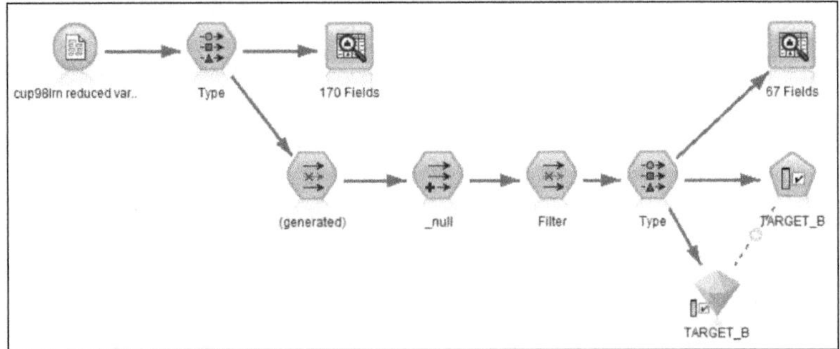

How it works...

There is no substitute for lots of hard work during Data Understanding. Some of the patterns here could be capitalized upon, and others could indicate the need for data cleaning. The *Using the Feature Selection node creatively to remove or decapitate perfect predictors* recipe in *Chapter 2, Data Preparation – Select*, shows how circular logic can creep into our analysis.

Note the large number of data and amount-related variables in the Generated model. These variables indicate that the potential donor did not give in those time periods. Failing to give in one time period is predicted with failing to give in another; it makes sense. Is this the best way to get at this? Perhaps a simple count would do the trick, or perhaps the number of recent donations versus total donations.

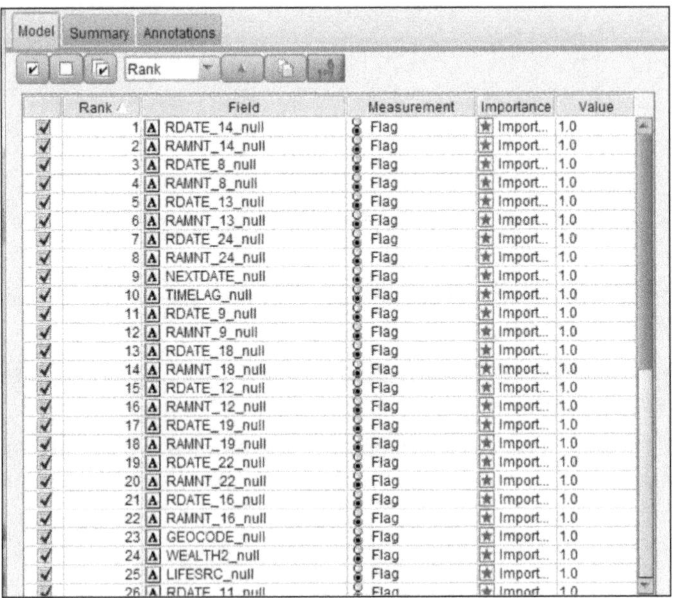

Rank	Field	Measurement	Importance	Value
1	RDATE_14_null	Flag	Import...	1.0
2	RAMNT_14_null	Flag	Import...	1.0
3	RDATE_8_null	Flag	Import...	1.0
4	RAMNT_8_null	Flag	Import...	1.0
5	RDATE_13_null	Flag	Import...	1.0
6	RAMNT_13_null	Flag	Import...	1.0
7	RDATE_24_null	Flag	Import...	1.0
8	RAMNT_24_null	Flag	Import...	1.0
9	NEXTDATE_null	Flag	Import...	1.0
10	TIMELAG_null	Flag	Import...	1.0
11	RDATE_9_null	Flag	Import...	1.0
12	RAMNT_9_null	Flag	Import...	1.0
13	RDATE_18_null	Flag	Import...	1.0
14	RAMNT_18_null	Flag	Import...	1.0
15	RDATE_12_null	Flag	Import...	1.0
16	RAMNT_12_null	Flag	Import...	1.0
17	RDATE_19_null	Flag	Import...	1.0
18	RAMNT_19_null	Flag	Import...	1.0
19	RDATE_22_null	Flag	Import...	1.0
20	RAMNT_22_null	Flag	Import...	1.0
21	RDATE_16_null	Flag	Import...	1.0
22	RAMNT_16_null	Flag	Import...	1.0
23	GEOCODE_null	Flag	Import...	1.0
24	WEALTH2_null	Flag	Import...	1.0
25	LIFESRC_null	Flag	Import...	1.0
26	RDATE_11_null	Flag	Import...	1.0

Also note the `TIMELAG_null` variable. It is the distance between the first and second donation. What would be a common reason that it would be NULL? Obviously the lack of a second donation could cause that problem. Perhaps analyzing new donors and established donors separately could be a good way of tackling this. The *Using a full data model/partial data model approach to address missing data* recipe in *Chapter 3, Data Preparation - Clean*, is built around this very idea. Note that neither imputing with the mean, nor filling with zero would be a good idea at all. We have no reason to think that one time and two time donors are similar. We also know for a fact that the time distance is never zero.

Note the `Wealth2_null` variable. What might cause this variable to be missing, and for the missing status alone to be predictive? Perhaps we need a new donor to be on the mailing list for a substantial time before our list vendor can provide us that information. This too might be tackled with a new donor/established donor approach.

See also

- The *Using the Feature Selection node creatively to remove or decapitate perfect predictors* recipe in *Chapter 2, Data Preparation - Select*
- The *Using CHAID stumps when interviewing an SME* recipe in this chapter
- The *Binning scale variables to address missing data* recipe in *Chapter 3, Data Preparation - Clean*
- The *Using a full data model/partial data model approach to address missing data* recipe in *Chapter 3, Data Preparation - Clean*

Creating an Outlier report to give to SMEs

It is quite common that the data miner has to rely on others to either provide data or interpret data, or both. Even when the data miner is working with data from their own organization there will be input variables that they don't have direct access to, or that are outside their day-to-day experience.

Are zero values normal? What about negative values? Null values? Are 1500 balance inquiries in a month even possible? How could a wallet cost $19,500? The concept of outliers is something that all analysts are familiar with. Even novice users of Modeler could easily find a dozen ways of identifying some. This recipe is about identifying outliers systematically and quickly so that you can produce a report designed to inspire curiosity.

There is no presumption that the data is in error, or that they should be removed. It is simply an attempt to put the information in the hands of Subject Matter Experts, so quirky values can be discussed in the earliest phases of the projects. It is important to provide whichever primary keys are necessary for the SMEs to look up the records. On one of the author's recent projects, the team started calling these reports **quirk reports**.

Getting ready

We will start with the `Outlier Report.str` stream that uses the `TELE_CHURN_preprep` data set.

How to do it...

To create an Outlier report:

1. Open the stream `Outlier Report.str`.

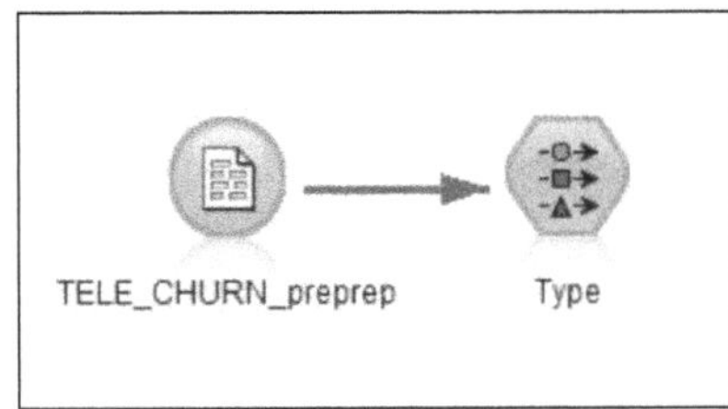

2. Add a Data Audit node and examine the results.

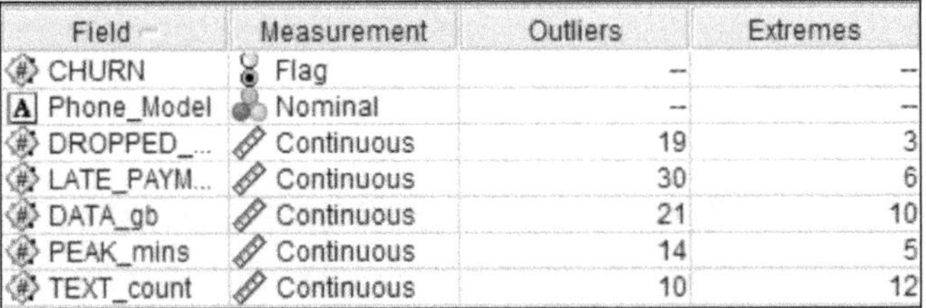

Field	Measurement	Outliers	Extremes
CHURN	Flag	--	--
Phone_Model	Nominal	--	--
DROPPED_...	Continuous	19	3
LATE_PAYM...	Continuous	30	6
DATA_gb	Continuous	21	10
PEAK_mins	Continuous	14	5
TEXT_count	Continuous	10	12

3. Adjust the stream options to allow for 25 rows to be shown in a data preview. We will be using the preview feature later in the recipe.

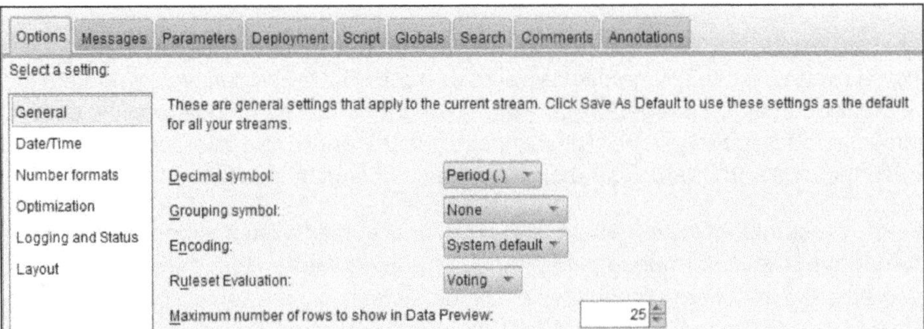

4. Add a Statistics node. Choose **Mean**, **Min**, **Max**, and **Median** for the variables `DATA_gb`, `PEAK_mins`, and `TEXT_count`. These three have either unusually high maximums or surprising negative values as shown in the Data Audit node.
5. Consider taking a screenshot of the Statistics node for later use.

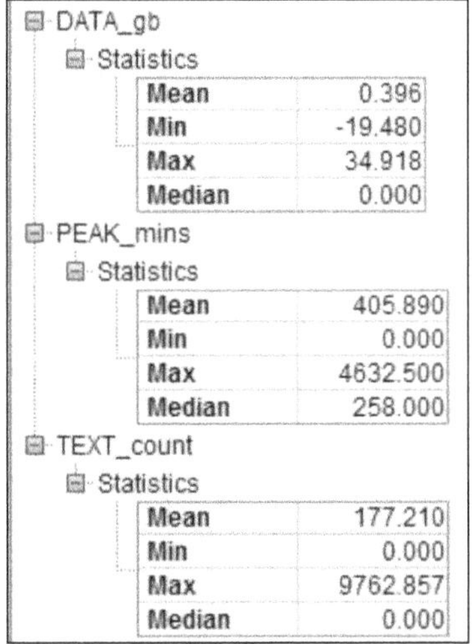

6. Add a Sort node. Starting with the first variable, `DATA_gb`, sort in ascending order.

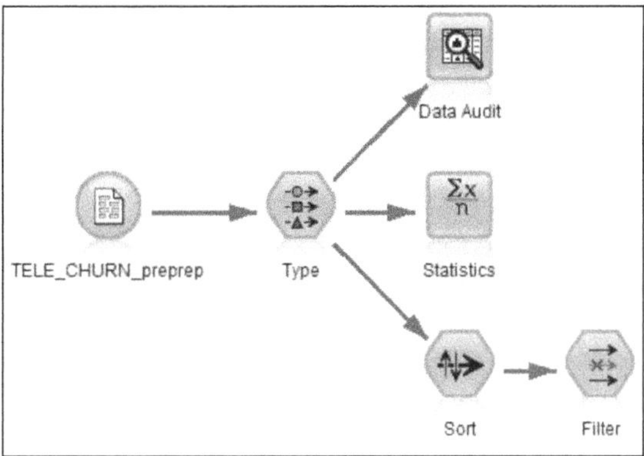

7. Add a Filter node downstream of the Sort node dropping `CHURN`, `DROPPED_CALLS`, and `LATE_PAYMENTS`. It is important to work with your SME to know which variables put quirky values into context.

Field	Filter	Field
ACCOUNT	→	ACCOUNT
CHURN	✕→	CHURN
Phone_Model	→	Phone_Model
DROPPED_CALLS	✕→	DROPPED_CALLS
LATE_PAYMENTS	✕→	LATE_PAYMENTS
DATA_gb	→	DATA_gb
PEAK_mins	→	PEAK_mins
TEXT_count	→	TEXT_count

8. Preview the Filter node. Consider the following screenshot:

	ACCOUNT	Phone_Model	DATA_gb	PEAK_mins	TEXT_count
1	7617	SG200	-19.480	329.167	0.000
2	3926	G5	-12.987	896.333	0.000

9. Reverse the sort, now choosing descending order, and preview the Filter node. Consider the following screenshot for later use:

	ACCOUNT	Phone_Model	DATA_gb	PEAK_mins	TEXT_count
1	3164	105D	34.918	541.833	0.000
2	9552	SG200	25.974	1213.167	0.000
3	1139	SG200	25.974	820.000	0.000
4	495	X23	19.480	419.833	126.857
5	5041	SG200	19.480	271.000	0.000

10. Sort in descending order on the next variable, `PEAK_mins`. Preview the Filter node.

	ACCOUNT	Phone_Model	DATA_gb	PEAK_mins	TEXT_count
1	9498	105D	0.000	4632.500	0.000
2	219	X23	0.000	3614.333	0.000
3	3498	SG200	0.000	3117.667	0.000
4	1932	G5	0.000	3059.000	176.571
5	773	SG200	0.000	2740.167	0.000
6	3867	SG200	0.000	2489.333	0.000
7	3410	100D	0.000	2457.333	0.000
8	5770	SG200	0.000	2443.500	0.000
9	9680	X5000	0.000	2296.500	42.857
10	5645	X5000	0.000	2242.167	41.143
11	2889	300M	0.000	2156.000	0.000
12	3128	SG200	0.000	2141.833	373.714
13	511	SG200	14.930	2094.333	0.000
14	8598	SG200	0.000	2092.500	0.000
15	1321	105D	0.000	2023.000	18.857
16	992	X5000	0.000	2009.167	0.000

11. Finally sort the variable, `TEXT_count`, in descending order and preview the Filter node.

	ACCOUNT	Phone_Model	DATA_gb	PEAK_mins	TEXT_count
1	7981	SG200	0.000	107.333	9762.857
2	6079	120S	0.000	0.000	9673.714
3	2692	X5000	0.000	1215.833	8753.143
4	4421	X5000	0.000	144.667	5736.000
5	1538	X5000	0.000	848.833	5374.286
6	7215	100D	0.000	98.500	5122.286
7	1896	SG200	0.000	15.000	4112.571
8	4594	SG200	0.000	96.667	4032.000
9	175	X25	0.000	68.333	3884.571
10	2747	X5000	0.000	1.667	3867.429
11	3652	X5000	0.000	333.500	3857.143
12	9512	SG200	0.000	333.333	3804.000
13	6152	G5	0.000	600.500	3629.143
14	6277	105D	0.000	246.333	3584.571
15	6238	G5	0.000	33.000	3325.714
16	7175	SG200	0.000	1.667	3257.143
17	1101	X23	0.000	27.833	3106.286

12. Examine `Outliers.docx` to see an example of what this might look like in Word.

How it works...

There is no deep theoretical foundation to this recipe; it is as straightforward as it seems. It is simply a way of quickly getting information to an SME. They will not be frequent Modeler users. Also summary statistics only give them a part of the story. Providing the min, max, mean and median alone will not allow an SME to give you the information that you need. If there is a usual min such as a negative value, you need to know how many negatives there are, and need at least a handful of actual examples with IDs. An SME might look up to values in their own resources and the net result could be the addition of more variables to the analysis. Alternatively, negative values might be turned into nulls or zeros. Negative values might be deemed out of scope and removed from the analysis. There is no way to know until you assess why they are negative. Sometimes values that are exactly zero are of interest. High values, NULL values, and rare categories are all of potential interest. The most important thing is to be curious (and pleasantly persistent) and to inspire collaborators to be curious as well.

See also

- The *Selecting variables using the CHAID Modeling node* recipe in *Chapter 2, Data Preparation – Select*
- The *Removing redundant variables using correlation matrices* recipe in *Chapter 2, Data Preparation – Select*

Detecting potential model instability early using the Partition node and Feature Selection node

Model instability would typically be described as an issue most noticeably during the evaluation phase. Model instability usually manifests itself as a substantially stronger performance on the Train data set than on the Test data set. This bodes ill for the performance of the model on new data; in other words, it bodes ill for the practical application of the model to any business problem. Veteran data miners see this coming well before the evaluation phase, however, or at least they hope they do. The trick is to spot one of the most common causes; model instability is much more likely to occur when the same inputs are competing for the same variance in the model. In other words, when the inputs are correlated with each other to a large degree, it can cause problems. The data miner can also get themselves into hot water with their own behavior or imprudence. *Overfitting*, discussed in the *Introduction* of *Chapter 7, Modeling – Assessment, Evaluation, Deployment, and Monitoring*, can also cause model instability. The trick is to spot potential problems early. If the issue is in the set of inputs, this recipe can help to identify which inputs are at issue. The correlation matrix recipe and other data reduction recipes can assist in corrective action.

This recipe also serves as a cautionary tale about giving the Feature Selection node a heavier burden than it is capable of carrying. This node looks at the bivariate relationships of inputs with the target. Bivariate simply means two variables and it means that Feature Selection is blind to what might happen when lots of inputs attempt to collaborate together to predict the target. Bivariate analyses are not without value, they are critical to the Data Understanding phase, but the goal of the data miner is to recruit a team of variables. The team's performance is based upon a number of factors, only one of which is the ability of each input to predict the target variable.

Getting ready

We will start with the `Stability.str` stream.

How to do it...

To detect potential model instability using the Partition and Feature Selection nodes, perform the following steps:

1. Open the stream, `Stability.str`.

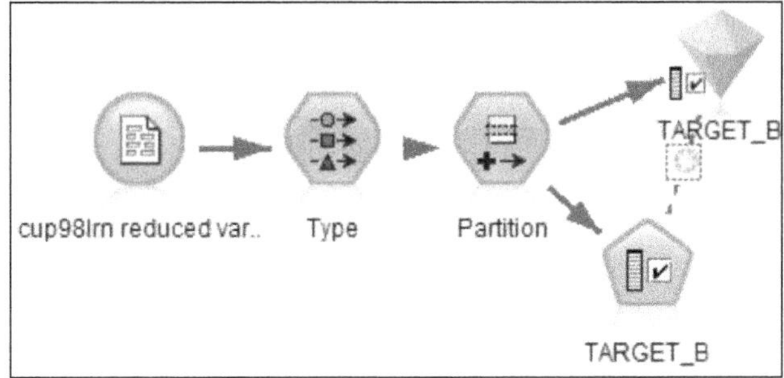

2. Edit the Partition node, click on the **Generate** seed button, and run it. (Since you will not get the same seed as the figure shown, your results will differ. This is not a concern. In fact, it helps illustrate the point behind the recipe.)

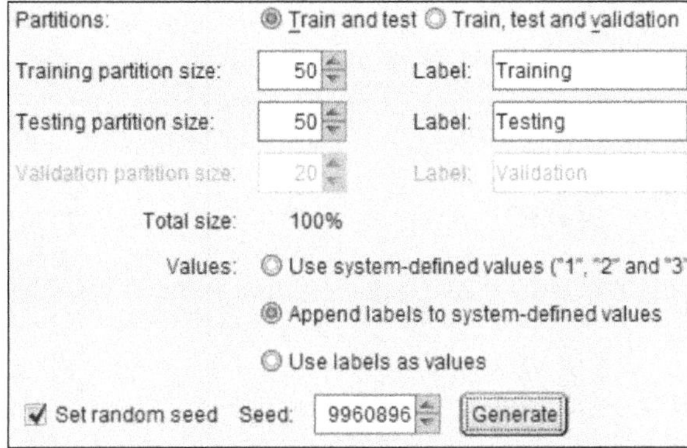

3. Run the Feature Selection Modeling node and then edit the resulting generated model. Note the ranking of potential inputs may differ if the seed is different.

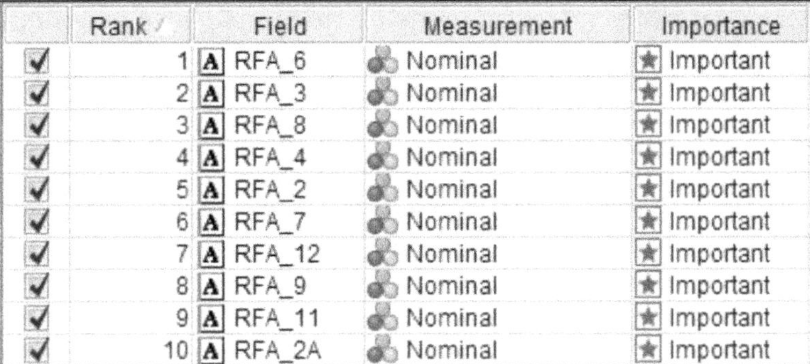

	Rank	Field	Measurement	Importance
✔	1	RFA_6	Nominal	Important
✔	2	RFA_3	Nominal	Important
✔	3	RFA_8	Nominal	Important
✔	4	RFA_4	Nominal	Important
✔	5	RFA_2	Nominal	Important
✔	6	RFA_7	Nominal	Important
✔	7	RFA_12	Nominal	Important
✔	8	RFA_9	Nominal	Important
✔	9	RFA_11	Nominal	Important
✔	10	RFA_2A	Nominal	Important

4. Edit the Partition node, generate a new seed, and then run the Feature Selection again.

5. Edit the Feature Selection generated model.

	Rank	Field	Measurement	Importance
✓	1	RFA_6	Nominal	Important
✓	2	RFA_4	Nominal	Important
✓	3	RFA_3	Nominal	Important
✓	4	RFA_8	Nominal	Important
✓	5	RFA_2	Nominal	Important
✓	6	RFA_11	Nominal	Important
✓	7	RFA_2A	Nominal	Important
✓	8	RFA_2F	Continuous	Important
✓	9	RFA_5	Nominal	Important
✓	10	CARDGIFT	Continuous	Important

6. For a third and final time, edit the Partition node, generate a new seed, and then run the Feature Selection. Edit the generated model.

	Rank	Field	Measurement	Importance
✓	1	RFA_4	Nominal	Important
✓	2	RFA_3	Nominal	Important
✓	3	RFA_6	Nominal	Important
✓	4	RFA_8	Nominal	Important
✓	5	RFA_2	Nominal	Important
✓	6	RFA_7	Nominal	Important
✓	7	RFA_12	Nominal	Important
✓	8	RFA_11	Nominal	Important
✓	9	RFA_9	Nominal	Important
✓	10	RFA_2A	Nominal	Important

How it works...

At first glance, one might anticipate no major problems ahead. `RFA_6`, which is the donor status calculated six campaigns ago, is in first place twice and is in third place once. Clearly it provides some value, so what is the danger in proceeding to the next phase? The change in ranking from seed to seed is revealing something important about this set of variables. These variables are behaving like variables that are similar to each other. They are all descriptions of past donation behavior at different times. The larger the number after the underscore, the further back in time they represent. Why isn't the most recent variable, `RFA_2`, shown as the most predictive? Frankly, there is a good chance that it is the most predictive, but these variables are fighting over top status in the small decimal places of this analysis. We can trust Feature Selection to alert us that they are potentially important, but it is dangerous to trust the ranking under these circumstances, and it certainly doesn't mean than if we were to restrict our inputs to the top ten that we would get a good model.

The behavior revealed here is not a good indication of how these variables will behave in a model, a classification tree, or any other multiple input techniques. In a tree, once a branch is formed using `RFA_6`, the tendency would be for the model to seek a variable that sheds light on some other aspect of the data. The variable used to form the second branch would likely not be the second variable on the list because the first and second variables are similar to each other. The implication of this is that, if `RFA_4` were chosen as the first branch, `RFA_6` might not be chosen at all.

Each situation is different, but perhaps the best option here is to identify what these related variables have in common and distill it into a smaller set of variables. To the extent that these variables have a unique contribution to make—perhaps in the magnitude of their distance in the past—that too could be brought into higher relief during data preparation.

See also

- The *Selecting variables using the CHAID Modeling node* recipe in *Chapter 2, Data Preparation - Select*
- The *Removing redundant variables using correlation matrices* recipe in *Chapter 2, Data Preparation - Select*

2
Data Preparation – Select

In this chapter, we will cover:

- Using the Feature Selection node creatively to remove or decapitate perfect predictors
- Running a Statistics node on an anti-join to evaluate the potential missing data
- Evaluating the use of sampling for speed
- Removing redundant variables using correlation matrices
- Selecting variables using the CHAID Modeling node
- Selecting variables using the Means node
- Selecting variables using single-antecedent Association Rules

Introduction

This chapter focuses on just the first task, Select, of the data preparation phase:

Decide on the data to be used for analysis. Criteria include relevance to the data mining goals, quality, and technical constraints such as limits on data volume or data types. Note that data selection covers selection of attributes (columns) as well as selection of records (rows) in a table.

Ideally, data mining empowers business people to discover valuable patterns in large quantities of data, to develop useful models and integrate them into the business quickly and easily. The name data mining suggests that large quantities of data will be involved, that the object is to extract rare and elusive bits of the data, and that data mining calls for working with data in bulk—no sampling.

New data miners are often struck by how much selection and sampling is actually done. For some, the stereotypical data miner dives in and looks at everything. It is unclear how such an unfocused search would yield any deployable results. Years ago, some Modeler documentation told the tale of the vanishing terabyte—the name alone communicates the basic idea. The data miner in the story, terrified that their systems can't handle the volume, begins the actual act of choosing the relevant data only to discover that they only have a few hundred instances of fraud.

One could argue that the fear of Big Data stems from a misunderstanding of selection and sampling. Large data warehouses filled to the brim with data are a reality, but one doesn't data-mine the undifferentiated whole. Some of the discussion about large data files assumes that all questions require all rows of data as far back in time as they are stored. This is certainly not true. One might use only a small fraction of one's data, that fraction that allows you to accurately and efficiently answer the problem as defined during the business understanding phase.

Also, a data miner does not select data in the way that a statistician does. Statisticians do much more heavy lifting during their variable selection phase. They emerge from that phase with perhaps just a handful of variables, possibly a dozen or two at the absolute most, but never hundreds. The data miner might very well start with a presumption that there will be dozens of inputs, with hundreds being common, and thousands not unheard of. In statistics, hypotheses determine the independent variables from the offset. That is not the nature of the selection discussed here. If you are selecting a subset of rows, it is for relevance, balancing, speed, or a combination of them. Another way to summarize this difference is, if the statistician favors parsimony at this stage, the data miner favors comprehensiveness. A statistician might lean towards variables that have proven to be valuable; the data miner excludes only those variables that are going to cause problems. (The recipe on decapitation is a prime example of avoiding problems.)

Despite the advantage of favoring comprehensiveness, in practice, it is difficult to make discoveries and build models quickly when working with massive quantities of data. Although data mining tools may be designed to streamline the process, it still takes longer for each operation to complete on a large amount of data than it would with a smaller quantity. In the course of a day, the data miner will run many operations, importing, graphing, cleaning, restructuring, and so on. If each one takes an extra minute or two due to the quantity of data involved, the extra minutes add up to a large portion of the day. As the data set grows larger, the time required to run each step also increases, and the data miner spends more time waiting, leaving less time for critical thinking.

So, what's more important, working quickly or working with all the available data? The answer is not the same in every case. Some analyses really do focus on rare and elusive elements of the data. An example can be found in the network security field, where the object is to discover the tracks of a lone intruder among a sea of legitimate system users. In that case, handling a large mass of data is a practical necessity. Yet most data mining applications do not focus on such rare events. Buyers among prospects are a minority, but they are not rare. The same can be said for many other applications. Data miners are most often asked to focus on behavior that is relatively common.

If the pattern of interest happens frequently, perhaps once in a hundred cases, rather than once in a million, it is not necessary to use large masses of data at every step in order to uncover the pattern. Since that is a common situation, most data miners have the opportunity to improve their own productivity by using smaller quantities of data whenever possible. Judicious use of sampling allows the data miner to work with just enough data for any given purpose, reducing the time required to run each of many operations throughout the day.

Having said all that, it is a terribly important set of decisions. Data miners, in principle, want all the data to have an opportunity to speak. However, variables included have to have some possibility of relevance and can't interfere with other variables. One tries to keep the subjectivity at bay, but it is a challenging phase. All of these recipes deal with deciding which rows to keep, and deciding which variables to keep; as one begins to prepare a modeling data set. Modeling will likely be weeks away at this point, but this is the start of that ongoing process. In the end, the goal would be to have every relevant phenomenon measured in some form, preferably in exactly one variable. Redundancy, while perhaps not causing the same problems that it causes in statistical techniques, does nonetheless cause problems. The correlation matrix recipe, among others, addresses this issue.

Although selection includes selecting rows (cases), some of the toughest choices involve Variables. Variable selection is a key step in the data mining process. Several reasons for variable filtering or removal include:

- Removing redundant variables; redundant variables waste time and computational bandwidth needlessly. Moreover, they can introduce instabilities in some modeling algorithms, such as linear regression.
- Removing variables without any information (constants or near constants).
- Reducing the number of variables in the analysis because there are too many for efficient model building.
- Reducing the cost of deploying models. When variables are expensive to collect, assessing if the added benefit justifies its inclusion, or if other, less expensive variables can provide the same or nearly the same accuracy.

The first and the second reasons should be done during the select data step of the data preparation stage. Sometimes it is obvious which variables are essentially identical, though often highly correlated variables or near-zero variance variables are only discovered through explicit testing.

The third reason can be done during data preparation or modeling. Some modeling algorithms have variable selection built-in, such as decision trees or stepwise regression. Other algorithms do not have variable selection built-in, such as nearest neighbor and Neural Networks. However, even if an algorithm has some form of variable selection built-in, variable selection prior to modeling can still be advantageous for efficiency so the same poor or redundant predictors aren't considered over and over again.

The fourth reason is usually done after models are built when one can assess directly the value of variables in the final models.

Five of the chapter's recipes focus on selecting variables prior to modeling, making modeling more efficient. The most common approach to removing variables is to perform single-variable selection based upon the relationship of the variable with the target variable. The logic behind this kind of variable selection is that variables that don't have a strong relationship with the target variable by themselves are unlikely to combine well with other variables in a final model. This is certainly the case with forward selection algorithms (decision trees, forward selection in regression models, to name two examples), but of course isn't always the case.

The Feature Selection node in Modeler is effective in removing variables with no or little variance as well as variables with a weak relationship to the target variable. However, the feature selection node does not identify redundant variables. In addition, despite its ability to select variables with significant association to the target variable, the degree of the association between the input variable and the target variable is not transparent from the Feature Selection node. It focuses, instead, on the statistical significance of the relationship. The Feature Selection node can also remove too aggressively if you have not addressed issues with the missing data.

Four of the variable recipes here (selecting variables using correlations, CHAID, the Means node, and Association Rules) rely on exporting reports from Modeler into Microsoft Excel to facilitate the selection process.

Using the Feature Selection node creatively to remove or decapitate perfect predictors

In this recipe, we will identify perfect or near perfect predictors in order to insure that they do not contaminate our model. Perfect predictors earn their name by being correct 100 percent of the time, usually indicating circular logic and not a prediction of value. It is a common and serious problem.

When this occurs we have accidentally allowed information into the model that could not possibly be known at the time of the prediction. Everyone 30 days late on their mortgage receives a late letter, but receiving a late letter is not a good predictor of lateness because their lateness caused the letter, not the other way around.

The rather colorful term decapitate is borrowed from the data miner *Dorian Pyle*. It is a reference to the fact that perfect predictors will be found at the top of any list of key drivers ("caput" means head in Latin). Therefore, to decapitate is to remove the variable at the top. Their status at the top of the list will be capitalized upon in this recipe.

The following table shows the three time periods; the past, the present, and the future. It is important to remember that, when we are making predictions, we can use information from the past to predict the present or the future but we cannot use information from the future to predict the future. This seems obvious, but it is common to see analysts use information that was gathered after the date for which predictions are made. As an example, if a company sends out a notice after a customer has churned, you cannot say that the notice is predictive of churning.

	Past	**Now**	**Future**	
	Contract Start	**Expiration**	**Outcome**	**Renewal Date**
Joe	January 1, 2010	January 1, 2012	Renewed	January 2, 2012
Ann	February 15, 2010	February 15, 2012	Out of Contract	Null
Bill	March 21, 2010	March 21, 2012	Churn	NA
Jack	April 5, 2010	April 5, 2012	Renewed	April 9, 2012
New Customer	24 Months Ago	Today	???	???

Getting ready

We will start with a blank stream, and will be using the `cup98lrn reduced vars2.txt` data set.

How to do it...

To identify perfect or near-perfect predictors in order to insure that they do not contaminate our model:

1. Build a stream with a Source node, a Type node, and a Table then force instantiation by running the Table node.
2. Force **TARGET_B** to be flag and make it the target.

3. Add a Feature Selection Modeling node and run it.

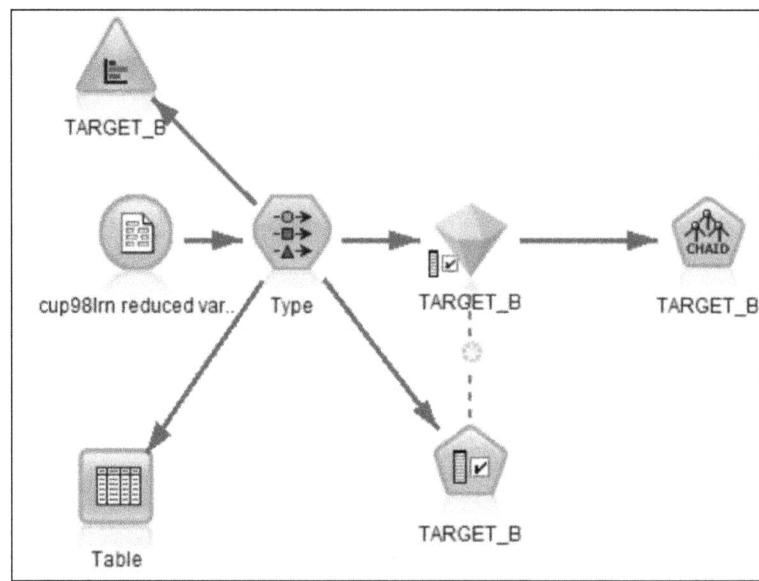

4. Edit the resulting generated model and examine the results. In particular, focus on the top of the list.

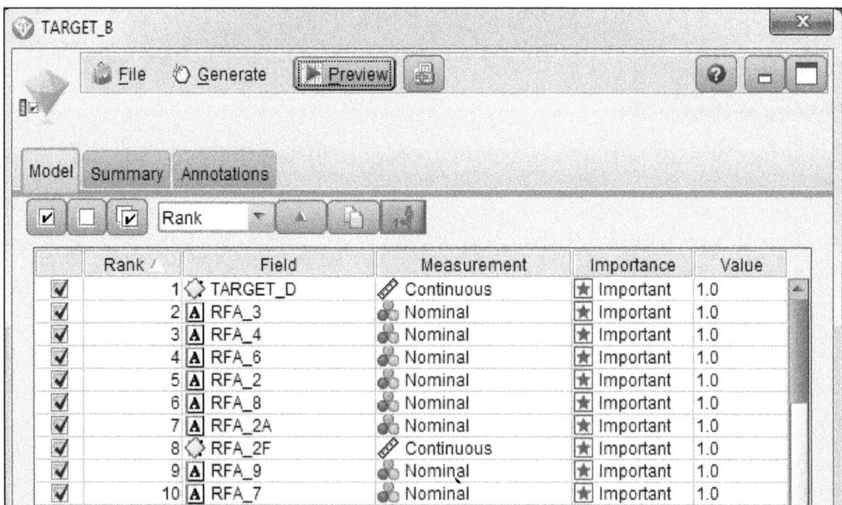

	Rank	Field	Measurement	Importance	Value
✓	1	TARGET_D	Continuous	Important	1.0
✓	2	RFA_3	Nominal	Important	1.0
✓	3	RFA_4	Nominal	Important	1.0
✓	4	RFA_6	Nominal	Important	1.0
✓	5	RFA_2	Nominal	Important	1.0
✓	6	RFA_8	Nominal	Important	1.0
✓	7	RFA_2A	Nominal	Important	1.0
✓	8	RFA_2F	Continuous	Important	1.0
✓	9	RFA_9	Nominal	Important	1.0
✓	10	RFA_7	Nominal	Important	1.0

5. Review what you know about the top variables, and check to see if any could be related to the target by definition or could possibly be based on information that actually postdates the information in the target.

6. Add a CHAID Modeling node, set it to run in **Interactive** mode, and run it.
7. Examine the first branch, looking for any child node that might be perfectly predicted; that is, look for child nodes whose members are all found in one category.

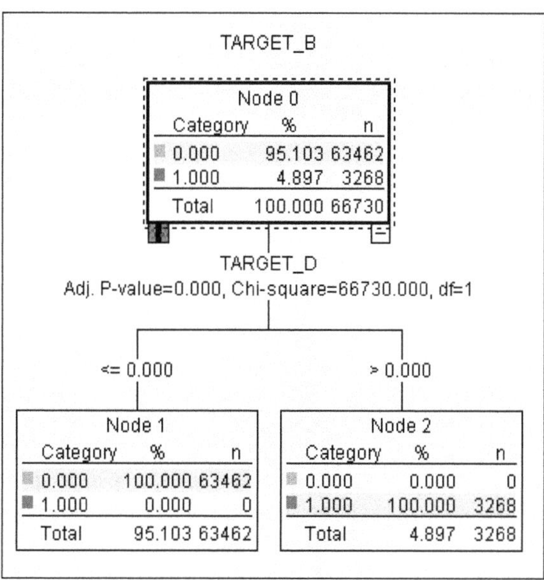

8. Continue steps 6 and 7 for the first several variables.

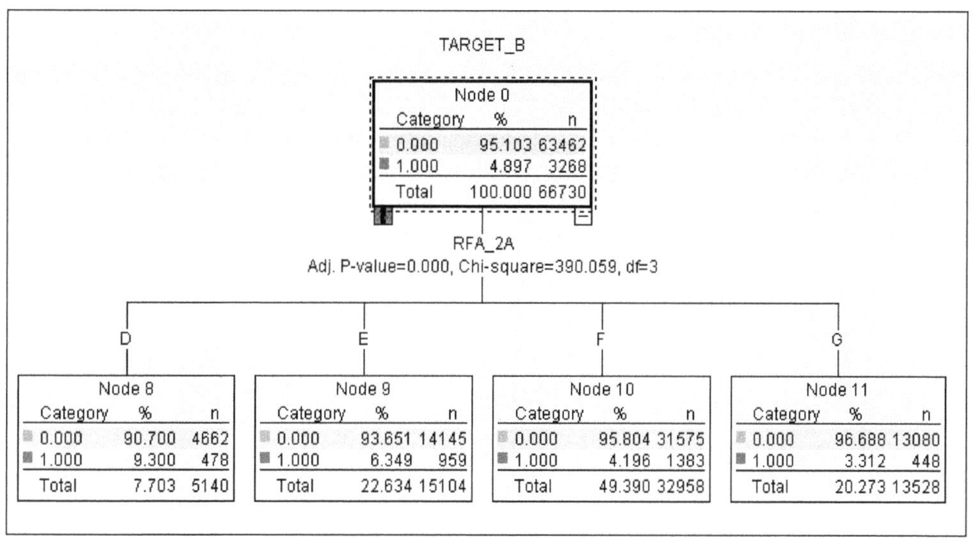

9. Variables that are problematic (steps 5 and/or 7) need to be set to **None** in the Type node.

How it works...

Which variables need decapitation? The problem is information that, although it was known at the time that you extracted it, was not known at the time of decision. In this case, the time of decision is the decision that the potential donor made to donate or not to donate. Was the amount, **Target_D** known before the decision was made to donate? Clearly not. No information that dates after the information in the target variable can ever be used in a predictive model.

This recipe is built of the following foundation—variables with this problem will float up to the top of the Feature Selection results.

They may not always be perfect predictors, but perfect predictors always must go. For example, you might find that, if a customer initially rejects or postpones a purchase, there should be a follow up sales call in 90 days. They are recorded as *rejected offer* in the campaign, and as a result most of them had a follow up call in 90 days after the campaign. Since a couple of the follow up calls might not have happened, it won't be a perfect predictor, but it still must go.

Note that variables such as `RFA_2` and `RFA_2A` are both very recent information and highly predictive. Are they a problem? You can't be absolutely certain without knowing the data. Here the information recorded in these variables is calculated just prior to the campaign. If the calculation was made just after, they would have to go. The CHAID tree almost certainly would have shown evidence of perfect prediction in this case.

There's more...

Sometimes a model has to have a lot of lead time; predicting today's weather is a different challenge than next year's prediction in the farmer's almanac. When more lead time is desired you could consider dropping all of the `_2` series variables. What would the advantage be? What if you were buying advertising space and there was a 45 day delay for the advertisement to appear? If the `_2` variables occur between your advertising deadline and your campaign you might have to use information attained in the `_3` campaign.

See also

- The *Using an @NULL multiple Derive to explore missing data* recipe in *Chapter 1, Data Understanding*
- The *Using CHAID stumps when interviewing an SME* recipe in *Chapter 1, Data Understanding*

Running a Statistics node on anti-join to evaluate the potential missing data

There is typically some data loss when various data tables are integrated. Although we won't discuss data integration until a later chapter, it is important to gauge what (and how much) is lost at this stage. Financial variables are usually aggregated in very different ways for the financial planner and the data miner. It is critical that the data miner periodically translate the data of the data miner back into the form that middle and senior management will recognize so that they can better communicate.

The data miner deals with transactions and individual customer data, the language of individual rows of data. The manager speaks, generally, the language of spreadsheets: regions, product lines, months rolled up into aggregated cells in Excel.

On a project, we once discovered that a small percentage of missing rows represented a larger fraction of revenue than average—much larger actually. We suddenly revisited our decision to drop those rows. Dropping them seemed the right decision—they were just bad IDs weren't they? Well, it is never that simple. There are few accidents in data. That experience produced a lesson:

Always include a revenue assessment in your decisions even when revenue is neither your input nor your target.

In this recipe we will learn a simple trick for assessing these variables at times when there is the potential for data loss.

Getting ready

We will start with a blank stream, and will be using the retail `Transactions` file and the `Products_Missing` file.

How to do it...

To evaluate potential missing data when integrating data:

1. Build a stream with both of the Source nodes, two Type nodes, and a Merge node.

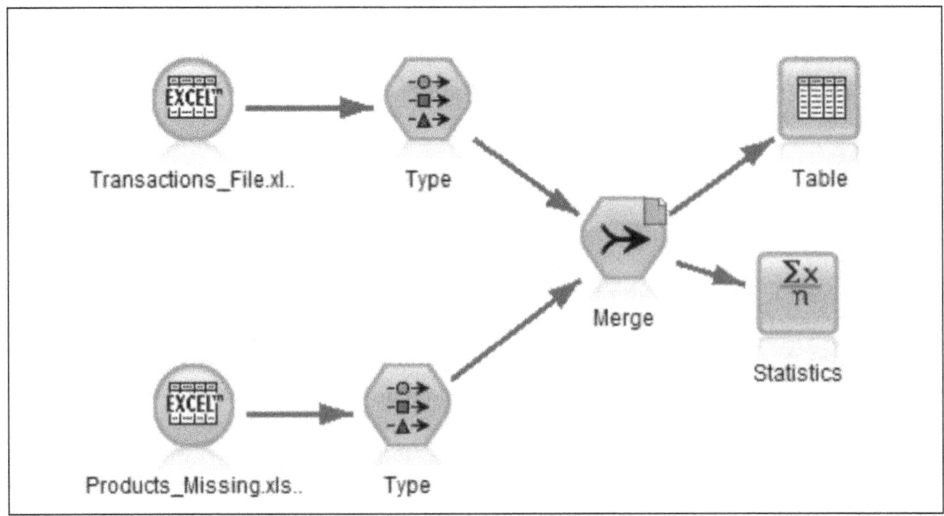

2. Perform an anti-join and make a note of the record count.
3. Run a Statistics node and request: **Count**, **Sum**, **Mean**, and **Median**.

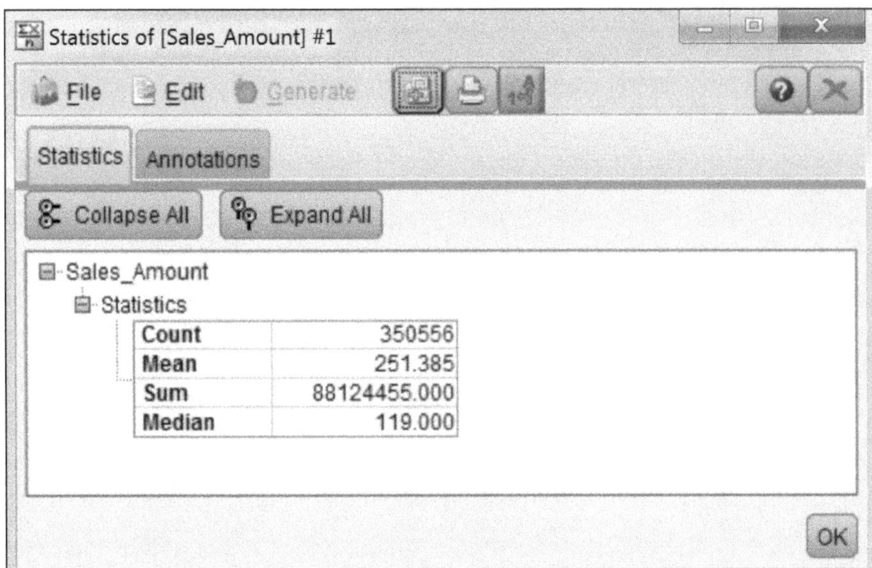

Count	350556
Mean	251.385
Sum	88124455.000
Median	119.000

4. Set **Products_Missing** to be the first input, and run the Merge node making a note of the record count. Since there is only one record we will not run a Stats node.
5. Reverse the inputs and repeat the merge, again making note of the record count.

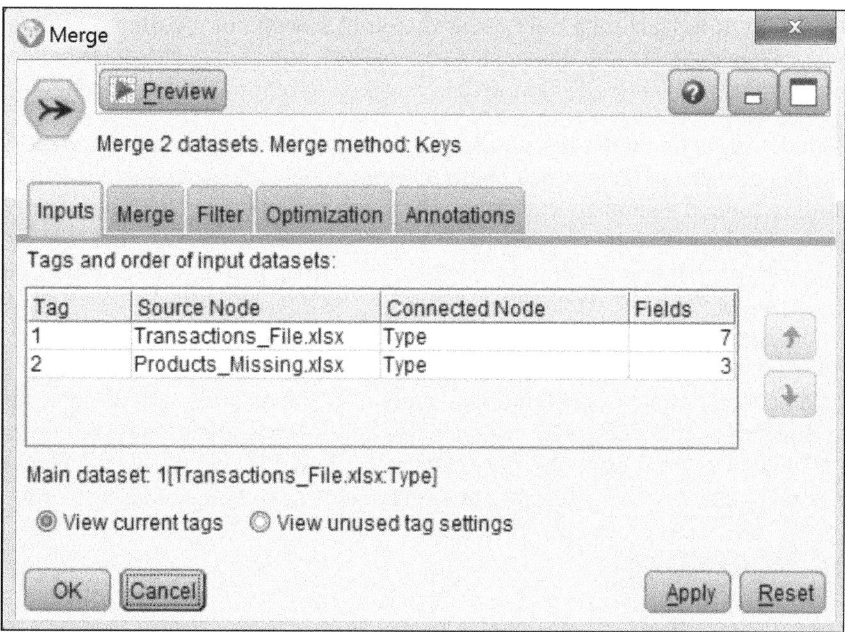

6. Re-run the Statistics node.

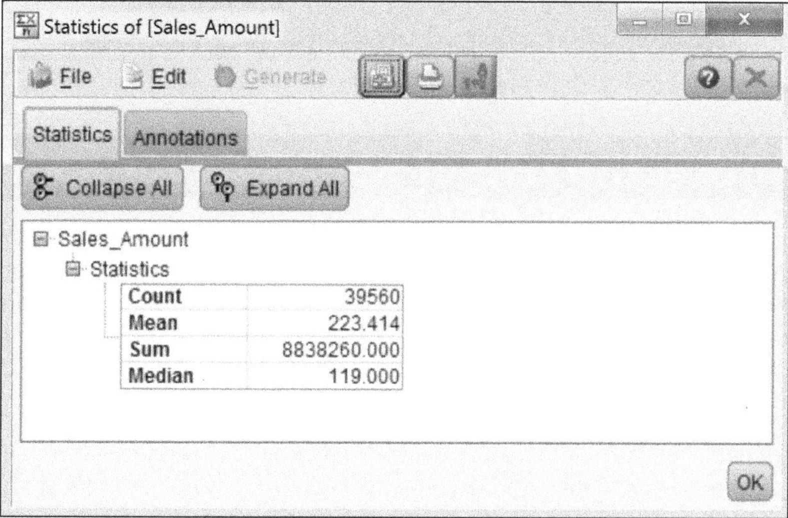

How it works...

Years ago on a project we discovered that 5 percent of the data—data that happened to be missing—represented more than 20 percent of the revenue. We expect, or perhaps more likely, we hope, that missing data will not derail us, but sometimes it certainly threatens the whole project. This recipe is about choosing your battles, identifying when missing data is a particularly serious problem and when we can move on to other aspects of the project.

Here, the bad news is that there is a substantial amount of missing data in the products file. How could this ever occur? The novice might be surprised. It occurs frequently. Perhaps the company just acquired a smaller retailer and there are issues in the old transactional data of the old vendor not matching up properly. There is good news, however. The average and median of the inner join and the anti-join suggest that we appear to have missing data that is missing at random and not systematically. It would be a much bigger problem if the usual customers (maybe even our best customers) were the ones that were missing. This is not usually the case although sometimes it takes detective work to figure out why. There is one additional bit of bad news, however; the total amount of the missing data points is not trivial. While it is dwarfed by the nearly 90 million that we can analyze, the missing 8 million might be large enough to warrant extensive data cleaning. One would now move to diagnose the problem, and if it seems achievable, and at a reasonable cost, address the problem.

See also

- The *Using an @NULL multiple Derive to explore missing data* recipe in *Chapter 1, Data Understanding*
- The *Creating an Outlier report to give to SMEs* recipe in *Chapter 1, Data Understanding*
- The *Using a full data model/partial data model approach to address missing data* recipe in *Chapter 3, Data Preparation – Clean*

Evaluating the use of sampling for speed

Modern data mining practice is somewhat different from the ideal. Data miners certainly do develop valuable models that are used in the business and many have massive resources of data to mine, even more data than might have been foreseen a generation ago. But not all data miners meet the profile of a business user, someone whose primary work responsibility is not data analysis and who is not trained in, or concerned with, statistical methods. Nor does the modern data miner shy away from sampling.

In practice, it has been difficult to make discoveries and build models quickly when working with massive quantities of data. Although data mining tools may be designed to streamline the process, it still takes longer for each operation to complete on a large amount of data than it would with a smaller quantity. This sampling can be extremely useful.

Getting ready

We will start with a blank stream, and will be using the `cup98lrn reduced vars2.txt` data set.

How to do it...

To evaluate the need for sampling:

1. Build a stream with a Source node, a Type node, and a Table node then force instantiation by running the Table node.
2. Force **TARGET_B** to be flag and make it the target. Set **TARGET_D** to **None**.
3. Add a Partition node downstream of the Type node.
4. Add a Feature Selection Modeling node and run it. (It will act like a filter, but it is critical not to trust it unless the data is clean.)
5. Add an Auto Classifier node and edit it. Choose to use 9 Models (the default is 3).

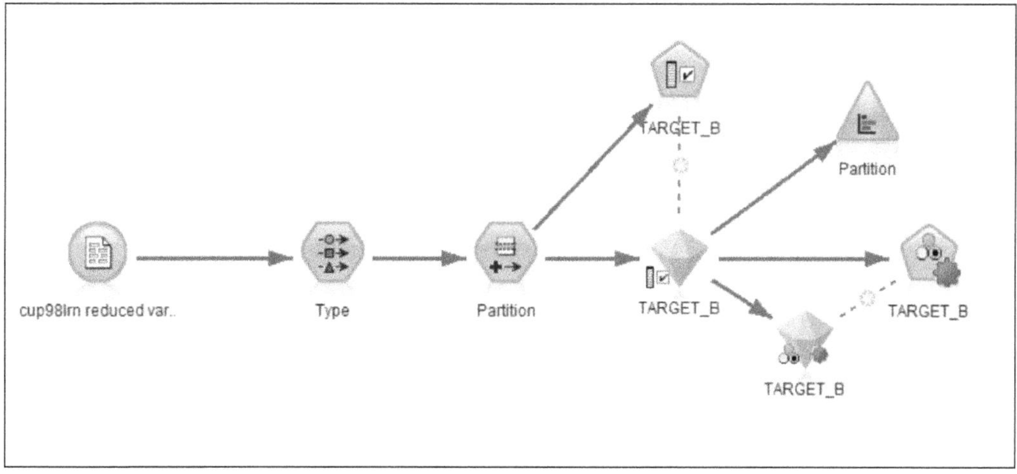

6. If you run the stream at this stage be prepared for a potentially long wait. The results of the stream at this stage are shown in the *How it works* section of this recipe.
7. Add a Sample node set to `10` percent in between the Source node and the Type node.

8. Cache the Sample node and force execution by running a table off the Sample node.

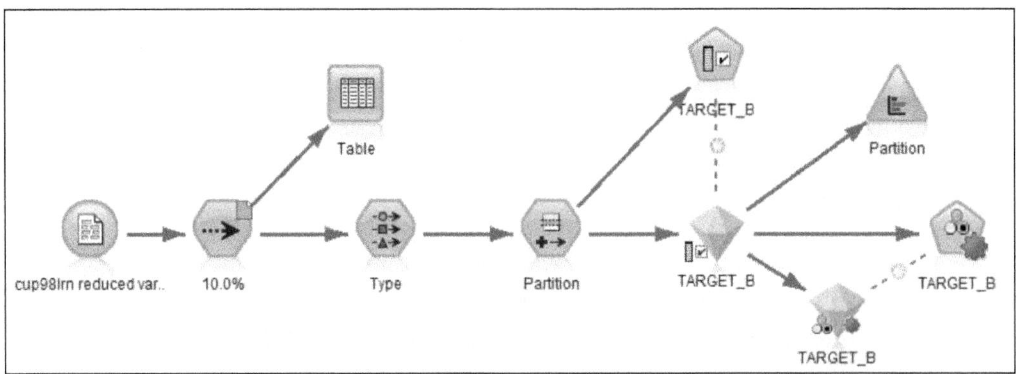

9. Run the **Auto Classifier**, and make note of the duration. (A test run on a newer machine took about 1 minute for the sampled data versus 13 minutes on the complete data.)
10. Add in **SVM** and **KNN** in the Auto Classifier and re-run. Note the duration. (A test run on complete data using all 11 classifiers was manually halted after running 3.5 hours.)
11. Take action to save your cache for future sessions:
    - Either right-click on the Sample node and save the cache
    - Or write the Sample node out to an external file

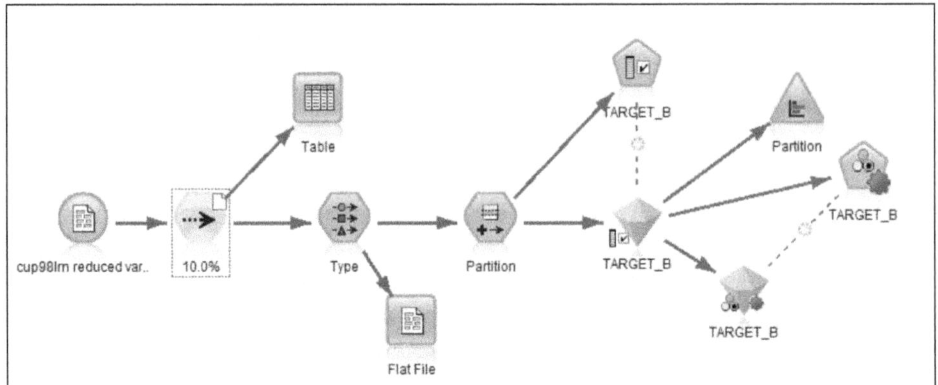

How it works...

This recipe is a demonstration of sorts. These steps are indeed the steps in sampling for speed. However, eventually your instincts will tell you that a model (or set of models) is going to be time-consuming. One does not need to run the stream in step 6 because we know, in advance, that it will take a long time. It is critical to remember that you are not in the modeling phase at this stage. You are merely planning. Notice that the Auto Classifier deselects SVMs and KNN as they are computationally expensive. It would be imprudent to be so skittish about sampling that you actually reduced the number of classifier models that you considered. (A test run on complete data using all 11 classifiers was manually halted after running 3.5 hours, but even a run on the sample failed. Unclean data is rougher on some algorithms than others.)

It is also critical to not trust the Feature Selection node to choose the best variables. We are simply using its ability to temporarily filter out variables that need cleaning to such an extent that they would cause the classifiers to fail. You won't get an early assessment of your data if the Auto Classifier turns red and fails to run.

Why not just select the most recent data or the current month? This actually can be quite effective, but it has risks as well. If the Target variable is affected by seasonality it probably is better to take a random sample of a year than to select a month.

This recipe will not be effective unless you pay careful attention to the caching of the Sample node. When you turn this feature on, the node will have an icon with the appearance of a white piece of paper. Once the cache turns green, the data has been stored. If you don't force it to cache before you model, it is performing the randomization and the modeling in the same step, and you won't notice an increase in speed until the second time that you run the model.

The bottom line is that, when you are doing initial exploration of the data, it is often appropriate to do bivariate and univariate analyses on all of your data; that is, use Distribution nodes and Data Audit nodes, because they run quickly on large files. Also, you generally use all of your data when you merge your data. But, it doesn't always make sense to run experimental, exploratory multivariate models on the entire data set when a random sample will give similar results. Running all the data will tend to change your behavior in a negative way, you will avoid computationally expensive algorithms, and/or you will avoid tuning the model properly.

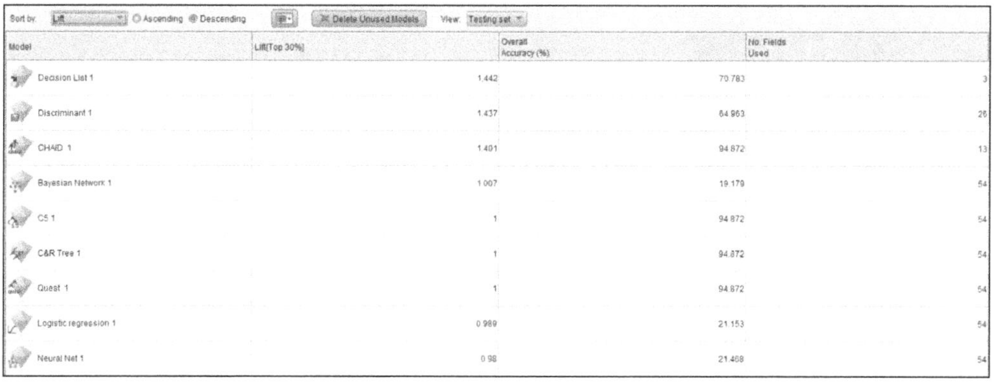

Sort by: Lift ○ Ascending ◉ Descending Delete Unused Models View: Testing set

Model	Lift{Top 30%}	Overall Accuracy (%)	No. Fields Used
Decision List 1	1.442	70.783	3
Discriminant 1	1.437	64.963	26
CHAID 1	1.401	94.872	13
Bayesian Network 1	1.007	19.179	54
C5 1	1	94.872	54
C&R Tree 1	1	94.872	54
Quest 1	1	94.872	54
Logistic regression 1	0.989	21.153	54
Neural Net 1	0.98	21.468	54

Note that the results on the sampled data (shown in the following screenshot) and the result of the complete data (shown in the previous screenshot) are similar. At first glance, they may not look similar, but if you scratch the surface, you would learn what you need at this stage from the sample. The CHAID model on complete data uses more variables, but that is a consequence of CHAID's stopping rules. It is noteworthy that the accuracy of using 13 variables is nearly the same as using only four. What have you learned? Merely that those four variables are probably worth a closer look, and that it might be a good idea to run CHAID interactively to better understand what is going on. It would also be a useful exercise to compare the top variables in each of these models. In short, you've learned which clean variables have promise, but the potential of the variables that need cleaning is still a complete mystery.

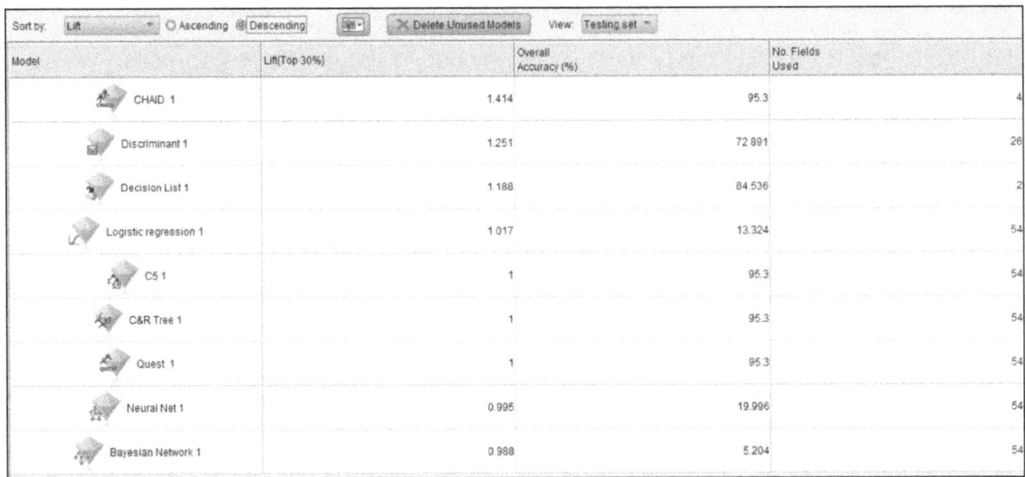

Sort by: Lift ○ Ascending ◉ Descending | Delete Unused Models | View: Testing set

Model	Lift{Top 30%}	Overall Accuracy (%)	No. Fields Used
CHAID 1	1.414	95.3	4
Discriminant 1	1.251	72.891	26
Decision List 1	1.188	84.536	2
Logistic regression 1	1.017	13.324	54
C5 1	1	95.3	54
C&R Tree 1	1	95.3	54
Quest 1	1	95.3	54
Neural Net 1	0.995	19.996	54
Bayesian Network 1	0.988	5.204	54

It is critical to always test and validate against unbalanced data. Modeler automatically uses unbalanced data for the test. However, if you have taken a simple random sample you have effectively removed that data from the available data processed in the stream. Validation, unlike modeling, is fast so you almost always want complete data when you validate. Typically the most recent month is a great *dress rehearsal*. On most projects, the most recent month did not exist when the project began so it makes a perfect test. Run all of that most recent month—unbalanced and complete—as a validation.

There's more...

Remember that sampling must not always be simple random sampling (the kind that we demonstrate here). Balancing is a kind of sampling. Building models with and without new donors is a variation on the theme. The Sampling node also supports complex sampling. While not covered here, it is a topic in its own right.

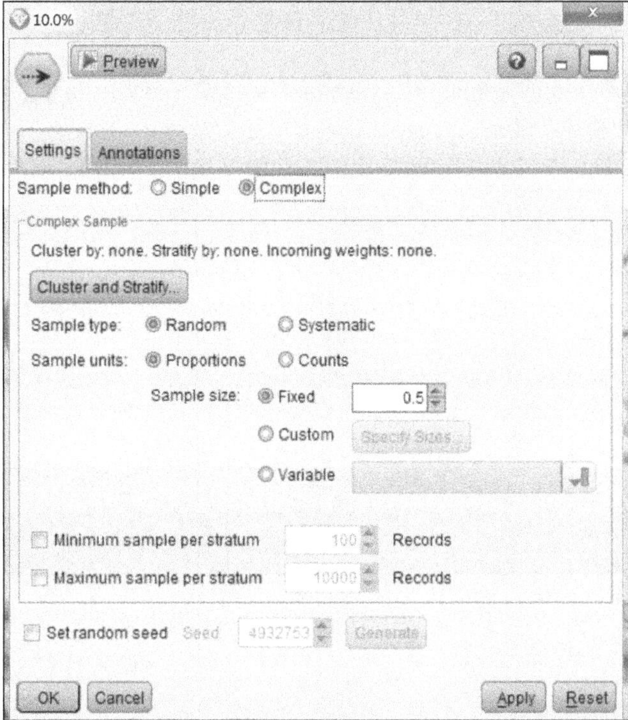

It is also important to not get too excited that there are a handful of variables that seem to show promise. It is only a handful, and there is a long road ahead at this stage. The emphasis would immediately turn to cleaning the data and saving some of the variables filtered out by the Feature Selection node. Many variables were dropped because they need attention, not because they hold no value.

Why bother with all of this when we won't use these models as the final model?

- It is disheartening to spend weeks cleaning data with little sense of where you stand.
- It is not a bad idea to spend more time on the top three classifiers models and less time on the bottom three classifiers. While this is common sense, be forewarned that when you rerun on clean data the ranking may change dramatically.
- As you add more and more clean variables to the models it can be useful (and rewarding) to find that new variables are continuously joining the top ten. During this lengthy process it would be pointless to run algorithms that are taking hours; after all, you are still shoulder-deep in data prep at that point.

After the lengthy process of data prep draws to a close and you enter into the modeling phase, you may possibly decide to increase the percentage of your sample and/or eliminate it altogether. After all, at that stage you will have clean data and will have narrowed your modeling approach to your "semi-finalists". Why not just let it run overnight?

See also

- The *Using an empty aggregate to evaluate sample size* recipe in *Chapter 1, Data Understanding*
- The *Evaluating the need to sample from the initial data* recipe in *Chapter 1, Data Understanding*
- The *Using a full data model/partial data model approach to address missing data* recipe in *Chapter 3, Data Preparation - Clean*
- The *Speeding up merge with caching and optimization settings* recipe in *Chapter 5, Data Preparation - Integrate and Format*
- The *How (and why) to validate as well as test* recipe in *Chapter 7, Modeling - Assessment, Evaluation, Deployment, and Monitoring*

Removing redundant variables using correlation matrices

In this recipe we will remove redundant variables by building a correlation matrix that identifies highly correlated variables.

Getting ready

This recipe uses the datafile, `nasadata.txt` and the stream file, `recipe_variableselection_correlations.str`.

You will need a copy of Microsoft Excel to visualize the correlation matrix.

How to do it...

To remove redundant variables using correlation matrices:

1. Open the stream, `recipe_variableselection_correlations.str` by navigating to **File** | **Open Stream**.
2. Make sure the datafile points to the correct path to the file `nasadata.txt`.
3. Open the Type node named `Correlation Types`. Notice that there are several variables of type continuous whose direction values have been set to **Input**, and a single continuous variable has its direction set to **Target**. The variable set to Target can be any variable that won't be an input to the model. If you don't have a good candidate, you can create a random variable and set that one to be the Target, as is done in this stream.

4. Open the generated model, `random_target`, and click on the **Advanced options**. Note that **Descriptives** is selected. This is the option that creates the correlation matrix for you. Note that this Linear Regression node is the old Modeler regression node. The new Regression node no longer provides a correlation matrix.

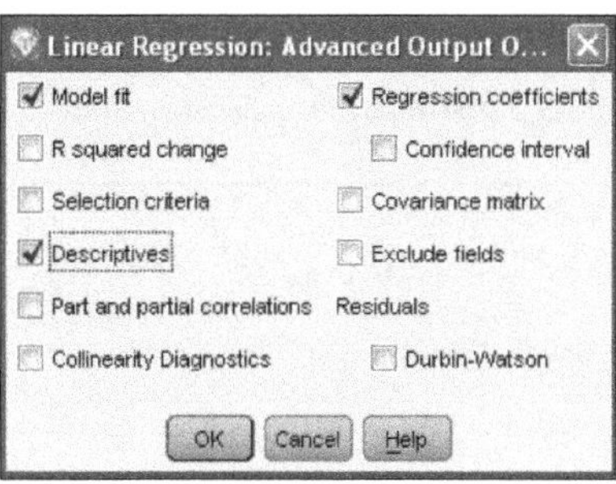

5. Build the linear regression model. Open the resulting generated model and click on the **Advanced** tab. You will see the advanced report that includes a **Pearson correlation** matrix similar to what appears in the following screenshot. However, with many variables, this report is difficult to browse to identify the correlations. Navigate to **File** | **Export** | **Advanced** and save the advanced report as an `html` file. Any name will work but save it as `Correlations.html` for this recipe.

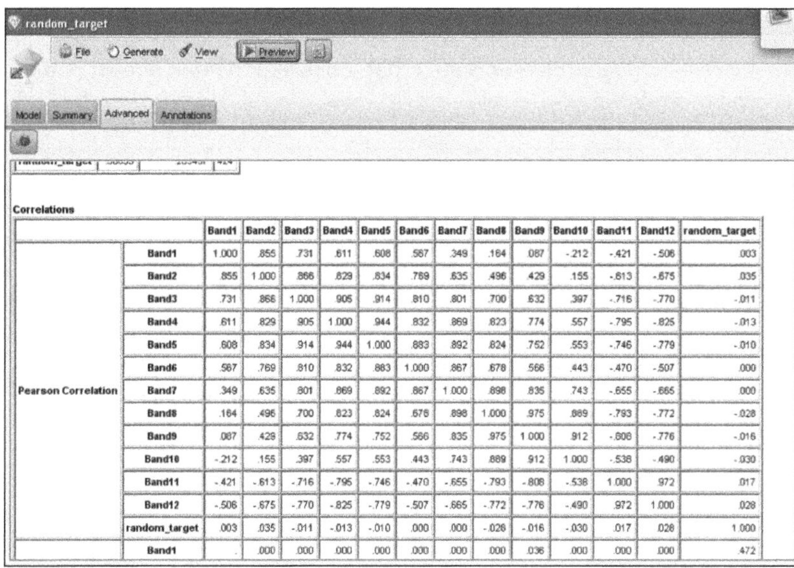

Correlations

		Band1	Band2	Band3	Band4	Band5	Band6	Band7	Band8	Band9	Band10	Band11	Band12	random_target
Pearson Correlation	Band1	1.000	.855	.731	.611	.608	.567	.349	.164	.087	-.212	-.421	-.506	.003
	Band2	.855	1.000	.866	.829	.834	.769	.635	.496	.429	.155	-.613	-.675	.035
	Band3	.731	.866	1.000	.905	.914	.810	.801	.700	.632	.397	-.716	-.770	-.011
	Band4	.611	.829	.905	1.000	.944	.832	.869	.823	.774	.557	-.795	-.825	-.013
	Band5	.608	.834	.914	.944	1.000	.883	.892	.824	.752	.553	-.746	-.779	-.010
	Band6	.567	.769	.810	.832	.883	1.000	.867	.678	.566	.443	-.470	-.507	.000
	Band7	.349	.635	.801	.869	.892	.867	1.000	.898	.835	.743	-.655	-.665	.000
	Band8	.164	.496	.700	.823	.824	.678	.898	1.000	.975	.889	-.793	-.772	-.028
	Band9	.087	.429	.632	.774	.752	.566	.835	.975	1.000	.912	-.808	-.776	-.016
	Band10	-.212	.155	.397	.557	.553	.443	.743	.889	.912	1.000	-.538	-.490	-.030
	Band11	-.421	-.613	-.716	-.795	-.746	-.470	-.655	-.793	-.808	-.538	1.000	.972	.017
	Band12	-.506	-.675	-.770	-.825	-.779	-.507	-.665	-.772	-.776	-.490	.972	1.000	.028
	random_target	.003	.035	-.011	-.013	-.010	.000	.000	-.028	-.016	-.030	.017	.028	1.000
	Band1	.	.000	.000	.000	.000	.000	.000	.000	.036	.000	.000	.000	.472

6. Open Microsoft Excel and open the file you just created called `Correlations.html`. Note that, if you are using a version of Excel prior to Excel 2007, you can only import up to 255 variables. If you are using Excel 2007 or later, you can import 16,384 variables, but it may take some time for the file to load. Save the file `Correlations.xls` or `Correlations.xlsx` if you would like to save the work done in Excel.

7. The only part of the table we need is the correlation matrix itself, labeled **Pearson Correlation**. It is helpful to delete non-correlation matrix rows and columns, but one can still proceed without editing the Excel document. The correlation matrix generated from the `nasadata.txt` data set begins at row 17. If you wish, color-code the values of the cells using conditional formatting so it is easier to see correlation values that have a large magnitude (close to 1 or -1). If you are using Excel 2007, one suggestion is to use the conditional formatting **Format** option as shown in the following screenshot.

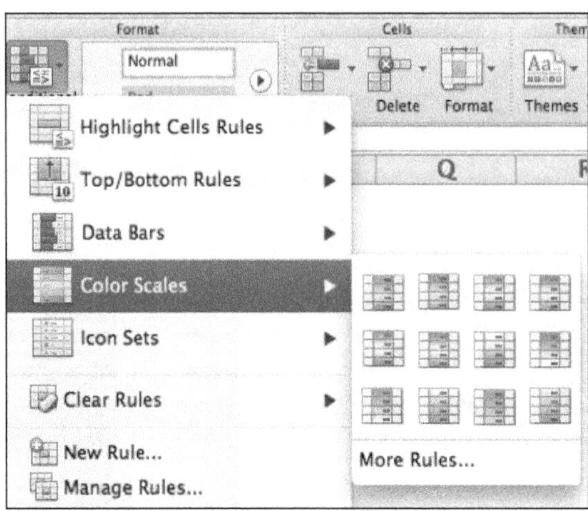

This will result in a correlation matrix that looks like the one shown in the following screenshot.

Correlations														
		Band1	**Band2**	**Band3**	**Band4**	**Band5**	**Band6**	**Band7**	**Band8**	**Band9**	**Band10**	**Band11**	**Band12**	**random_target**
Pearson Correlation	**Band1**	1	0.855	0.731	0.611	0.608	0.567	0.349	0.164	0.087	-0.212	-0.421	-0.506	0.003
	Band2	0.855	1	0.866	0.829	0.834	0.769	0.635	0.496	0.429	0.155	-0.613	-0.675	0.035
	Band3	0.731	0.866	1	0.905	0.914	0.81	0.801	0.7	0.632	0.397	-0.716	-0.77	-0.011
	Band4	0.611	0.829	0.905	1	0.944	0.832	0.869	0.823	0.774	0.557	-0.795	-0.825	-0.013
	Band5	0.608	0.834	0.914	0.944	1	0.883	0.892	0.824	0.752	0.553	-0.746	-0.779	-0.01
	Band6	0.567	0.769	0.81	0.832	0.883	1	0.867	0.678	0.566	0.443	-0.47	-0.507	0
	Band7	0.349	0.635	0.801	0.869	0.892	0.867	1	0.898	0.835	0.743	-0.655	-0.665	0
	Band8	0.164	0.496	0.7	0.823	0.824	0.678	0.898	1	0.975	0.889	-0.793	-0.772	-0.028
	Band9	0.087	0.429	0.632	0.774	0.752	0.566	0.835	0.975	1	0.912	-0.808	-0.776	-0.016
	Band10	-0.21	0.155	0.397	0.557	0.553	0.443	0.743	0.889	0.912	1	-0.538	-0.49	-0.03
	Band11	-0.42	-0.61	-0.72	-0.795	-0.746	-0.47	-0.655	-0.793	-0.808	-0.538	1	0.972	0.017
	Band12	-0.51	-0.68	-0.77	-0.825	-0.779	-0.507	-0.665	-0.772	-0.776	-0.49	0.972	1	0.028
	random_target	0.003	0.035	-0.01	-0.013	-0.01	0	0	-0.028	-0.016	-0.03	0.017	0.028	1

If you are using Excel 2003 or older, you can use the conditional formatting options shown in the following screenshot.

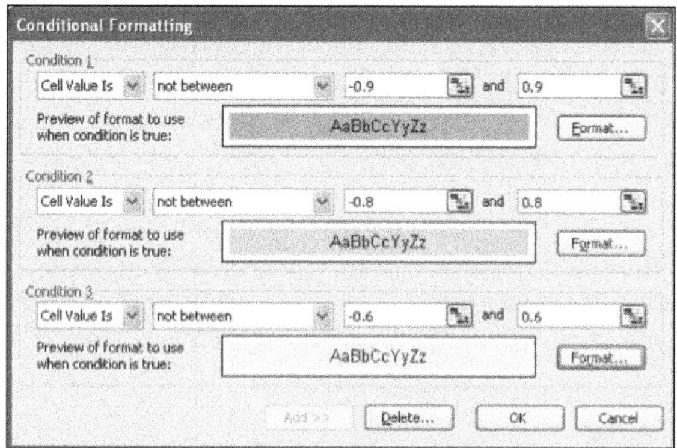

This will result in a correlation matrix such as the one shown in the following screenshot:

	A	B	C	D	E	F	G	H	I	J	K	L	M	N
1	**Field**	**Band1**	**Band2**	**Band3**	**Band4**	**Band5**	**Band6**	**Band7**	**Band8**	**Band9**	**Band10**	**Band11**	**Band12**	**random_target**
2	**Band1**	1	0.855	0.731	0.611	0.608	0.567	0.349	0.164	0.087	-0.212	-0.421	-0.506	0.003
3	**Band2**	0.855	1	0.866	0.829	0.834	0.769	0.635	0.496	0.429	0.165	-0.613	-0.675	0.036
4	**Band3**	0.731	0.866	1	0.906	0.914	0.81	0.801	0.7	0.632	0.397	-0.716	-0.77	-0.011
5	**Band4**	0.611	0.829	0.906	1	0.944	0.832	0.869	0.823	0.774	0.557	-0.795	-0.825	-0.013
6	**Band5**	0.608	0.834	0.914	0.944	1	0.883	0.892	0.824	0.752	0.553	-0.746	-0.779	-0.01
7	**Band6**	0.567	0.769	0.81	0.832	0.883	1	0.867	0.678	0.566	0.443	-0.47	-0.507	0
8	**Band7**	0.349	0.635	0.801	0.869	0.892	0.867	1	0.898	0.835	0.743	-0.655	-0.665	0
9	**Band8**	0.164	0.496	0.7	0.823	0.824	0.678	0.898	1	0.975	0.889	-0.793	-0.772	-0.028
10	**Band9**	0.087	0.429	0.632	0.774	0.752	0.566	0.835	0.976	1	0.912	-0.808	-0.776	-0.016
11	**Band10**	-0.212	0.165	0.397	0.557	0.553	0.443	0.743	0.889	0.912	1	-0.538	-0.49	-0.03
12	**Band11**	-0.421	-0.613	-0.716	-0.795	-0.746	-0.47	-0.656	-0.793	-0.808	-0.538	1	0.972	0.017
13	**Band12**	-0.506	-0.675	-0.77	-0.826	-0.779	-0.507	-0.665	-0.772	-0.776	-0.49	0.972	1	0.028
14	**random_target**	0.003	0.036	-0.011	-0.013	-0.01	0	0	-0.028	-0.016	-0.03	0.017	0.028	1

8. When you see two variables that are highly correlated with each other, make a determination which variable you would like to keep and which one you would like to remove. If more than two variables are highly correlated with each other, select only one representative of the idea. In the nasadata example, the variables `Band4` and `Band5` are correlated at greater than 0.9 with `Band3`, and therefore can be safely removed from analysis. One can also argue that `Band9`, `Band10` and `Band 12` can be removed.

9. In the Modeler stream, connect a Type node to the right of the correlations Type node. Double-click on the Type node, and set the direction of the variables that were discarded based on the correlation matrix shown in Excel to **None**. One can also use a Filter node to remove `Band4`, `Band5`, `Band9`, `Band10`, and `Band12`.

How it works...

When you desire to identify variables that are highly correlated with each other so that you can remove redundant variables, there is no single node that will perform the task. Only the Regression node and the Discriminant nodes create a correlation matrix, with only the former allowing one to export the resulting matrix. This recipe provides a method to identify the redundant variables so they can be removed.

The first five steps load the data and build the regression model so that the correlation matrix can be exported and operated on in Excel. Steps 6 to 8 show how to identify highly correlated variables in Excel so that a list of redundant variables can be created. Step 9 shows how to apply that list to a Type node or Filter node to remove the redundant fields from further analysis.

There's more...

If there are more than a dozen variables removed from analysis, it can become quite tedious to set each of these individually in a Type node or Filter node. Running a script to set the remove variables to None in a Type node or de-selecting variables in a Filter node can speed up the process significantly and reduce the likelihood of errors made in the selection process.

See also

- The *Using Neural Network for Feature Selection* recipe in *Chapter 6, Selecting and Building a Model*
- *Selecting variables using the CHAID Modeling node* in this chapter

Selecting variables using the CHAID Modeling node

In this recipe we will identify and select variables to include as model inputs using the CHAID node.

You will need a copy of Microsoft Excel to visualize and select the chi-square values for each variable.

Getting ready

This recipe uses the datafile `cup98lrn_reduced_vars3.sav` and the stream `recipe_variableselection_chaid.str`.

How to do it...

To identify and select variables to include as model inputs using the CHAID node:

1. Open the stream `variableselection_chaid.str` by navigating to **File** | **Open Stream** and selecting the stream.
2. Make sure the datafile points to the correct path for the file `cup98lrn_reduced_vars3.sav`.
3. Open the Type node named `CHAID Types`. Notice that there are several variables of type continuous whose direction values have been set to **Input**, and a single continuous variable has its direction set to Target. The variable set to Target should be the target variable **TARGET_B**.
4. Open the node **TARGET_B** and select the **Interactive Model** option.

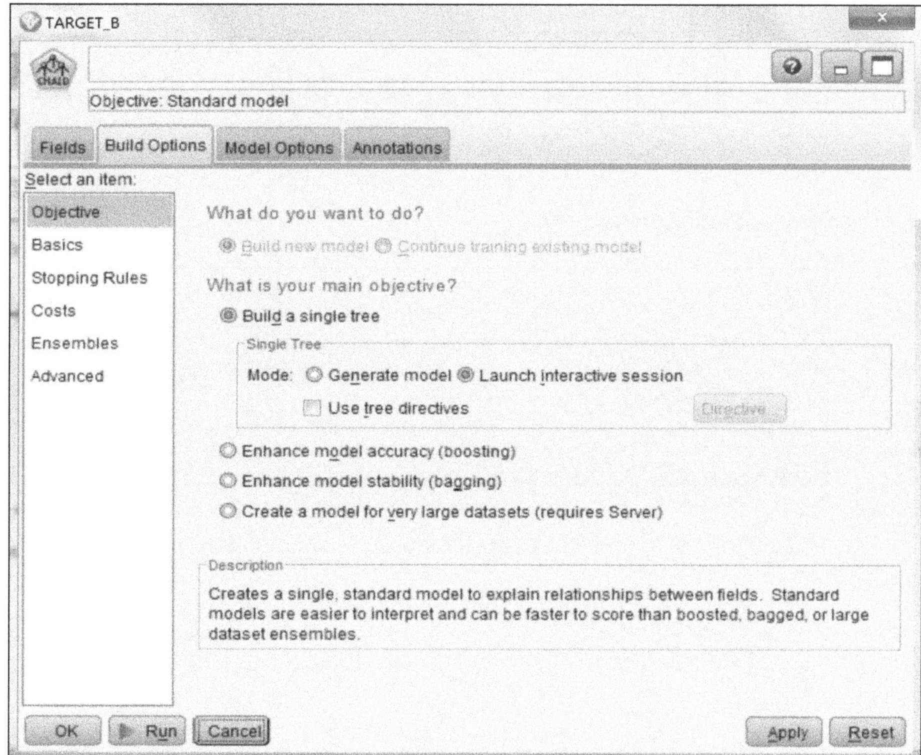

5. Begin to build the CHAID model by clicking on the **Run** button. When the interactive model split appears, click on the **Predictors...** button to reveal the chi-square statistic for all fields in order from the highest to lowest value.

To find the **Predictors...** button click on the **Grow Branch with Custom Split** button (Illustrated in the following screenshot).

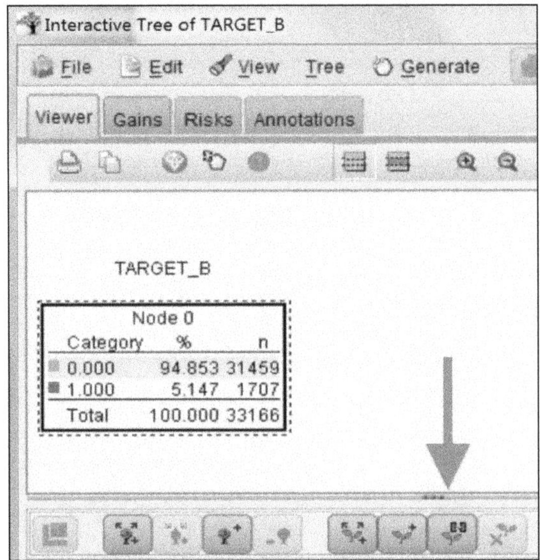

6. Click on the **Predictors...** button.

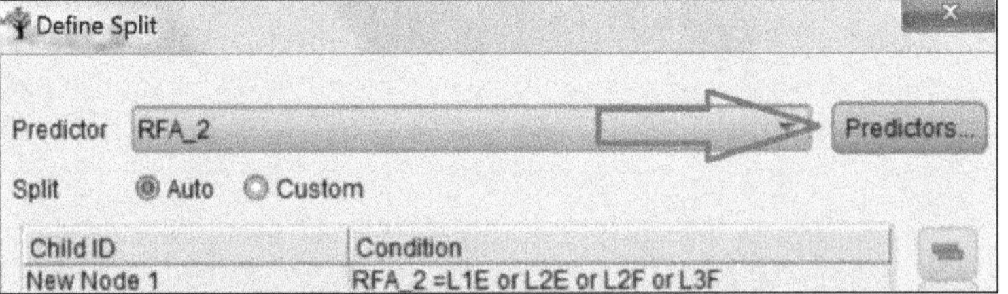

This reveals the list of predictors and their associated probabilities.

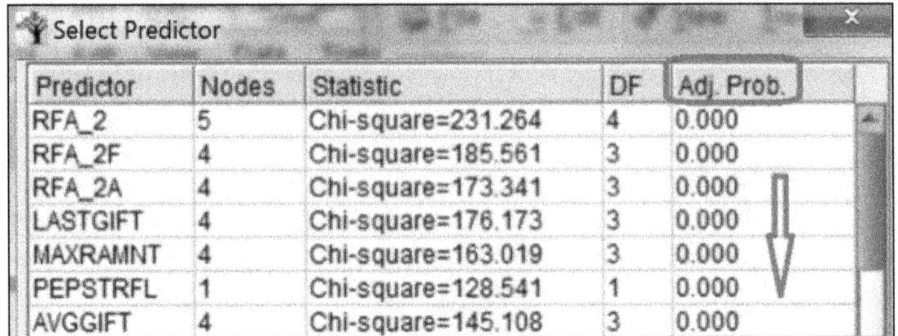

7. Click on any field in the list and press *Ctrl + A* to select all the variables in the list. Copy the selected variables with *Ctrl + C*. Open Microsoft Excel and create a new Workbook. Paste the buffer into Excel. This provides an easier way to identify which fields to keep.
8. Identify all fields whose chi-square statistic values have a p-value greater than 0.05. These are good candidates to remove.
9. In the Modeler stream, connect a Type node to the right of the CHAID Type node. Double-click on the Type node, and set variables that were selected in step 7 to **None**. As an alternative, one may use a Filter node to remove fields selected in step 7.

How it works...

In decision trees, the root (first or top) split identifies the variable that best separates the data into two or more subgroups that maximize a criterion of interest. A CHAID decision tree finds the single variable that has the largest chi-square statistic. However, to find this maximum, every variable must be examined and its chi-square statistic computed. The interactive mode reveals all of these values. The number of variables being tested doesn't affect this method significantly because computation for CHAID increases only linearly with the number of fields.

Once we have the chi-square statistic values and corresponding p values for every variable, we then can use this value to select which variables are good predictors on their own (that is, produce significant differences in the target variable values after the split). This variable list can then be used as a simple variable selection method.

There's more...

One doesn't need to use the 0.05 value to select variables; many reasonable metrics can be used to select fields. For example, once can choose the top 10 or 25 variables regardless of p-value. Or one can relax the p-value selection criterion from 0.05 to 0.1 or 0.15 to allow more variables to be included in the analysis. If large numbers of rows exist in the data, the p-values may be very small even for splits that don't appear to be very useful. In these cases, the splits may be statistically significant but not operationally significant. Feel free to adjust the threshold of p-values to one that reflects the operational significance of your problem.

As with the correlation matrix variable selection, selecting or removing a large number of variables may be tedious and prone to error, so writing a CLEM script to customize the Type node or Filter node can help.

Within the generated model, you have the option to create a Filter node that removes predictors or inputs that have not been used by the model or you can remove fields based on predictor importance:

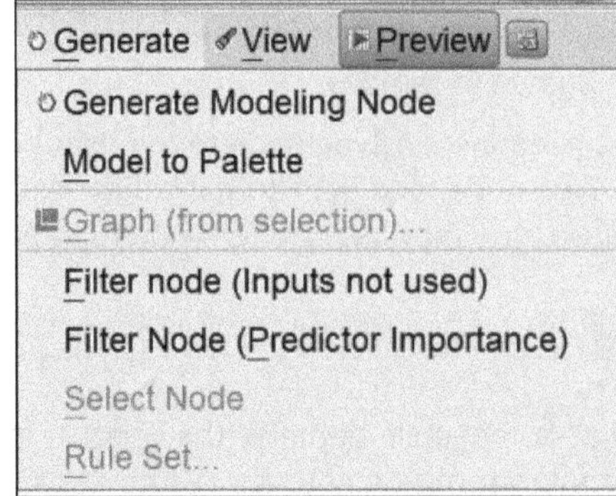

If you select to generate a Filter node based on predictor importance, you then have additional options to include or exclude a certain number of fields or to include or exclude fields based on a specified level of importance:

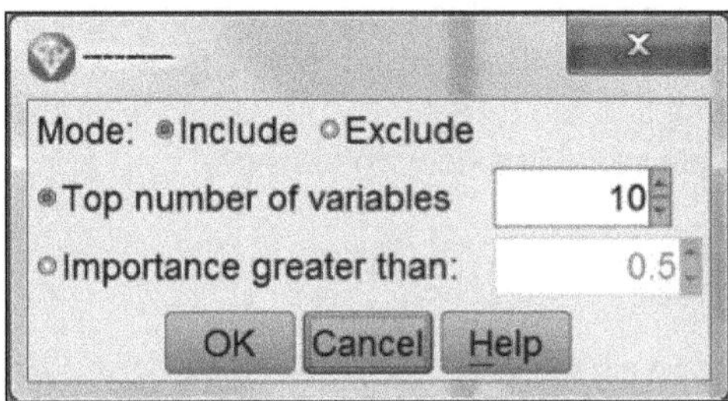

See also

- The *Selecting variables using the Means node* and *Selecting variables using single-antecedent Association Rules* recipes in this chapter

Selecting variables using the Means node

In this recipe we will identify and select variables to include as model inputs using the Means node.

Getting ready

This recipe uses the datafile `cup98lrn_reduced_vars3.sav` and the stream `recipe_variableselection_means.str`.

You will need a copy of Microsoft Excel to visualize the list of rules (optional).

How to do it...

To identify and select variables to include as model inputs using the Means node:

1. Open the stream `variableselection_means.str` by navigating **File** | **Open Stream**.
2. Make sure the datafile points to the correct path to the file `cup98lrn_reduced_vars3.sav`.
3. Open the Means node to look at the options. Note that the grouping variable is our target variable TARGET_B, and the test fields are all the continuous variables of interest as shown in the following figure.

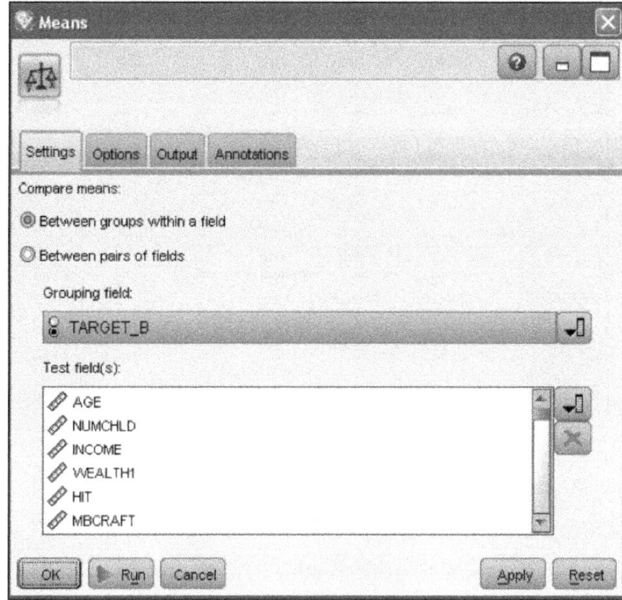

4. Run the Means node by clicking on **Run**.

5. Inside the output window, click on the `Importance` column twice so that the variables are sorted in descending order of **Importance** as shown in the following screenshot.
6. Identify variables whose importance score is greater than 0.9. These are good candidates to retain as inputs for your models.
7. Open the Type node, `MEANS types`. Press *Ctrl* + *A* to select all fields, left-click on any variable's **Role** value, and select **None**. For **TARGET_B**, change the **Role** to **Target**, and for every variable identified in step 7, select **Input** as the role. Note that you can keep both the Means node output and Type node open at the same time.

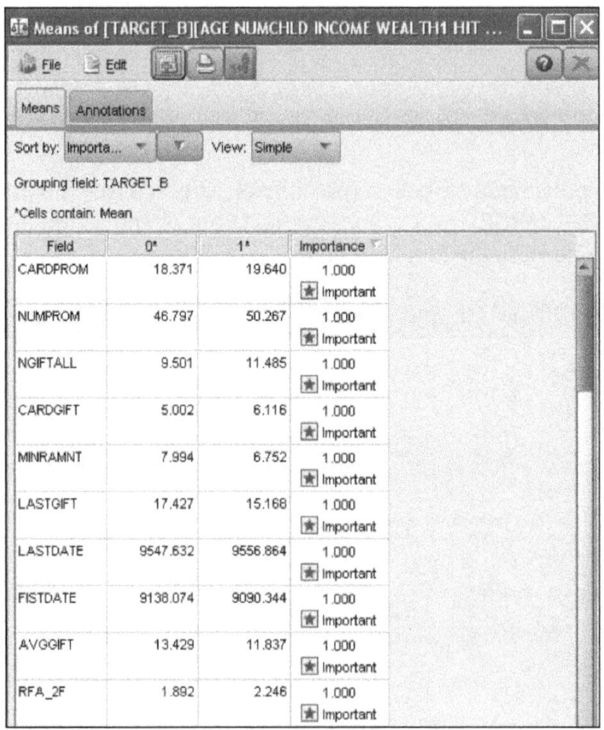

How it works...

The Means node is an excellent way to examine the differences on average between groups for a `Nominal`, `Ordinal`, or `Flag` target variable. When examining the difference of means based on a grouping variable in the Means node, Modeler generates an F Statistic value for each continuous (or Flag) variable and computes the associated significance value. This value is called **Importance** in Modeler, where a value of 1.0 represents highly significant differences in the mean values and values of 0.0 represent no difference in the mean values between groups.

The mean values for each input are shown in the columns, one value for each target variable value. For a `Flag` variable, there will be two values. For **TARGET_B**, the way to interpret the results is: for the **TARGET_B** having value `1`, the average **CARDPROM** value is `19.64`, whereas when **TARGET_B** with value `0`, the average **CARDPROM** value is `18.371`.

There is no right value to use as a cutoff indicating which variables are good or not. A value of 0.9 is a conservative cutoff. Note that the more records one has, the higher the **Importance** score tends to become. As a result, large datasets can show high **Importance** scores even when the difference in mean values is quite small. If this is the case, one can increase the **Importance** cut-off to 0.95 or even 0.99.

There's more...

More information about the F-test can be seen by navigating to the **View** | **Advance report** setting. In this report, the four values for each variable are the mean value, the standard deviation, the standard error (for the mean value), and the record count. In addition, the F-Test's F Statistic is revealed in addition to the **Importance** score shown in the simple report.

The F-statistic value itself can be revealed by navigating to the **View** | **Advanced** option (refer to the following screenshot). Unfortunately, as shown in the screenshot, sorting by the F-Test value does not sort numerically in all versions of Clementine and Modeler. Some versions sort by ASCII character set value so all leading 9 values will be at the top. To see a true numerically sorted list, one can export the report by navigating to **File** | **Export HTML** and load the report into Excel and sort it there.

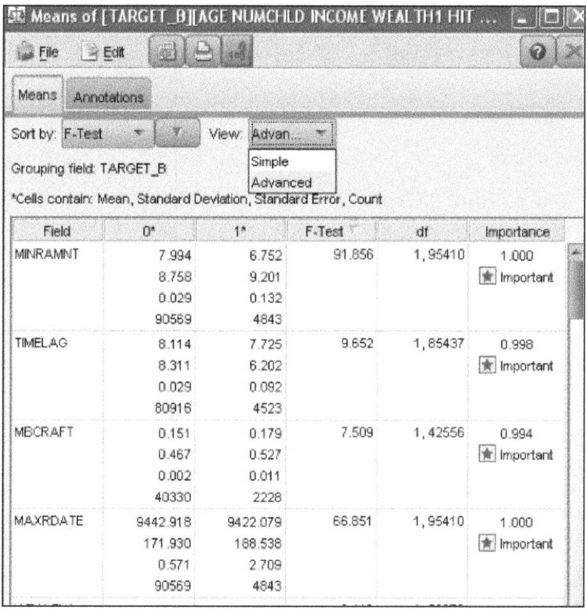

As with the correlation matrix variable selection, selecting or removing a large number of variables may be tedious and prone to error, so writing a CLEM script to customize the Type node or Filter node can help.

See also

- The *Selecting variables using the CHAID Modeling Node* and *Selecting variables using single-antecedent Association Rules* recipes in this chapter

Selecting variables using single-antecedent Association Rules

In this recipe we will identify and select variables to include as model inputs using the Apriori Association Rules node. We will select the top 24 predictors based on Association Rules variable selection. We will use the same `KDD Cup 1998` data set, but this version of the data was prepared with the stream `Recipe - variable selection apriori data prep.str` to create quintile versions of continuous variables. The target variable is the top quintile in donation amounts, TARGET_D between $20 and $200.

Getting ready

This recipe uses the datafile `cup98lrn_reduced_vars3_apriori.sav` and the stream `Recipe - variable selection apriori.str`.

You will need a copy of Microsoft Excel to visualize the list of rules.

How to do it...

To identify and select variables to include as model inputs using the Apriori Association Rules node:

1. Open the stream `Recipe - variable selection apriori.str` by navigating to **File | Open Stream**.
2. Make sure the datafile points to the correct path to the file `cup98lrn_reduced_vars3_apriori.sav`.
3. Open the Type node named `APRIORI Types`. Notice that only `Nominal` and `Flag` variables are used. The variable set to Target should be the target variable TARGET_D_TILE5_1.
4. Open the **Apriori** node and look at the options. Note that the **Minimum antecedent support** is set to `10` percent, Confidence percent is set to 1 percent and the number of antecedents to 1.

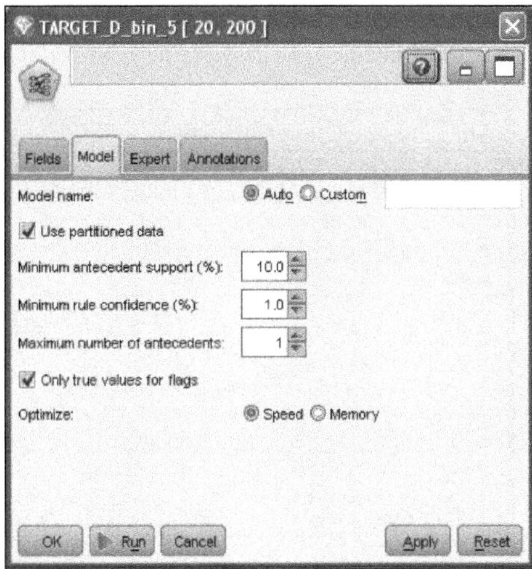

5. Build the Association Rules model by clicking on **Run**.
6. Open the generated model. In the show/hide criteria drop-down menu, add **Instances** and **Lift** to the report as shown in following screenshot. If the list is not sorted by Confidence or Lift any longer, click on the sort by arrow to the right of the **Confidence %** text until the sort order is descending.

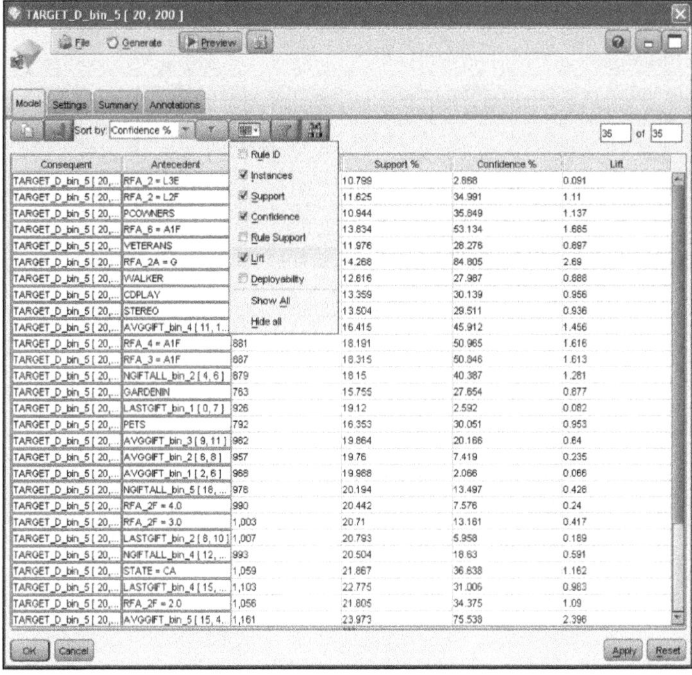

7. Export the rules by navigating to **File** | **Export HTML** | **Model** and save the file as `associationrules.html`.

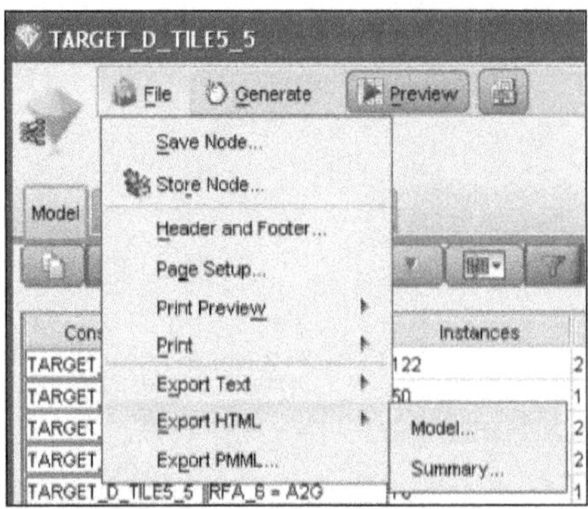

8. Identify rules of interest, such as the 12 rules with the highest confidence and the 12 rules with the lowest confidence. A sample list is shown in the following screenshot. Make a note of these rules so you can include these as inputs.

A	B	C	D	E	F	G	H
	Consequent	Antecedent	Instances	Support %	Confidence %	Lift	Select
1	TARGET_D_bin_5 [20, 200]	RFA_2A = G	691	14.268	84.805	2.69	Select
2	TARGET_D_bin_5 [20, 200]	LASTGIFT_bin_5 [20, 450]	1,337	27.607	79.581	2.524	Select
3	TARGET_D_bin_5 [20, 200]	AVGGIFT_bin_5 [15, 450]	1,161	23.973	75.538	2.396	Select
4	TARGET_D_bin_5 [20, 200]	RFA_2F = 1.0	1,794	37.043	53.344	1.692	Select
5	TARGET_D_bin_5 [20, 200]	RFA_6 = A1F	670	13.834	53.134	1.685	Select
6	TARGET_D_bin_5 [20, 200]	RFA_2 = L1F	1,173	24.221	52.259	1.657	Select
7	TARGET_D_bin_5 [20, 200]	RFA_4 = A1F	881	18.191	50.965	1.616	Select
8	TARGET_D_bin_5 [20, 200]	RFA_3 = A1F	887	18.315	50.846	1.613	Select
9	TARGET_D_bin_5 [20, 200]	AVGGIFT_bin_4 [11, 14]	795	16.415	45.912	1.456	Select
10	TARGET_D_bin_5 [20, 200]	RFA_2A = F	2,056	42.453	42.85	1.359	Select
11	TARGET_D_bin_5 [20, 200]	NGIFTALL_bin_2 [4, 6]	879	18.15	40.387	1.281	Select
12	TARGET_D_bin_5 [20, 200]	STATE = CA	1,059	21.867	36.638	1.162	Select
13	TARGET_D_bin_5 [20, 200]	PCOWNERS	530	10.944	35.849	1.137	
14	TARGET_D_bin_5 [20, 200]	RFA_2 = L2F	563	11.625	34.991	1.11	
15	TARGET_D_bin_5 [20, 200]	RFA_2F = 2.0	1,056	21.805	34.375	1.09	
16	TARGET_D_bin_5 [20, 200]	LASTGIFT_bin_4 [15, 19]	1,103	22.775	31.006	0.983	
17	TARGET_D_bin_5 [20, 200]	NGIFTALL_bin_3 [7, 11]	1,111	22.94	30.873	0.979	
18	TARGET_D_bin_5 [20, 200]	CDPLAY	647	13.359	30.139	0.956	
19	TARGET_D_bin_5 [20, 200]	PETS	792	16.353	30.051	0.953	
20	TARGET_D_bin_5 [20, 200]	STEREO	654	13.504	29.511	0.936	
21	TARGET_D_bin_5 [20, 200]	VETERANS	580	11.976	28.276	0.897	
22	TARGET_D_bin_5 [20, 200]	WALKER	611	12.616	27.987	0.888	
23	TARGET_D_bin_5 [20, 200]	GARDENIN	763	15.755	27.654	0.877	
24	TARGET_D_bin_5 [20, 200]	PEPSTRFL	2,885	59.571	21.109	0.669	Select
25	TARGET_D_bin_5 [20, 200]	AVGGIFT_bin_3 [9, 11]	962	19.864	20.166	0.64	Select
26	TARGET_D_bin_5 [20, 200]	NGIFTALL_bin_4 [12, 17]	993	20.504	18.63	0.591	Select
27	TARGET_D_bin_5 [20, 200]	NGIFTALL_bin_5 [18, 91]	978	20.194	13.497	0.428	Select
28	TARGET_D_bin_5 [20, 200]	RFA_2F = 3.0	1,003	20.71	13.161	0.417	Select
29	TARGET_D_bin_5 [20, 200]	RFA_2F = 4.0	990	20.442	7.576	0.24	Select
30	TARGET_D_bin_5 [20, 200]	AVGGIFT_bin_2 [6, 8]	957	19.76	7.419	0.235	Select
31	TARGET_D_bin_5 [20, 200]	LASTGIFT_bin_2 [8, 10]	1,007	20.793	5.958	0.189	Select
32	TARGET_D_bin_5 [20, 200]	RFA_2A = E	1,400	28.908	4.071	0.129	Select

9. In the Modeler stream, connect a Type node to the right of the `APRIORI` Type node. Double-click on the Type node, and set variables that were selected in step 8 to **Input**, and all other variables that were formerly inputs to **None**.

How it works...

The Association Rules model with only one antecedent is merely a convenient way to show the relationship between every categorical variable identified as `Input` and the `Target` variables. The figure of merit for this relationship is **Confidence %** which is the percentage of records matching the input variable value **True** with the Target variable value **True**.

Association rules require input and target variables to be categorical; in Modeler, these are the `Nominal`, `Ordinal`, or `Flag` variables. The data set analyzed in this recipe contained binned versions of continuous variables so that they could be assessed in addition to the variables that are nominal in their original state.

Once the association between the input variables and the target is listed along with the relationship to the target, one can choose to remove those fields with little relationship to the target, namely those whose lift is close to 1. Those with lift values larger or smaller than 1 have some relationship to the target, either the high-valued donors (donated $20-$200) or those who are not high-valued donors. The **Select** label in the previous screenshot was applied when the lift value was greater than 1.125 or less than 0.7. This selection criterion is subjective.

As a side note, the outcome of the last four recipes could be combined to determine which fields are consistently relevant across all methods.

There's more...

Note that the list in the previous screenshot only includes those variables or categories with greater than 10 percent support; this in itself reduces the number of variables. Try reducing the Support percent filter in the Apriori node from 10 percent to 1 percent and see how many more variables show up in the list.

The Association Rules do not provide a significance test to help assess the relationship between each input and the target variable. A chi-square test can be computed in Excel or one can use the CHAID modeling node to provide the chi-square statistic.

One can also expand the search for variables by adjusting the number of antecedents to two, thereby finding all pairwise combinations of inputs. This can sometimes be valuable because variables that are not good predictors on their own can sometimes be good predictors in combination with other variables.

As with the correlation matrix variable selection, selecting or removing a large number of variables may be tedious and prone to error, so writing a CLEM script to customize the Type node or Filter node can help.

See also

- The *Selecting variables using the CHAID Modeling node* and *Selecting variables using the Means node* recipes in this chapter

3
Data Preparation – Clean

In this chapter, we will cover:

- Binning scale variables to address missing data
- Using a full data model/partial data model approach to address missing data
- Imputing in-stream mean or median
- Imputing missing values randomly from uniform or normal distributions
- Using random imputation to match a variable's distribution
- Searching for similar records using a Neural Network for inexact matching
- Using neuro-fuzzy searching to find similar names
- Producing longer Soundex codes

Introduction

This chapter addresses the clean subtask of the data preparation phase. CRISP-DM describes this subtask in the following way:

> *Raise the data quality to the level required by the selected analysis techniques. This may involve selection of clean subsets of the data, the insertion of suitable defaults, or more ambitious techniques such as the estimation of missing data by modeling.*

While this chapter can't tackle the entire subject of cleaning data, it addresses three themes, and all three themes involve working with data that is incomplete in some way:

- Avoiding the missing data
- Imputing the missing data
- Fuzzy matching

The first two recipes address the first theme, that is, how to deal with missing data. Sometimes a null value indicates that a value is unknown, but very frequently a null value is the only appropriate value because for the particular case (customer) the value is non-applicable. In these instances imputation is usually not the best choice.

However, when the missing data truly is missing, that is, a certain value is to be expected, but that value is unknown, imputation can be an important tool to the data miner. For instance, in one of the following recipes we perform a random imputation, where the missing value is age. Certainly, there is no question of age being applicable.

The phrase in the CRISP-DM definition, "to the level required", is helpful here. For many techniques including Neural Nets, if any data is missing the entire case (row) is ignored. This makes some solution of missing data critical, and this can be accomplished by imputation, when appropriate, but it is also the idea behind an approach such as the example used in the *Using a full data model/partial data model approach to address missing data* recipe.

The last three recipes address the last theme. Perhaps the most difficult variable to have with missing data is a proper key; a way of easily matching records. Data miners would much prefer to have an accurate row ID in order to match by name, but sometimes it is unavoidable. How do we deal with names that are similar, but not identical? What if it is similarity, rather than identity, that we are after—similar crime reports are an example.

Binning scale variables to address missing data

This recipe will tackle the issue of null values that are non-applicable rather than values that are unknown. When transactions are processed for modeling, invariably there will be certain transactions that are missing for a given case. In this recipe our cases will be customers. Imagine the straightforward instance that a customer, Bill Johnson, did not rent a horror movie within the last 12 months. The *Using an @NULL multiple Derive to explore missing data* recipe in *Chapter 1, Data Understanding*, helps determine if the presence or absence of such a value is predictive of the target. This recipe prepares the original variable for modeling. The issue addressed in this recipe is virtually guaranteed to occur when preparing dates of transactions and that is the nature of this particular recipe. However, its application is not limited to date arithmetic on transactions. It can be used on any scale variable that has the possibility of a true null value. If the scale variable is always applicable, and the value is unknown, then imputation might be considered.

Getting ready

We will start with the existing stream called `Binning Null Scales.str`.

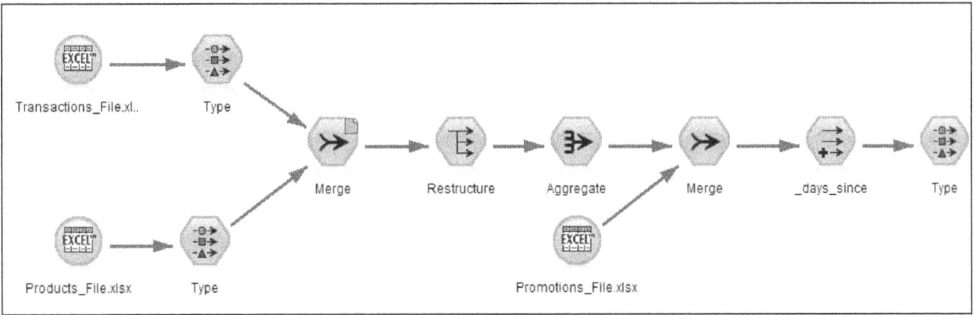

How to do it...

In order to determine if you need to bin scale variables to address missing data, perform the following steps:

1. Edit the Type node, verify that `Promo_3_Response` is the target variable, and ensure that only the seven days since variables are chosen as inputs.
2. Add a CHAID Modeling node and run it.
3. Examine the resulting model, and confirm that all of the cases were used. This can be confirmed by examining the root node. (The following figure only shows a small portion of the tree.)

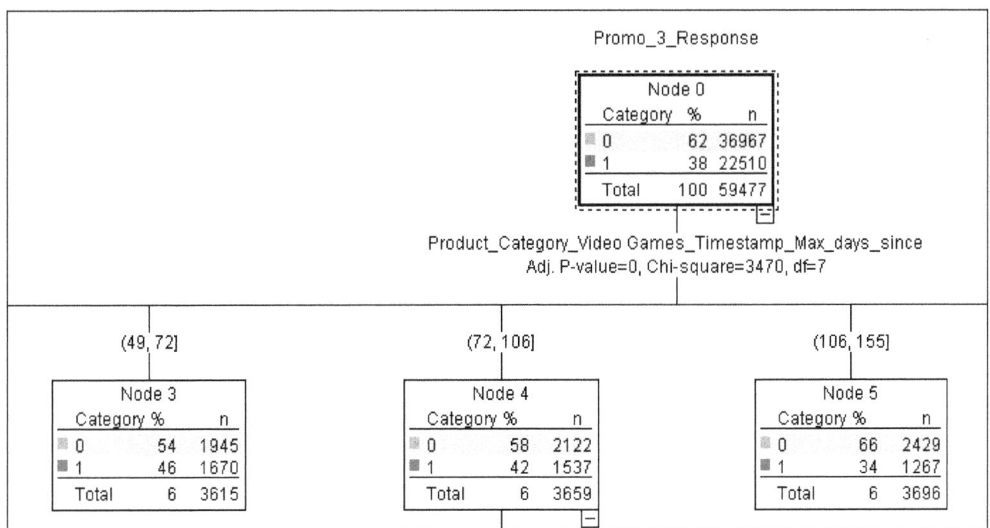

4. Add a Neural Net node and run it.
5. Examine the summary information of the resulting model and confirm that many cases were not used.

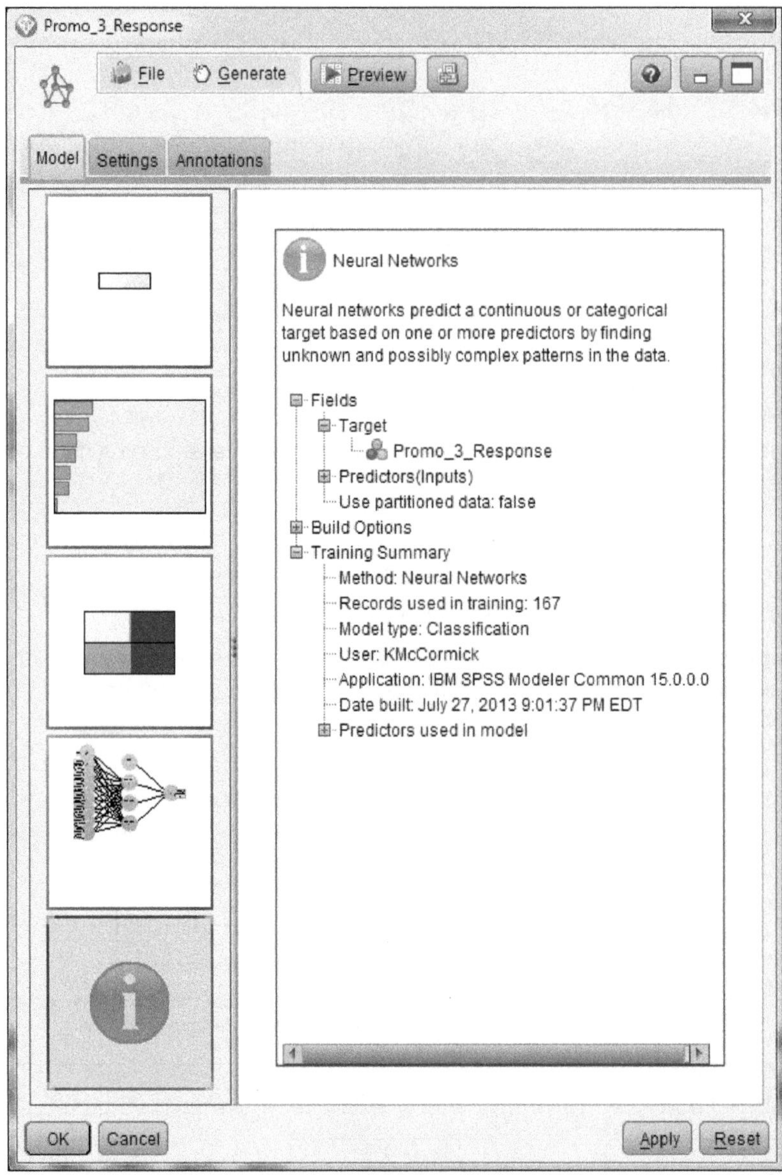

6. Before we take action to resolve the problem we need a better diagnosis. Add a Multiple Derive node that produces a null/not null flag for each day since the variable.

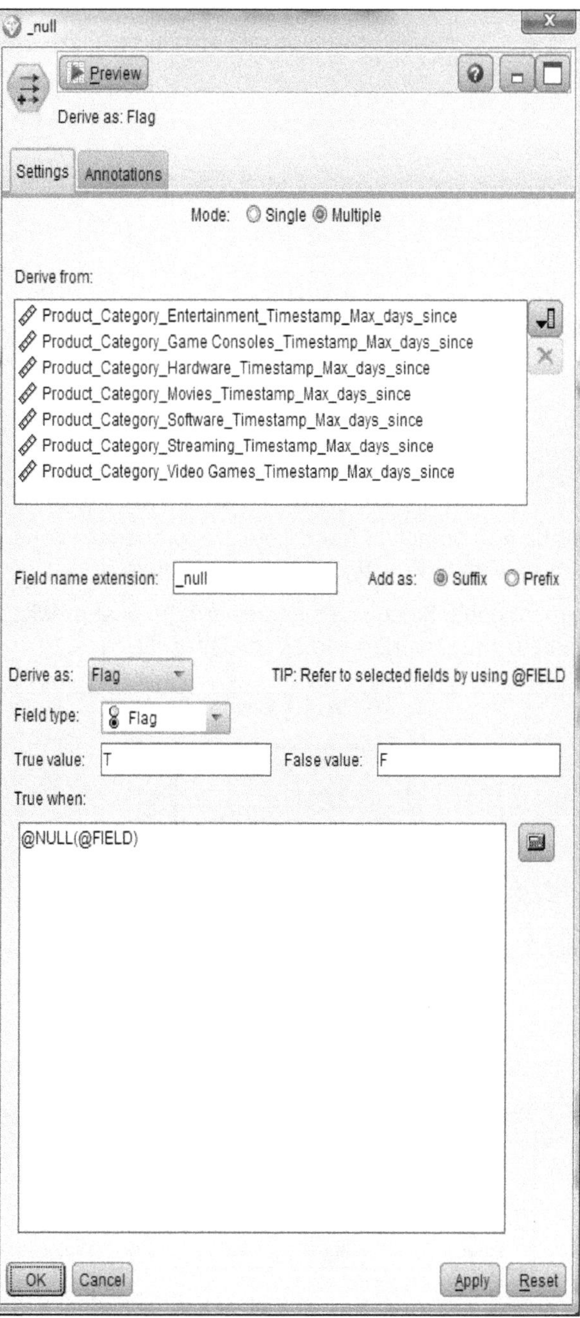

7. Insert the node in between the `_days_since` Derive node and the Type node.
8. Once again run the CHAID node but, this time, do so interactively and with the `_null` variables being added as additional inputs.

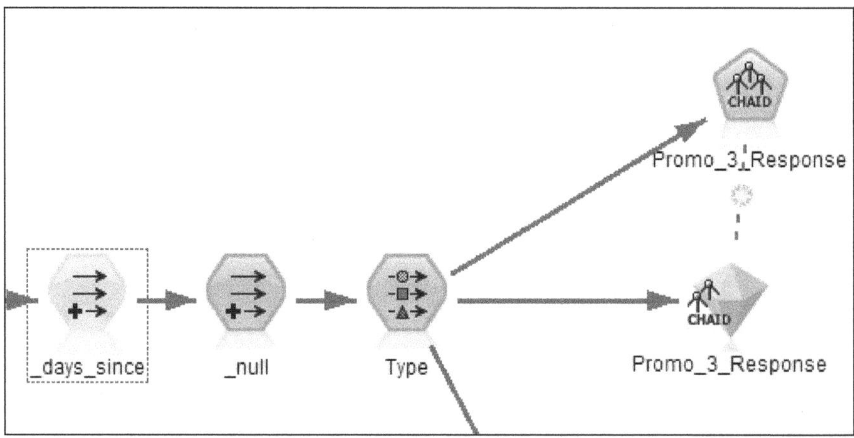

9. Allow the default first branch to form. Note that propensity generally drops from left to right and then we also have a separate node for nulls.
10. Return to the root node. Since video games are the best predictor of our target, force the Video Games' `_null` variable to be the first split.

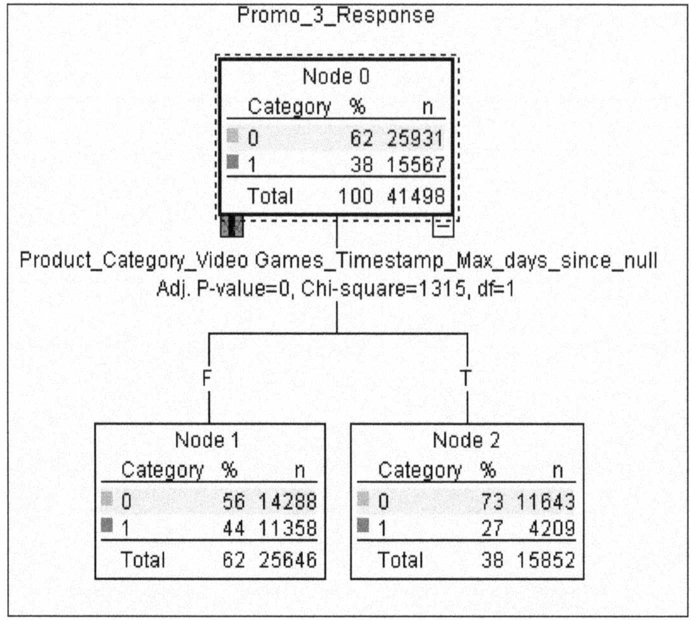

11. Now allow the Video Games' `_days_since` variable to branch beneath it.
12. Eight child nodes are formed, but use the custom settings to form only three. The resulting pattern remains similar, but is arguably clearer.

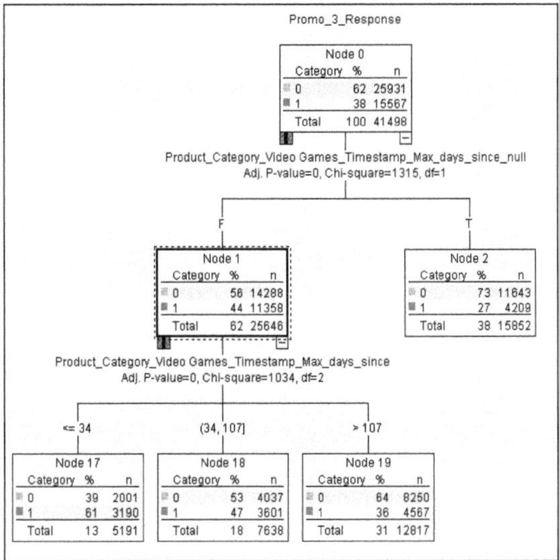

13. The four categories: **Node 17**, **Node 18**, **Node 19**, and **Node 2** (as shown in the previous figure) seem useful in that they clearly show different propensities. Add a new derive node that echoes this pattern for all of the `_days_since` variables.

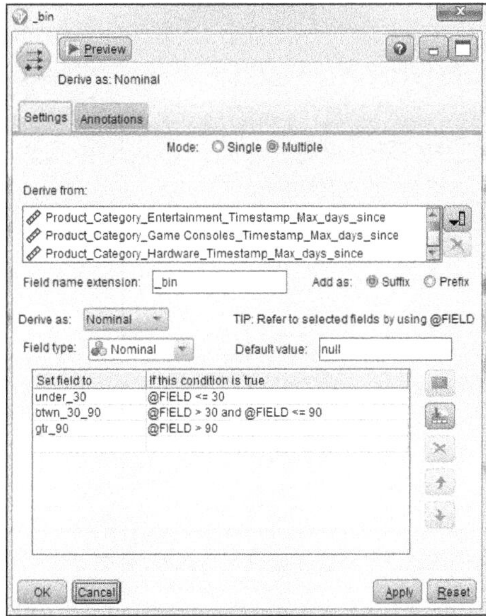

14. Run the Neural Net once again, using only these new variables.

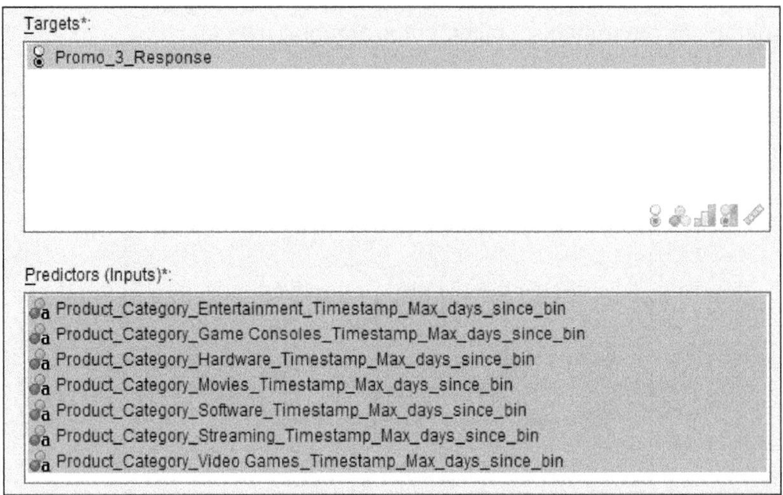

15. Examine the summary and confirm that the complete data set was used.

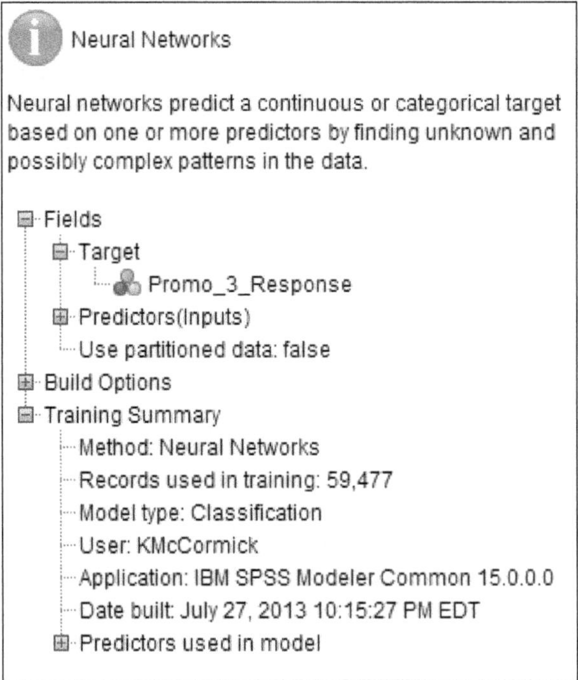

How it works...

The opening stream is interesting in that it takes three different retail data sets and determines the most recent date that a particular product category was purchased by the customer. The result is a series of date arithmetic calculations; those calculations, in days, are at the heart of this recipe.

By running CHAID and Neural Net we learn the following straightforward lesson: CHAID isn't tripped up by lots of null values, but Neural Net produces a disastrous result. We don't want to assume, however, that Neural Net (or any other technique that treats missing data this way) is ruled out. This is terribly important because the majority of modeling techniques in Modeler treat missing data the way that Neural Nets do, and we don't want to eliminate a potential algorithm over a concern that is easily addressed. We simply need to prepare the variable in a way that is more conducive to modeling.

We can rule out a couple of options starting with imputing. There are simply too many missing cases to impute. Also, do we have any reason to assume that the cases that are missing would have values that we can base on the customers that are not missing? They are certainly not missing randomly so this would be unwise. Also, as the Neural Net experiment makes clear, eliminating missing cases would be a disaster. Everyone is missing something, as few (or no) customers have bought something in every category.

The exercise of using interactive CHAID shows the effectiveness of this technique in deciding how to handle the missing data. It would be wise to look at a few variables, not only one in order to decide where the cut points should be. Here categories such as "under 30 days", "30-90 days", and "more than 90 days" seemed to make sense. In an actual project, you would want to base cut offs on more exploration.

The binned variables are easy to make, and easy to explain. It is always a shame to lose the variance in a true scale variable but it is better than losing the variable. Often variables such as these are prematurely screened. The Feature Selection node will invariably throw them out because of the high percentage of missing data, but there is no reason to throw them out. Date information is terribly important to data mining, but not in the form of dates themselves. Data arithmetic invariably produces nulls. The new variables (columns) have a good probability of being useful to the Neural Net (or other methods) and prevent the massive loss of rows.

See also

- The *Using CHAID stumps when interviewing an SME* recipe in *Chapter 1, Data Understanding*
- The *Using an @NULL multiple Derive to explore missing data* recipe in *Chapter 1, Data Understanding*

Using a full data model/partial data model approach to address missing data

It is common in data mining to have one category of customers more prone to having missing data. In fact, there may be a category of customers that are assured to have certain data missing. For instance, let's say that you have found in running your cell phone business that calculating the distance in time between phone upgrades is useful in estimating when the customer's next phone upgrade will be. A newly acquired customer will not have any prior phone history in the data set, but it would be risky to assume that your established customers are the same as your new customers.

How then to estimate the value of *average months between new phones*? One approach is to simply avoid the problem, and build a different model for your new customers and your established customers. In this recipe, we will learn how to diagnose the pattern of missing data and determine if this technique applies.

Getting ready

We will start with a blank stream.

How to do it...

In order to determine if you need to use the full data model/partial data model approach to address missing data, perform the following steps:

1. Build a stream with a Source node, a Type node, and a Table node, then force instantiation by running the Table node. Use the data `cup98lrn_reduced_vars2.txt`.
2. Create a Derive node that extracts the first letter of `RFA_3`.

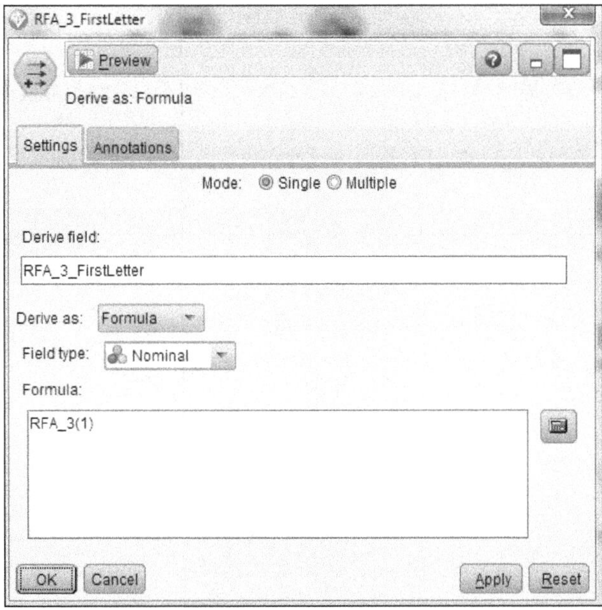

3. Go to the Type node and force `TARGET_B` to be flag and make it the target. Some variables, including `TARGET_D`, are perfect predictors and should be set to none before Modeling, but the recipe can proceed without this step.
4. Add a Select node that includes on the group `N` on the variable `RFA_3_FirstLetter`. The `N` group is the new donors.

   The following table shows the codes for `RFA3_FirstLetter`:

	Codes for RFA3_FirstLetter
F	`First time donor`: Anyone who has made their first donation in the last 6 months and has made just one donation.
N	`New donor`: Anyone who has made their first donation in the last 12 months and is not a first time donor. This is everyone who made their first donation 7-12 months ago, or people who made their first donation between 0-6 months ago and have made 2 or more donations.
A	`Active donor`: Anyone who made their first donation more than 12 months ago and has made a donation in the last 12 months.
L	`Lapsing donor`: A previous donor who made their last donation between 13-24 months ago.
I	`Inactive donor`: A previous donor who has not made a donation in the last 24 months. People who made a donation more than 25 months ago.
S	`Star donor`: Star donors are individuals who have given to 3 consecutive card mailings.

5. Run a Feature Selection node downstream of the Select node. Notice that some potentially interesting variables have been automatically filtered because they are frequently missing.

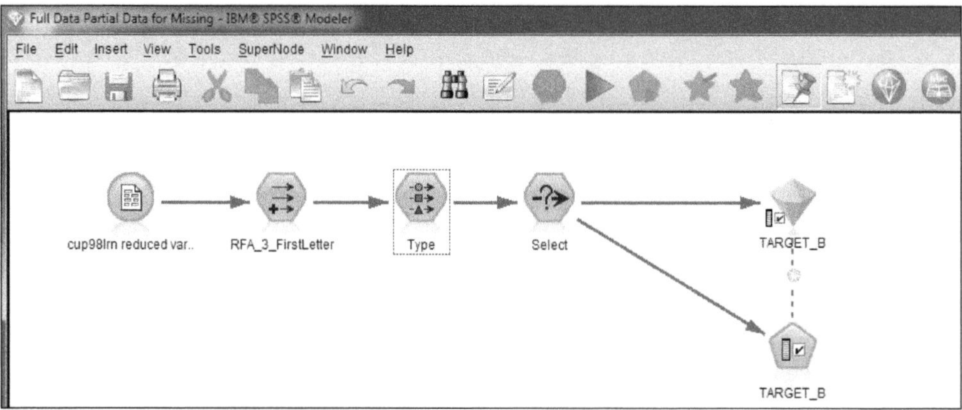

6. Repeat step 4 for the groups that are not `N`. Add another Select node to do this and run an additional Feature Selection node.

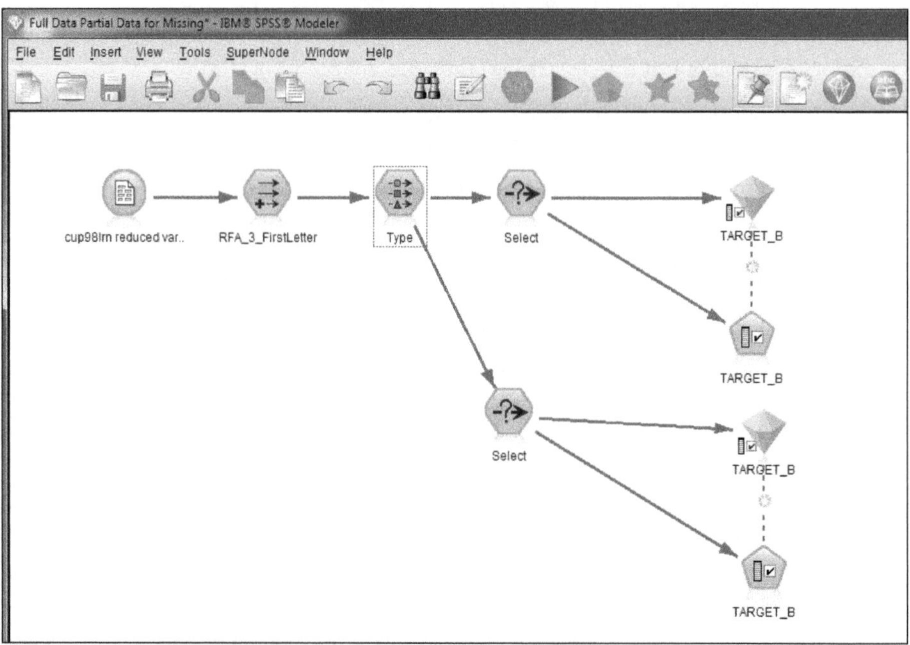

7. Edit both the Feature Selection generated models looking for differences between the two.

8. Look, in particular, for variables that have been filtered from the `N` group, but that have not been filtered from the non `N` group.
9. You would then proceed with building a different model for the two groups, and then appending the results into one data set.

How it works...

Certain information is collected for established customers (donors) but is not available when the customer is first acquired (at the time of first donation). For instance, `Wealth2` is not available for the new donors. Average gift doesn't look very useful for new donors, but that is only natural. There is no established pattern. Would we want to miss out on the modeling possibilities of either of these variables because they are not available for new donors?

How about imputing? Only 5 percent of donors are new donors. Should we guess (albeit an informed guess) how many times they will donate, and what their average will be? The idea of this recipe is that we use the information when it is available, and simply use other information when it is not available. This trick is extremely different from imputing, and is also unlike the idea of surrogates in C&RT. It can be quite effective.

How do you know when this trick is useful? Sometimes when modelers learn of this trick they are tempted to build different models for every category. That is not recommended. This is useful when:

- One data category is missing useful information systematically and for easily determined reasons; that is, they are brand-new donors
- The missing information is both present and useful in the other segment

Be careful not to trust Feature Selection to do all of your data exploration. It was expedient in this case, and revealed the necessary pattern. However, it can never replace the time and attention of a human data miner. Some of the variables that Feature Selection nodes keep might be redundant (best revealed in a correlation matrix) and some of the screened variables could be saved by proper data preparation. There is no substitute for the hard work of data exploration. When branching the data in the way that this recipe describes, it is usually revealed after many hours of exploration.

There's more...

This trick can be especially useful when the prior history is explicitly lacking. For instance, in cell phone churn data, new customers cannot possibly have information about their prior phone or their prior contract.

See also

- The *Removing redundant variables using correlation matrices* recipe in *Chapter 2, Data Preparation - Select*
- The *Using the Feature Selection node creatively to remove or decapitate perfect predictors* recipe in *Chapter 2, Data Preparation - Select*

Imputing in-stream mean or median

Filling missing values with the mean or median is a common approach to removing missing values. Modeler has mechanisms for computing and filling missing values using either the Set Globals node or the Data Audit node. Unfortunately, both of these are terminal nodes and therefore require the user to run them as a separate step or as a script. Moreover, the options for which values to impute with are limited to the mean, mid-point, or (in the case of the Data Audit node) a constant.

In this recipe we will impute missing values with the median of a variable in-stream, without the use of `@GLOBAL` variables.

Getting ready

This recipe uses the following files:

- Datafile: `cup98lrn_reduced_vars3.sav`
- Stream file: `Recipe - impute missing with fixed value.str`

How to do it...

To impute missing values with the median of a variable:

1. Open the stream (`Recipe - impute missing with fixed value.str`) by going to **File** | **Open Stream**.
2. Make sure the datafile points to the correct path to the datafile (`cup98lrn_reduced_vars3.sav`).
3. Run the `Stats Before` Data Audit node. Note that the variable `AGE` has only 71,707 valid values, fewer than the 95,412 records in the data set. Note also that the minimum `AGE` value is 1.

4. Open the Type Node named `set blanks`. For the variable `AGE`, left-click on the blank cell in the `Missing` column and select the **Specify** option, as shown in the following figure. Now click on the **OK** button.

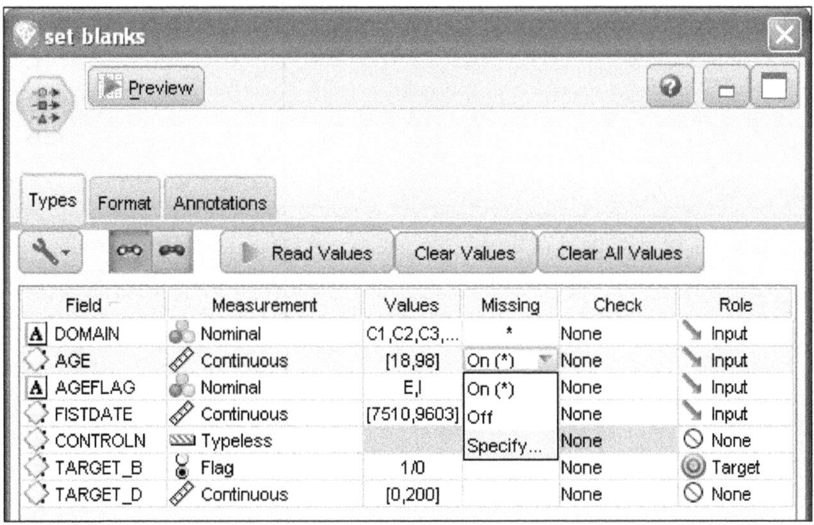

5. Select the **Define blanks** checkbox. Also, in the **Range** option, type `0` in the left box and `17` in the right box, as shown in the following figure. Click on the **OK** button to close this window, then again click on **OK**.

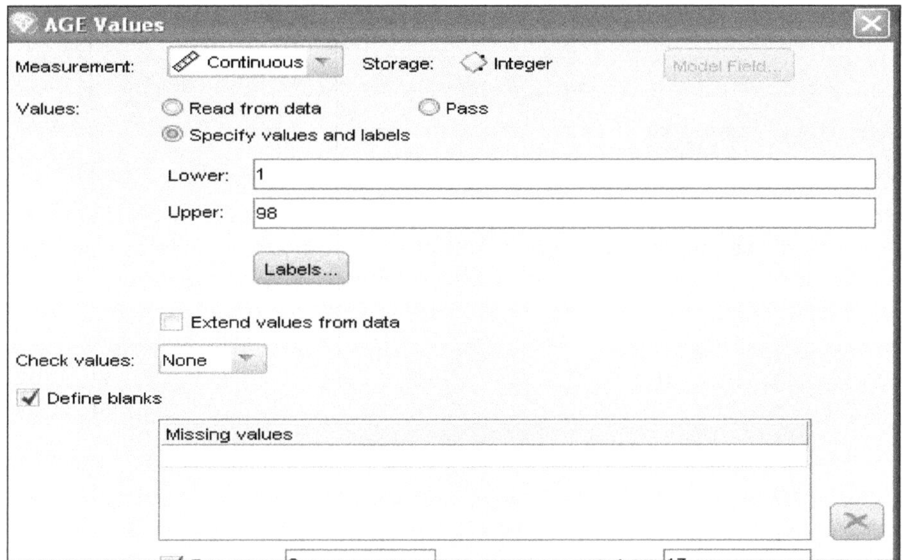

6. Add an Aggregate node to the stream. In the Aggregate node, do not add any key fields, but add `AGE` to the **Aggregate fields** as shown in the following screenshot. Only check the **Median** checkbox and then click on **OK**.

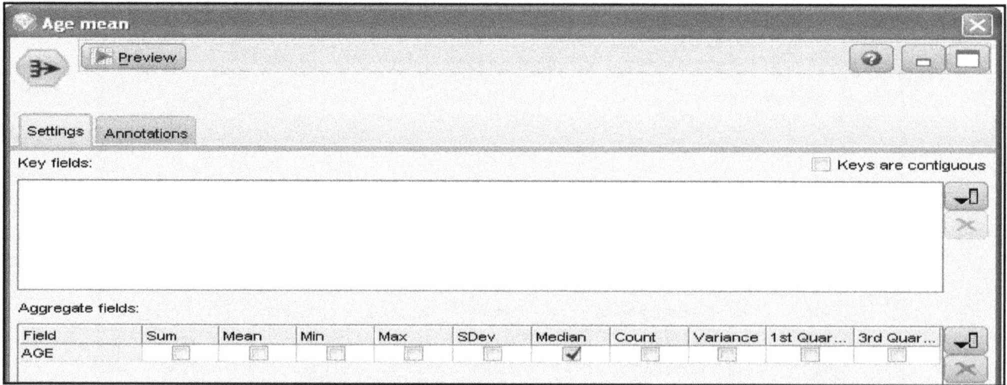

7. Add a Merge node to the stream, and connect both the `set blanks`, that is the Type node and the Aggregate node, to the Merge node. Inside the Merge node, select the **Keys** radio button for the **Merge Method** option. Now click on **OK**.
8. Add a Filler node to the stream connected to the Merge node. Open the Filler node, and select `AGE` as a fill in field. For the **Replace** option, select **Blank and null values**. Finally, in the **Replace with** box, type in `to_integer( AGE_Median)` and click on the **OK** button.
9. Attach a Data Audit node to the Filler node and run the node. Note that the number of valid values for `AGE` is now 95,412. Also note that the histogram for AGE has a spike near the center of its distribution. This is due to filling in the blank and null values with the median.

How it works...

In this recipe, missing values are imputed with the median, the value preferred by many practitioners because the median is a more robust statistic (the median is less sensitive to outliers) than the mean. But in addition to replacing only NULL values with the mean, the recipe also replaces values that are considered invalid with the median as well. In step 4, the range of ages between 0 and 17 is specified as blank, meaning they are considered as if they are missing. The Filler node described in step 8 operates on NULL values and BLANK, meaning that AGE values that are NULL or are specified as BLANK (i.e., AGE values between 0 to 17) are filled in.

The Aggregate node computed the summary statistics for all 95,412 records by not specifying any variable as **Key fields**. The Merge node set up in step 7 performs a full combinatoric join by specifying joining by a key, but without actually specifying any variable as the key to join on. Since the Aggregate node produced only one record, the effect of the join is to just add the median values (and `Record_Count`) as additional columns after the merge.

There's more...

One can fill the missing values with the mean by selecting the **Mean** button in the Aggregate node and using `AGE_Mean` in the Filler node. If one would rather compute a mid-point, one could compute both the min and max statistics in the Aggregate node, compute the mid-point, that is, *(AGE_Max - AGE_Min)/2*, and merge these values with the original data.

Note that, in step 9, the histogram for AGE has the spike in the middle as shown in the following figure. Imputing with a fixed value, either mean, median, or mid-point, fills all missing values with a single value, thereby distorting the distribution's standard deviation.

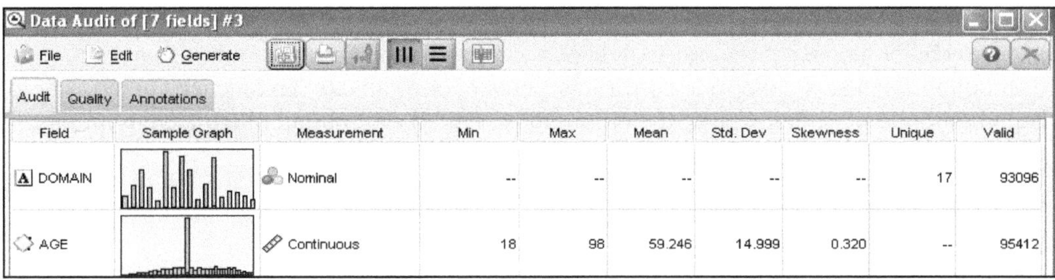

Field	Sample Graph	Measurement	Min	Max	Mean	Std. Dev	Skewness	Unique	Valid
DOMAIN		Nominal	--	--	--	--	--	17	93096
AGE		Continuous	18	98	59.246	14.999	0.320	--	95412

One simple alternative is to use another variable to adjust the imputed value. In this data set, there is a variable called `FISTDATE`, which is the date of the very first donation. Presumably, a first donation made 30 years ago must have been made by an older donor (at least 48 years old). If the Aggregate node is modified to have `FISTDATE` as the key field, and then one sets `FISTDATE` as the `Key` field in the subsequent Merge node, the resulting distribution has the chance of being smoother. In fact, it is, as is shown in the following figure:

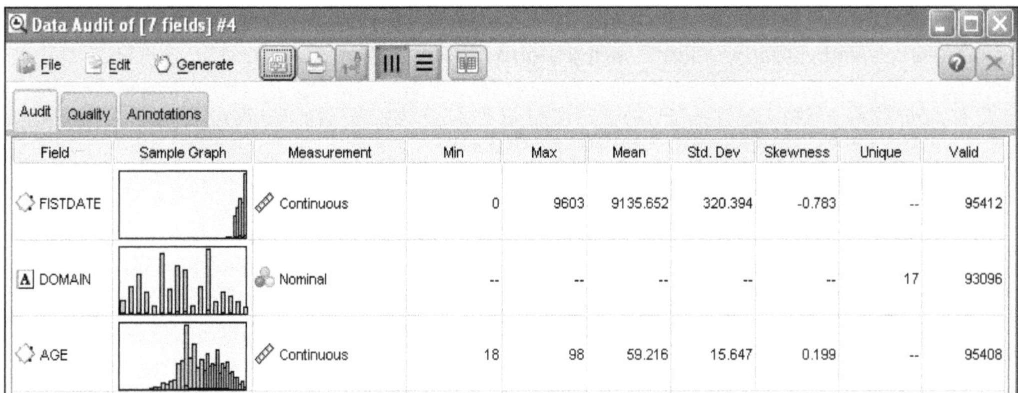

Field	Sample Graph	Measurement	Min	Max	Mean	Std. Dev	Skewness	Unique	Valid
FISTDATE		Continuous	0	9603	9135.652	320.394	-0.783	--	95412
DOMAIN		Nominal	--	--	--	--	--	17	93096
AGE		Continuous	18	98	59.216	15.647	0.199	--	95408

If one doesn't know which variable to use in conjunction with the Aggregate node, one can use the imputation available in the Data Audit node's **Quality** tab, selecting the `Algorithm` method to build a predictive model to impute the missing values.

See also

- The *Imputing missing values randomly from uniform or normal distributions* recipe in this chapter
- The *Using random imputation to match a variable's distribution* recipe in this chapter

Imputing missing values randomly from uniform or normal distributions

Filling missing values with a random number is often preferable to filling with a constant, such as the mean or median. If the distribution of a variable matches or nearly matches a known distribution, such as a uniform or normal distribution, one can use the functions in Modeler to generate random numbers, given the parameters needed to generate the random numbers.

In this recipe we will impute missing values with random distributions: uniform and normal.

Getting ready

This recipe uses the following files:

1. Datafile: `cup98lrn_variable cleaning random impute recipe.sav`
2. Stream file: `Recipe - impute random with known random distribution.str`

How to do it...

To impute missing values randomly with uniform or normal distributions:

1. Open the `Recipe - impute random with known random distribution.str` file by navigating to **File** | **Open Stream**.
2. Make sure the datafile points to the correct path to the file `cup98lrn_variable cleaning random impute recipe.sav`.
3. Open the `set blanks` Type node and specify blanks for `AGE`, just as with steps 4 and 5 in the *Imputing in-stream mean or median* recipe in this chapter.
4. Insert a Filler node and connect it to the `set blanks` Type node. Open the node and, from the drop-down variable list in the **Fill in fields** area, select `AGE`. In the **Replace** drop-down menu select **Blank and null values**. In the **Replace with** area, type `undef` as shown in the following screenshot. Click on the **Annotations** tab and rename the node as `replace 0-17 with NULL`. Now click on **OK**.

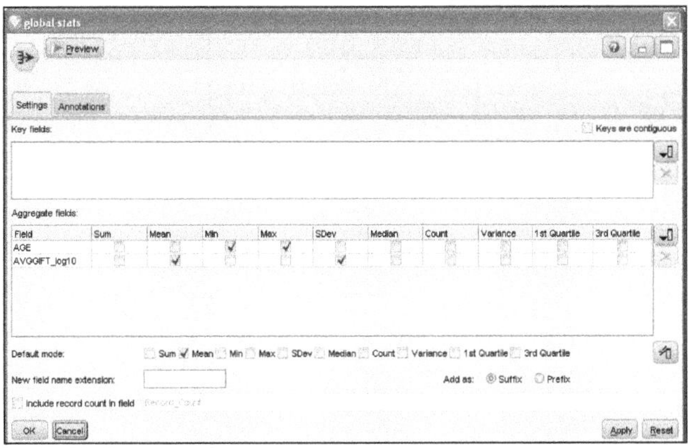

5. Insert an Aggregate node, place it above the `replace 0-17 with NULL` Filler node and connect it to the Filler node. Inside the Aggregate node, in the **Aggregate fields** section, select fields `AGE` and `AVGGIFT_log10`. For `AGE`, check the **Min** and **Max** checkboxes only. For `AVGGIFT_log10`, check the **Mean** and **SDev** checkboxes. Uncheck the **Include record count in field** checkbox. These options are shown in the following screenshot. Now click on the **OK** button.

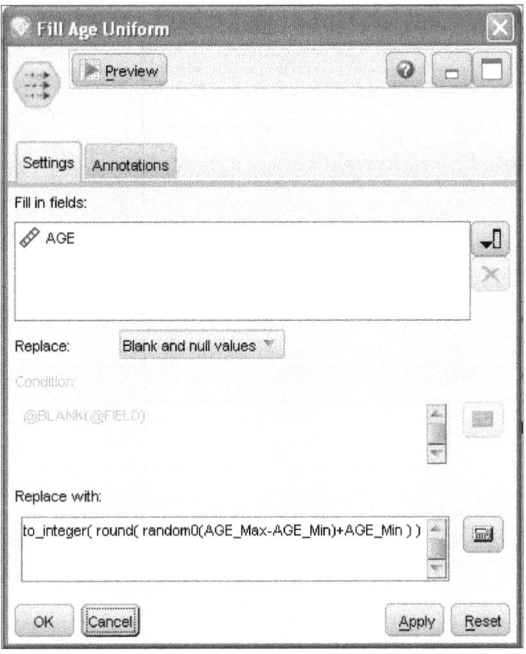

6. Insert a Merge node and connect to it first the `replace 0-17 with NULL` Filler node as discussed in step 4, then the Aggregate node as discussed in step 5. Now select the **Keys** radio button and click on **OK**.

7. Insert a Filler node and connect it to the Merge node. Open the Filler node and in the **Fill in fields** area select the variable `AGE`. From the **Replace** drop-down list, choose **Blank and null values**. In the **Replace with** box type in `to_integer( round( random0(AGE_Max-AGE_Min)+AGE_Min ) )` as shown in the following figure. Click on the **Annotations** tab and change the name of the node to `Fill Age Uniform` now click on **OK**.

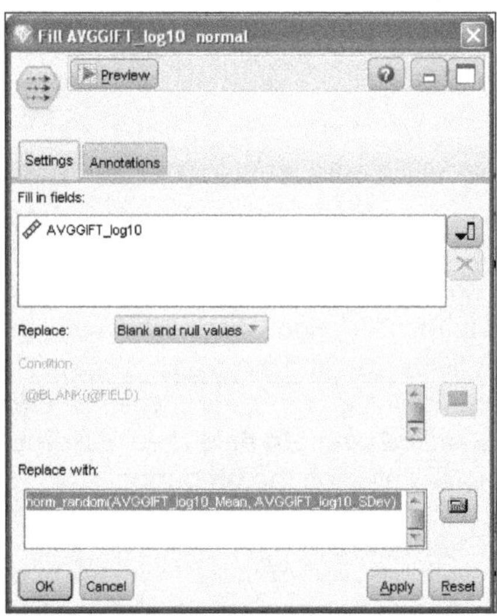

8. Insert a Filler node and connect it to the Filler node `Fill Age Uniform`. Open the Filler node and in the **Fill in fields** box, select the variable `AVGGIFT_log10`. From the **Replace** drop-down list, choose **Blank and null values**. and in the **Replace with** box, type in `norm_random(AVGGIFT_log10_Mean, AVGGIFT_log10_SDev)` as shown in the following figure. Click on the **Annotations** tab, change the name of the node to `Fill AVGIFT_log10 normal`, and then click on **OK**.

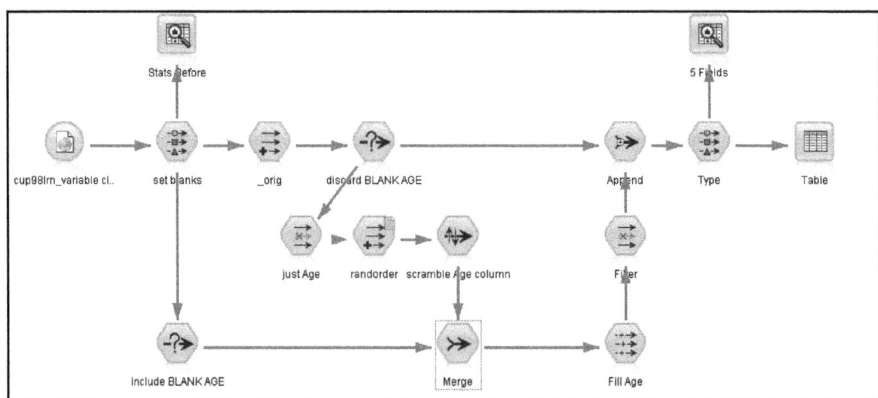

9. Insert a Type node and connect it to the `Fill Age Uniform` node. Then insert a Data Audit node and connect it to the Type node. Run the Data Audit node and examine the distributions for `AGE` and `AVGGift_log10`.

How it works...

For a uniform distribution, the minimum and maximum values are sufficient to specify the range of values to generate with the uniform random number function in Modeler: `random()`. For normal distributions, one needs the mean and the standard deviation of the distribution. These can be calculated in-stream with an Aggregate node (as mentioned in step 5).

Once the summary statistics have been calculated, the imputation itself is straightforward, using Filler nodes and Modeler functions for calculating random values for uniform and normal distributions.

There's more...

One can fine-tune the statistics used to generate the uniform and normal random numbers by adding a `Key` field to the Aggregate node. For example, one could compute the minimum and maximum `AGE` for each value of another field such as `FISTDATE` by using the Aggregate node, as done in the *Imputing in-stream mean or median* recipe in this chapter.

See also

- The *Imputing in-stream mean or median* recipe in this chapter
- The *Using random imputation to match a variable's distribution* recipe in this chapter

Using random imputation to match a variable's distribution

This recipe imputes missing values with actual values (selected at random) from the variable with missing values needing to be imputed. It is valuable when one does not want to impute with a constant but the variable has a distribution that isn't replicated well by a normal or uniform random imputation method.

In this recipe we will impute values for a missing or blank variable with a random value from the variable's own known values. This random imputation will therefore match the actual distribution of the variable itself.

Getting ready

This recipe uses the following files:

- Datafile: `cup98lrn_variable cleaning random impute recipe.sav`
- Stream file: `Recipe - impute missing with actual values.str`

How to do it...

1. Open the stream (`Recipe - impute missing with actual values.str`) by navigating to **File | Open Stream**.
2. Make sure the datafile points to the correct path and to the datafile (`cup98lrn_variable cleaning random impute recipe.sav`).
3. Open the `set blanks` Type node and specify blanks for `AGE`, just like step 4 and step 5 in the *Imputing in-stream mean or median* recipe in this chapter.
4. To the right of the `set blanks` Type node, insert a Derive node. Select the **Multiple** mode option and select the variable `AGE`. Add the field name extension `_orig` as a suffix and, in the formula area, type `@FIELD`.
5. To the right of the Derive node now named `_orig`, insert a Select node, select the **Discard** mode, and type `@BLANK(AGE)` into the condition area. Go to the **Annotations** tab and rename the node `discard BLANK AGE`.
6. Beneath the Select node specified in step 5, add a Filter node connected to the Select node. Open the Filter node and remove all fields except for `AGE`. In the 3rd column, change the name of this field to `fillAGE`. Go to the **Annotations** tab and change the name of the node to `just AGE`.
7. Insert a Derive node and connect it to `just AGE`. Rename this Derive field as `randorder`, and in the formula area type `random(1.0)`.
8. Insert a Sort node and connect it to the Derive node, `randorder`. Add the `randorder` field to the sort list, and sort it ascending (it doesn't matter which order one sorts, ascending or descending). Go to the **Annotations** tab and rename the node as `scramble AGE column`.
9. Copy the Select node, `discard BLANK AGE` and paste it in the stream. Move the pasted Select node to just below the `set blanks` Type node. Open the Select node and select the mode **Include** (changing it from **Discard**). Then go to the **Annotations** tab and change the name of the node to `include BLANK AGE`.
10. Insert a Merge node in the stream and connect the `scramble Age column` Sort node and the `include BLANK AGE` Select nodes to it. Open the Merge node and choose the **Order** radio button for the Merge method. Leave the merge as an inner join and then click on **OK**.

11. Insert a Filler node and in the **Fill in fields** area select the field AGE. In the **Replace with** box type fillAGE, and then click on **OK**.
12. Insert a Filter node and connect it to the Filler node from step 11. Open the Filter node and remove fields fillAGE, and randorder. Now click on the **OK** button.
13. Insert an Append node and place it above the Filter node from step 12. First connect the discard BLANK AGE Select node to the Append node, then connect the Filter node from step 13 to the Append node. Open the Append node and make sure the output field column contains all the variables of interest. Check the **Tag records by including source dataset in field** checkbox and type Ageimputed in the text box to its right.
14. While still in the Append node, click on the **Inputs** tab. Type the word No in the **Tag** column for the row containing the main data (it should have as the connected node discard BLANK AGE). Type the word Yes in the **Tag** column with the connected node, that is, Filter. Now click on **OK**.
15. Insert a Type node and connect it to the Append node.
16. Insert a Data Audit node and connect it to the Type node from step 15. Move it above the Type node.
17. Run the Data Audit node to examine the resulting AGE values, including its mean, standard deviation, and number valid.

How it works...

The top path of the stream discards the values of AGE leaving only the BLANK values, namely the NULL values and those values less than or equal to 17. These records will be retained as it is.

The downward path that goes through the include BLANK AGE Select node contains all the records with BLANK AGE values. The AGE values will be replaced, but the remaining fields will be retained as is.

The values to impute are created in the middle path of the stream, below the discard BLANK AGE Select node. First, we remove all other fields; only AGE matters in this path. A random number is generated to rearrange (randomly) the order of the AGE values. The Sort node scrambles the AGE values in the order of the random numbers. The AGE field is renamed to fillAGE and contains the randomized AGE values that will replace the BLANK values.

The Merge node combines the middle and bottom paths by order. The number of records that are retained after the merge is the smaller of the number of records for the two paths.

The final stream should look something like the one shown as follows:

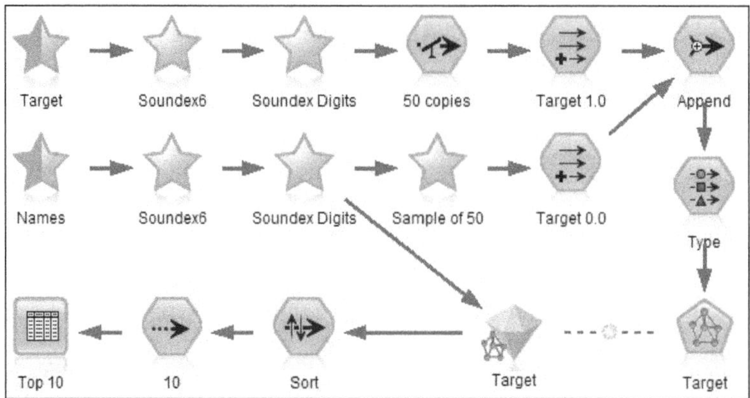

There's more...

Random imputation is a common method for missing value imputation because it is an unbiased method to fill in the missing values. However, whenever a random number is created, it is different from the last time. Every time one runs this Modeler stream, the imputed values will be different, and can become problematic when one is trying to replicate an analysis or particular results.

If one only needs a temporary freeze on these random values, one can cache the `randorder` Derive node to keep the same random numbers as long as the cache is retained. It will be flushed if anything in the stream before the `randorder` node has changed, or upon re-opening the stream.

An alternative is to save the random values by exporting the random values as a `.sav` file. This list of random numbers can be brought back into the stream and added to the data using a Merge node. Another way to save the random numbers is by creating and filling a cache for the `randorder` node and then exporting that cache to a file. The next time one runs the stream, one can load the cache from the saved file.

If the field being filled is more than 50 percent missing, one will have to replicate the populated values 2 or more times to ensure there are enough values to fill in. For example, if 75 percent of the values are missing (leaving only 25 percent populated), the 25 percent populated records will have to be replicated three times.

See also

- The *Imputing in-stream mean or median* recipe in this chapter
- The *Imputing missing values randomly from uniform or normal distributions* recipe in this chapter

Searching for similar records using a Neural Network for inexact matching

Many applications require the matching of names, and although exact matching is often used, inexact matching is useful when we want to take into account the possibility of spelling errors. Soundex codes can provide a form of inexact matching but even exact matching of Soundex codes can miss obvious matches like *fog* and *phogg*. Neuro-fuzzy Soundex combines the extended Soundex codes provided by the Soundex supernode with neuro-fuzzy (inexact) matching to provide a very flexible name and word matching technique.

Getting ready

This recipe uses the following files:

- Datafile: `names.txt`
- Stream file: `Neuro_Fuzzy_Soundex.str`
- Supernode library file: `Soundex_Digits.slb`

How to do it...

To search for similar records using a neural network for inexact matching, perform the following steps:

1. Open the stream file (`Neuro_Fuzzy_Soundex.str`) by going to **File** | **Open Stream.**

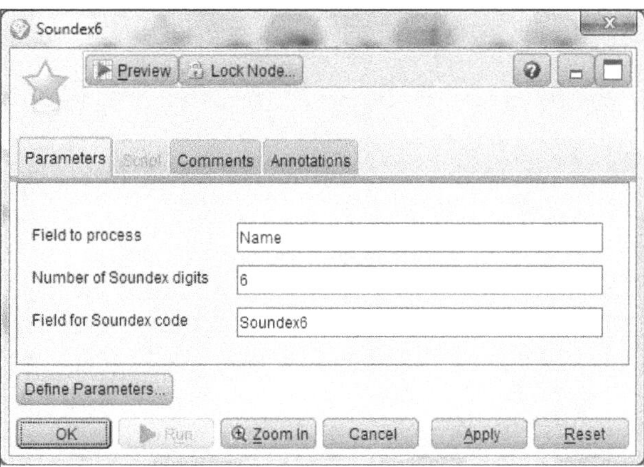

2. Zoom in to the supernode **Target**. This selects a specific target record from the datafile `names.txt`.

3. Zoom in to the supernode **Names**. This selects all except the target record from the datafile `names.txt`.
4. Double-click on one of the Soundex6 supernodes to show its parameters as shown in the following screenshot. The settings produce a Soundex code with 6 numeric digits from the field `Name` into a new field called `Soundex6`.

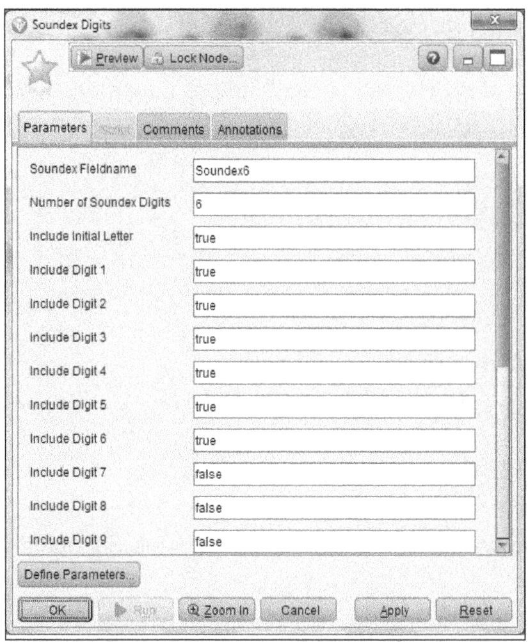

5. Double-click on one of the **Soundex Digits** supernodes to show its parameters as shown in the following figure:

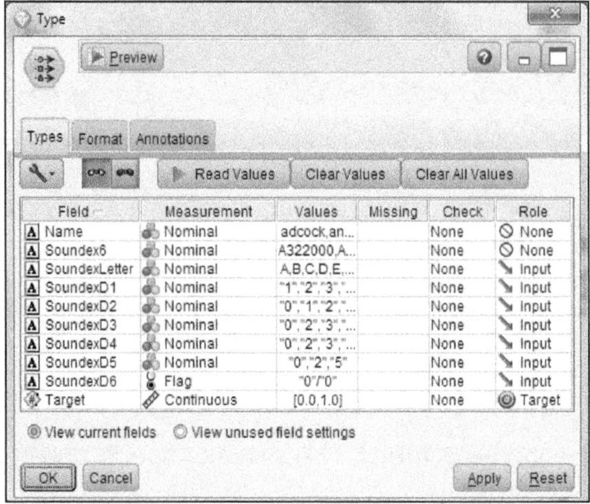

This supernode (also available from the supernode library file, Soundex_Digits.slb) decomposes a Soundex code into several fields, one for each character of the Soundex code. These fields are called SoundexLetter for the initial letter, SoundexD1 for the initial digit, SoundexD2 for the second digit, and so on. The parameters are the name of the field holding the Soundex code, the number of numeric digits from this code to be processed, and then a flag for each character to determine whether it should be output (this allows you to select a subset of the digits in the Soundex code if you do not need all of them).

6. The rest of the stream replicates the neuro-fuzzy searching recipe. Open the Type node to see the roles of fields in the neural network model as shown in the following figure:

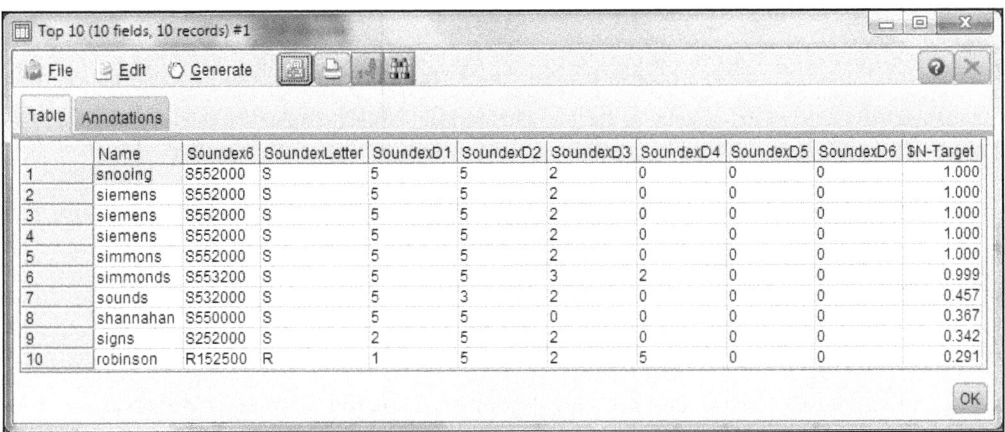

	Name	Soundex6	SoundexLetter	SoundexD1	SoundexD2	SoundexD3	SoundexD4	SoundexD5	SoundexD6	$N-Target
1	snooing	S552000	S	5	5	2	0	0	0	1.000
2	siemens	S552000	S	5	5	2	0	0	0	1.000
3	siemens	S552000	S	5	5	2	0	0	0	1.000
4	siemens	S552000	S	5	5	2	0	0	0	1.000
5	simmons	S552000	S	5	5	2	0	0	0	1.000
6	simmonds	S553200	S	5	5	3	2	0	0	0.999
7	sounds	S532000	S	5	3	2	0	0	0	0.457
8	shannahan	S550000	S	5	5	0	0	0	0	0.367
9	signs	S252000	S	2	5	2	0	0	0	0.342
10	robinson	R152500	R	1	5	2	5	0	0	0.291

7. Run the Table node `Top 10`. The result is shown in the following figure:

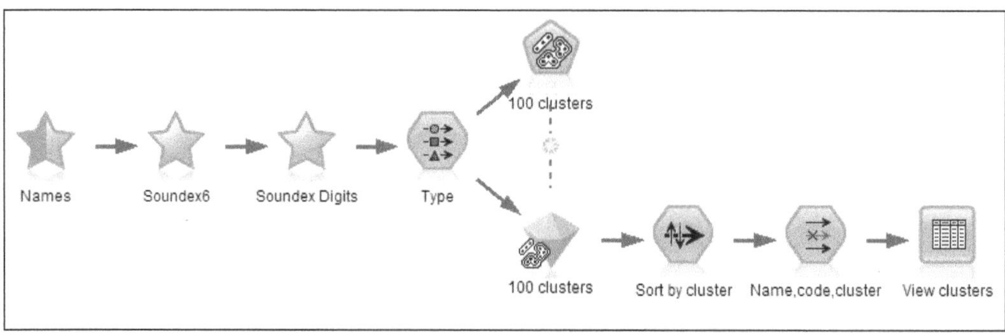

The table shows the words or names, their Soundex6 codes, the decomposition of these codes, and the score from the neural network model. Words with a Soundex6 code identical to Simmons (S552000) get a score of 1.0; words with other Soundex6 codes get lower scores, but a degree of similarity is being detected and has been used to rank all the words in `names.txt` to find those most similar to **simmons**.

How it works...

The neuro-fuzzy Soundex stream works in the following way:

1. Creating extended Soundex codes for names using the Soundex supernode.
2. Decomposing the Soundex codes into their individual characters in separate fields using the Soundex Digits supernode.
3. Using the separate characters from the Soundex code as the attributes of each example, use the neuro-fuzzy searching technique to locate words that sound like the target.

There's more...

Decomposing Soundex codes into their component characters opens up a world of possibilities. For example, here's a stream that takes a list of names and produces groups of those that sound alike using clustering:

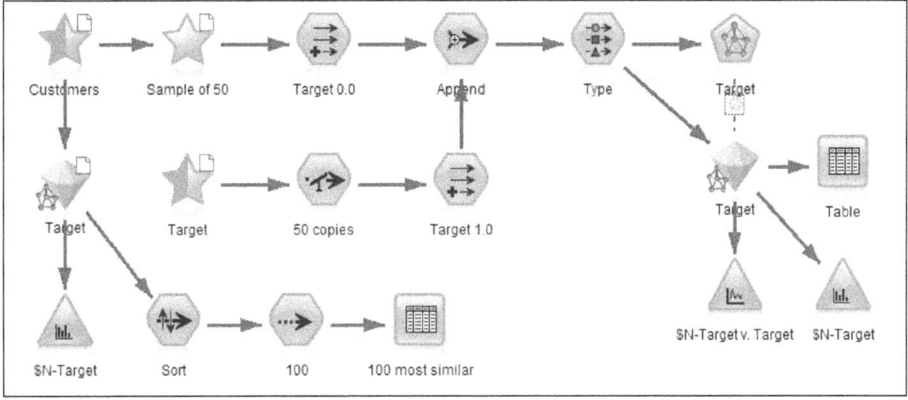

See also

- The *Using neuro-fuzzy searching to find similar names* recipe in this chapter
- The *Producing longer Soundex codes* recipe in this chapter

Using neuro-fuzzy searching to find similar names

Searching for a record in a data set is a commonplace operation in data processing and analysis. When the match to the target is exact, the operation is straightforward, but many searches must be inexact, for example, searching for similar faces, or searching for similar crimes. We call this kind of search *fuzzy*, not in the mathematical sense as it is used in fuzzy logic, but in the everyday sense of inexact. When this kind of fuzzy searching is performed using a neural network, we call it **neuro-fuzzy searching**.

Neuro-fuzzy searching is accomplished by training a neural network model to recognize the target, the object of the search, and produce a score that rates the similarity of an example to the target. This model is then used to score the database to be searched, and we can then select the example or examples that are most similar to the target.

Getting ready

This recipe uses the following files:

- Datafile: `cup98LRN.txt`
- Stream file: `Neuro_Fuzzy_Searching.str`

How to do it...

To use neuro-fuzzy searching to find similar names:

1. Open the stream file (`Neuro_Fuzzy_Searching.str`) by going to **File | Open Stream**.

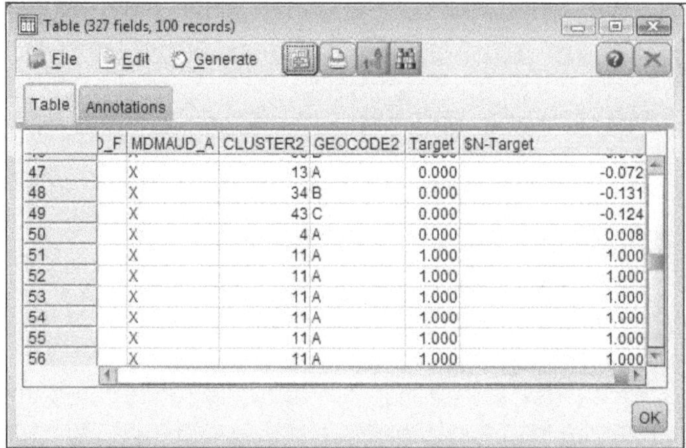

	D_F	MDMAUD_A	CLUSTER2	GEOCODE2	Target	$N-Target
47		X	13	A	0.000	-0.072
48		X	34	B	0.000	-0.131
49		X	43	C	0.000	-0.124
50		X	4	A	0.000	0.008
51		X	11	A	1.000	1.000
52		X	11	A	1.000	1.000
53		X	11	A	1.000	1.000
54		X	11	A	1.000	1.000
55		X	11	A	1.000	1.000
56		X	11	A	1.000	1.000

2. Zoom in to the supernode `Customers`. This supernode reads the datafile `cup98LRN.txt` and performs minor cleaning operations to remove missing data; the aim is to produce a data set that is fully populated, but of a substantial size, and excludes the target record.
3. Zoom in to the supernode `Sample of 50`. This supernode uses 2 sample nodes to produce a small sample from the much larger data set.
4. Zoom in to the supernode `Target`. This supernode selects the target record; the stream searches for other records that are similar to the target.
5. Edit the Balance node `50 copies`. This node produces 50 copies of the target record.
6. Open the Derive node `Target 1.0`. This node creates the field `Target` with the value 1.0, which indicates that this is the target record. A similar Derive node creates the same field with the value `0.0` for the records that are not the target.
7. Edit the Type node; note that `Target` is set to be the target for training, and that the `ID` field is set to direction `NONE` (not to be used in training).
8. The Neural Net node, `Target`, uses the default settings for this node and, when run, produces the model `Target`. Run the Table node, `Table`, to see the output of the model.

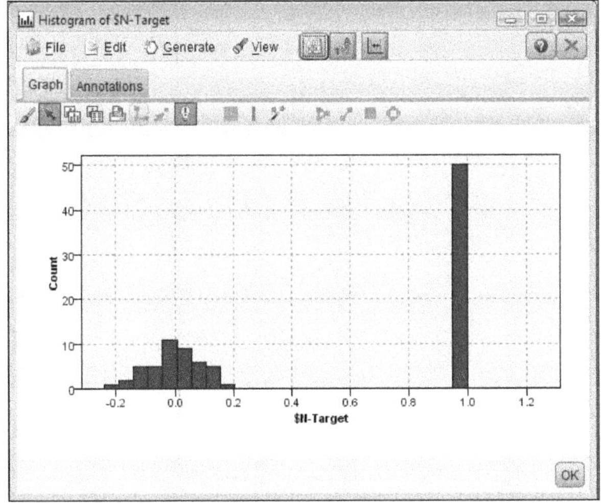

The preceding figure is arranged to show the key feature of this output; on the training data, target records produce a predicted value of 1.0. Non-target records produce much smaller values, mostly less than 0.2, indicating dissimilarity from the target record.

9. Run the Histogram node `$N-Target` on the far right of the stream.

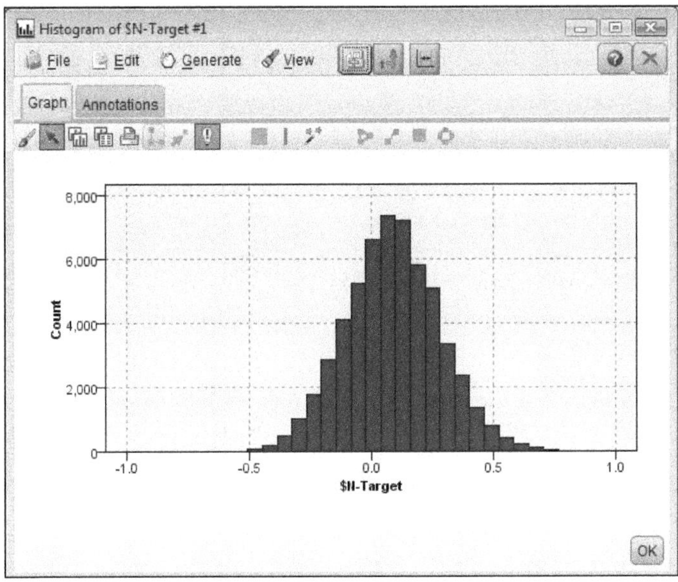

You can see from the preceding screenshot that the separation of the target records from others is perfect for the training data.

10. Run the Histogram node `$N-Target` on the far left of the stream.

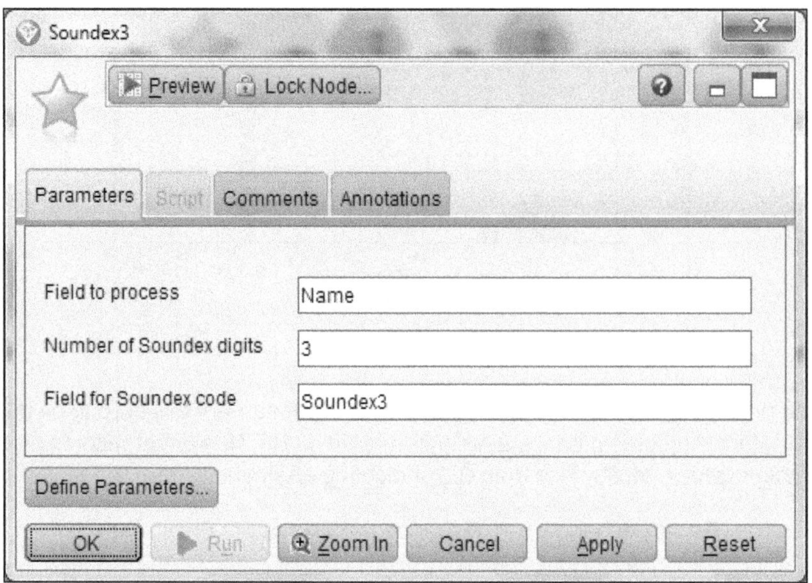

You can see from the preceding screenshot that, for the full data set, the model produces a much wider range of values. Some of these are greater than 0.5, indicating similarity to the target record.

11. Run the Table node `100 most similar`. The Sort node and Sample node that feed this table simply select the 100 records with the highest `$N-Target` scores, that is the 100 records that, according to the model, are most similar to the target variable. The most similar record overall will be at the top of this list.

How it works...

Neuro-fuzzy searching means using a neural network, which has been trained to recognize a target instance, to search a database for similar instances. The beauty of this technique is that the model is trained on a very small data set, in this example only 100 records, composed of 50 copies of the target and 50 other records.

The indicator in the training set that shows whether a record is the target or not (the derived field `Target`) is a real-valued number and not an integer or a Boolean. This is important, because the neural network is a scoring model, producing a real-valued output, so that different degrees of similarity to the target can be indicated.

It is possible for the modeling step in this recipe to fail. If the non-target examples chosen for training included, by chance, a record very similar to the target, then the model would not produce good separation and this would be reflected in the preceding histogram figure showing model output `$N-Target` for the training data. If this happens, the solution is to pick a different random sample of non-target variables and try again.

There's more...

All data mining algorithms operate by creating a definition of similarity based on the training data, and neural networks perform a search among different definitions of similarity; this makes them particularly powerful when the problem is explicitly about similarity. Neuro-fuzzy searching is one domain in which exploring different neural network topologies can be advantageous. For example, for some data sets, this technique has been found effective when using a neural network with two hidden layers instead of the default single hidden layer.

This technique has been used to find similar faces and similar crime reports.

See also

- The *Searching for similar records using a Neural Network for inexact matching* recipe in this chapter
- The *Producing longer Soundex codes* recipe in this chapter

Producing longer Soundex codes

Soundex coding is an abstract way to represent the sound of a word; it was invented to help identify when the same name might be spelt differently over a period of time, but is used more generally to help identify variant spellings of the same name or word. For example *spelled* and *spelt* would have the same Soundex code.

Normally, a Soundex code represents a word by its initial letter capitalized, followed by three numeric digits (0-6) representing groups of letters that might be substituted for one another. The numeric digit codes correspond to letters of the alphabet as follows:

Numeric Digit Group Code	Letters
1	B P F V
2	C S K G J Q X Z

Numeric Digit Group Code	Letters
3	D T
4	L
5	M N
6	R

All other letters (vowels plus Y, H & W) are ignored, as are adjacent repetitions of the same code. If the result contains fewer than 3 numeric digits, the length is padded with zeros.

Modeler includes a built-in function to generate Soundex codes, but this will produce only codes with 3 numeric digits. If a longer code is required, the Soundex supernode can produce a code of up to 19 numeric digits, but the maximum code is shorter when repetitions must be skipped.

This recipe illustrates the function of the Soundex supernode and when longer Soundex codes can be useful.

Getting ready

This recipe uses the following files:

- Datafile: `names.txt`
- Stream file: `Soundex_Supernode.str`
- Supernode library file: `Soundex_Supernode.slb`

How to do it...

1. Open the stream (`Soundex_Supernode.str`) by going to **File** | **Open Stream**.
2. Make sure that the Var. file node points to the datafile `names.txt`.
3. Double-click on the supernode `Soundex3`; the parameters of the supernode have been set to process the field Name and produce a 3-digit Soundex code in a new field called `Soundex3`.

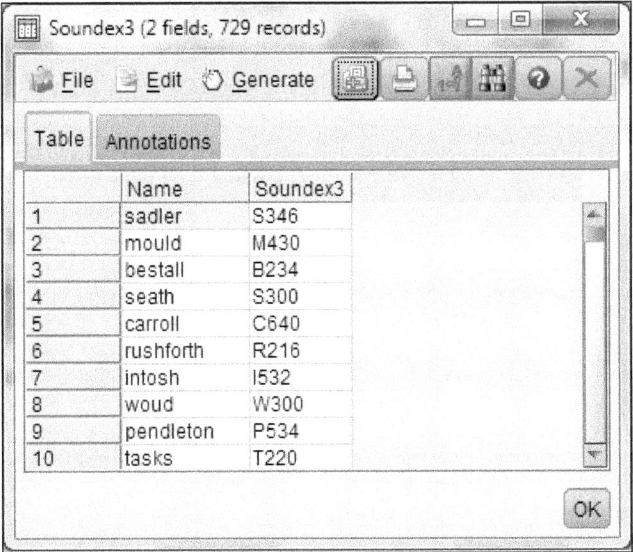

	Name	Soundex3
1	sadler	S346
2	mould	M430
3	bestall	B234
4	seath	S300
5	carroll	C640
6	rushforth	R216
7	intosh	I532
8	woud	W300
9	pendleton	P534
10	tasks	T220

4. Run the Table node `Soundex3`, producing the following output; note that the `Name` field contains many values that are not names, and the second field `Soundex3` is the Soundex code created by the Soundex supernode. This code is the same as Modeler's Soundex built-in function one would create.

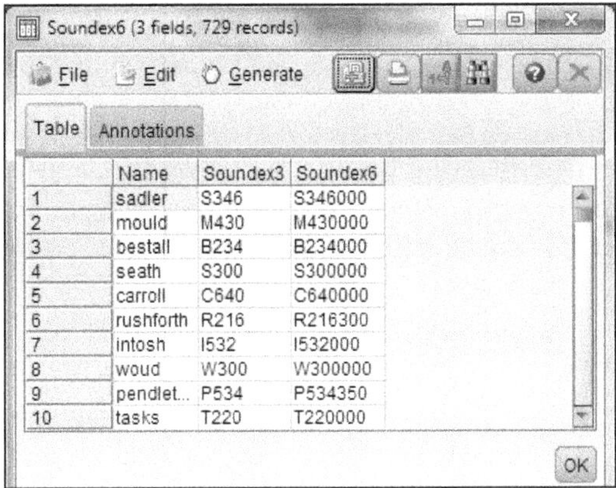

	Name	Soundex3	Soundex6
1	sadler	S346	S346000
2	mould	M430	M430000
3	bestall	B234	B234000
4	seath	S300	S300000
5	carroll	C640	C640000
6	rushforth	R216	R216300
7	intosh	I532	I532000
8	woud	W300	W300000
9	pendlet...	P534	P534350
10	tasks	T220	T220000

5. Double-click on the supernode `Soundex6`; the parameters of the supernode have been set to process the field `Name` and produce a 6-digit Soundex code in the new field `Soundex6`.

6. Run the Table node `Soundex6`, producing the following output. Note that the codes in the field `Soundex6` have 6 numeric digits instead of 3 and that in many but not all cases the last 3 numeric digits are zeros.

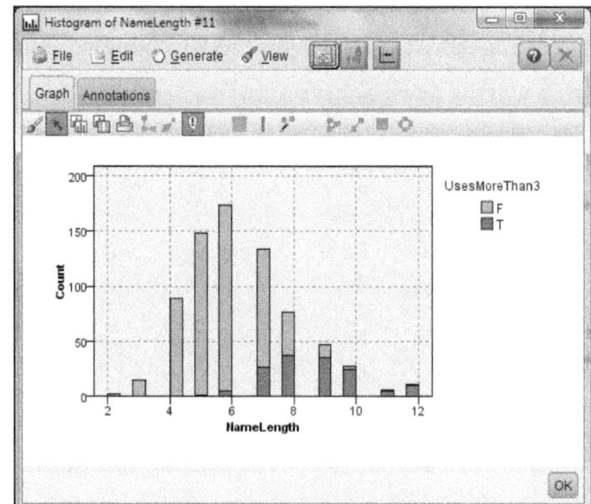

7. Open the Derive nodes `NameLength` and `UsesMoreThan3`. `NameLength` is simply the length of the `Name` string. `UsesMoreThan3` is a Boolean indicating whether more than three digits of the Soundex6 code are actually being used, based on the expression:

   Soundex6 /= Soundex3 >< "000"

   In other words this Boolean is `false` when Soundex6 and Soundex3 are the same except for 3 trailing zeros, otherwise `true`.

8. Run the Histogram node `NameLength`; this is overlaid with `UsesMoreThan3` to produce the following graph. Note that longer names have a higher chance of using more than 3 Soundex digits, and that a substantial proportion of data overall use more than 3.

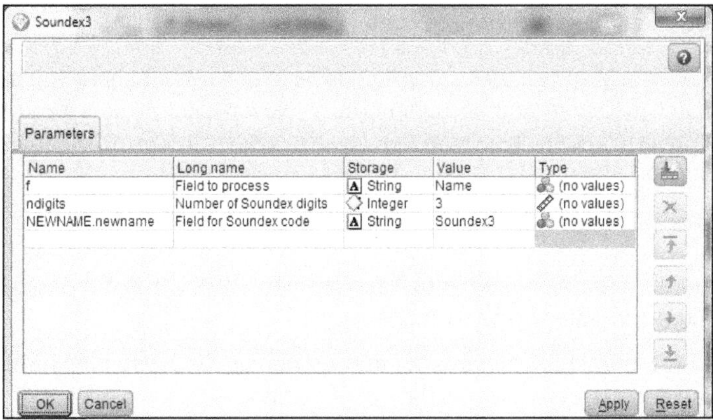

9. Run the final table node `UsesMoreThan3`, showing only the strings which have this property; note that surprisingly common names such as Watkins and Jenkins make use of more than 3 digits.

How it works...

The Soundex supernode takes three parameters, the name of the field for that the code should be generated, the number of numeric digits in the desired code, and the name of the field in which to produce the Soundex code. The supernode works by creating successive characters of the Soundex code with a series of derive nodes, then filling or stripping the result to the correct length.

The following expression is used in most of the derive nodes, and implements the key translation of letters to codes. This instance examines the third letter in the word and derives a new field called `c3`.

```
if length(s) < 3 then '0'
elseif member(s(3),[B P F V]) and c2 /= '1' then '1'
elseif member(s(3),[C S K G J Q X Z]) and c2 /= '2' then '2'
elseif member(s(3),[D T]) and c2 /= '3' then '3'
elseif s(3) = 'L' and c2 /= '4' then '4'
elseif member(s(3),[M N]) and c2 /= '5' then '5'
elseif s(3) = 'R' and c2 /= '6' then '6'
else '' endif
```

Downloading the example code

You can download the example code files for all Packt books you have purchased from your account at http://www.packtpub.com. If you purchased this book elsewhere, you can visit http://www.packtpub.com/support and register to have the files e-mailed directly to you.

Several features of this expression are notable:

- The initial `if` branch implements filling the code with zeros if the word is too short to contain the character being examined
- The `elseif` branches implement letter groupings, and also eliminate repeated letters and codes by looking at the previous code
- The `else` branch returns an empty string so that a character can simply be skipped if it is to be ignored

The supernode parameters are defined as follows:

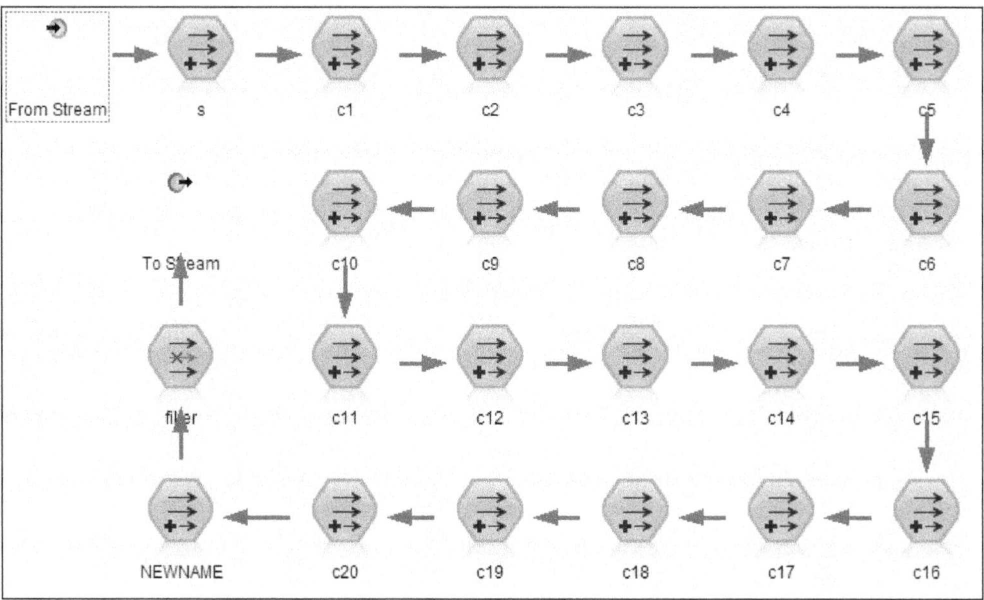

Note that the final parameter is a slot parameter, referring to a parameter called `newname`, which is modified in the Derive node named `NEWNAME`. This Derive node creates the new field containing the results of the Soundex supernode.

Zoomed in, the Soundex supernode looks like this:

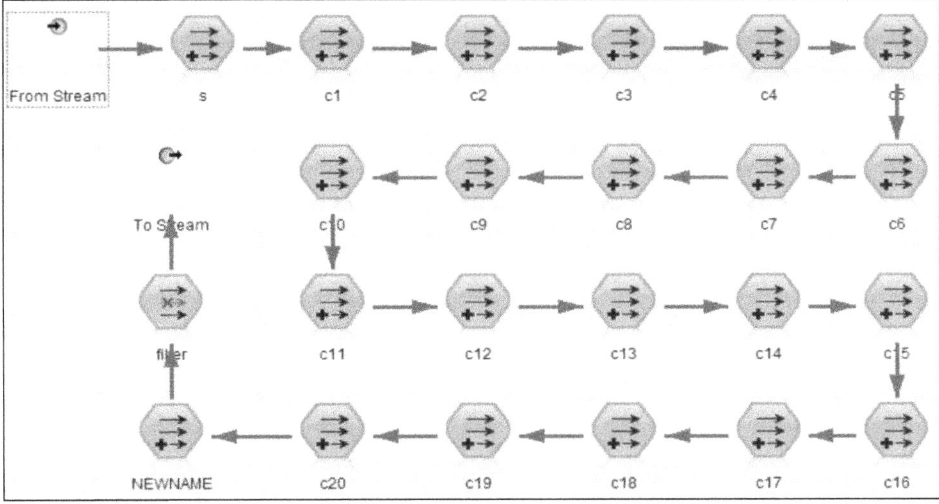

- The derived field **s** is calculated using the built-in function `lowertoupper`, so that letters extracted from the string will always be uppercase. This function is applied to the parameter `$P-f`, that is the first parameter of the supernode.
- The derived field `c1` is the initial letter of the string, and the derived fields `c2` to `c20` are the numeric digits of the Soundex code, calculated using the preceding expression except that `c2` is simpler because it does not have to check the value of the previous digit.
- The derive node `NEWNAME` simply appends `c1` to `c20` together with trailing zeros and then truncates the string to the length requested by the second supernode parameter. The new field it creates has the name supplied by the third supernode parameter.
- The final filter node removes all the derived fields except for that created by `NEWNAME`.

There's more...

This recipe explores the properties of Soundex codes, particularly those with more digits than the standard 3. In addition, it illustrates how supernode parameters can be used to make them reusable. It also illustrates the advanced feature of *structured parameters*, which can be used to control the setting of nodes within a supernode when the required control is beyond the scope of an ordinary parameter.

The Soundex supernode itself is supplied in the file `Soundex Supernode.slb`; this can be inserted for use in any stream when Soundex coding is required.

See also

- The *Searching for similar records using a Neural Network for inexact matching* recipe in this chapter
- The *Using neuro-fuzzy searching to find similar names* recipe in this chapter

4
Data Preparation – Construct

In this chapter, we will cover:

- Building transformations with multiple Derive nodes
- Calculating and comparing conversion rates
- Grouping categorical values
- Transforming high skew or kurtosis variables using a multiple Derive mode
- Creating flag variables for aggregation
- Using Association Rules for interaction detection/feature creation
- Creating time-aligned cohorts

Introduction

This chapter will focus on the Construct subtask of CRISP-DM's data preparation phase. The CRISP-DM document describes it as follows:

> *This task includes constructive data preparation operations such as the production of derived attributes, entire new records, or transformed values for existing attributes.*

Of all the subtasks in CRISP-DM, the Construct subtask is a good candidate for the one that many novices fail to plan enough time for. Everyone knows that the data must be cleaned and braced for that task to take a long time. "What needs to be constructed?", one might ask. The example that frequently inspires the Aha! experience is dates. Dates—quite simply—are nearly useless in the modeling phase. They are stored as merely points in time. The modeling algorithms have to work awfully hard to spot an interesting date—perhaps spotting a difference between big dates and little dates. One needs to give the algorithms a major helping hand. But, what is interesting are the distances between dates, or the number of events between dates. No one stores their dates in this way. Absolute dates are the best way to store date information, but relative date information is the best way to model this information. The *Creating time-aligned cohorts* recipe of this chapter, one of the longest recipes, addresses this and other related issues of time. For certain projects, this critical issue may cost projects several days.

Stepping back for the broader view, often what we are constructing is a customer-level view of our data. Of course, "customer" could be a patient, or a traveler, an insurance claimant, or even something like a machine engine, but it differs from data that is explored at the group level. It also differs from data at the transactional level. Predictive methods that treat the customer base as one large unit are limiting in many ways. They offer little explanatory power, so the organization may have a departmental forecast, but without much understanding of how, on a per-person basis, to alter the outcome. Decision makers may end up with a prediction without guidance for taking action.

A better advantage is to examine individual behavior, as seen through the lens of the individual's transactions. Models built only on the individual's characteristics, such as demographics, are not rich, and often fail to illuminate beyond what "everybody knows" about the data. Working at the individual level provides information that forms a strong basis for decision making. These new variables that we construct are summaries of past behavior and as such are a great source of insight about future behavior. There is more than a dose of psychology often present in such analyses. Although there is but one recipe on aggregation, *Creating flag variables for aggregation*, aggregation is at the core of this activity. Reducing many rows of data, usually transactional in nature, into a single row summary, often with hundreds of columns of data, that is how aggregation describes a single actor and its behavior.

Along the way, many other issues on the subject of construction or "Data Augmentation" will be addressed. In the first recipe, we learn a basic, but important trick: how to use the Derive node to produce, not just one variable, but instead a related set of variables. In the second recipe, pursuing a similar theme we calculate a large number of ratios. These ratios will resemble our target, but for a different time period. By arraying them over time we can get a sense of whether we are trending in a particular direction. There is also a recipe, *Transforming high skew or kurtosis variables using a multiple Derive node*, that, in a sense, cleans the data, correcting for a skew, but does so by creating alternate versions of the original variables.

Set variables with a very large number of categories are found in nearly every project. As with date manipulation, it is a skill that one cannot succeed without. However, it is usually done manually or based on business knowledge. In other words, one uses ones knowledge to craft a taxonomy, and uses it to reduce the number of categories, boiling down the subtleties until one has fewer categories. This is often not as easy as it sounds. What if you have product SKU, but no product category? It happens more often than you might think. The *Grouping categorical variables* recipe takes a stab at tackling this issue from the data only when external group information is not available.

Building transformations with multiple Derive nodes

In this recipe we will create several new variables with a single Derive node by invoking the **multiple** radio button.

Getting ready

This recipe uses the datafile `cup98lrn_reduced_vars3.sav` and the stream `Recipe - variable construct multiple derive.str`.

How to do it...

1. Open the stream `Recipe - variable construct multiple derive.str` by clicking on **File** | **Open Stream**.
2. Make sure the datafile points to the correct path to the datafile `cup98lrn_reduced_vars3.sav`.
3. Add a Derive node to the stream and connect it to the Type node called `First Type`.
4. Open the Derive node, click on the **Multiple** radio button. In the **Derive from** region, select all of the RFA variables, from **RFA_2** to **RFA_24**. You can select multiple variables by clicking on **RFA_2**, scrolling down to **RFA_24** and *Shift*-clicking on **RFA_24**. Then click on **OK**.
5. In the **Field name extension** box, change the text **_Derive** to `R`.

6. In the **Field Type** drop-down list, select **Nominal**. This is shown in the following screenshot:

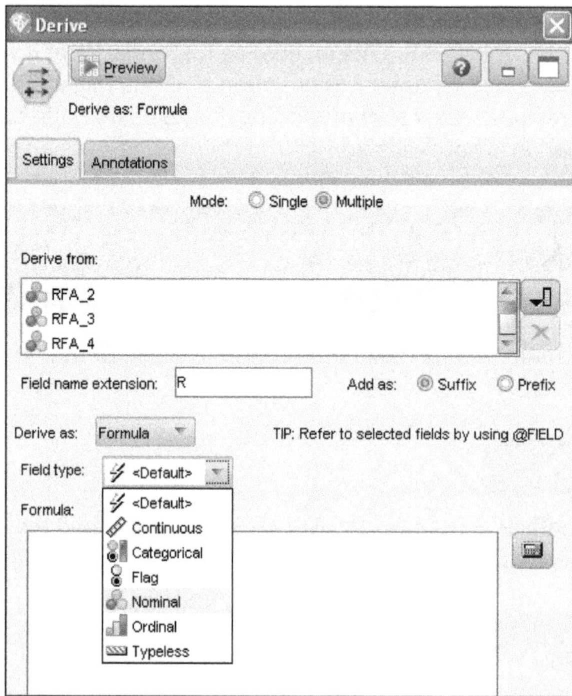

7. Inside the **Formula** box, type the formula `startstring( 1, @FIELD )`.
8. Click on **OK** to exit the Derive node.

How it works...

The **Multiple** option in a Derive node is a very powerful way to apply the same transformation to as many variables as one needs. Any transformation that can be created for a single variable can also be created for multiple variables.

The key syntax element for the multiple mode is the `@FIELD` function. `@FIELD` serves as a placeholder that represents each variable listed in the **Derive from** box above in the order they are listed.

This particular transformation is applied to all of the `RFA` variables, where RFA stands for **Recency, Frequency, and Monetary**. Each of these variable values is three characters, containing a Recency character (the first), a Frequency character (the second), and a Monetary character (third). The transformation desired here is to split out each of the three characters into their own variables. The first of the three is the Recency character, hence the field name extension `R`. Using `startstring( 1, @FIELD)` takes the first character at the beginning of each variable as the derived value.

The result of this Derive node will be new variables named `RFA_2R`, `RFA_3R`, through `RFA_24R`. If one connects the Derive node now called `R` (for the extension typed into the **Field name extension** field) to a Distribution node, one will see for `RFA_3R`, the distribution shown in the following screenshot:

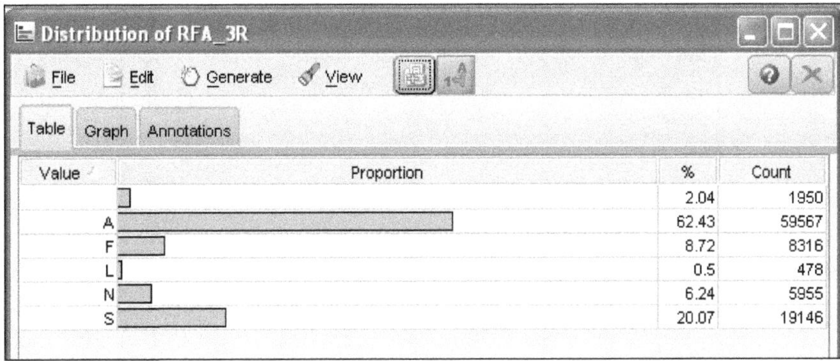

There's more...

For the first transformation, the `R` node, the CLEM syntax was supplied. However, one can always use the Expression Builder to build out a formula.

A second transformation can be built to return the middle character of the RFA string. Use the field name extension `F` for this node. While there are many ways one can do this, one way is to create a substring between the second character and the second character, inclusive, which is shown in the Expression Builder screenshot at the end of this recipe with the function `substring_between(2, 2)` or `@FIELD(2)`. This will return a string with values `1`, `2`, `3`, or `4`. If one would like to have this string returned as an integer instead, one can convert the string to an integer by transforming the result with the `to_integer()` function.

So far we have only been using formulas to build multiple new variables in a single Derive node. However, any variable type can be created in this way. Try changing the **Derive as** drop-down box to **Flag**. Now, instead of a formula, one enters into the textbox a condition that can be **True** or **False**, such as if the first character is an "S", return the value **True** else **False** as shown in the following screenshot:

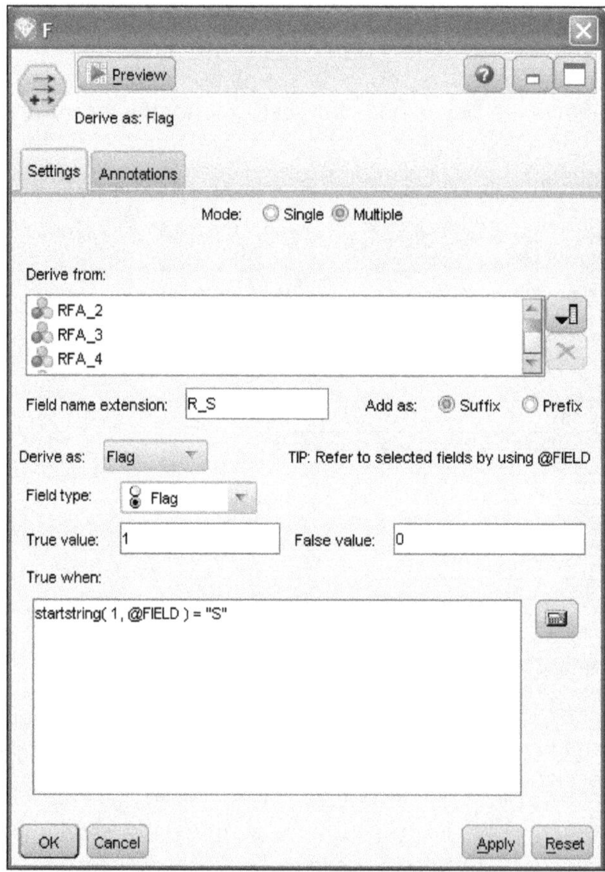

If one would like to also build derived variables to create variables containing other bytes of the RFM rollup, such as exposing the F (frequency) byte, one would use a string operator to return the second character of the three. The `substring_between()` function is one way to accomplish this, as is shown in the following screenshot:

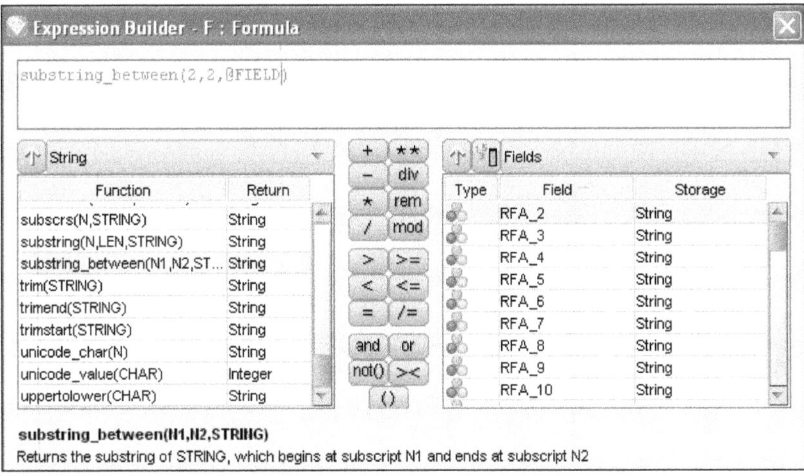

Calculating and comparing conversion rates

There are times when you need to transform a variable to be able to better answer a question or to gain additional insight. In this recipe we will calculate the ratio of donors to total prospective donors. The data set already has a donate/not donate variable in the form of `TARGET_B`. We will calculate something similar for all of the campaigns, allowing us to present results on a line chart and look at trends.

Getting ready

We will start with the `Conversion Rates.str` stream.

How to do it...

1. Open the stream and edit the Derive node. Note that it is a multiple derive and it is producing several new variables:

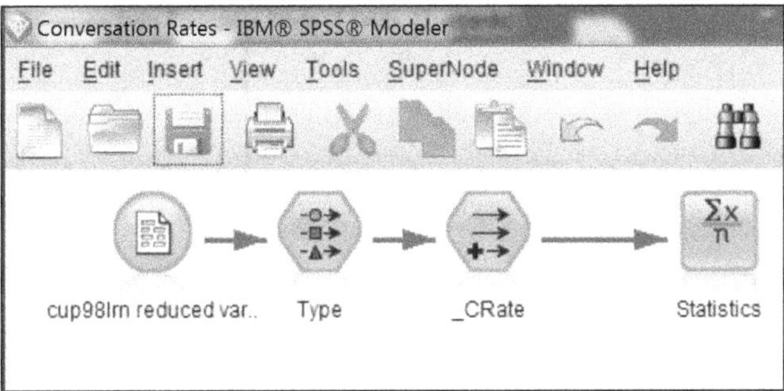

2. Edit the Statistics node, verify that it is requesting **Mean** only and run:

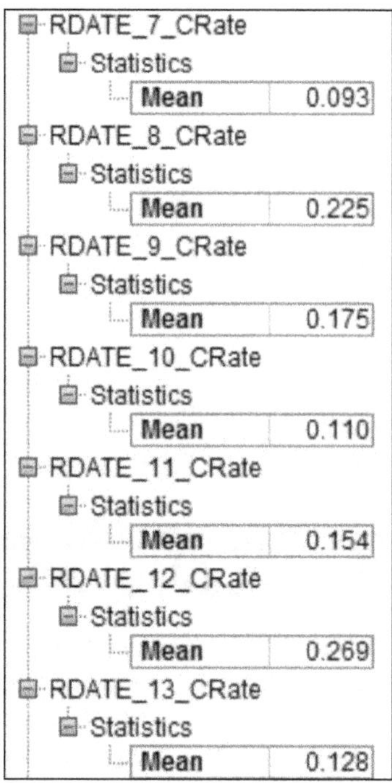

3. Add an Aggregate node with no key variables, but with all of the new campaign date variables from `RDATE_7_CRate` through `RDATE_24_CRate`:

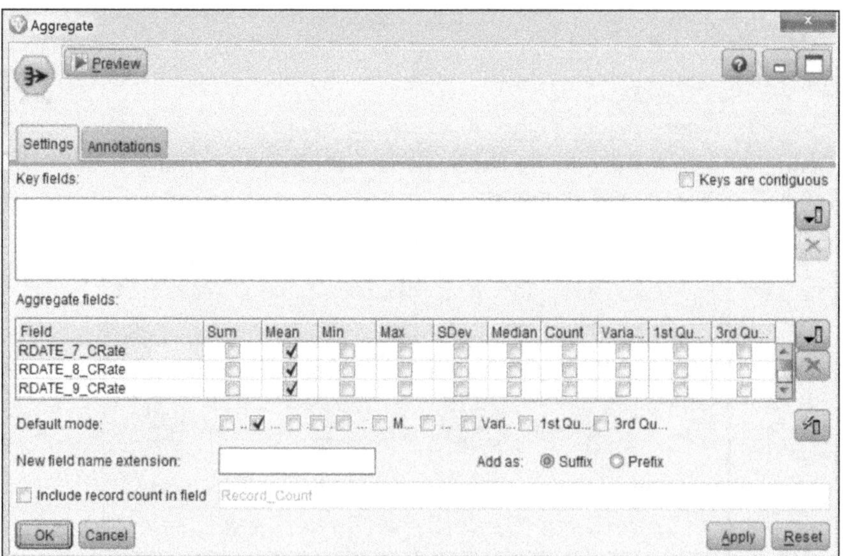

4. Add a Transpose node. We will use the prefix `CRate` and we only need one new variable:

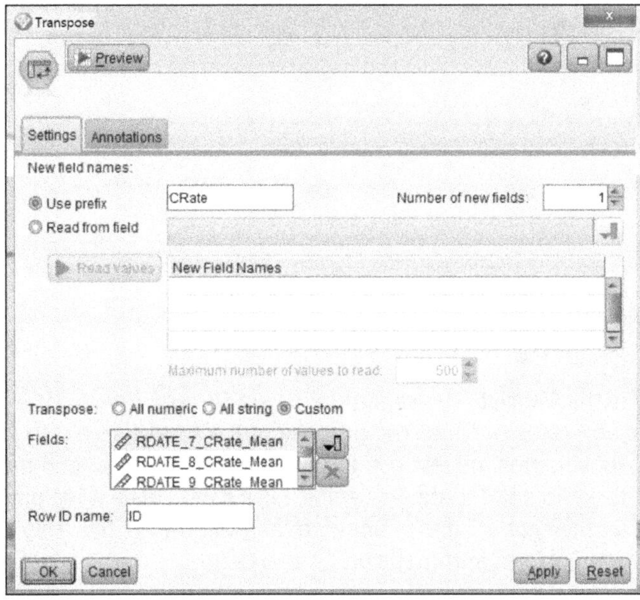

5. Add a Derive node with `@INDEX` as the formula. We will call the new variable `CampaignID`.
6. Add a Multiplot node with our new variable `CampaignID` as the **X field**, and `CRate1` as the **Y field**. Make sure to select **Use all data** as shown in the following screenshot:

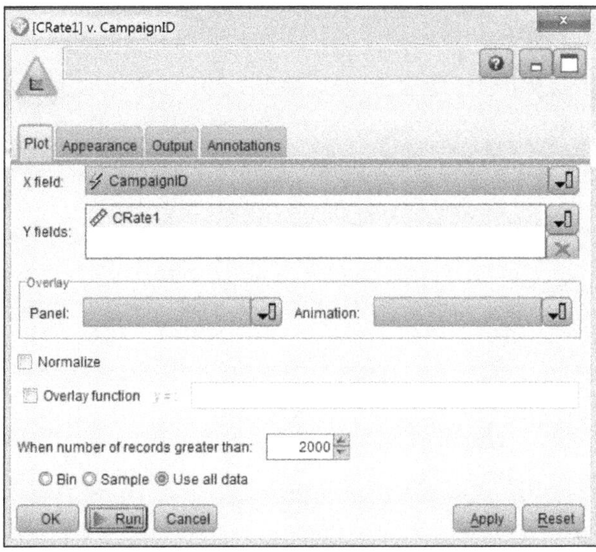

7. You should have added four new nodes to the stream. Run the Multiplot:

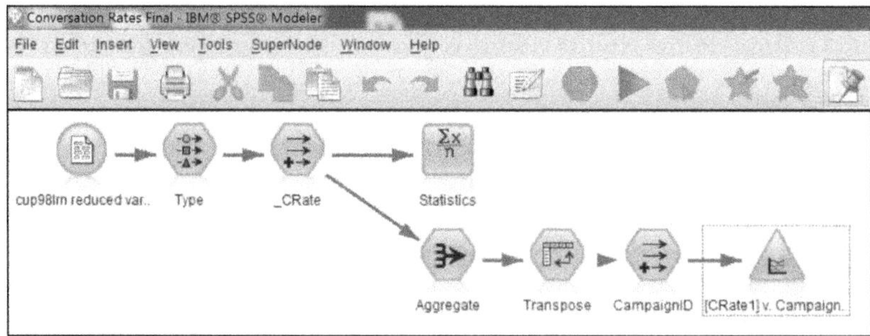

How it works...

The calculation uses the **Multiple** derive feature of the Derive node. `RDate_3` through `RDate_6` have very low rates because the purpose of the analysis was to look for lapsed donors. Therefore, those dates are left out. Simply, if there is a date then they donated, and if there is no date, they did not donate. Assigning a `1` for the **False** value produces a more intuitive result in that they get a 1 if they donated, and 0 if they didn't. This is better than T and F because we can perform arithmetic on 1s and 0s:

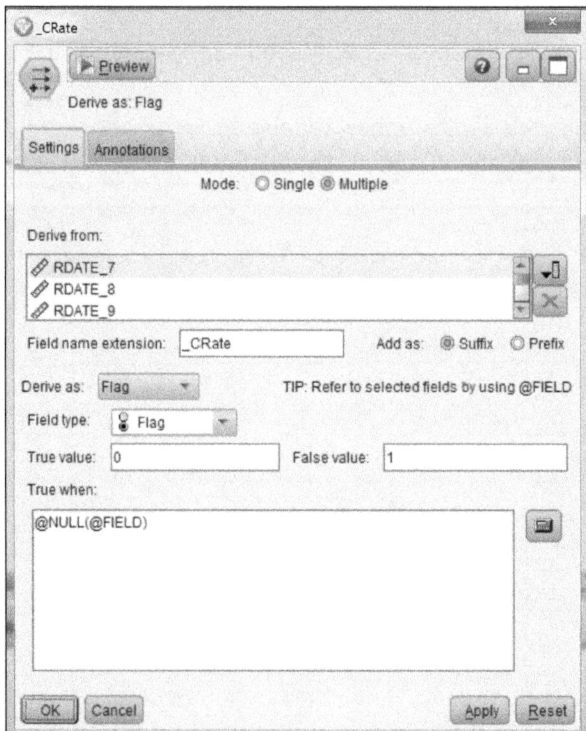

The Statistics node, in theory, gives us the result that we want, but with some manipulation we can make it much easier to look at the trend over time.

The Aggregate node produces the mean for each campaign, which importantly is the same as the percentage. This is a valuable trick. However, it produces a wide data set with only one row. The values are the ones that we need, but it is not a convenient shape for producing a plot.

The Derive node simply allows us to force the proper order. We will use the resulting variable as the *X* axis in our plot forcing the campaigns to run from the most recent on the left-hand side and the most distant in time to the right-hand side, which can be displayed in the Multiplot. The rates seem to fluctuate considerably. We would want to investigate this. Perhaps it is the type of campaign, or time of year, or other factors:

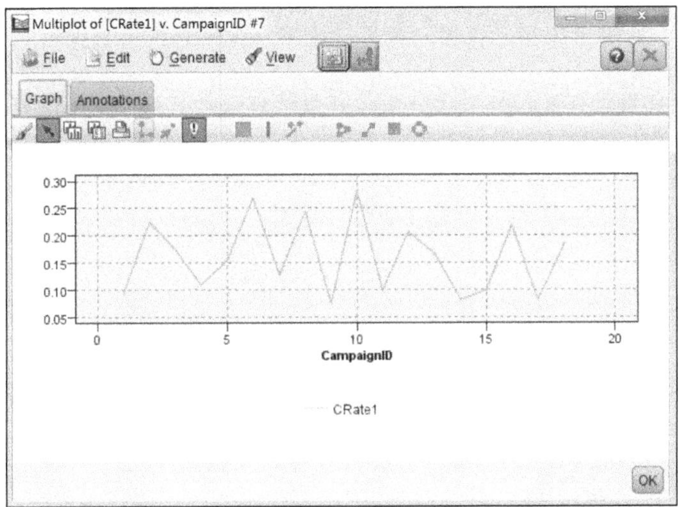

There's more...

What if we want to repeat the same process for two groups?

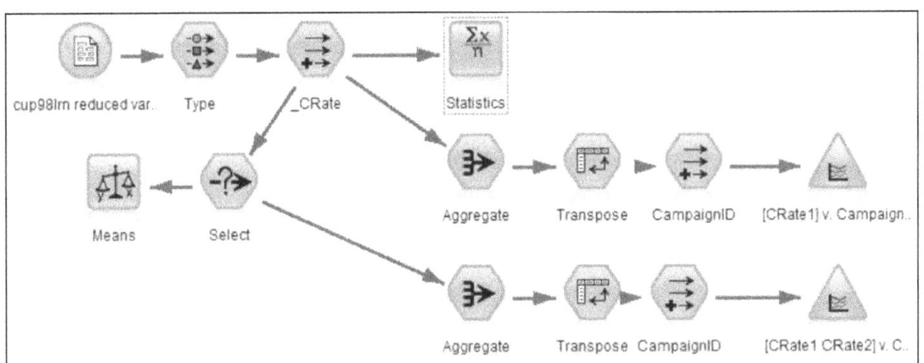

The `More` stream adds two features. It screens out genders that are not M or F. Other "genders" include Unknown and Joint Account. Now the **Means** node can compare the two groups. Also, the Aggregate now produces the conversion rates for both groups, which then can be displayed side by side in the Multiplot as shown in the following screenshot:

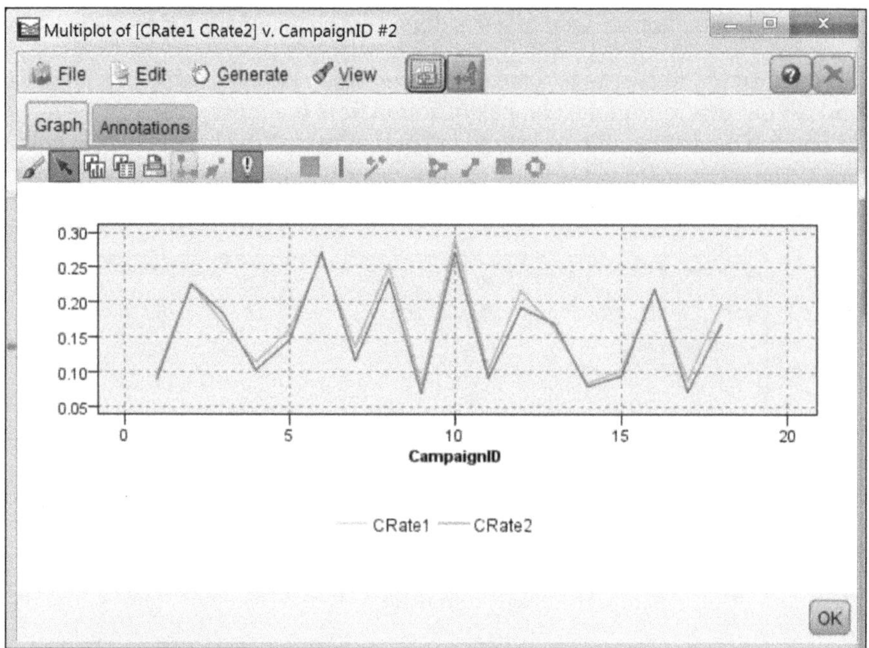

See also

- The *Building transformations with multiple Derive nodes* recipe in this chapter

Grouping categorical values

In the data used for modeling, we frequently find attributes with a large number of different categorical values. A typical example is product codes, identifying a product purchased by a customer.

A data attribute with many different values can cause problems for data mining algorithms; complex data can make the algorithms run slowly, and may make it more difficult to find the patterns in the data, leading to less accurate models. A useful step in data preparation is to simplify this kind of complex data by grouping the values of a categorical variable into a smaller range of values, where the grouping has a relationship to the problem to be solved.

This recipe shows how to group product codes by their relation to a target response variable. It produces product groups, which are groupings of product codes, based on deciles of the response rates for each product code.

Getting ready

This recipe uses the following files:

- Datafile: `Transactions_File.txt`
- Datafile: `Promotions_File.txt`
- Stream file: `Categorical_Grouping.str`

How to do it...

1. Open the stream `Categorical_Grouping.str` by clicking on **File** | **Open Stream**.
2. Edit the Type node to the left of the stream; this provides the types and modeling roles of the data fields created by the source supernode `Response`, as shown in the following screenshot. The data represents the most expensive item purchased by each customer, including the cost (`Sales_Amount`), method of payment and product code, and also the predictive target response used for modeling:

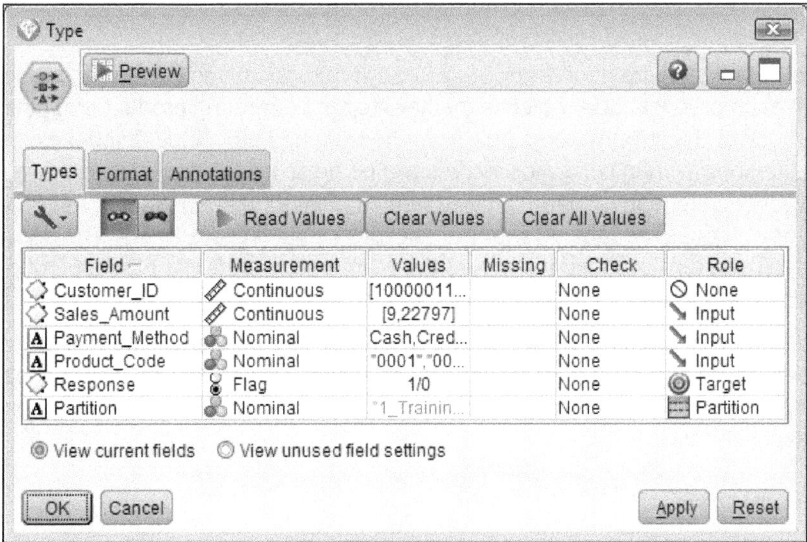

3. Run the Distribution node `Product_Code`; this displays the product codes with their associated response propensity, as shown in the following screenshot. Only a few customers, usually fewer than 100, are connected with each product code, and there are several hundred product codes.

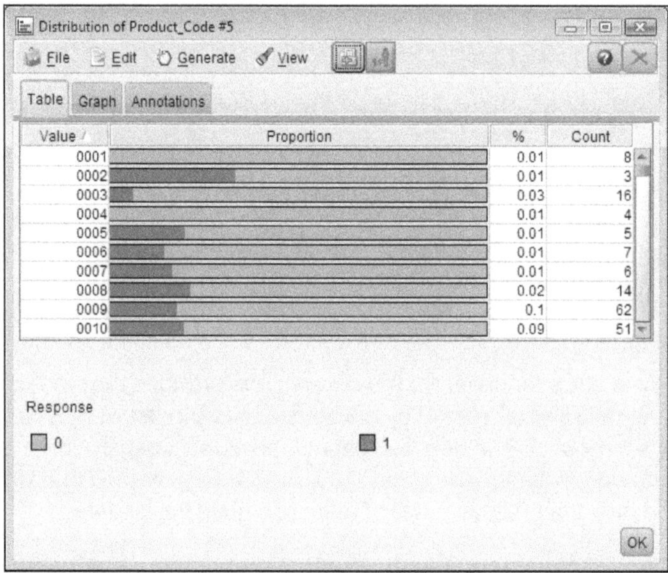

4. Edit the Aggregate node `Response Rate`; this calculates the average response rate for each product code, which is the key step in generating product groupings. This branch of the stream works only from the training data, since response rates would be unknown when customer records are being scored by a deployed model. Once the product code response rates have been calculated, response rates are deciled and product codes are labeled with the relevant decile label (1 to 10). The decile label is then used as a product group, and the merge node adds the product group to each customer record.
5. Run the Distribution node `Product_Group`; this displays the product groups with their associated response propensity, as shown in the following screenshot. Because of the way they were created, these product groups have an orderly relation to response rates.

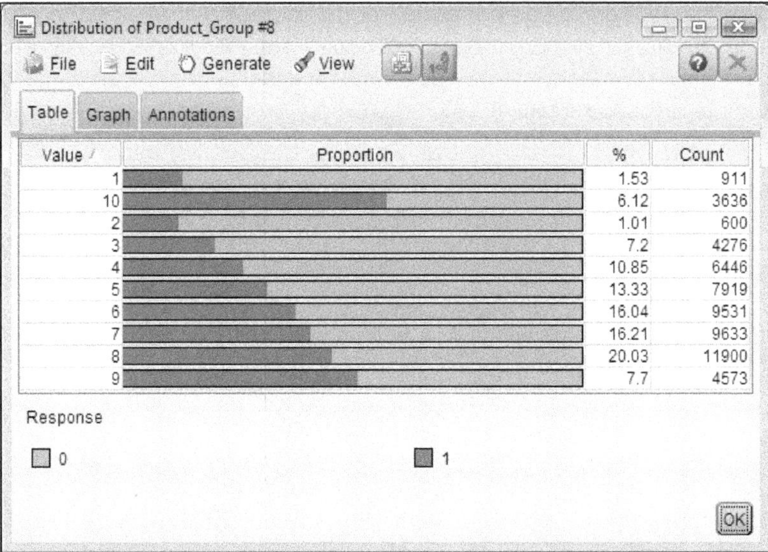

6. Browse the C5.0 decision tree model `Response NG`; this was produced without the product groups but with the product codes. The following screenshot shows a fragment of this complex decision tree; the model makes heavy use of product codes and its complexity is related to the large number of different codes.

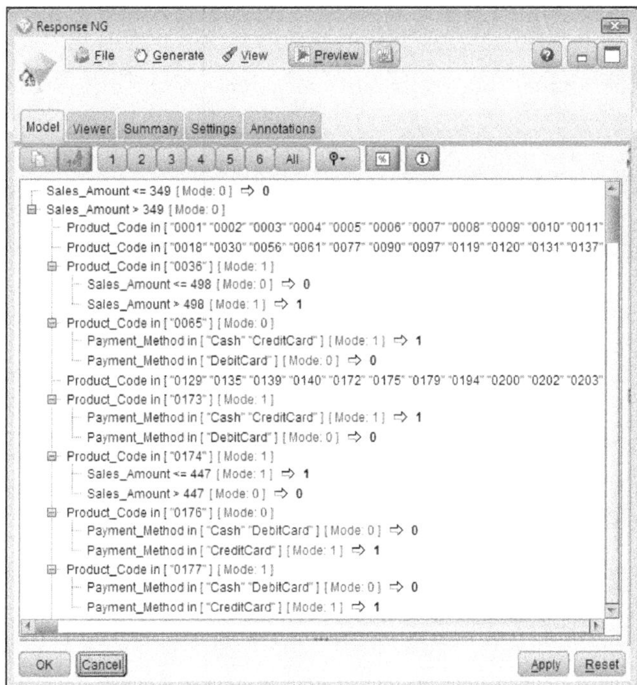

7. Browse the C5.0 decision tree model `Response WG`; this was produced with the product groups but without the product codes. The following screenshot shows the much simpler decision tree; the model makes use of product groups and their relation to response rates.

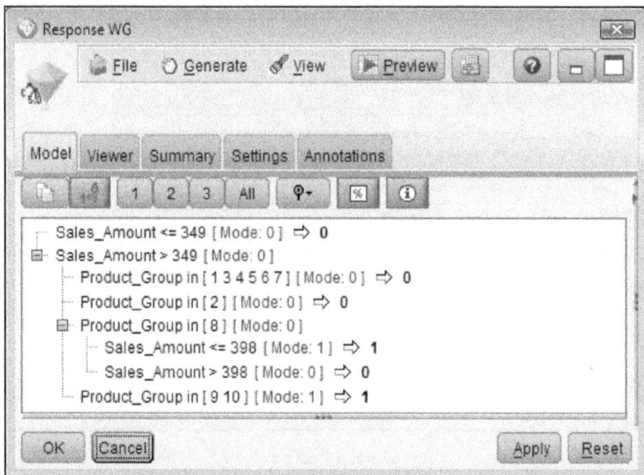

8. Run the Analysis node; the output shows that, on the test data, the model using product groups instead of product codes is comparable (only very slightly more accurate). The main advantage of product groups in this case is the simplicity of the model; this difference in complexity is so strong that it could make the difference between a model that can be deployed and one that cannot.

How it works...

This recipe shows a simple way to group categorical values and the stream is easy to construct. The groups are the deciles of response rates associated with individual values; this guarantees that the groups provide information about the predictive target (in this case response). The response rates are calculated by aggregation.

The branch of the stream that calculates the product groupings produces a mapping of product code to product group, and this is used as a lookup table by the Merge node, to augment the customer records with the product group as an additional variable.

This process augments the data mining algorithm by finding general-purpose information about the target and its association with a categorical variable before the algorithm is applied. Because it is effectively an addition to the algorithm, the groups must be generated from the training data and not the test data.

This technique provides a simple equivalent to Modeler's "optimal binning", but for categorical instead of numeric attributes.

There's more...

This technique can be adapted in three ways:

- First, the granularity of the grouping can be modified by using different *N*-tiles, such as quartiles (4), quintiles (5), or vigntiles (20) in the Binning node. The only additional modification required would be in the filter node to rename a different tile field to be Product_Group.
- Secondly, the technique could be applied to several different categorical variables in the same data set. Each variable to be grouped requires a separate sequence of Aggregate, Binning, Filter, and Merge nodes; each sequence could be brought together in a Merge node to simplify the stream.
- Finally, the mappings of categorical variables to groups could be stored as separate tables of data; each mapping would be a table with two columns. This is useful if a mapping is to be used several times, for example, in several different data preparation and modeling streams.

Transforming high skew and kurtosis variables with a multiple Derive node

In this recipe we will create transformations of numeric variables with high skew or kurtosis that makes them more normally distributed with a single Derive node by invoking the **Multiple** radio button. For many algorithms, normal distributions are assumed and therefore one often transforms variables so that this assumption is more nearly met.

Getting ready

This recipe uses the datafile `cup98lrn_reduced_vars3.sav` and the stream `Recipe - variable construct multipleskew.str`.

How to do it...

1. Open the stream `Recipe - variable construct multipleskew.str` by clicking on **File** | **Open Stream**.
2. Make sure the datafile points to the correct path to the datafile `cup98lrn_reduced_vars3.sav`.
3. Add a Derive node to the stream and connect it to the Type node called `First Type`.

4. Open the Derive node and click on the **Multiple** radio button. In the **Derive from** region, select all monetary variables, including `RAMNTALL_2` through `TARGET_D`. You can select multiple variables by clicking on `RAMNT_2`, scrolling down to `TARGET_D`, and *Shift*-clicking on `TARGET_D`. Then click on **OK**. Another way to select all of the variables is to click on the variable of interest and then click on **Apply**. Repeat this for every variable to be included in the list to be transformed.

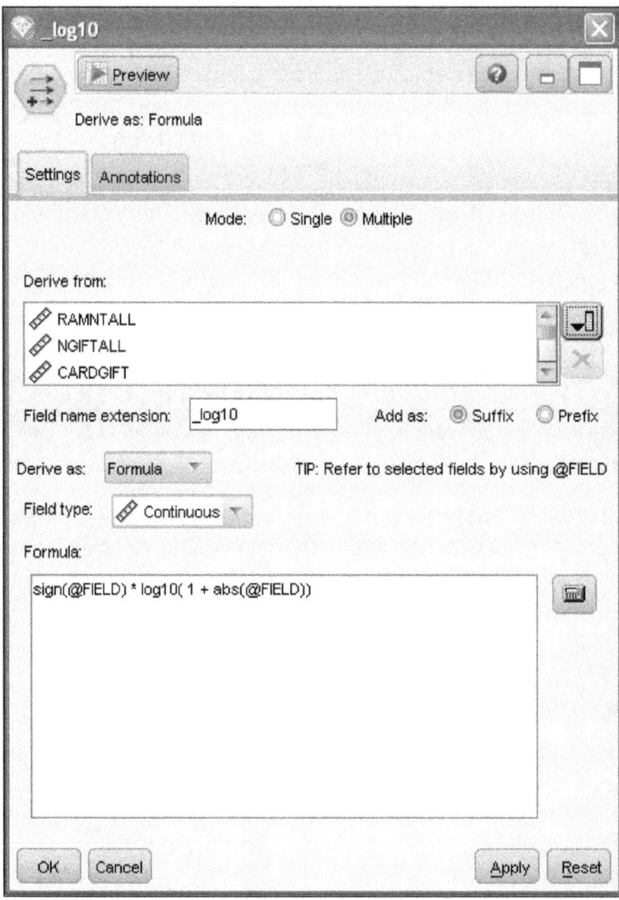

5. In the **Field name extension** box, change the text `_Derive` to `log10`.
6. In the **Field type** drop-down box, select **Continuous**.
7. Inside the **Formula** box, type the formula `sign(@FIELD)*log10(1+abs(@FIELD))`.
8. Click on **OK** to exit the Derive node.

How it works...

This recipe is a variation of the *Building transformations with multiple Derive nodes* recipe that described how to take advantage of the **Multiple** option in a Derive node. In this case, however, a numeric transformation is applied rather than a categorical. For many algorithms, normal distributions are assumed and therefore one often transforms the variable so that this assumption is more nearly met. The most common transformation to apply when one observes a positive skew in a distribution is a **log transform**, with log10 being one of most common transforms to apply. The CLEM syntax for a log transform in a Derive node with the **Multiple** option selected is `log10( @FIELD )`.

Severe negative skew causes the same problems for some algorithms. However, the log transform is undefined for negative values and will return a NULL value for any values of a variable that is negative. Moreover, a log transform of the number 0 is also undefined.

A solution to these problems is to modify the argument of the log transform so that it is never negative or zero. One can achieve this by adding 1 to the value (so that one never takes the log transform of the number 0) and by taking the absolute value of the variable (so that it is never negative). The CLEM syntax for these operations is `log10( 1 + abs(@FIELD))`.

We have introduced a new problem, however, which is that any negative numbers are now positive in the data, and the log transforms will reflect a positive value for those variables. We can however reintroduce the negative sign of the log transformed version of the variable by multiplying the log transformed variable by its original sign: positive numbers remain positive after the log transform, and negative numbers now are given a negative log transformed value. The CLEM syntax for this complete expression, the one referred to in the recipe, is `sign(@FIELD)*log10( 1 + abs(@FIELD))`.

High kurtosis in a variable can be seen in a histogram as a spike in the middle of the distribution, and long tails on both sides of the spike. Sometimes variables with that represent profit and loss that will have skewed profit values and skewed loss values (those are negative). This recipe will transform these profit/loss variables into new ones that are more normally distributed.

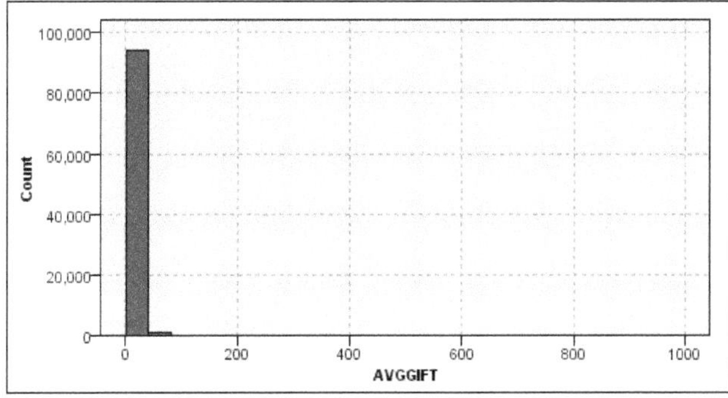

A result of transformations is shown in the preceding and following screenshots. In the preceding screenshot, we see a Histogram node output with the natural distribution of `AVG_GIFT`. After the log transformation, the following screenshot shows the transformed variable with a normal distribution overlay, clearly a more normal distribution. The normal curve overlay can be turned on in the **Histogram Node Options** tab.

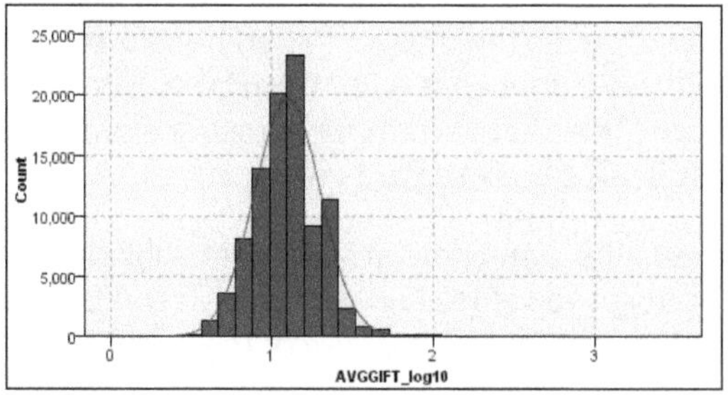

There's more...

This recipe works for positively skewed variables whose skew is not too severe. If the skew is very severe, one may have to transform the variable twice to achieve a transformed variable that is closer to a normal distribution.

For a negative skew, this recipe only works when the negative skew is a result of negative values of the variable. If there is negative skew but the variable is always positive, consider applying a power transform (squaring or cubing the variable) to achieve a distribution closer to normal.

As an alternative to experimenting through the use of a Derive variable, one may prefer to use the Transform node, a very convenient node for this purpose. The Transform node shows a sequence of transformations that can be applied to a variable and demonstrates what the resulting variable looks like after the transformation:

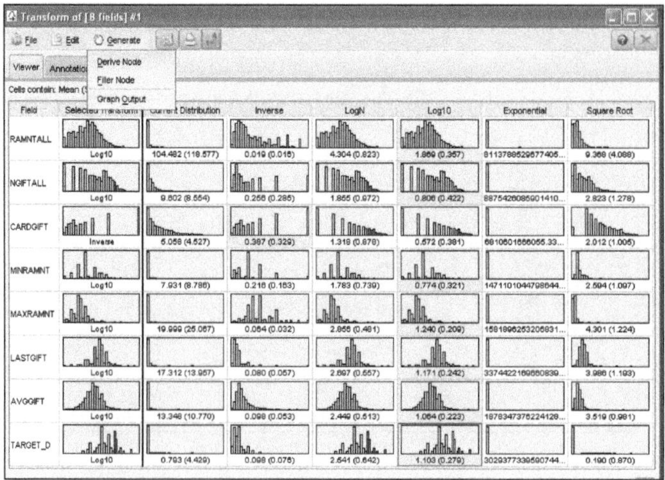

The preceding screenshot shows the output of a Transform node after applying a log10 transform to each of the continuous variables except for `CARDGIFT` where an inverse transform was applied.

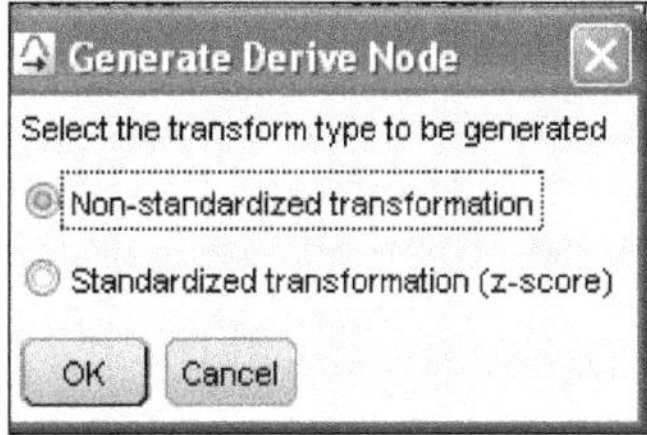

One can then generate a supernode from the Transform node through the menu option **Generate** | **Derive Node** and then select the scaling you would like to apply to the transformation (check the preceding screenshot). This creates a supernode containing a separate Derive node for every variable that has been transformed. However, even if one applies the exact same transformation to every variable in the supernode, there is a still a separate Derive node for every variable (check the following screenshot). This recipe collects all of the transformed variables using the same transformation in the same Derive node. Moreover, the Transform node cannot de-skew a negative number with the log transform as was done in this recipe.

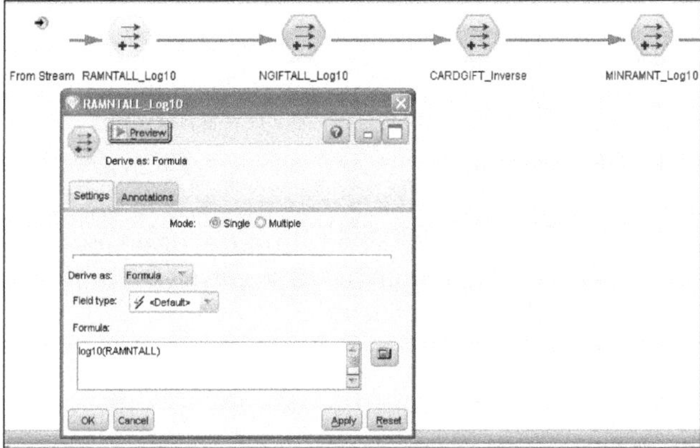

However, the Transform node can be used to identify a good transformation prior to executing this recipe. If one first identifies the transformation of interest and the variables one would like to apply the transformation to, one can then create a Derive node for all of those variables in the same manner as was done in this recipe.

Creating flag variables for aggregation

The SetToFlag node is a very convenient node that converts a single nominal variable into as many binary columns as desired, one column for each nominal variable value. However, the default values for the node are `T` and `F`, which unfortunately cannot be used for any nodes that require numeric values. In this recipe we will create flag variables that can be used in Aggregate nodes, Means nodes, and other numeric operations. Using numeric values (`1` and `0` in this recipe) will work with any nodes that require flag or nominal values such as Association Rules and the grouping variable for the Means node (as T and F will), but will also work as numeric values in nodes such as the Aggregate node.

Getting ready

This recipe uses the datafile `cup98lrn_reduced_vars3.sav` and the stream `recipe_variableconstruct_flags.str`.

How to do it...

1. Open the stream `recipe_variableconstruct_flags.str` by clicking on **File** | **Open Stream**.
2. Make sure the datafile points to the correct path to the file `cup98lrn_reduced_vars3.sav`.
3. Open the Type node named `Types`. Notice that the Filter node preceding this type removed most of the fields so that only a few remained. The variable set to **Target** should be the variable `TARGET_B`.
4. Open the node `SetToFlag` and select the variable `RFA_2A`. The values of that variable should appear in the **Available set values** region as shown in the following screenshot. Click on the yellow arrow so these values will be in the **Create flag fields** region. Click on **OK** to close the window:

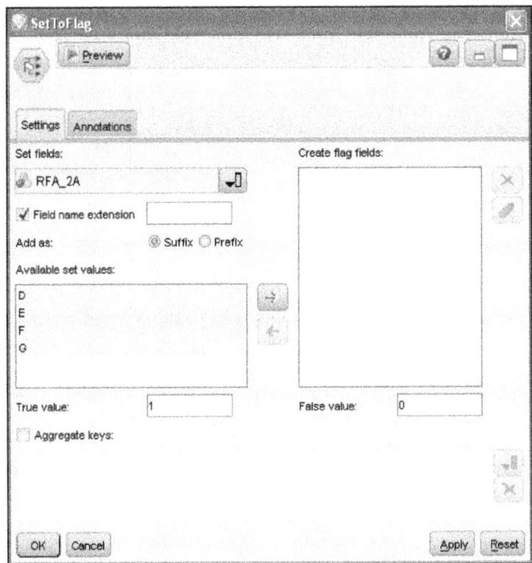

5. Open the **Set Inputs** Type node and scroll to the bottom to see these four new flag variables.
6. Open the Aggregate node. Notice that the four flag variables are included in the **Aggregate fields** region with mean values to be calculated.
7. Click on the Table node and run the selection.

How it works...

Two examples of nodes that may be used with the SetToFlag node in this stream are the Aggregate node and the Means node. In the Means node, since the flag variables are numeric, they can be used as test fields. The example in the stream shows the relationship between the target variable (`TARGET_B`) and each of the values of the variable `RFA_2A`; this variable could not be included as a test field if it were nominal.

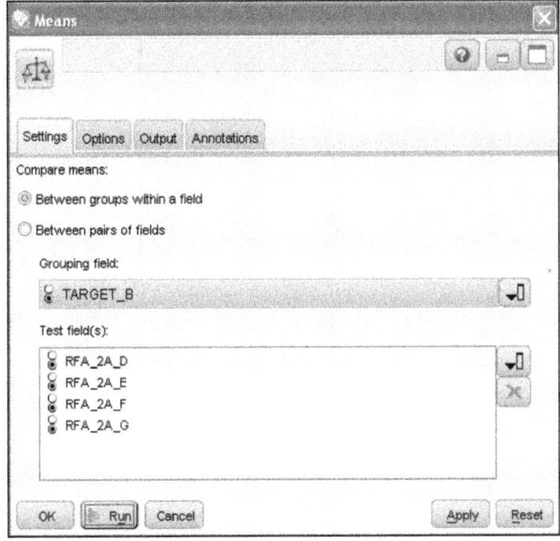

There's more...

The SetToFlag node is a very convenient way to include flag versions of many nominal variables in one node; there is no limit to the number of variables that can be expanded into flag variables.

Sometimes it is convenient to check the **Aggregate keys** checkbox to collapse the flag variables by the grouping variable. For example, one may have multiple transactions for each customer ID and want to identify if he or she has ever purchased amounts of different bins: $0-$50, $51-$100, $100-200, or $200 and above. If each of these bins is converted to a flag in the SetToFlag node, the Aggregate key can be set to the customer ID, and each field will then indicate if a customer has *ever* had a transaction in that bin. It works the same as running an Aggregate node with the **Max** option checkbox selected for each flag variable without adding the `_Max` extension to the variables.

Using Association Rules for interaction detection/feature creation

Interactions allow one to see the combined effect of more than one variable. Unfortunately, interactions are not automatically calculated by many algorithms. The Association Rules created here are intended to find interactions between nominal, ordinal, and flag variables in the data. In this recipe we will create 10 new interactions to use as model inputs using the A Priori Association Rules node. This recipe builds from the *Selecting variables using single-antecedent Association Rules* recipe from *Chapter 2, Data Preparation – Select*, including using the same target variable: the `TARGET_D` quintile between $20 and $200.

Getting ready

This recipe uses the datafile `cup98lrn_reduced_vars3_apriori.sav` and the stream `Recipe - variable construction apriori.str`.

You will need a copy of Microsoft Excel to visualize the list of rules.

How to do it...

1. Open the stream `Recipe - variable construction apriori.str` by clicking on **File** | **Open Stream**.
2. Make sure the datafile points to the correct path to the file `cup98lrn_reduced_vars3_apriori.sav`.
3. Open the Type node named `APRIORI Types`. Notice that only **Nominal** and **Flag** variables are present. The variable set to **Target** should be the target variable `TARGET_D_TILE5_1`.

4. Open the Apriori node and look at the options. Note that the minimum antecedent support is set to `5` percent, the confidence percentage is set to `1` percent and the number of antecedents to `2`:

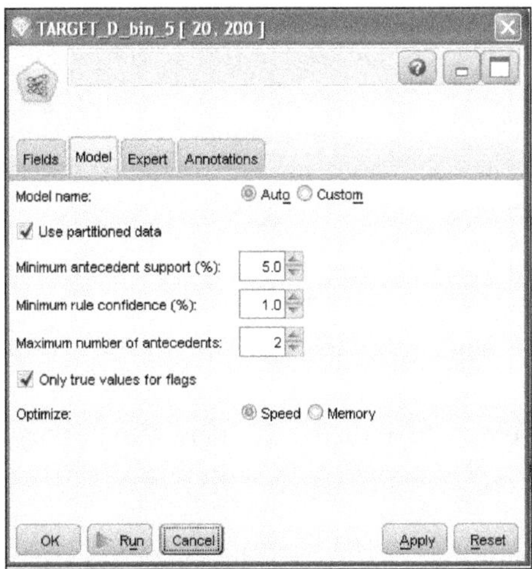

5. Build the Association Rules model by clicking on **Run**.

6. Open the generated model. In the show/hide criteria drop-down menu, add **Instances** and **Lift** to the report as shown in the following screenshot. If the list is not sorted by confidence or lift any longer, click on the "sort by" arrow to the right of the **Confidence %** text twice or until the sort order is descending:

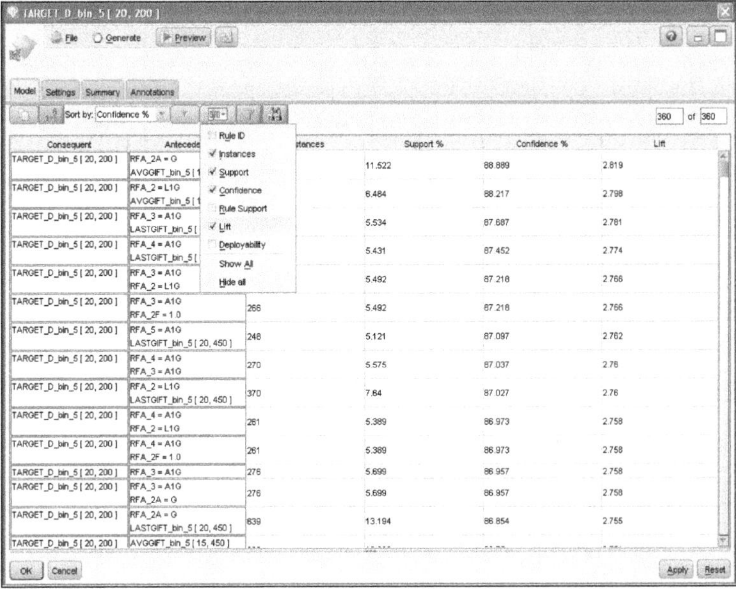

7. Export the rules by selecting **File** | **Export HTML** | **Model...** and save the file as `associationrules 2 antecedents.html`.

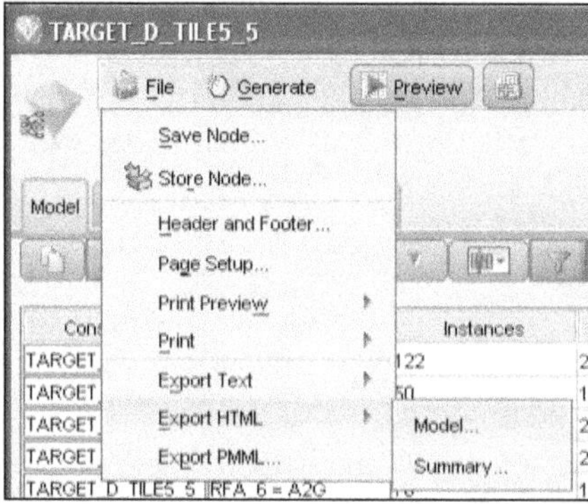

8. Identify rules of interest, such as the 10 rules with the highest confidence and the 10 rules with the lowest confidence. Make a note of these rules so you can include these as inputs.

9. In the Modeler stream, connect a Derive node to the stream, creating a new flag variable for the top interaction, `RFA_2A = G + AVGGIFT_bin_5 [ 15, 450 ]`, as shown in following screenshot:

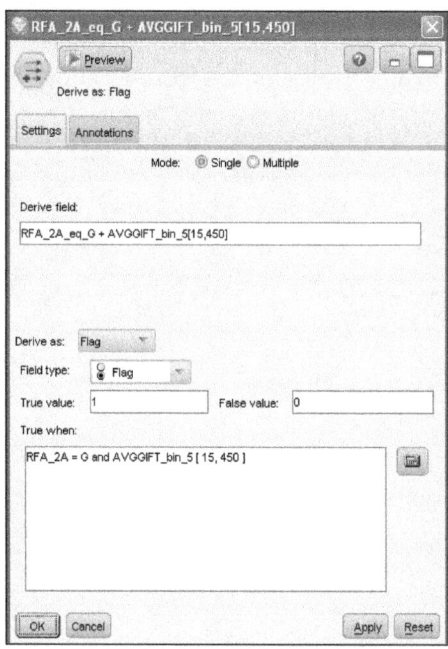

10. Repeat step 9 for each additional interaction variable found through the 2-antecedent Association Rules model.

How it works...

The Association Rules created here are intended to find interactions between nominal, ordinal, and flag variables in the data. Interactions are particularly useful for algorithms that only consider main effects such as linear and logistic regression. While decision trees can be used to find interactions between variables—continuous and categorical—they have two deficiencies for variable selection. First, trees are greedy search algorithms, finding the best split at each level. Trees therefore can miss the best interactions if they are fooled into keeping a suboptimal split. Second, trees return the best model only; one would need to rebuild trees, forcing different root-node splits to find a wide range of interactions.

Association Rules, on the other hands, identify *all* combinations of variables. In this recipe, all 2-antecedent Association Rules with support greater than 5 percent are discovered, sorted by **Confidence** % or **Lift** to make more clear which interactions have the strongest relationship to the target.

One may want to identify 10 interactions that have a very high or very low association with the target variable. For example, note that the top rule has support greater than 10 percent so it matches a large segment of the population and has nearly 90 percent association with the top quintile of donors. `AVGGIFT` and `RFA_2A = G` are both measures of how much a donor has given historically, but this rule indicates that their gift size in the past year is high *and* their average donation amount over their lifetime is high. The interaction gives the model an additional bump in performance.

	A	B	C	D	E	F	G
1		Consequent	Antecedent	Instanc	Support	Confidence	Lift
2	1	TARGET_D_bin_5 [20, 200]	RFA_2A = G and AVGGIFT_bin_5 [15, 450]	558	11.522	88.889	2.819
3	2	TARGET_D_bin_5 [20, 200]	RFA_2 = L1G and AVGGIFT_bin_5 [15, 450]	314	6.484	88.217	2.798
4	3	TARGET_D_bin_5 [20, 200]	RFA_3 = A1G and LASTGIFT_bin_5 [20, 450]	268	5.534	87.687	2.781
5	4	TARGET_D_bin_5 [20, 200]	RFA_4 = A1G and LASTGIFT_bin_5 [20, 450]	263	5.431	87.452	2.774
6	5	TARGET_D_bin_5 [20, 200]	RFA_3 = A1G and RFA_2 = L1G	266	5.492	87.218	2.766
7	6	TARGET_D_bin_5 [20, 200]	RFA_3 = A1G and RFA_2F = 1.0	266	5.492	87.218	2.766
8	7	TARGET_D_bin_5 [20, 200]	RFA_5 = A1G and LASTGIFT_bin_5 [20, 450]	248	5.121	87.097	2.762
9	8	TARGET_D_bin_5 [20, 200]	RFA_4 = A1G and RFA_3 = A1G	270	5.575	87.037	2.76
10	9	TARGET_D_bin_5 [20, 200]	RFA_2 = L1G and LASTGIFT_bin_5 [20, 450]	370	7.64	87.027	2.76
11	10	TARGET_D_bin_5 [20, 200]	RFA_4 = A1G and RFA_2 = L1G	261	5.389	86.973	2.758
12	11	TARGET_D_bin_5 [20, 200]	RFA_4 = A1G and RFA_2F = 1.0	261	5.389	86.973	2.758

Unfortunately, this process does not automate the selection and building of interactions; they must be added manually to the stream. Note that one limitation is that continuous fields cannot be used to identify interactions unless they have been binned.

There's more...

After loading the Association Rules into Excel, one can examine not only the strongest interactions but also the relative improvement in predicting the target variable when considering the interaction over and above the single variables. If one opens the file `associationrules 2-antecendents final.xlsx`, the list of interactions is shown with additional columns that identify rules with some key variables in them.

In the spreadsheet `associationrules 2-antecedents.xlsx`, also shown in the following screenshot, rules with `AVGGIFT_bin_5` are selected by filtering the rules. One can see that `AVGGIFT_bin_5` on its own has a 75 percent association with the target, but the interaction has an 89-percent association with the target. Formulas for identifying the number of antecedents and the variables themselves are included in the spreadsheet:

B	C	D	E	F	G	H	I	J
Consequent	Antecedent	Instan	Support	Confidence	Lif	# Anteceder	RFA_2A = G	AVGGIFT_bin_5 [15, 450]
TARGET_D_bin_5 [20, 200]	RFA_2A = G and AVGGIFT_bin_5 [15, 450]	558	11.522	88.889	2.819	2	RFA_2A = G	AVGGIFT_bin_5 [15, 450]
TARGET_D_bin_5 [20, 200]	RFA_2 = L1G and AVGGIFT_bin_5 [15, 450]	314	6.484	88.217	2.798	2		AVGGIFT_bin_5 [15, 450]
TARGET_D_bin_5 [20, 200]	AVGGIFT_bin_5 [15, 450] and LASTGIFT_bin_5 [20, 450]	883	18.233	86.75	2.751	2		AVGGIFT_bin_5 [15, 450]
TARGET_D_bin_5 [20, 200]	STATE = CA and AVGGIFT_bin_5 [15, 450]	321	6.628	80.997	2.569	2		AVGGIFT_bin_5 [15, 450]
TARGET_D_bin_5 [20, 200]	AVGGIFT_bin_5 [15, 450] and PEPSTRFL	347	7.165	78.386	2.486	2		AVGGIFT_bin_5 [15, 450]
TARGET_D_bin_5 [20, 200]	RFA_2F = 2.0 and AVGGIFT_bin_5 [15, 450]	249	5.141	77.51	2.458	2		AVGGIFT_bin_5 [15, 450]
TARGET_D_bin_5 [20, 200]	AVGGIFT_bin_5 [15, 450]	1,161	23.973	75.538	2.396	1		AVGGIFT_bin_5 [15, 450]
TARGET_D_bin_5 [20, 200]	AVGGIFT_bin_5 [15, 450] and RFA_2F = 1.0	759	15.672	75.099	2.382	2		AVGGIFT_bin_5 [15, 450]
TARGET_D_bin_5 [20, 200]	AVGGIFT_bin_5 [15, 450] and RFA_2 = L1F	442	9.127	66.063	2.095	2		AVGGIFT_bin_5 [15, 450]
TARGET_D_bin_5 [20, 200]	AVGGIFT_bin_5 [15, 450] and RFA_2A = F	598	12.348	63.545	2.015	2		AVGGIFT_bin_5 [15, 450]

There is one way to automate the use of interactions in Modeler. One can connect the generated model to the stream, open the generated model, modify the **Settings** tab to include only one prediction, and ignore the basket predictions (see the following screenshot). Attach a Type node to the generated model, and change the type of **$A-Rule_ID-1** to **Nominal**. Now *every* rule can be included as an input to models, though the number of rules can be quite large, and the actual variables that are included in the rule are not self-evident.

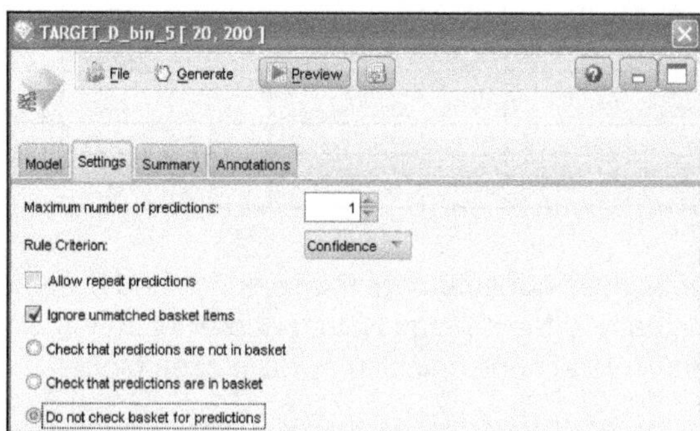

There is one last item of note in this recipe. There are several fields in the Association Rules that are bins with values for that bin contained within brackets. This can be done quite simply in Modeler. In this recipe, these bins were all quintiles created with the Binning node. Make sure you select **Tiles** for the **Binning method** and **Quintile (5)** for the number of tiles. In the example shown in the following screenshot, three fields are included in the Binning node. The explanation here however will focus on the field `TARGET_D`:

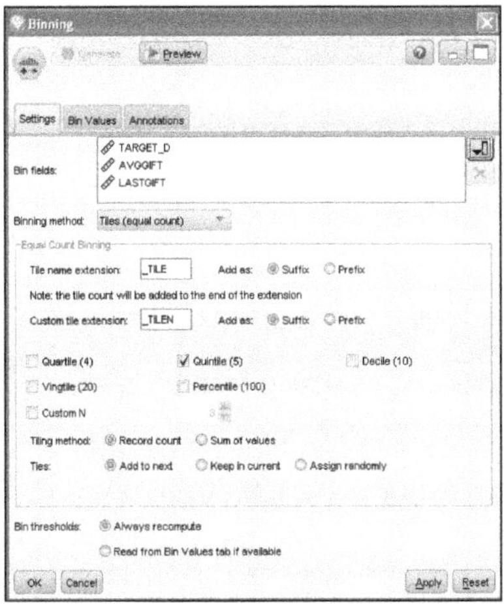

Insert an Aggregate node, group by `TARGET_D_TILE5`, and in the **Aggregate fields** section, compute the minimum and maximum values of `TARGET_D`. You can deselect computing `Record_Count` as this won't be needed. Next, add a Derive node, call the new field `TARGET_D_Bin`, set the **Field type** option to **Nominal**, and use the following CLEM code to construct the bin label: `"TARGET_D_[" >< TARGET_D_Min >< ", " >< TARGET_D_Max >< " ]"`. This uses the concatenate operator to build up the string with the left square bracket indicating "greater than or equal to" and the right square bracket indicating "less than or equal to".

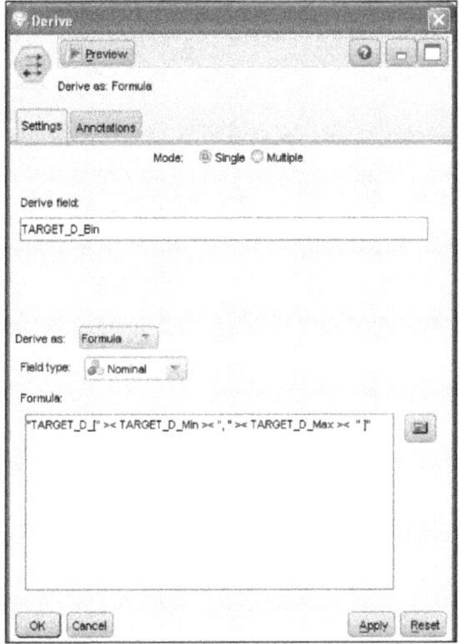

The result of this Derive node is shown in the following table. All that is left to do now is remove the `Min` and `Max` values using a Filter node, and then fold the new field `TARGET_D_Bin` into the stream using a Merge node with the key `TARGET_D_TILE5`.

TARGET_D_Min	TARGET_D_Max	TARGET_D_TILE5	TARGET_D_Bin
1	7	1	`TARGET_D_[1, 7 ]`
8	9	2	`TARGET_D_[8, 9 ]`
10	14	3	`TARGET_D_[10, 14 ]`
15	19	4	`TARGET_D_[15, 19 ]`
20	200	5	`TARGET_D_[20, 200 ]`

Creating time-aligned cohorts

In this recipe we will create a table that combines customer information, monthly statements, and churner identifiers conditioned by cohort information.

Why we would do this is best explained by means of an example. Suppose we wish to identify the best predictors of whether a customer is going to churn. To do this we might be tempted to throw everyone into a pot of data and see what algorithm best predicts who are churners and who are not churners. There are two immediate problems with this: one, the results would be skewed where we would have many more non-churners than churners going into the analysis, and two, the process used would be insensitive to everything going on within similar customer traits. After all, while John churned in January 2012, Sally (who came from the same region) has not churned. Wouldn't it make more sense to fine-tune the analysis so that we are comparing customers with similar experiences but different outcomes? That way we get the same number of churners and non-churners. And also, they are matched up, at least from a sampling perspective, on the basis of common characteristics.

Getting ready

This recipe uses three kinds of datafiles to represent three kinds of information: customer monthly statement information (`TELE_MONTHLY_STATEMENTS.sav`), customer personal information including features selected (`TELE_CUSTOMER.sav`), and customer churn information including cohort identification (`TELE_CHURN.sav`).

One of the additional calculations we're going to perform is to create variables that, by means of ratios, give us some indication of a customer's change in behavior prior to churning. It is frequently noted by people who have considerable experience with churn behavior that there are typically clues in the last couple of months, "red flags" indicating they're about to switch. While it is possible the company might not be able to do anything about it, knowing it is about to happen can be helpful. The company can either make an offer to the customer or they can note that material will have to be returned by the customer when they stop subscribing.

How to do it...

1. Open the stream `Recipe - customer churn.str` by clicking on **File** | **Open Stream**.
2. Make sure the datafiles point to the correct path for each of the three tables.

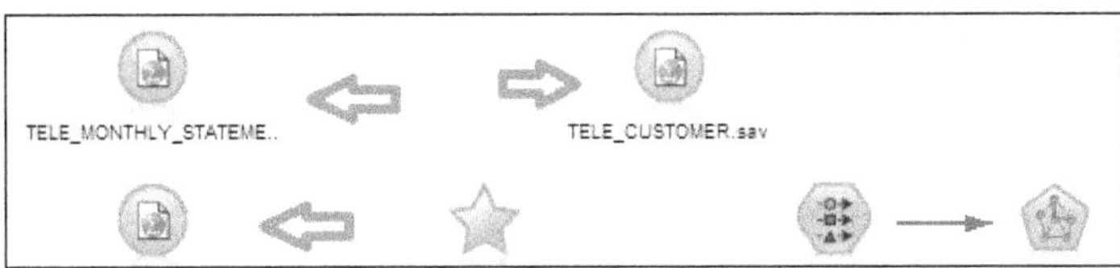

3. Add Merge nodes to the stream. Connect the datafiles to the Merge nodes as shown in the following screenshot. Connect the final Merge node to the Type node:

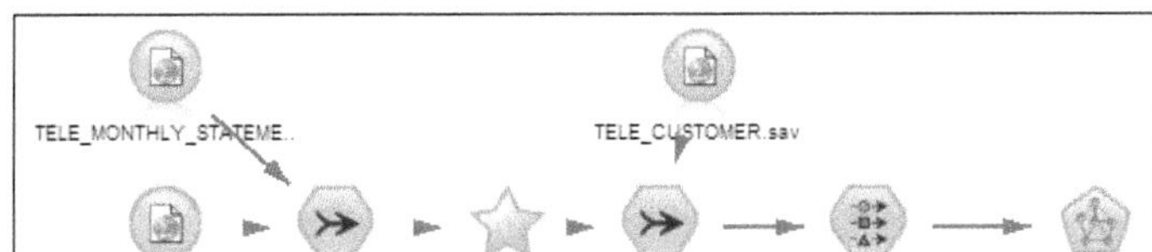

4. Open each Merge node. You will notice a grayed out **ACCOUNT** on the left-hand side. Click on the **Keys** radio button (it will become ungrayed). Click on **ACCOUNT**. Click on the right arrow to move **ACCOUNT** under **Keys for merge:**. Click on **OK**:

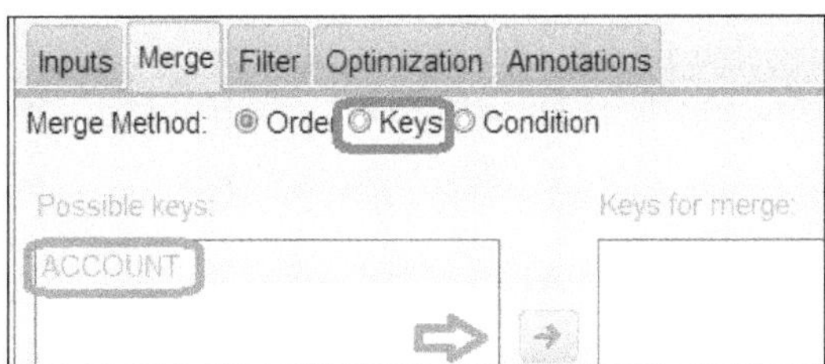

5. Open the second Merge node and do exactly the same in the second Merge node as you did in the first Merge node.

6. Right-click on the node labeled **CHURN** on the right and click on **Run**. You will get the following results:

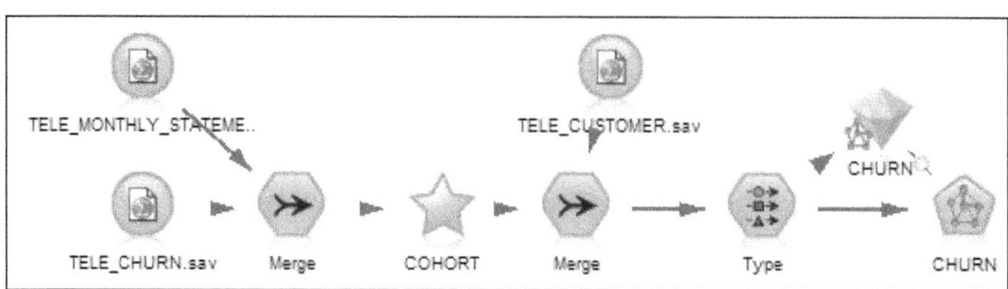

7. You are encouraged to double-click on the **CHURN**-generated model and investigate what is in the model.

How it works...

This recipe described how to join multiple tables together in order to produce a data set, that can be analyzed for the predict CHURN. What we need to do is combine information about customers, information about monthly statements, and information about who churned and the matching non-churning customer. It increased the sensitivity of the analysis and balanced their contributions by pulling only cohorts from the pool of customers who did not churn. It also created ratios that give us indications of change in behavior of any customers over the last months before the churn.

The manner in which datafiles are combined is by means of the Merge node. We used an inner join in the first merge in order to select out only those customers who churned and the cohorts of the churned customers. In our example, we used the Merge node to combine data on the basis of **ACCOUNT**.

In the second merge, we attached the personal customer information such as the features they had selected for their phones. In this manner we had combined personal customer information, summary transaction data, and churn/cohort data in order to give us a balanced and sensitive analysis of churn.

We also created ratios of behavior just prior to the churn over long term behavior. To see how this is done, we need to drill into the **COHORT** supernode (right-click on the supernode and click on **Zoom in**).

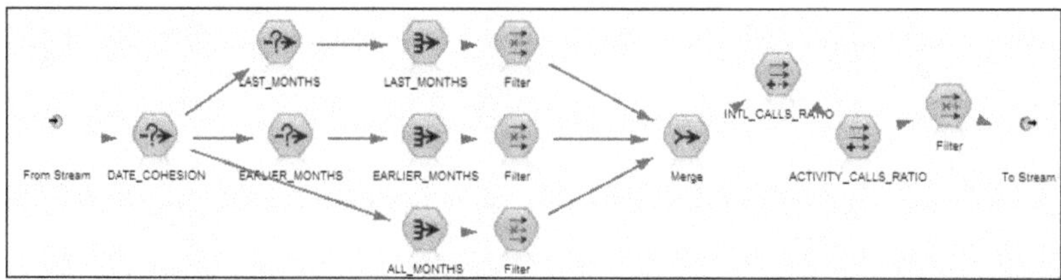

Often, as in our example, it is necessary to normalize data. Since we are merging on **ACCOUNT**, we need one observation per account. The manner in which this is typically done is by means of the Aggregate node and the Select node.

We have the following three conditions we need to consider:

- The most recent behaviors (last 2 months)
- Earlier behavior (prior to 2 months ago)
- All behaviors

In the case of All behaviors, we are interested in the number of missing payments. In the case of international calls and all activities, we want to find the ratio of the number of calls of the most recent months over all months prior to that.

If you open the Aggregate nodes (illustrated in the following screenshot), we see that the data is aggregated on **ACCOUNT**. We also see that CHURN information is passed along and we calculate the mean for the number of calls dropped, number of international calls, total activity on the part of the customer, and the number of late payments, as shown in the following screenshot:

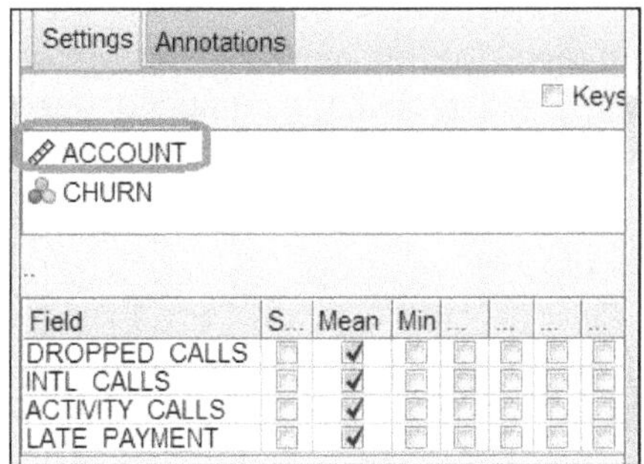

There's more...

There is a lot of preparation that goes into properly analyzing a churn. Of particular importance is the information found in the `TELE_CHURN` file. This file contains `ACCOUNT`, `CHURN`, `DATE_START`, `DATE_END`, and `ACCOUNTX`. This is the table that identifies those accounts that are churning and those accounts that are cohorts. We use the information we have about those who churn in order to censor non-churn behavior:

Field	Filter	Field
ACCOUNT	⟶	ACCOUNT
CHURN	⟶	CHURN
ACCOUNTX	⟶	ACCOUNTX
DATE_START	⟶	DATE_START
DATE_END	⟶	DATE_END

Finally, we can run the CHURN model and then investigate the relationships by going into the CHURN generated model.

If we double-click on the resulting neural network model, we get the following results:

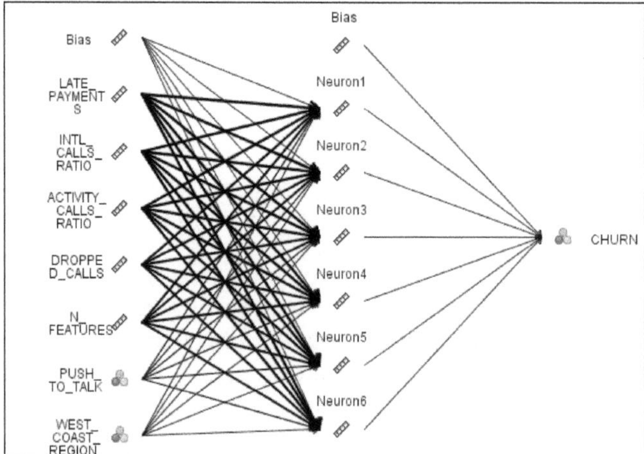

We can see that the strongest predictors of churn are: `LATE_PAYMENTS` (the number of late payments), `Intl_calls_ratio` (the drop in the number of international calls), `ACTIVITY_CALLS_RATIO` (the drop in overall activity related to the account), and `DROPPED_CALLS` (the number of dropped calls).

5

Data Preparation – Integrate and Format

In this chapter, we will cover:

- Speeding up a merge with caching and optimization settings
- Merging a lookup table
- Shuffle-down (nonstandard aggregation)
- Cartesian product merge using key-less merge by key
- Multiplying out using Cartesian product merge, user source, and derive dummy
- Changing large numbers of variable names without scripting
- Parsing nonstandard dates
- Parsing and performing a conversion on a complex stream
- Sequence processing

Introduction

This set of recipes contains tricks and shortcuts for tasks that most analysts would anticipate as central to data preparation. Two subtasks are addressed, integrate and format. The first four recipes involve aspects of integration and the last two involve aspects of format.

The first recipe makes use of the optimization settings in the Merge node. By combining this feature with some preparation steps in the stream, one can handle data sets of considerable size. The next recipe takes as its starting point the flexibility that can come from using the core features of Modeler that date back to the earliest versions. Many recently added nodes automate routine tasks, such as SetToFlag. However, many of these same tasks were possible in Modeler in earlier versions. With convenience sometimes come limitations. Shuffle Down uses this approach to produce a nonstandard aggregation. The next two recipes address typical merge conditions. Finally, the issue of formatting is addressed with a trick for renaming variables and an example of the somewhat laborious process of dealing with nonstandard (unsupported) dates.

Speeding up merge with caching and optimization settings

In this recipe, we will start with a simple stream involving two Merge nodes. Although the sample size in the example is not extremely large, we will explore how you could speed up this stream if you were experiencing performance issues. In effect, we are performing a trade, trading available hard drive space to make it easier on the processor. One should be able to process millions of rows even if you are restricted to a client copy of Modeler. Note that, if you are experiencing these kinds of problems during Deployment, you should probably pursue a more complete solution. If, however, it is a data prep challenge, this should be helpful in getting you past the problem, and then during modeling you should consider a random sample.

Getting ready

We will start with the stream `SpeedUpMerge.str`.

How to do it...

To speed up a Merge node by using a cache and optimization settings:

1. Open the stream `SpeedUpMerge.str`. To run the entire stream on very large data sets might take a while. While the number of rows is not trivial, it is far from being Big Data so there is no harm in running it in its current form.

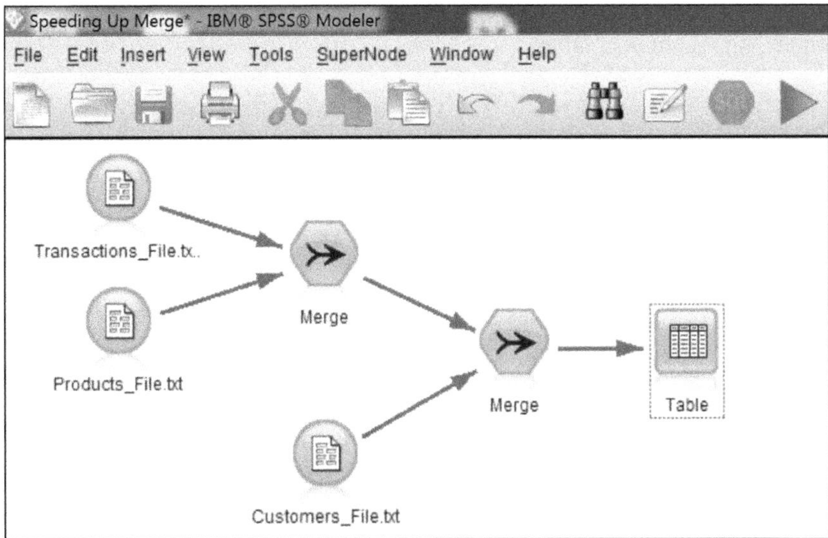

2. Add a Sort node to the Transactions file, enable cache, and run an empty Aggregate and Table (see the *Using an empty aggregate to evaluate sample size* recipe in *Chapter 1, Data Understanding*, for more on this.)

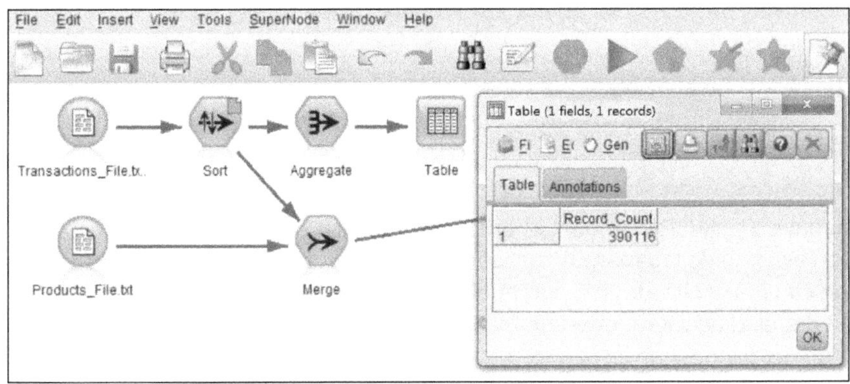

3. Add a Sort node to the `Products_File` source node, enable cache, and run an empty Aggregate and Table.

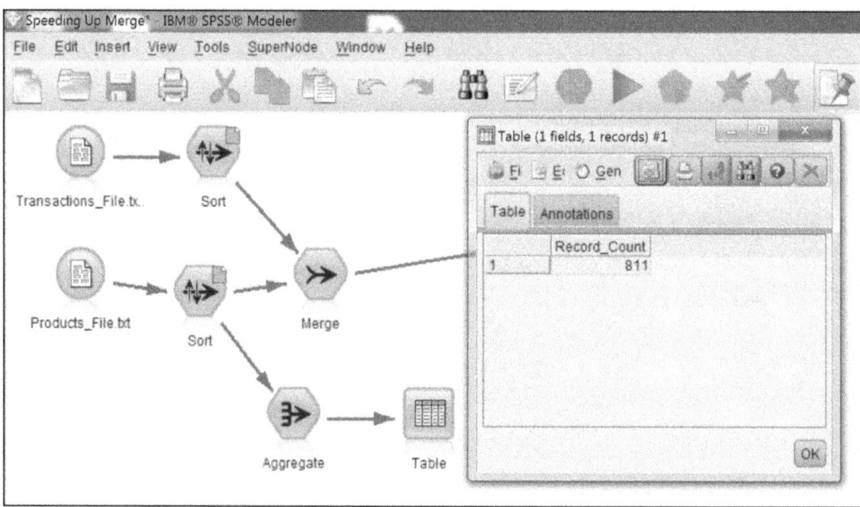

4. Since it is now true that our data from both sources is sorted, we will inform the Merge node of that fact. In the optimization settings select **One input dataset is relatively large** and **All inputs are already sorted by key fields**.
5. Enable cache for the Merge node and force it to run. Here we will run an Aggregate node and Table node.

How it works...

When you have a very large amount of data, perhaps 10s of millions of rows, Modeler may bog down if you ask it to do too many things at once. Assuming that you have plenty of hard drive space, you can make a trade. You can effectively trade your hard drive space in exchange for a reduced demand on your processor. By caching the results of the sort, you are ensuring that the sort is no longer an issue when the merge is attempted. The optimization settings can then be used, and by caching the Merge node itself you store a copy of the results and prevent having to do it again. One can extend this one step further by creeping along, one node at a time in a computationally expensive merge. Further, as is demonstrated in the next section, you can send the results out to an external file. It is important to note that this is not a deployment stream, nor is this something that you would want to repeat in multiple modeling sessions. The idea is to push the limits of what your processor can do.

SQL pushback note: These recommendations for optimal aggregation and merging do not apply when using SQL pushback. Doing sorts prior to merges will in most cases result in degradation of performance. Its precise effect depends on the implementation of the database and is rooted in the fact that order does not exist in a true relational database. As such, sorting (one common form of order) will, in most relational databases, result in a forced termination of pushback. Furthermore, many modern databases take advantage of the non-ordered nature of relational databases by using massively parallel systems when creating aggregates or running merges.

See also

- The *Using an empty aggregate to evaluate sample size* and *Evaluating the need to sample from the initial data* recipe *in Chapter 1, Data Understanding*
- The *Evaluating the use of sampling for speed* recipe in *Chapter 2, Data Preparation - Select*

Merging a lookup table

Nominal variables with more than several categories pose a potential problem. First, fields with a large number of categories can significantly increase processing time. Second, these fields can potentially have categories with very few cases, which can become problematic (for example, they might be outliers or just difficult to understand). Third, these fields might not even be used by certain models (see the following screenshot). Finally, fields with a large number of categories might not really get at the crux of the real characteristics of interest. Many new users of Modeler don't realize that many algorithms are automatically transforming nominal variables behind the scenes. Within the **General Setting** in **Stream Properties**, there are two options designed to prevent this problem from getting out of hand.

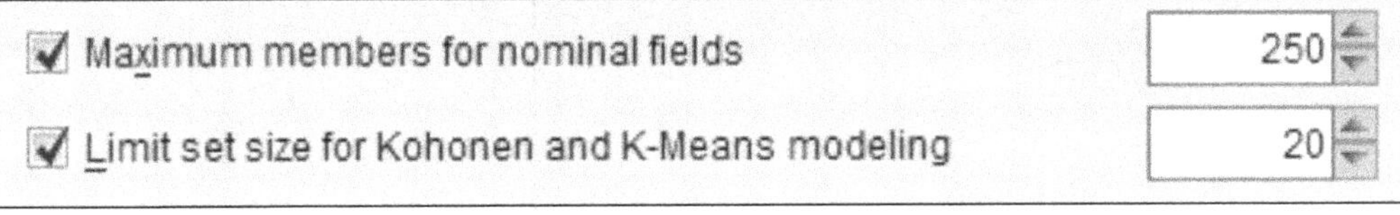

As mentioned earlier, many times fields with a large number of categories might not really get at the real characteristics of interest and therefore sometimes it is much better to leave them out. If this is done, it is wise to associate information stored in other fields with the qualities that describe the categories. So, for example, instead of using a field such as **Phone_ID**, we can use a lookup table to match the phone IDs with phone characteristics. What qualities do we want the variables to have. Quite simply, they should be scales, flags, or sets with just a handful of categories. Variables such as storage capacity, or camera_flag, or smart phone/flip phone.

Getting ready

This recipe uses the `CHURN_with_MODELS` data set and well as the `PHONE MODELS.xlsx` spreadsheet. We will begin with an empty stream.

How to do it...

To create a lookup table:

1. Place a new source node to read in the `CHURN_with_MODELS` data set. Add a Type node, verifying that our **Target**, **Churn**, has been declared and that **ACCOUNT** is **typeless**. Add and run a Data Audit node.

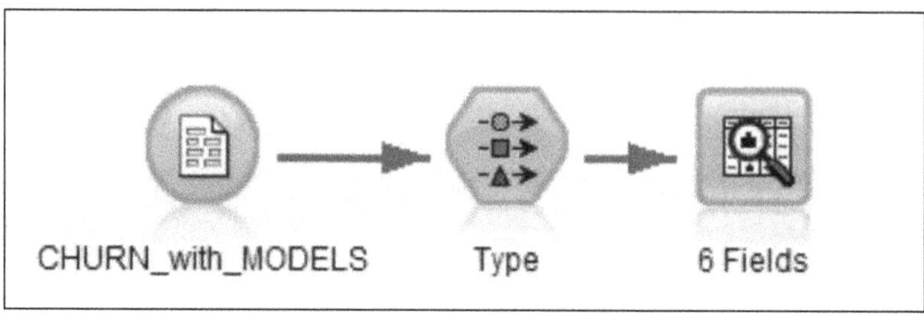

2. Edit the resulting Data Audit, and pay particular attention to Phone_ID. In the screenshot we have double-clicked on **Phone_ID** to take a closer look. What if we determined that B50 has high churn? It looks like it does, but it would be hard to take action on it because we wouldn't know what aspect of the phone was driving churn. We will now take steps to rectify this.

Value	Proportion	%	Count
1005		1.56	20
100D		10.03	129
105D		20.76	267
120S		4.51	58
300M		1.56	20
50CX		0.78	10
AA10		0.93	12
B50		10.58	136
G5		8.94	115
S50		1.4	18
SG200	0.0894245723172628 3	20.61	265
X23		2.72	35
X25		3.03	39
X5000		12.6	162

3. Add a source node for our lookup table, the `PHONE MODELS.xlsx` spreadsheet, and connect both sources to a Merge node.

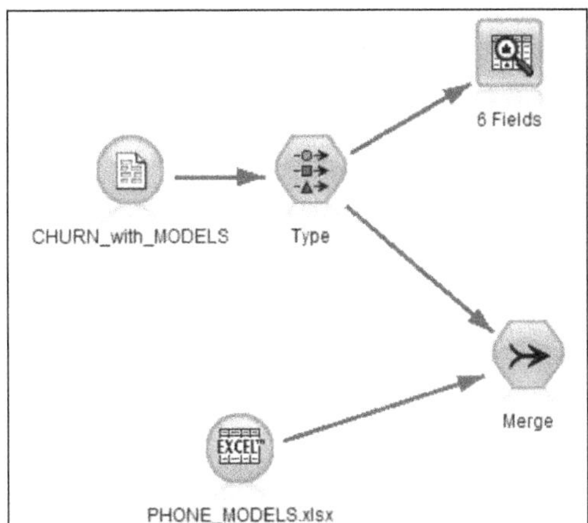

4. Adjust the settings in the Merge node to reflect that we are performing a **partial outer join**.

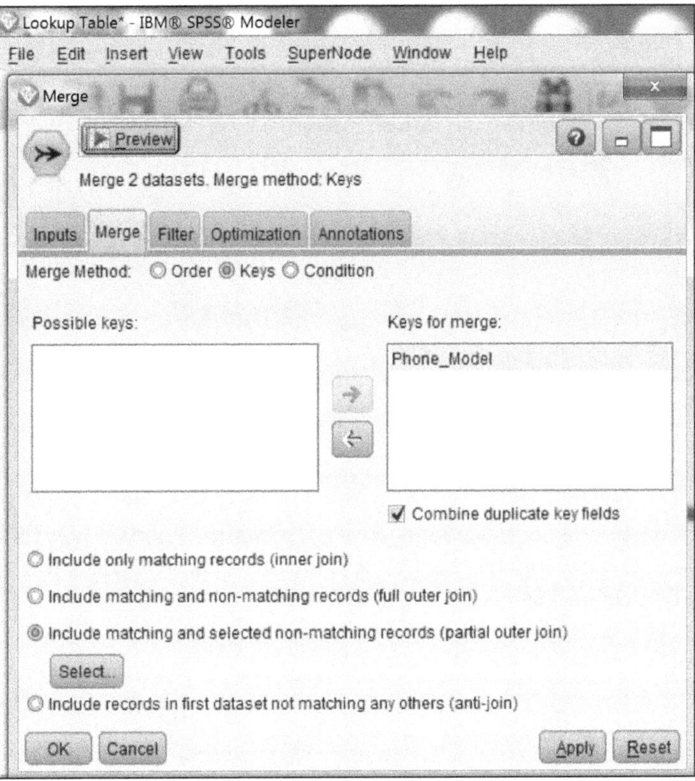

5. Click on the **Select** button and edit the check boxes to reflect our larger data set. **CHURN_with_MODELS** is to have **Outer Join** checked so that all of its cases are merged, and our lookup table should have no check, so only cases that match the **CHURN_with_MODELS** data set are merged.

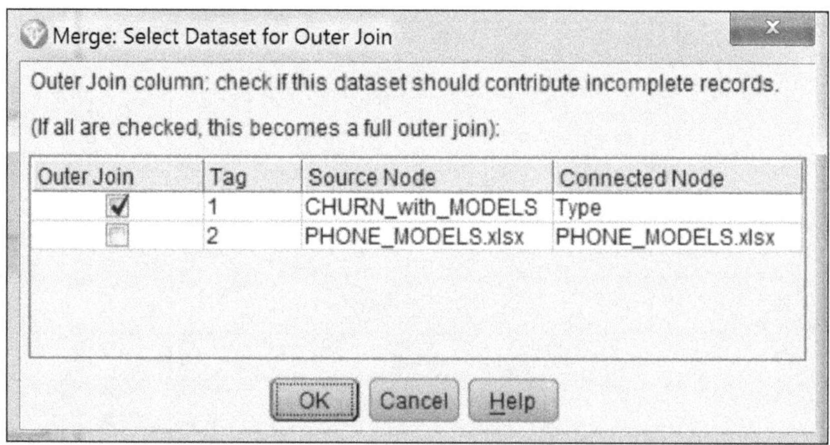

6. Add a Type node and Data Audit downstream of the Merge node.

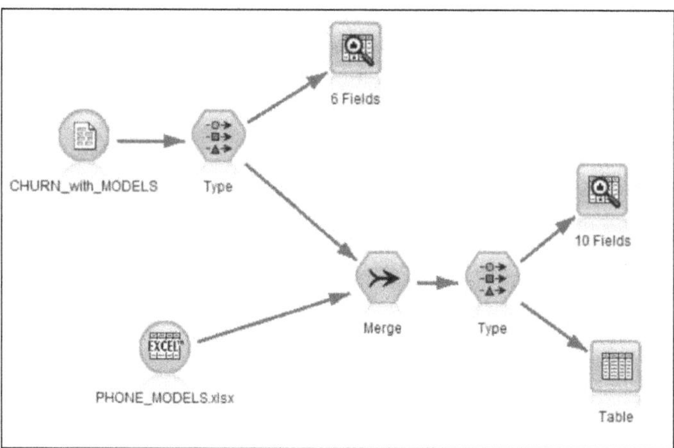

7. Edit the Type node so that **Phone_ID** is set to **None**. Since we now have the phone characteristics it would be redundant to include Phone_ID. Also, the new variables should be declared as Flag.

8. Run the Data Audit node. Some of the characteristics look as if they might be related to the target CHURN. In particular, **Touch** looks as if it has a different relationship from the other variables. More red (churn) on the smaller group on the left (no touch command), and less red on the right (touch command).

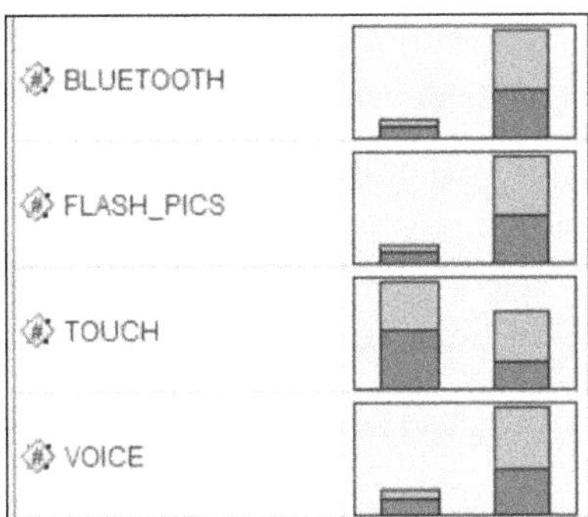

How it works...

As mentioned previously, fields with a large number of categories can be problematic. The key to this recipe is to replace fields with a large numbers of categories with fields that better represent the underlying characteristics of the field to be discarded. If this can be done, this can benefit the analyst in several ways. First this helps by addressing the issues that were mentioned previously, that is, speeding up processing, not having to worry about categories with a few cases, and actually using the fields. Second, the analyst can greatly benefit from representing the underlying characteristics of a field by not just making predictions of how a specific category (that is, product) might be related to churn, but instead being able to predict how an underlying characteristic is related to churn so that we can have some information about how new products might fare once do they become available.

See also

- The *Running a Statistics node on an anti-join to evaluate the potential missing data* recipe in *Chapter 2, Data Preparation – Select*
- The *Speeding up merge with caching and optimization settings* recipe in this chapter

Shuffle-down (nonstandard aggregation)

Some applications require a form of aggregation not directly supported in Modeler, for example, aggregating a set of Booleans or Flags with a logical or Boolean operator such as `OR`. This recipe shows how to combine sorting with sequence functions in filler nodes to perform nonstandard aggregations.

This technique originates with basket analysis using versions of Modeler that pre-date the inclusion of the SetToflag node. Without the Set-to-flag node, when an analysis required aggregating a set of Booleans, it was necessary to construct the required technique out of the then-existing nodes. Typically, this processing step started with multiple records for each customer, with several fields representing the presence of different products in the basket, one basket per record. It is then required to perform an aggregation using a Boolean `OR` operation to produce one record per customer showing the products in all the baskets (that is, whether the customer has ever had each product).

The shuffle-down technique makes heavy use of Modeler's sequence functions, which is the ability for a CLEM expression to refer to values in other records than the one currently being processed. The presence of these functions makes Modeler's data manipulation more powerful than standard SQL, because it enables operations that make use of the order of records in the data set. This makes Modeler particularly useful for processing time-series data.

Getting ready

This recipe requires no data file because the example data is generated by a User Input source node and other operations inside a supernode, and the required stream file is `Shuffle_Down.str`.

How to do it...

To combine sorting with sequence functions in filler nodes to perform non-standard aggregations:

1. Open the stream `Shuffle_Down.str` by navigating to **File** | **Open Stream**.
2. Run the Table node `Baskets`; this displays the input data for the shuffle-down operation. Each record represents one basket, and four baskets are included for each customer (identified by the ID). Note that the records for a given ID are all adjacent in the data; this is necessary for the shuffle-down operation, and is achieved by the sort operation.

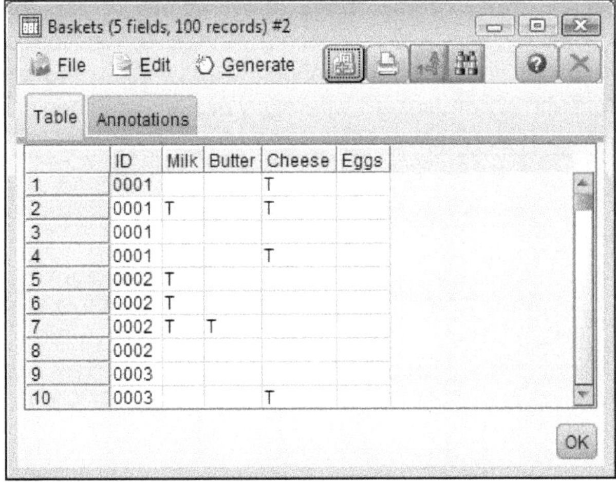
Baskets (5 fields, 100 records) #2

	ID	Milk	Butter	Cheese	Eggs
1	0001			T	
2	0001	T		T	
3	0001				
4	0001			T	
5	0002	T			
6	0002	T			
7	0002	T	T		
8	0002				
9	0003				
10	0003			T	

3. The source supernode in this stream produces a random set of data that is then cached; this means that, when you run the stream, you will probably see different data from that shown here.
4. Edit the Filler node; this performs the main shuffle-down operation. Note that all the Boolean fields are selected for processing. Each field is set to `T` if the current record is not the first for its ID (its ID is the same as the previous record), the previous value for the same field is T, and the value is not already T.

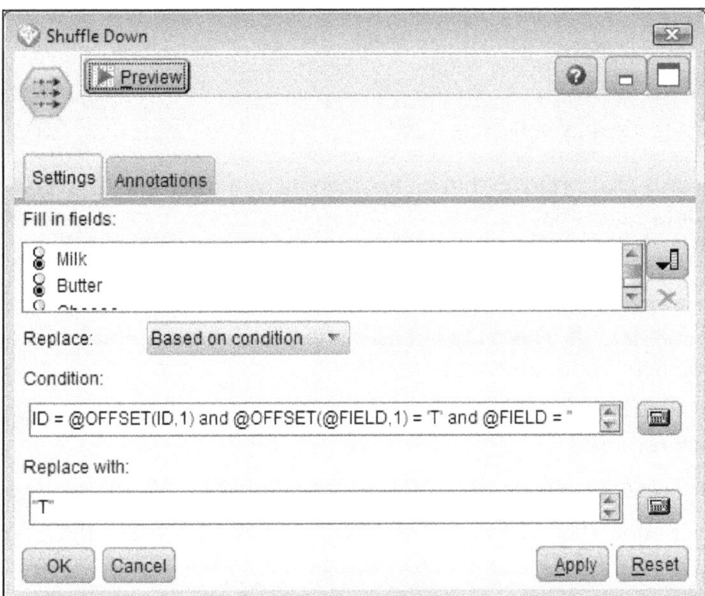

5. Run the Table node, `Processed`; this displays the intermediate form of shuffled-down data. Each basket for a given ID has been combined, using a logical OR, with the previous record; this has the effect of shuffling true values down the page, so that the final record of each ID contains a T where any basket contained a T, otherwise not.

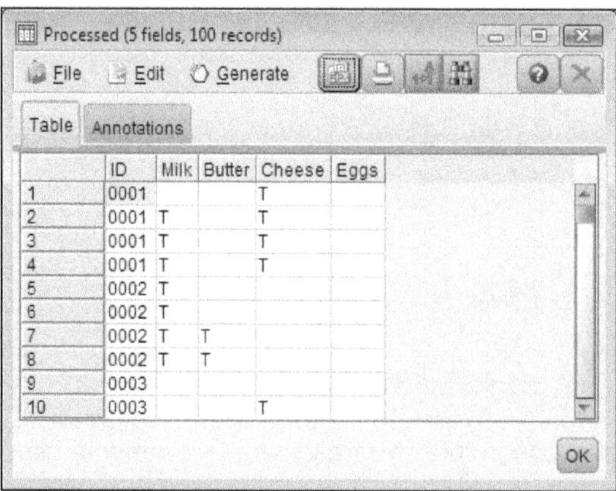

	ID	Milk	Butter	Cheese	Eggs
1	0001			T	
2	0001	T		T	
3	0001	T		T	
4	0001	T		T	
5	0002	T			
6	0002	T			
7	0002	T	T		
8	0002	T	T		
9	0003				
10	0003			T	

6. Edit the Select node, `Last of each`, this selects the last record for each ID, that is those records whose ID is different from the ID of the next record.
7. Run the Table node, `Merged Baskets`. This displays one record per ID, where all of the original records for the ID have been combined, or aggregated, with a logical OR operation, so that a field is T if it was T in any of the records of the same ID.

How it works...

The shuffle-down technique works like this:

1. The records are sorted so that all the records with the same ID will be adjacent in the data.
2. The Filler node processes all of the required flag fields.
3. The Filler node's condition processes all except the first record for each customer, that is only records where the last ID is the same as the current one, expressed by the condition: `ID = @OFFSET(ID,1)`.
4. The function @OFFSET is used to retrieve values, in a given field, in previous or following records.
5. For the flags to be processed, true is represented by T and false by the empty string "".
6. The Filler node's condition processes only those values where the previous value of the same field is T. The condition becomes: `ID = @OFFSET(ID,1)` and `@OFFSET(@FIELD,1) = "T"`

7. The Filler node only needs to modify false values, so the condition becomes: `ID = @OFFSET(ID,1),@OFFSET(@FIELD,1) = "T"`, and `@FIELD=""`
8. If the condition is true, the value is replaced with `"T"`.
9. The Filler node therefore has the effect of shuffling true values "down" the sequence of records, so that the final record for each ID contains a `"T"` in each field that had a `"T"` in any previous record for the same ID.
10. The final step is to select only the last record for each ID, using a Select node with the condition: `ID /= @OFFSET(ID,-1).`

There's more...

This technique is not restricted to aggregation using a logical OR operation; any aggregation can be performed in this way, so shuffle-down is useful when data preparation requires any kind of aggregation that is not supported directly by Modeler.

For example, aggregation to count the `T` values for a given ID would have the same structure, except that the filler node would provide numeric values and perform arithmetic on them.

See also

- The *Creating flag variables for aggregation* recipe in *Chapter 4, Data Preparation – Construct*
- The *Sequence processing* recipe in this chapter

Cartesian product merge using key-less merge by key

Preparing data for analysis requires a wide range of different operations, because each different kind of analysis requires the data to be in the appropriate form for that analysis. In some examples, two or more lists of items must be joined together in such a way that the result is every possible combination of items, one from each of the lists. This is called a Cartesian product, and in Modeler this is performed using a *merge by key* operations where no key is specified.

Getting ready

This recipe requires no datafile because the example data is generated by user input source nodes and the stream file required is `Cartesian_Product.str`

How to do it...

To perform a Cartesian product merge where no key is specified:

1. Open the stream `Cartesian_Product.str` by navigating to **File** | **Open Stream**.
2. Run the four Table nodes to the left, **ABC**, **PQR**, **XYZ**, and **123**. This will display the four data sets, generated by the user input source nodes, that will be used to illustrate the technique.

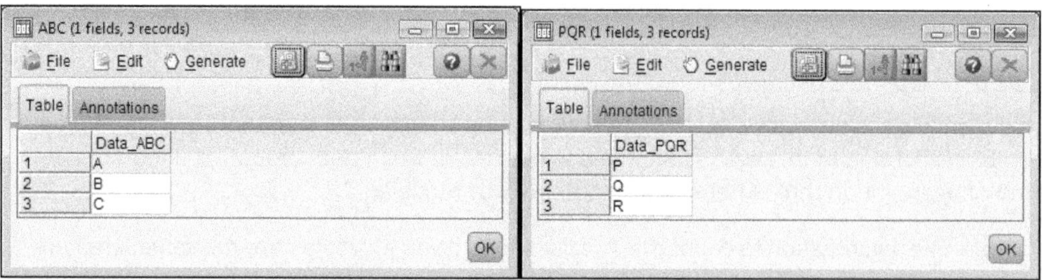

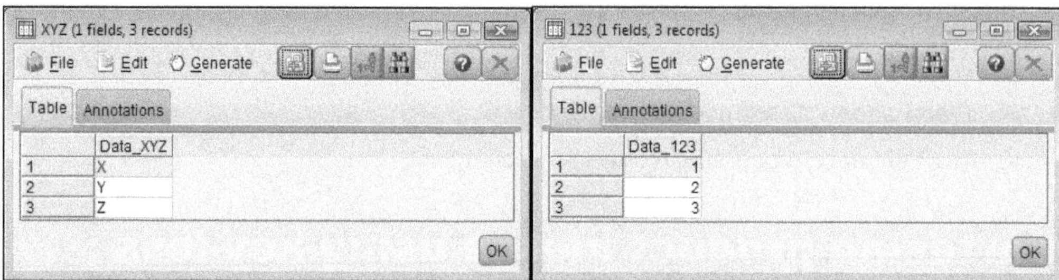

3. Run the Table node, `Results 3`. This shows the results of applying Modeler's default *"merge by order"* to these data sets; 3 records are produced, each one combining four data items from the example data, based on the order of records in the input data sets.
4. Edit the Merge node, `Cartesian`. Note that the node is set to *merge by key*, but no key is selected; these settings produce a Cartesian product of all the inputs to the Merge node.

5. Run the Table node, `Results 81`; this displays the result of the Cartesian product merge operation. Note that 81 records are produced, one for each possible combination of one record from each of the input data sets; each data set contains three records, and there are four data sets, so the number of records in the resultant data set is three to the power of four, that is, 81 cases.

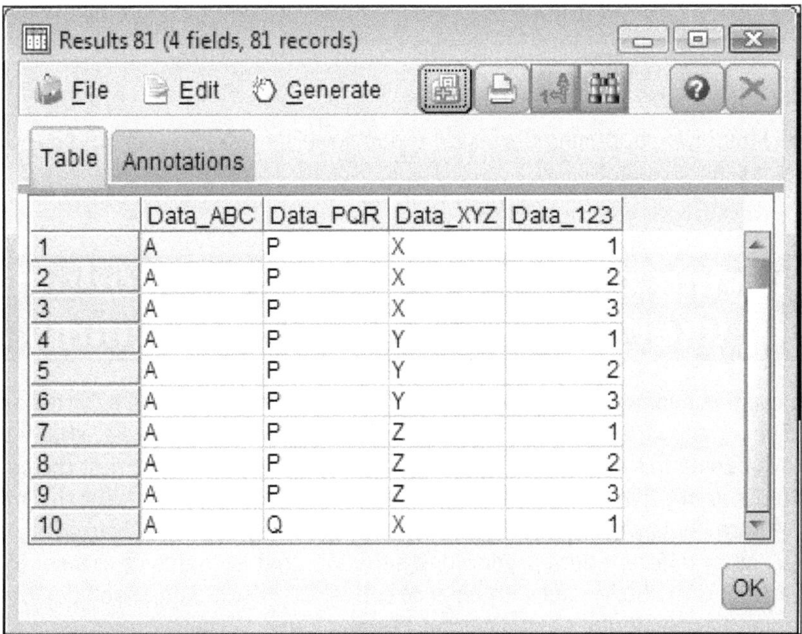
Results 81 (4 fields, 81 records)

	Data_ABC	Data_PQR	Data_XYZ	Data_123
1	A	P	X	1
2	A	P	X	2
3	A	P	X	3
4	A	P	Y	1
5	A	P	Y	2
6	A	P	Y	3
7	A	P	Z	1
8	A	P	Z	2
9	A	P	Z	3
10	A	Q	X	1

How it works...

This recipe shows the key-less merge technique for generating a Cartesian product in Modeler. Prior to the introduction of a key-less merge, the same effect was accomplished by deriving a key for each input to the merge, where both the name and the value of the key were identical in each branch (sometimes called a dummy key). A merge using this key would then produce a Cartesian product because every record from every branch would match all the records from the other branches, so every combination of records represents a match. The key-less merge does the same thing, but without the overhead of creating and later removing the dummy key.

There's more...

Note that a Cartesian product potentially produces a very large amount of data. For example, if each data set input to the merge consisted of 1000 records, then the Cartesian product would contain one trillion (10 to the power of 12) records. Cartesian products are therefore normally only used when all, or all but one, of the data sets contains only a few records.

See also

- The *Multiplying out using Cartesian product merge, user source, and derive dummy* recipes in this chapter

Multiplying out using Cartesian product merge, user source, and derive dummy

To produce every combination from two or more sets of records requires a Cartesian product operation. The recipe *Cartesian product merge using key-less merge by key* shows the simplest way of doing this in Modeler, by using a key-less merge. The current recipe shows a different method of generating a Cartesian product that uses dummy keys; this method dates from before the key-less merge operation was included in the software. This recipe also illustrates a slightly different data preparation situation; that is, in this case a set of 1000 customer records is multiplied out with a set of codes, the result being each customer record is duplicated and appended to each available code.

Getting ready

This recipe uses the datafile, `cup98LRN.txt` and the stream file, `Multiply_Out.str`

How to do it...

To perform a Cartesian product merge by using dummy keys:

1. Open the stream `Multiply_Out.str` by navigating to **File** | **Open Stream**.
2. Run the Table node, `1000 Customers`. This displays the main input to the multiply-out operation, that is, a set of 1000 customer records.

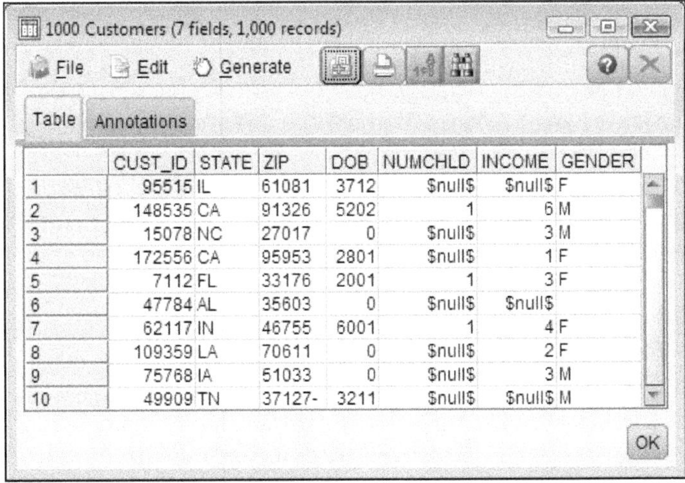

	CUST_ID	STATE	ZIP	DOB	NUMCHLD	INCOME	GENDER
1	95515	IL	61081	3712	$null$	$null$	F
2	148535	CA	91326	5202	1	6	M
3	15078	NC	27017	0	$null$	3	M
4	172556	CA	95953	2801	$null$	1	F
5	7112	FL	33176	2001	1	3	F
6	47784	AL	35603	0	$null$	$null$	
7	62117	IN	46755	6001	1	4	F
8	109359	LA	70611	0	$null$	2	F
9	75768	IA	51033	0	$null$	3	M
10	49909	TN	37127-	3211	$null$	$null$	M

3. Run the Table node `ABCDEF`. This displays the set of codes with which the customer records will be combined.

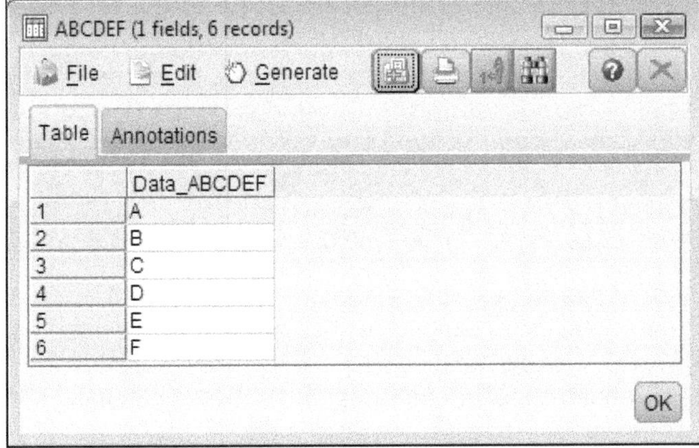

	Data_ABCDEF
1	A
2	B
3	C
4	D
5	E
6	F

4. Edit one of the **DUMMY** Derive nodes. Note that the value for this variable will be the same in all of the derive nodes for this variable, and for every record.
5. Edit the Merge node. The derived field **DUMMY** has been chosen as the merge key.
6. Run the Table node, `Results 6000`. This displays the 6000 records produced by the Cartesian product operation in the merge node. Each customer record is duplicated six times, each copy with one of the possible codes appended to it. The key field DUMMY has been removed by the filter node.

How it works...

The Cartesian product operation is exactly the same as it would be produced by a key-less merge. This recipe shows an alternative method. The use of dummy keys is no longer required for built-in merge or aggregation operations in Modeler, because a key-less operation does the same thing and is supported by these nodes; however, this technique can be required in less common situations where other built-in operations or non-standard processing does not support a key-less operation.

There's more...

The creation of dummy variables that always have the same value illustrates a more general point about using a visual programming interface for data preparation. Rather than providing a wizard interface, with interactive dialogs to guide the user through standard data preparation steps, Modeler provides something closer to a general programming interface. This means that the user of Modeler can construct operations that were not predicted by the designers, in order to overcome what would otherwise be built-in limitations in the design.

See also

- The *Cartesian product merge using key-less merge by key* recipe in this chapter

Changing large numbers of variable names without scripting

In this recipe we learn how to change variable names by adding suffixes or prefixes using a Derive node. The data sources for this recipe were developed by computing the average value of several key fields after aggregating by the variable `STATE` and then by `DOMAIN`. The Aggregate node, as a default, appends the string `_Mean` (when obtaining a mean) to each of the variables so that the variable names come from both.

Getting ready

This recipe uses the datafiles `cup98lrn_reduced_vars3_varchange state.sav` and `up98lrn_reduced_vars3_varchange domain.sav`, and the stream `Recipe - change variable names.str`.

How to do it...

To change variable names by adding suffixes or prefixes using a Derive node:

1. Open the stream `Recipe - change variable names.str` by navigating to **File | Open Stream**.
2. Make sure the datafile points to the correct path to the `cup98lrn_reduced_vars3_varchange state.sav` and `cup98lrn_reduced_vars3_varchange domain.sav`.
3. Open the Type node, `STATE Feed Types`. Note the variable names with the suffix `_Mean`. Now open the Type node `DOMAIN Feed Types` and note that this stream branch has the same variable names.
4. Add a **Derive** node to the top stream branch and connect it to the `STATE Feed Types` node.
5. Open the Derive node, click on the **Multiple** radio button, and select the five variables **RAMNTALL_Mean**, **NGIFTALL_Mean**, **LASTGIFT_Mean**, **FISTDATE_Mean**, and **RFA_2F_Mean**. In the field name extension box, replace the string with `State_` and click on the radio button, **Prefix**, next to the text **Add as:**. In the Formula region, type `@FIELD`. These options are shown in following screenshot. Click on **OK**.

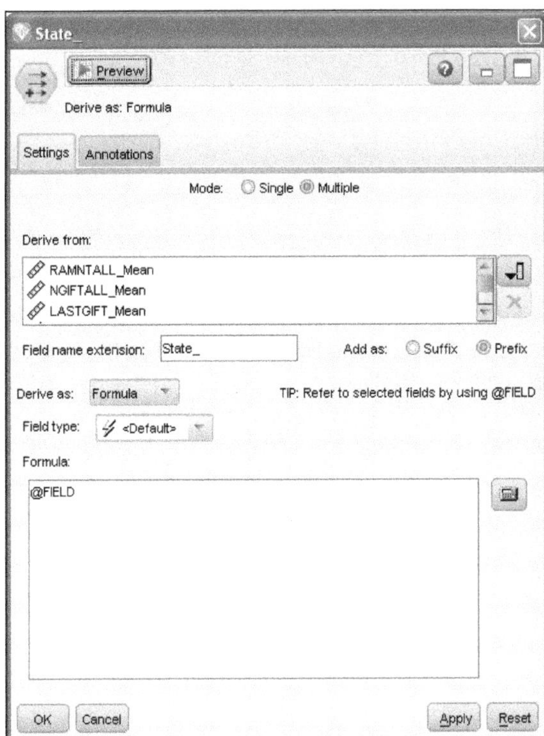

6. Copy the node that was configured in step 5, now labeled `State_`, and paste it to the stream. Move the pasted node to the right of the Type node, `DOMAIN Feed Type`, and connect it.
7. Open the node created in step 6 and change the string `State_` to `Domain_`. Click on **OK**. In the stream, this node should now be labeled as `Domain_`.

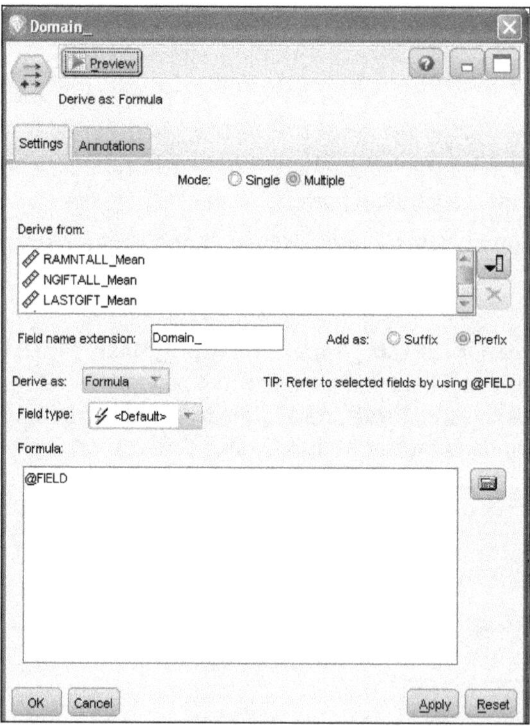

8. Add a Filter node to the stream and connect it to node, `State_`.
9. Open the Filter node. Click on the field name, **RAMNTALL_Mean** in the first column and press *Shift* + click (left-click on he mouse) on the row, **RFA_2F_Mean**, to select the five fields with suffix _Mean. Click on an arrow (second column) for any of the five selected fields. This will change the arrows to the symbol, **x**. Click on **OK**.

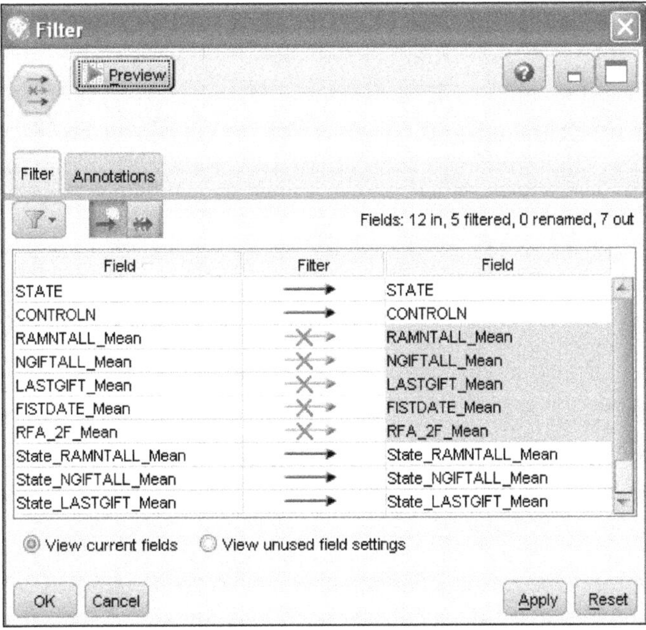

10. Repeat steps 8 and 9, but connect the Filter node to the node `Domain_`.
11. Add a Merge node to the stream and connect the two Filter nodes to the Merge node.
12. Open the Merge node. Click on the **Keys** radio button. Next, in the **Possible Keys** list, click on **CONTROLN**, and, using the right-arrow, add **CONTROLN** to the **Keys for merge** list. Click on **OK**.
13. Add a Table node to the stream and connect it to the Merge node.

How it works...

Predictive analytics applications often combine data from multiple sources into the same stream. This stream uses a simple example where five fields with the same names are combined into a single stream with a field prefix indicating the source of the field. In other examples, one may have dozens or hundreds of fields from different sources, even without the problem of them having the same names. In these cases, it can be very useful to label the fields with an indicator of the source of the data, such as coming from the `customer` table, the `product` table, or from an external demographic data source.

The most straightforward way to change field names in Modeler is by manually changing the name of each field in a Filter node. However, this is very tedious when there are several, dozens, or even hundreds of fields one would like to change.

In situations where it suffices to merely add a suffix or prefix to the field name. The two key steps in this recipe take advantage of the multiple options in the Derive node and the ease of multiple field selection in a Filter node.

In the Derive node, the CLEM language keyword `@FIELD` is used as a placeholder in the formula box to indicate that we desire to create a new variable that is merely a copy of every variable in the list specified in the **Derive from:** list. The field name extension text string can be a prefix or a suffix (a prefix was chosen for this recipe).

The Filter node then can be used to remove the original copy of each field that was renamed by a simple contiguous selection of the variables, and then clicking on the arrow to remove the fields from the stream.

There's more...

Usually, it is advantageous to rename the fields prior to a merge to combine fields from multiple data sources to make the selection of the fields to rename simpler. This is not always possible, however. If the fields that were duplicated are not in sequence, selecting the fields in the Derive node and de-selecting the fields in the Filter node can be very tedious as well. In this case one may use a Field Reorder node to put all of the fields to be renamed in consecutive columns, such as at the end of the field list. Now, one can use simple *Shift* + click operations to select the variables to rename easily.

See also

- The *Building transformations with multiple Derive nodes* recipe in *Chapter 4, Data Preparation – Construct*
- The *Changing formatting of fields in a Table node* recipe in *Chapter 7, Modeling – Assessment, Evaluation, Deployment, and Monitoring*

Parsing nonstandard dates

The `KDD98` data set uses a YYMM date format, which is not one of the supported date formats in Modeler. In this recipe we will use Derive nodes to parse the existing date information and reassemble it into a supported format. In this recipe we will extract the month portion of information contained in a variable that combines the month and year in a string. The starting stream has already addressed the year information. We will modify the stream so that it also addresses the month information.

Getting ready

We will start with the `Parsing Nonstandard Dates.str` stream, which uses the `cup98lrn reduced vars2.txt` data set.

How to do it...

1. Open the `Parsing Nonstandard Dates.str` stream.
2. Run a preview of the Derive node. Scroll to the far right of the table to see the new variable, and then edit the Derive node. The variable is the `Year_str` variable. Note that the original variable, `DOB`, has the two-digit year on the left, and the two digits for the month on the right of a four character string.
3. Copy and paste the Derive node and modify it for the month information. The Derive field will be **Month_str**. The `IF and Then:` condition will be the same, but the `Else:` condition will be different. The new `Else:` condition is **substring(3,2, to_string(DOB))**.

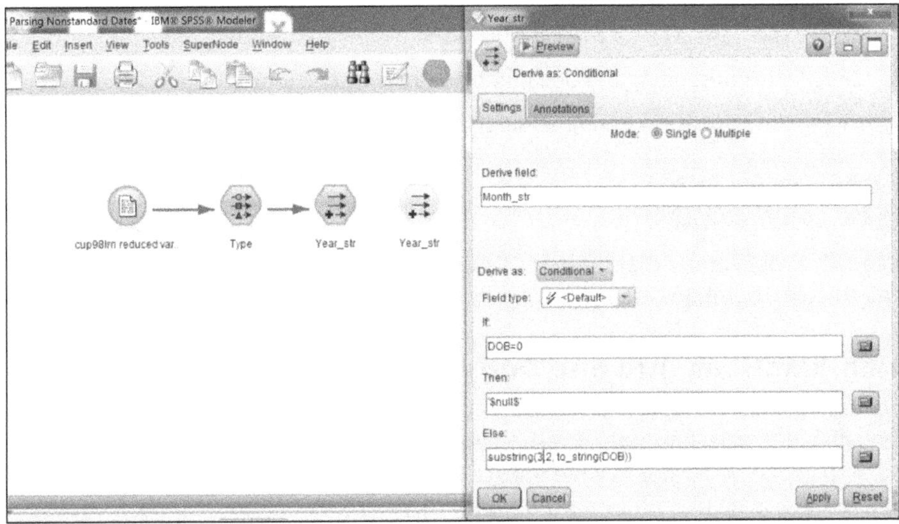

4. Add an additional Derive to assemble the year and month pieces into a new DOB variable named `DOB_date`. The formula will be `datetime_date(to_integer(Year_str),to_integer(Month_str),15)`. Note that we have arbitrarily chosen the 15th as the day of the month.
5. To make use of our new variable, we will calculate the potential donors' age at the time of the campaign. We will use February, 15th, 1997 as the campaign date. The formula for the new Derive node, **Age_at_Campaign**, will be `intof(date_years_difference(DOB_date, datetime_date(1997,2,15)))`.
6. Add a Table node, run it, and then examine the results.

How it works...

Nonstandard or unsupported dates are generally no fun. As we have seen, it often requires converting back and forth between strings and numeric. It gets more complicated that the string length is not constant. Here the constant 4 digits length was helpful. The zero for missing dates was a bit odd in this data set, but was easily resolved with the `if...then...else` grammar of the Derive node.

Functions in the CLEM expression language used in the recipe included:

- `to_string()` and `to_integer()` for conversion
- `substring()` for dividing the 4-character dates into year and month
- `datetime_date()` for reassembling the pieces into a supported date
- `intof()` for dropping the decimal places in our calculated age
- `><` for concatenation (string addition) of the `'19'` and the two digit year

There's more...

Now let's talk about some other options. We chose the route that was the easiest to follow the first time through, but there are more elegant ways of performing this calculation.

Nesting functions into one Derive node

Many veteran coders would prefer using nested functions instead of the three-step process that we outlined to calculate `DOB_date`. However when we combine multiple functions in a single step, it can be harder to write and/or to read. There is really no wrong way, but the following formula is an alternate way that many more experience coders might choose:

```
datetime_date(to_integer('19' >< substring(1,2, to_string(DOB))),to_
integer(substring(3,2, to_string(DOB))), 15)
```

Note that the three lines are the three components: year, month, and day. All the pieces were present before, but this new else condition combines three derives into one.

Performing clean downstream of a calculation using a Filter node

Having created `DOB_date` we don't need the original ingredients anymore. Although Modeler forces us to create a new name for new variables, we can use a Filter node to revert back to the original name. (In other words, Modeler's grammar does not allow C=C+1.) Note that in the Filter node we have given our new variable `DOB_date` the old, and original, name of DOB. We have also dropped the variables `DOB`, `Year_str`, and `Month_str`.

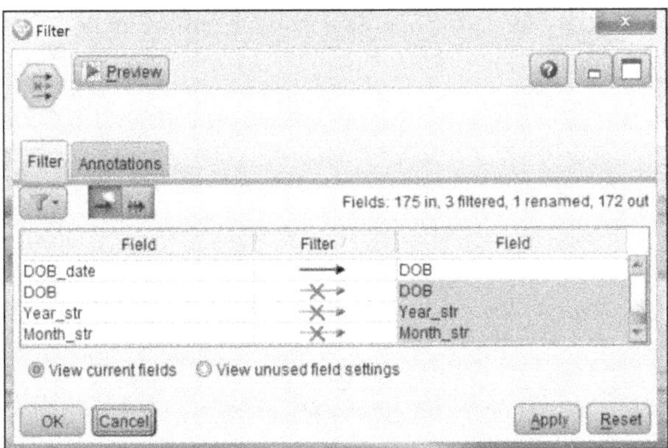

Using parameters instead of constants in calculations

This recipe's solution calculates the age of the potential donor at the launch of the most recent campaign. What if we were interested in another campaign? What if we wanted to update the stream for next month's campaign? We could make changes to the CLEM code in the Derive node, but a better option is a parameter. Examine the following modification.

```
intof(date_years_difference(DOB_date,'$P-parameter0' ))
```

One can set the parameters in the designated areas of the menus under **Tools** | **Stream Properties**. By using this feature we can update the date without having to change the code. Changing working code can be risky; one can introduce errors. Note that you can use this feature for more than one parameter. The menu is straightforward. We have used the default name parameter, but have labeled the long name, `Campaign_Date`, and provided the date `1997-02-15`.

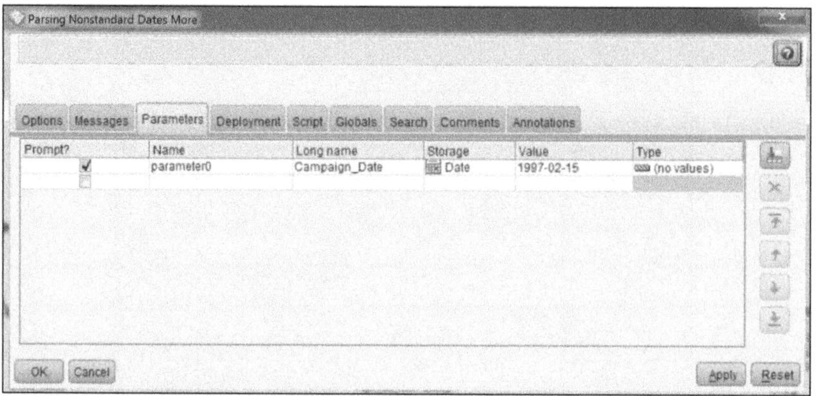

See also

- The *Parsing and performing a conversion on a complex stream* recipe in this chapter

Parsing and performing a conversion on a complex stream

In this example we have data from a call center in the Philippines. The managers at the call center want to determine the call volume between midnight and 8 AM so they can staff the call center accordingly. To get this information, there is a timestamp variable that indicates the time when the customer called and the time zone where the customer was located (in this case all customers are in the Pacific time zone). Now there are two wrinkles in this timestamp variable. First, the timestamp variable does not have a constant string length. This variation in position makes it more difficult to extract the actual times because we cannot just specify to extract all characters between position x and position `y`. Second, even though all customers called from the Pacific time zone, some called during Pacific Standard Time and others during Pacific Daylight Time, and in the Philippines this time change does not occur, so we'll need to add an hour to the call times for those customers that called during Pacific Standard Time. In this recipe we will use a series of Derive nodes to parse a timestamp variable. In addition, we will show how to perform date arithmetic on a timestamp variable.

Getting ready

We will start with the `Parsing Example Stream.str` that uses datafile `Parsing Example.txt`.

How to do it...

To parse a timestamp variable and perform date arithmetic:

1. Open the stream `Parsing Example Stream.str`.
2. Make sure the source node points to the correct path to the datafile `Parsing Example.txt`.
3. Run the Table node to view the data. Note that there are 10,000 cases and that the starting position of the actual call time varies within each row.

	Email	Full Name	TimeStamp	Account ID
1	Molly@victor.co.uk	Shyann Bins	Wednesday Mar 28 2012 03:55:18 GMT-0700 (Pacific Standard Time)	42709
2	Manley@sandy.org	Candido Kutch	Saturday Aug 10 1985 04:55:11 GMT-0700 (Pacific Standard Time)	76136
3	Hollis.Lind@lacy.org	Santos Effertz	Friday Apr 16 2010 09:34:45 GMT-0700 (Pacific Standard Time)	59965
4	Archibald@aniya.us	Kirsten Beahan	Sunday Nov 20 2005 07:32:54 GMT-0800 (Pacific Daylight Time)	13920
5	Bell@georgianna.us	Taya Nienow	Thursday Jun 17 2004 14:52:49 GMT-0700 (Pacific Standard Time)	42231
6	Angie_Kunze@mariela.tv	Alice Dietrich	Tuesday Feb 13 1990 15:06:00 GMT-0800 (Pacific Daylight Time)	60069
7	Freeman_Schiller@madelyn.us	Arturo Schultz MD	Wednesday Jul 24 1991 10:48:39 GMT-0700 (Pacific Standard Time)	28356
8	Madisyn@verda.biz	Cordelia Dickinson	Monday May 17 2004 21:01:26 GMT-0700 (Pacific Standard Time)	21205
9	Cathryn@layla.ca	Nestor Nicolas	Sunday Oct 29 2000 14:18:51 GMT-0700 (Pacific Standard Time)	44213
10	Santa_Dach@sanford.me	Durward Wiegand	Wednesday Jul 11 1990 00:49:28 GMT-0700 (Pacific Standard Time)	48880
11	Devan@destiny.info	Amaya Kirlin	Sunday Oct 31 1982 00:48:24 GMT-0700 (Pacific Standard Time)	57579
12	Ara@bonnie.net	Cora Dicki II	Monday Dec 06 2010 00:18:05 GMT-0800 (Pacific Daylight Time)	24370
13	Maya.Fisher@serenity.co.uk	Reyna Ferry	Tuesday Jul 25 2006 22:11:53 GMT-0700 (Pacific Standard Time)	19557
14	Sandrine_Langosh@andrew.ca	Ms. Lula Connelly	Wednesday Jan 21 2004 18:04:50 GMT-0800 (Pacific Daylight Time)	14129
15	Louisa@elroy.org	Marcia Altenwerth ...	Monday May 08 2000 16:24:22 GMT-0700 (Pacific Standard Time)	73933
16	Krista_Abshire@rodrick.us	Wiley Cormier	Sunday Oct 11 1992 14:56:04 GMT-0700 (Pacific Standard Time)	16123
17	Liliane_Dickens@dane.com	Fannie Pfannerstill	Wednesday Dec 16 1987 07:43:18 GMT-0800 (Pacific Daylight Time)	75811
18	Brooke.Brekke@eduardo.ca	Trinity Hansen	Sunday Dec 10 1995 23:58:04 GMT-0800 (Pacific Daylight Time)	19247
19	Tianna@eudora.com	Mack Kozey DVM	Monday Jun 16 1997 23:03:33 GMT-0700 (Pacific Standard Time)	15893
20	Larry.Gulgowski@kody.ca	Rae Reichel	Friday Jun 14 2013 16:23:00 GMT-0700 (Pacific Standard Time)	52630

4. Connect a Derive node to the Source node.
5. Edit the Derive node and name it `Find:`.

6. In the formula box specify the following expression, `locchar (`:`, 1, TimeStamp)`. The `locchar` function, `locchar(CHAR, N, STRING)`, searches the string (the variable `Timestamp`) for the character `CHAR` (`:` in single back quotes) starting at position N (`1`) and returns the position where the `CHAR` (`:`) was found.

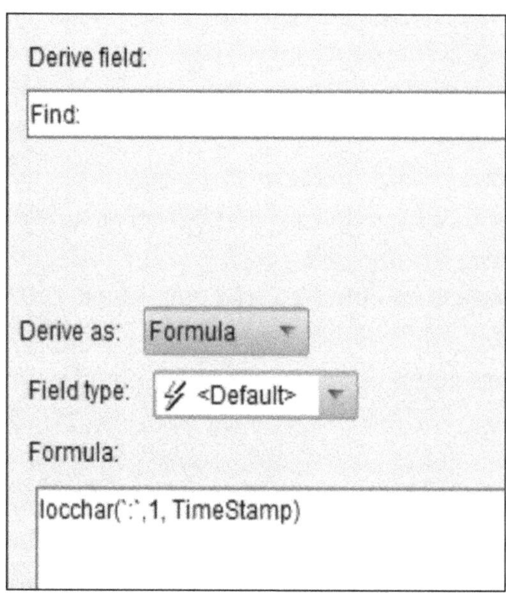

This creates a new variable, `Find:`, that then identifies the number of characters to the starting position of the colon within the actual call time.

TimeStamp	Account ID	Find:
Wednesday Mar 28 2012 03:55:18 GMT-0700 (Pacific Standard Time)	42709	25
Saturday Aug 10 1985 04:55:11 GMT-0700 (Pacific Standard Time)	76136	24
Friday Apr 16 2010 09:34:45 GMT-0700 (Pacific Standard Time)	59965	22
Sunday Nov 20 2005 07:32:54 GMT-0800 (Pacific Daylight Time)	13920	22
Thursday Jun 17 2004 14:52:49 GMT-0700 (Pacific Standard Time)	42231	24
Tuesday Feb 13 1990 15:06:00 GMT-0800 (Pacific Daylight Time)	60069	23
Wednesday Jul 24 1991 10:48:39 GMT-0700 (Pacific Standard Time)	28356	25
Monday May 17 2004 21:01:26 GMT-0700 (Pacific Standard Time)	21205	22
Sunday Oct 29 2000 14:18:51 GMT-0700 (Pacific Standard Time)	44213	22
Wednesday Jul 11 1990 00:49:28 GMT-0700 (Pacific Standard Time)	48880	25

7. Now we can remove the day and date information. Connect a new Derive node to the `Find:` Derive node.
8. Edit the Derive node and name it `RemoveDate`.

9. In the formula box specify the following expression, `allbutfirst ("Find:" -3, TimeStamp)`. The `allbutfirst` function, `allbutfirst(N, STRING)`, returns a string consisting of all characters within string (the variable `Timestamp`) except for the first N characters (`"Find:"-3`—the length specified by the field `Find:` minus 3 characters is used since the field `Find:` specifies the position of the colon and we want the position of the actual call time); that is, it removes the first N characters of the string.

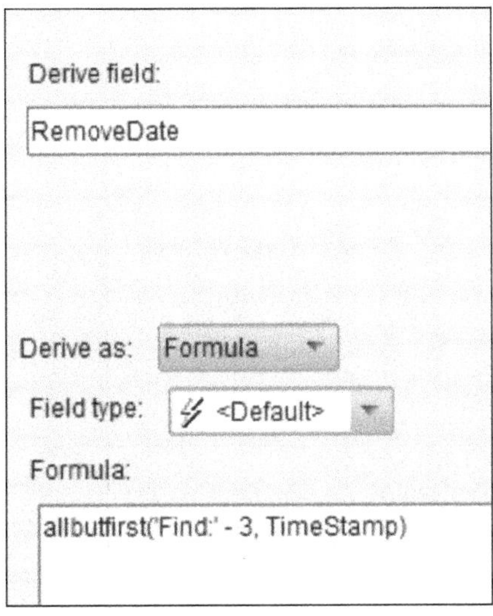

Now that we have a cleaner field, we can easily remove the actual call time.

TimeStamp	Account ID	Find:	RemoveDate
Wednesday Mar 28 2012 03:55:18 GMT-0700 (Pacific Standard Time)	42709	25	03:55:18 GMT-0700 (Pacific Standard Time)
Saturday Aug 10 1985 04:55:11 GMT-0700 (Pacific Standard Time)	76136	24	04:55:11 GMT-0700 (Pacific Standard Time)
Friday Apr 16 2010 09:34:45 GMT-0700 (Pacific Standard Time)	59965	22	09:34:45 GMT-0700 (Pacific Standard Time)
Sunday Nov 20 2005 07:32:54 GMT-0800 (Pacific Daylight Time)	13920	22	07:32:54 GMT-0800 (Pacific Daylight Time)
Thursday Jun 17 2004 14:52:49 GMT-0700 (Pacific Standard Time)	42231	24	14:52:49 GMT-0700 (Pacific Standard Time)
Tuesday Feb 13 1990 15:06:00 GMT-0800 (Pacific Daylight Time)	60069	23	15:06:00 GMT-0800 (Pacific Daylight Time)
Wednesday Jul 24 1991 10:48:39 GMT-0700 (Pacific Standard Time)	28356	25	10:48:39 GMT-0700 (Pacific Standard Time)
Monday May 17 2004 21:01:26 GMT-0700 (Pacific Standard Time)	21205	22	21:01:26 GMT-0700 (Pacific Standard Time)
Sunday Oct 29 2000 14:18:51 GMT-0700 (Pacific Standard Time)	44213	22	14:18:51 GMT-0700 (Pacific Standard Time)
Wednesday Jul 11 1990 00:49:28 GMT-0700 (Pacific Standard Time)	48880	25	00:49:28 GMT-0700 (Pacific Standard Time)
Sunday Oct 31 1982 00:48:24 GMT-0700 (Pacific Standard Time)	57579	22	00:48:24 GMT-0700 (Pacific Standard Time)
Monday Dec 06 2010 00:18:05 GMT-0800 (Pacific Daylight Time)	24370	22	00:18:05 GMT-0800 (Pacific Daylight Time)
Tuesday Jul 25 2006 22:11:53 GMT-0700 (Pacific Standard Time)	19557	23	22:11:53 GMT-0700 (Pacific Standard Time)
Wednesday Jan 21 2004 18:04:50 GMT-0800 (Pacific Daylight Time)	14129	25	18:04:50 GMT-0800 (Pacific Daylight Time)
Monday May 08 2000 16:24:22 GMT-0700 (Pacific Standard Time)	73933	22	16:24:22 GMT-0700 (Pacific Standard Time)
Sunday Oct 11 1992 14:56:04 GMT-0700 (Pacific Standard Time)	16123	22	14:56:04 GMT-0700 (Pacific Standard Time)
Wednesday Dec 16 1987 07:43:18 GMT-0800 (Pacific Daylight Time)	75811	25	07:43:18 GMT-0800 (Pacific Daylight Time)
Sunday Dec 10 1995 23:58:04 GMT-0800 (Pacific Daylight Time)	19247	22	23:58:04 GMT-0800 (Pacific Daylight Time)
Monday Jun 16 1997 23:03:33 GMT-0700 (Pacific Standard Time)	15893	22	23:03:33 GMT-0700 (Pacific Standard Time)
Friday Jun 14 2013 16:23:00 GMT-0700 (Pacific Standard Time)	52630	22	16:23:00 GMT-0700 (Pacific Standard Time)

10. Connect a new Derive node to the `RemoveDate` Derive node.
11. Edit the Derive node and name it `Time`.

12. In the formula box specify the following expression, `datetime_time(substring(1,8, RemoveDate))`. The substring function, `substring(N, LEN, STRING)`, returns a string consisting of LEN characters (8) within STRING (the variable `RemoveDate`) starting from the character at position N (1). The `datetime_time` function, `datetime_time(ITEM)`, returns the time value of a given item (the newly extracted information based on the substring function).

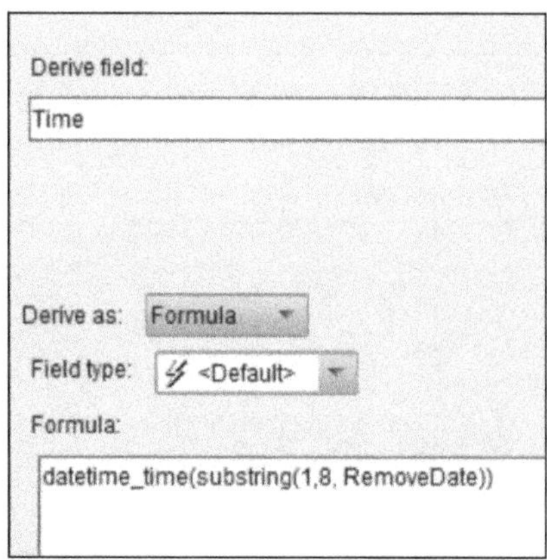

You can see that we correctly extracted the actual call time.

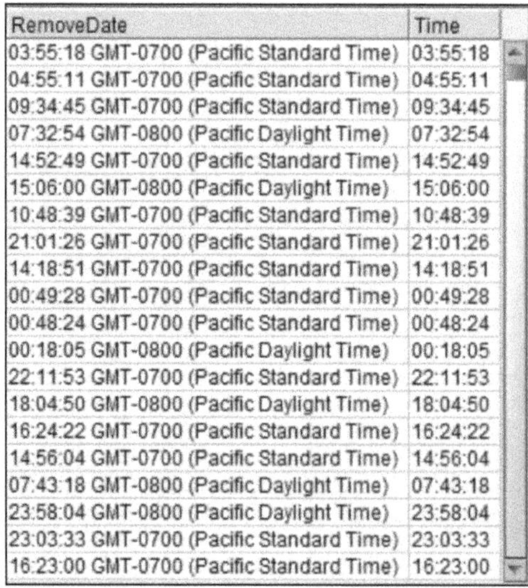

RemoveDate	Time
03:55:18 GMT-0700 (Pacific Standard Time)	03:55:18
04:55:11 GMT-0700 (Pacific Standard Time)	04:55:11
09:34:45 GMT-0700 (Pacific Standard Time)	09:34:45
07:32:54 GMT-0800 (Pacific Daylight Time)	07:32:54
14:52:49 GMT-0700 (Pacific Standard Time)	14:52:49
15:06:00 GMT-0800 (Pacific Daylight Time)	15:06:00
10:48:39 GMT-0700 (Pacific Standard Time)	10:48:39
21:01:26 GMT-0700 (Pacific Standard Time)	21:01:26
14:18:51 GMT-0700 (Pacific Standard Time)	14:18:51
00:49:28 GMT-0700 (Pacific Standard Time)	00:49:28
00:48:24 GMT-0700 (Pacific Standard Time)	00:48:24
00:18:05 GMT-0800 (Pacific Daylight Time)	00:18:05
22:11:53 GMT-0700 (Pacific Standard Time)	22:11:53
18:04:50 GMT-0800 (Pacific Daylight Time)	18:04:50
16:24:22 GMT-0700 (Pacific Standard Time)	16:24:22
14:56:04 GMT-0700 (Pacific Standard Time)	14:56:04
07:43:18 GMT-0800 (Pacific Daylight Time)	07:43:18
23:58:04 GMT-0800 (Pacific Daylight Time)	23:58:04
23:03:33 GMT-0700 (Pacific Standard Time)	23:03:33
16:23:00 GMT-0700 (Pacific Standard Time)	16:23:00

Now that we have parsed a timestamp variable, we need to perform date arithmetic. The first thing we need to do is identify which callers were on daylight saving time versus those that were on standard time.

13. Connect a Derive node to the `Time` Derive node.
14. Edit the Derive node and name it `Find`.
15. In the formula box specify the following expression, `locchar (`(`, 1, RemoveDate)`. The `locchar` function will now search, starting at position 1, for the open parenthesis in the field `RemoveDate`, and return with the position of where the open parenthesis was found.

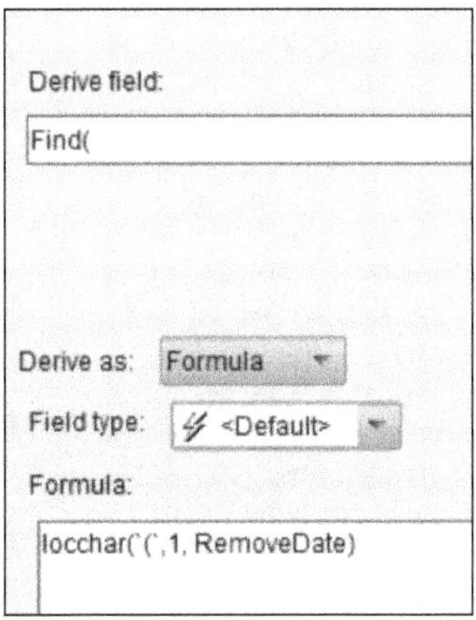

Now that we have identified the location of the open parenthesis, we can extract the time zone information.

16. Connect a new Derive node to the `Find` Derive node.
17. Edit the Derive node and name it `TimeZone`.
18. In the formula box specify the following expression, `allbutfirst ("Find(", RemoveDate)`. The `allbutfirst` function will now remove the first `Find` (characters from the field `RemoveDate` and return the remainder, that is, the time zone.

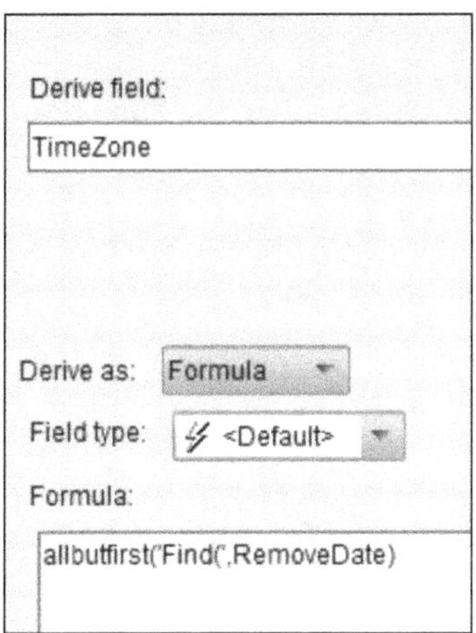

You can see that we correctly extracted the time zone.

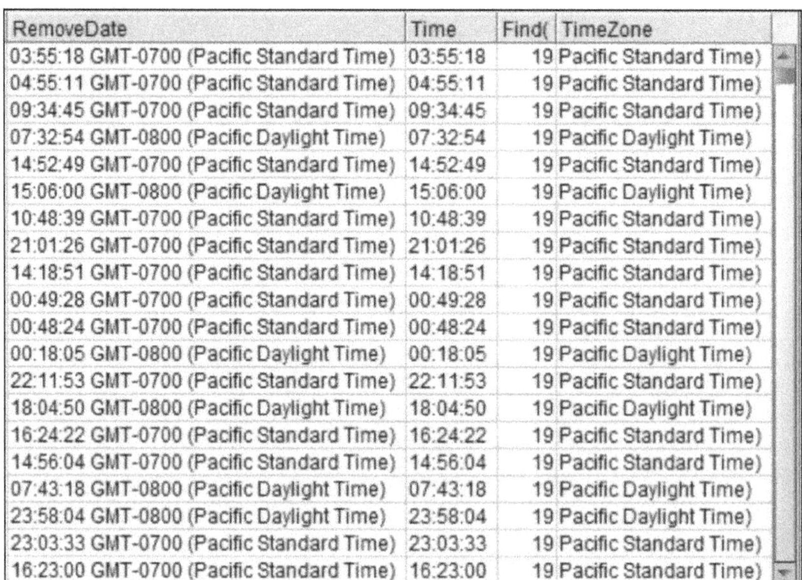

RemoveDate	Time	Find(	TimeZone
03:55:18 GMT-0700 (Pacific Standard Time)	03:55:18	19	Pacific Standard Time)
04:55:11 GMT-0700 (Pacific Standard Time)	04:55:11	19	Pacific Standard Time)
09:34:45 GMT-0700 (Pacific Standard Time)	09:34:45	19	Pacific Standard Time)
07:32:54 GMT-0800 (Pacific Daylight Time)	07:32:54	19	Pacific Daylight Time)
14:52:49 GMT-0700 (Pacific Standard Time)	14:52:49	19	Pacific Standard Time)
15:06:00 GMT-0800 (Pacific Daylight Time)	15:06:00	19	Pacific Daylight Time)
10:48:39 GMT-0700 (Pacific Standard Time)	10:48:39	19	Pacific Standard Time)
21:01:26 GMT-0700 (Pacific Standard Time)	21:01:26	19	Pacific Standard Time)
14:18:51 GMT-0700 (Pacific Standard Time)	14:18:51	19	Pacific Standard Time)
00:49:28 GMT-0700 (Pacific Standard Time)	00:49:28	19	Pacific Standard Time)
00:48:24 GMT-0700 (Pacific Standard Time)	00:48:24	19	Pacific Standard Time)
00:18:05 GMT-0800 (Pacific Daylight Time)	00:18:05	19	Pacific Daylight Time)
22:11:53 GMT-0700 (Pacific Standard Time)	22:11:53	19	Pacific Standard Time)
18:04:50 GMT-0800 (Pacific Daylight Time)	18:04:50	19	Pacific Daylight Time)
16:24:22 GMT-0700 (Pacific Standard Time)	16:24:22	19	Pacific Standard Time)
14:56:04 GMT-0700 (Pacific Standard Time)	14:56:04	19	Pacific Standard Time)
07:43:18 GMT-0800 (Pacific Daylight Time)	07:43:18	19	Pacific Daylight Time)
23:58:04 GMT-0800 (Pacific Daylight Time)	23:58:04	19	Pacific Daylight Time)
23:03:33 GMT-0700 (Pacific Standard Time)	23:03:33	19	Pacific Standard Time)
16:23:00 GMT-0700 (Pacific Standard Time)	16:23:00	19	Pacific Standard Time)

Now we have to instantiate the data so that it is read correctly by Modeler.

1. Connect a new Type node to the `TimeZone` Derive node.
2. Edit the Type node and click on the **Read Values** button. Now that the data has been instantiated, we are ready to perform date arithmetic.
3. Connect a new Derive node to the Type node.
4. Edit the Derive node and name it `Time Corrected`.
5. Change the **Derive As** drop-down menu from **Formula** to `Conditional`.
6. In the **If** box specify the following expression, `TimeZone = "Pacific Standard Time)"`. This is saying that if on the field `TimeZone` you have a value of Pacific Standard Time, then the expression in the **Then** box applies; or else if you have any other value on the field `TimeZone`, then the expression in the **Else** box applies.

7. In the **Then** box specify the following expression, `datetime_time(datetime_in_seconds(Time) + 1 * 60 * 60)`. In this case, this means that for those people that are on Pacific Standard Time we have to add one hour to their actual call time on the time field. The `datetime_in_seconds` function, `datetime_in_seconds(DATETIME)`, returns the value in seconds of a `DATETIME` field (`Time`). Here we want to add one hour to those people that were on Pacific Standard Time, so we need to add (1) to increase the actual call time hour by one hour; we need to add (60) to have no effect on the actual call time minutes, because adding 60 minutes to :05 for example still gives us :05—this is just affecting minutes and nothing else. We need to add (60) to have no effect on the actual call time seconds, because adding sixty seconds to :05 for example still gives us :05—this is just affecting seconds and nothing else. The datetime_time function just returns the time value of the newly calculated information.
8. In the **Else** box specify the following expression, **Time**. In this case this means that those people that are on Pacific Daylight Time just keep their value on the time field.

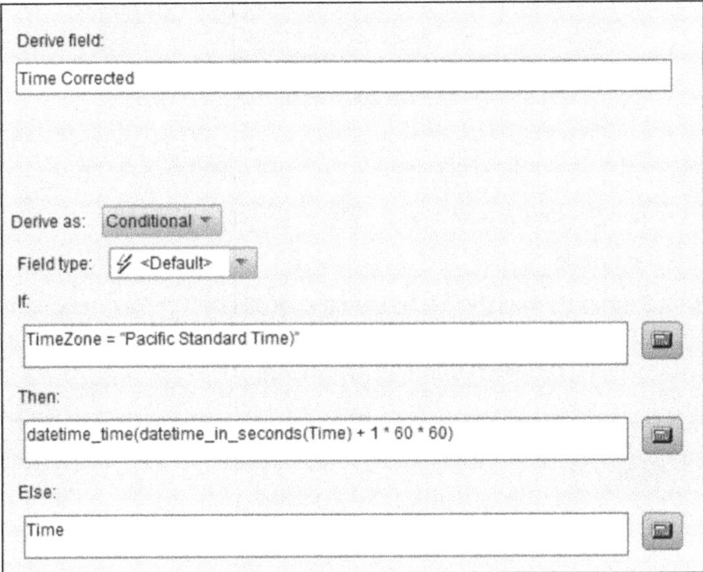

You can see that we correctly performed the date arithmetic.

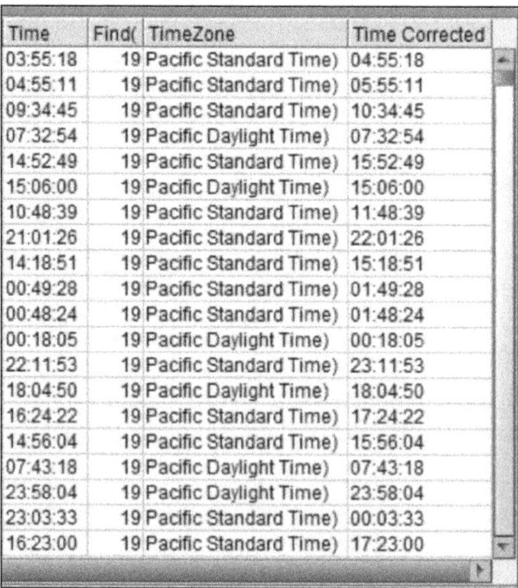

Time	Find(	TimeZone	Time Corrected
03:55:18	19	Pacific Standard Time)	04:55:18
04:55:11	19	Pacific Standard Time)	05:55:11
09:34:45	19	Pacific Standard Time)	10:34:45
07:32:54	19	Pacific Daylight Time)	07:32:54
14:52:49	19	Pacific Standard Time)	15:52:49
15:06:00	19	Pacific Daylight Time)	15:06:00
10:48:39	19	Pacific Standard Time)	11:48:39
21:01:26	19	Pacific Standard Time)	22:01:26
14:18:51	19	Pacific Standard Time)	15:18:51
00:49:28	19	Pacific Standard Time)	01:49:28
00:48:24	19	Pacific Standard Time)	01:48:24
00:18:05	19	Pacific Daylight Time)	00:18:05
22:11:53	19	Pacific Standard Time)	23:11:53
18:04:50	19	Pacific Daylight Time)	18:04:50
16:24:22	19	Pacific Standard Time)	17:24:22
14:56:04	19	Pacific Standard Time)	15:56:04
07:43:18	19	Pacific Daylight Time)	07:43:18
23:58:04	19	Pacific Daylight Time)	23:58:04
23:03:33	19	Pacific Standard Time)	00:03:33
16:23:00	19	Pacific Standard Time)	17:23:00

Finally we can select the calls that occurred between midnight and 8 AM.

1. Connect a new Select node to the Time Corrected Derive node.
2. Edit the Select node.
3. In the **Condition** box specify the following expression, `'Time Corrected' > "00:00:00" and 'Time Corrected' < "08:00:00"`. This is selecting those calls that occurred between midnight and 8 AM.

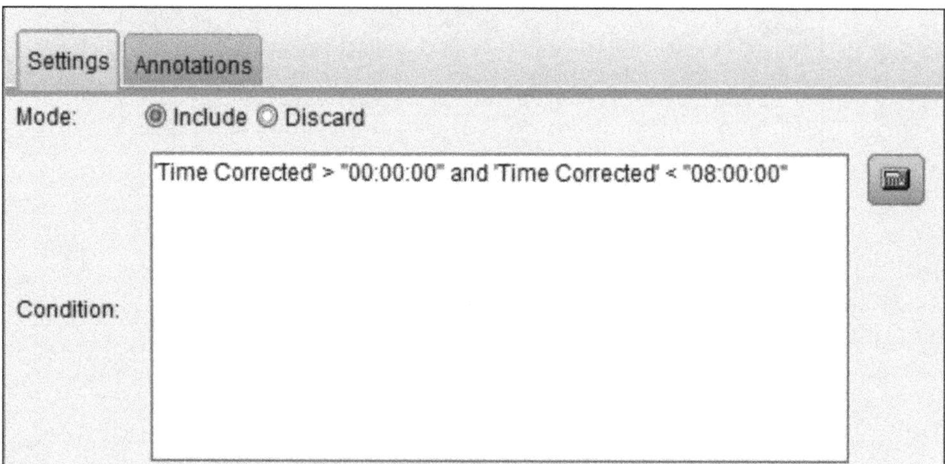

Running a Table node indicates that 3293 calls occurred during the hours of interest. Now the managers at the call center can staff the call center appropriately given the call volume during these hours.

How it works...

This recipe had two goals:

1. To show how to parse a field where we did not have a constant string length.
2. To show how to perform date arithmetic.

Regarding the first goal, the real trick in parsing any field that does not have a constant string length is to identify a character of interest and then use the `locchar` function to identify the number of characters needed to reach the character of interest. Once this is done, and in some instances you may have to do this several times, there are many functions that can allow you to obtain the information you need.

Regarding the second goal, the key to performing date arithmetic in Modeler is to remember that, when you want to add or subtract a constant, you need to transform the field and the constant into seconds using the `datetime_in_seconds` function. There are a lot of other functions that can be used to perform arithmetic with dates, for example, calculating the time between two dates, but in our experience adding or subtracting a constant can prove to be tricky in Modeler.

See also

- The *Parsing nonstandard dates* recipe in this chapter

Sequence processing

Many applications require the discovery of patterns in data representing a sequence of events; examples include quality control and fault diagnosis and prevention in industrial and mechanical processes. Data in these applications typically takes the form of logs; that is time-stamped sets of measurements that form a sequence. The measurements may be very simple, even a single variable, but the patterns are found in how these measurements vary over time. Modeler includes a variety of features for processing sequential data of this sort. This recipe illustrates some of these sequence processing operations and how they are used to build up a set of variables describing the changes in measurement over time.

Getting ready

This recipe requires no datafile because the example data is generated by a user input source node and other operations inside a source supernode. The stream file required is `Sequence_Processing.str`.

How to do it...

1. Open the stream file (`Sequence_Processing.str`) by navigating to **File** | **Open Stream**.
2. Run the Table node, `Log data`; this displays the raw log data that will be used to demonstrate sequence processing, shown in the following screenshot. The log data contains a series of 100 logs, identified by the field **LogID**, each with up to 100 entries identified by the field **LogEntry**. The field **Timestamp** shows seconds from the start of the log, and the field **Temp** contains a temperature measurement.

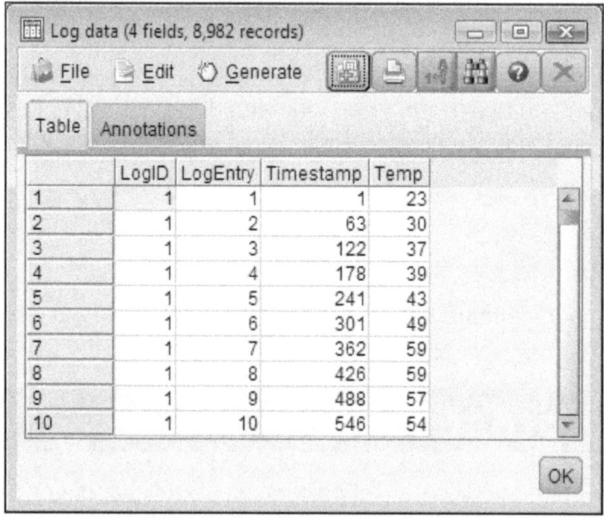

	LogID	LogEntry	Timestamp	Temp
1	1	1	1	23
2	1	2	63	30
3	1	3	122	37
4	1	4	178	39
5	1	5	241	43
6	1	6	301	49
7	1	7	362	59
8	1	8	426	59
9	1	9	488	57
10	1	10	546	54

Note that this output (and subsequent outputs in this recipe) will not be exactly the same when you run the stream; although always in the same form, the data is synthesized by the supernode, and therefore will be different in detail each time the stream is used. The data is cached so that further results in the same session will remain consistent.

3. Run the Table node, `Log sizes`; this displays the number of entries in each log, shown in the following screenshot.

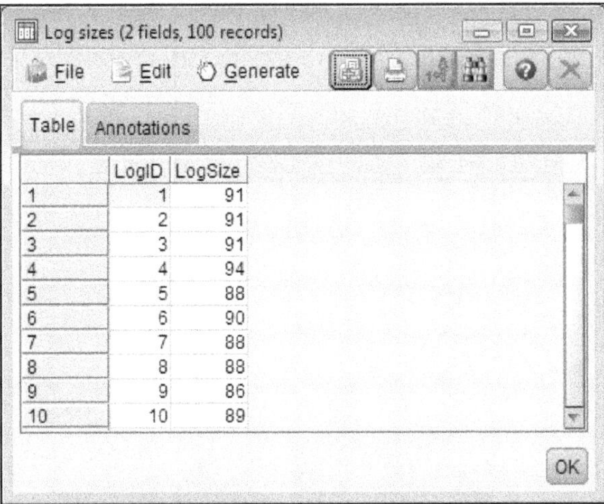

	LogID	LogSize
1	1	91
2	2	91
3	3	91
4	4	94
5	5	88
6	6	90
7	7	88
8	8	88
9	9	86
10	10	89

4. Edit the Derive node, `TempAcc`. In this example we wish to monitor the temperature acceleration, that is, the rate at which the temperature changes. This will be zero at the beginning of a log (because there has been no change) and each subsequent log entry will calculate this as the change in temperature since the last log entry divided by time since the last log entry.

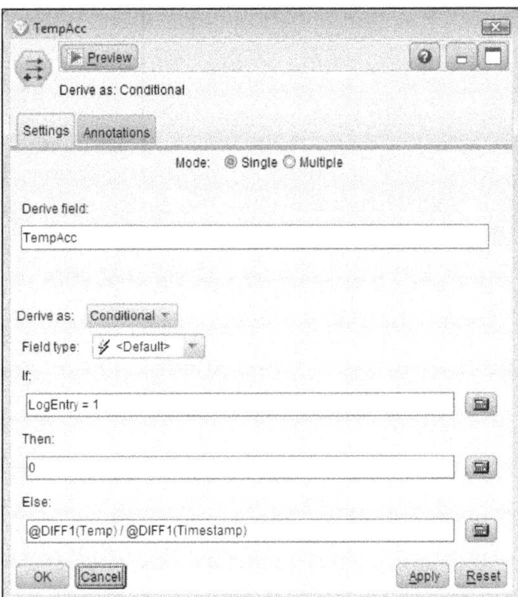

Modeler provides a built-in sequence function for calculating change in a sequence of records. The expression @DIFF1(Temp) gives the difference between Temp in the current record and Temp in the previous record, and @DIFF1(Timestamp) does the same for Timestamp. The ratio of these is the rate of change in temperature.

5. Run the Histogram node, `TempAcc`; this displays a graph of the temperature acceleration calculated in step 4, which ranges from just below -0.1 to just over 0.2.

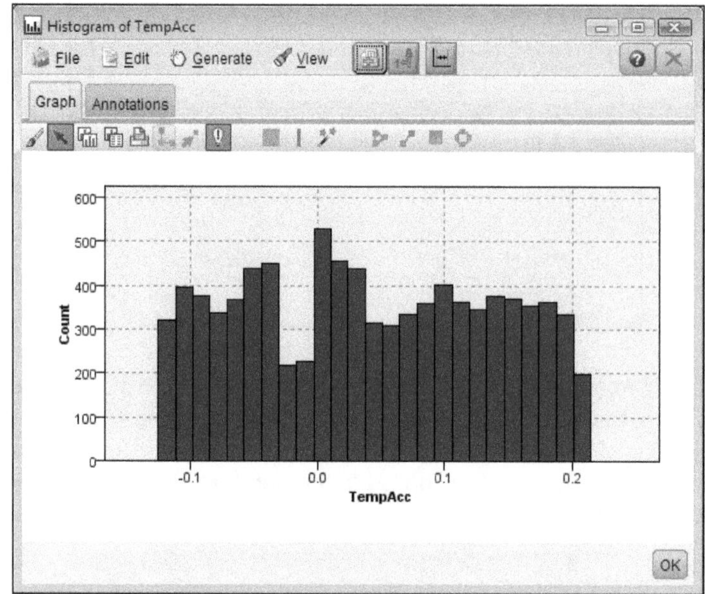

In this example, the temperatures relate to a measurement taken from a piece of equipment during a process, and equipment failure is believed to be related to temperature acceleration. It is rare for temperature acceleration to reach 0.2, but the risk of failure is high when it does; the risk becomes low again after acceleration drops below 0.15.

6. Edit the Derive node, `TempRisk`.

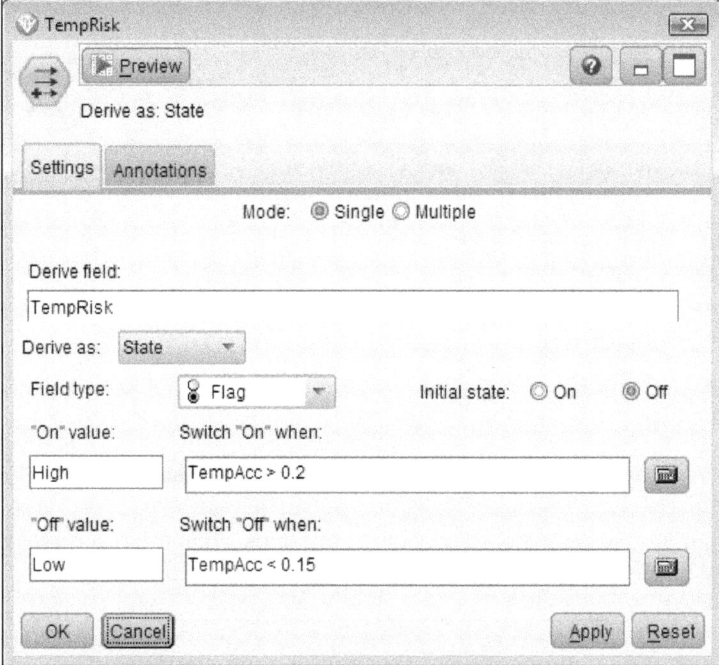

This is a special kind of Derive node called a Derive State; it creates a state variable, a flag in sequential data whose value remains the same unless changed by specific conditions. This kind of Derive node allows us to model a state variable whose value depends on the previous state as well as the details of the current record.

The new state variable `TempRisk` begins with the off value `Low`, meaning low risk, switches to the on value `High` if `TempAcc` exceeds `0.2`, and switches back to `Low` when `TempAcc` drops below `0.15`.

7. Run the Table node, `Log Risk Counts`. This displays the number of low-risk and high-risk entries for each log. Most, but not all, logs have at least one high-risk entry.

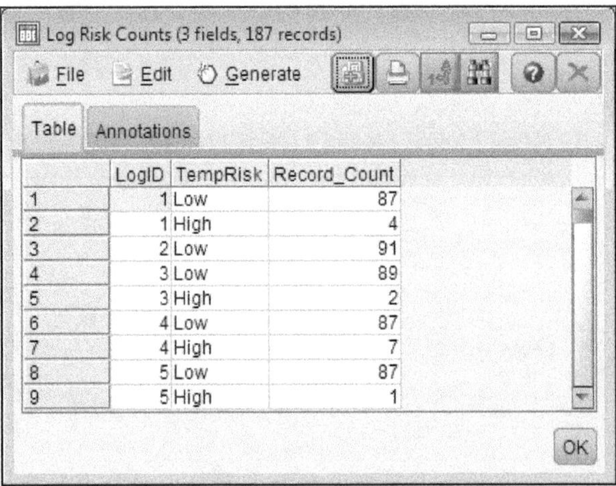

	LogID	TempRisk	Record_Count
1	1	Low	87
2	1	High	4
3	2	Low	91
4	3	Low	89
5	3	High	2
6	4	Low	87
7	4	High	7
8	5	Low	87
9	5	High	1

8. A further area to be explored concerns occasions when the risk remains high over several consecutive log entries. Edit the Derive node, `CountHigh`.

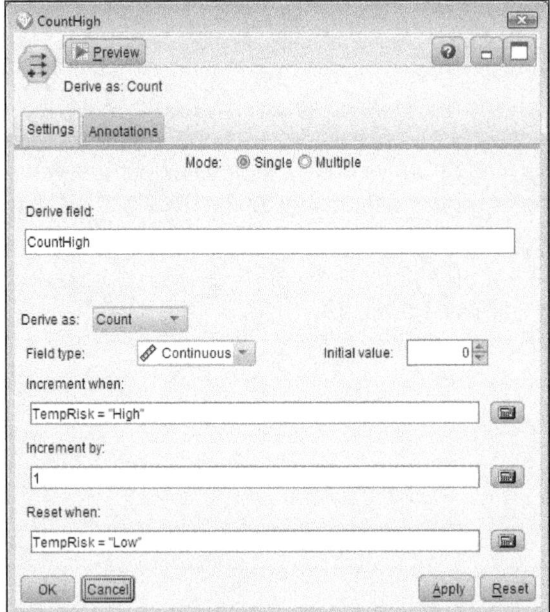

This is a special kind of Derive node called a Derive Count; it implements a counter to indicate how many times a specific condition has been true, with a specified initial value, increment amount, and reset condition.

The new counter `CountHigh` counts the number of consecutive times that the temperature acceleration risk has been high.

9. Run the Table node `N counts high`; this displays the number of instances for each level of the consecutive high-risk counter.

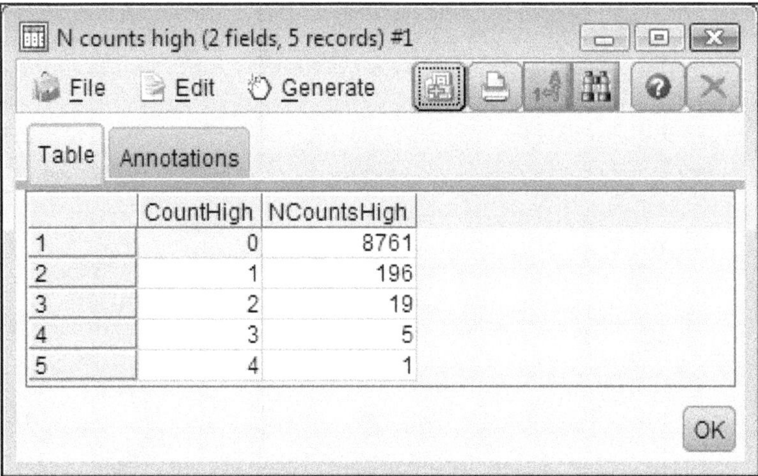

	CountHigh	NCountsHigh
1	0	8761
2	1	196
3	2	19
4	3	5
5	4	1

In this example, the highest level is 4 consecutive high-risk log entries, which only occurs once. (It is possible for the stream to show higher levels than this; see the note on step 2.)

10. Edit the Derive node, `MaxTimeHigh`. This explores the amount of time spent in a high-risk state rather than the number of log entries. Because it is unknown exactly when a high-risk state began, what is calculated is not the time spent at high risk, but the maximum time that could have been spent.

This node calculates the difference between timestamps from the current record and a previous record. This is not necessarily the immediately previous record; rather it is the last record in which the risk was low. Two of Modeler's sequence functions are used: @SINCE, which returns the offset from the current record of the last record where a condition was true, and @OFFSET, which returns the value of a variable at a given offset from the current record. These two functions are often used together to access a targeted piece of data from previous records in a sequence.

The expression `@OFFSET(Timestamp,@SINCE(TempRisk="Low"))` returns the timestamp from the most recent record with a low temperature acceleration risk.

11. Run the Plot node, `CountHigh v. MaxTimeHigh`. This displays a scatter-plot of the number of consecutive entries at high risk against the time spent at high risk.

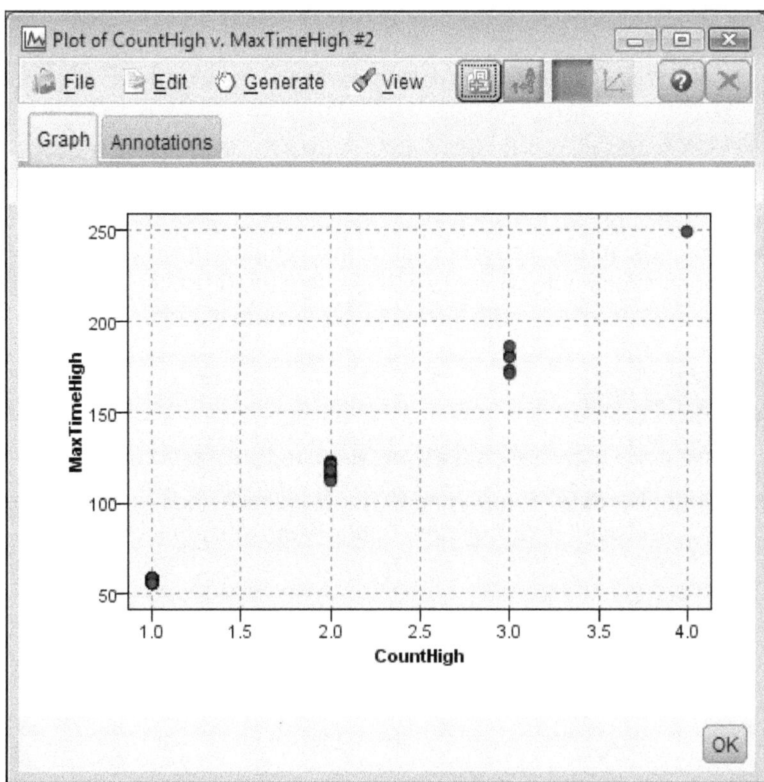

This shows a property that is the consequence of log entries having irregular timing–the greater the number of high-risk log entries, the wider the spread of possible times spent at high risk.

How it works...

This recipe illustrates a typical sequence of data preparation steps for sequential data. In certain kinds of applications, rather than simple trends over time, we are interested in rates of change, states, counts, and other descriptions of sequential phenomena. This recipe illustrates 5 specific features in Modeler that are used for this kind of data preparation:

- **Derive State nodes**: These create a variable whose value remains the same over time unless changed by specific conditions
- **Derive Count nodes**: These create a counter that is incremented and resets under specific conditions

- **Sequence function @DIFF1**: It calculates the difference between the current value and the immediately previous value of the same variable
- **Sequence function @OFFSET**: It accesses previous values of a variable
- **Sequence function @SINCE**: It returns the offset from the current record when a specific condition was true and is often used to identify a target record for @OFFSET

There's more...

Modeler contains additional features for sequential processing not shown in this recipe; these include the History node, further sequence functions including moving averages, maxima and minima, additional functions similar to @DIFF1, and the @THIS function sometimes used within @SINCE. All are described in the Modeler user documentation.

See also

- The *Shuffle-down (non-standard aggregation)* recipe in this chapter
- The *Reformatting data for reporting with a Transpose node* recipe in *Chapter 7, Modeling – Assessment, Evaluation, Deployment, and Monitoring*

6

Selecting and Building a Model

In this chapter, we will cover:

- Evaluating balancing with Auto Classifier
- Building models with and without outliers
- Using Neural Network for Feature Selection
- Creating a bootstrap sample
- Creating bagged logistic regression models
- Using KNN to match similar cases
- Using Auto Classifier to tune models
- Next-Best-Offer for large data sets

Introduction

Given the obvious importance of Modeling, why only one Chapter? Certainly, one could easily write 1000 pages on the various algorithms and the proof is in the large number of books that have done just that. The goal of this Cookbook, however, is to direct the reader to areas that they might otherwise spend too little time on, or to suggest approaches that are non-obvious.

There is much about the many algorithms that is non-obvious. They demand study. Thankfully, they also reward that study but in ways that can be frustrating to the intermediate-level data miner. It is often said, and can actually be shown, that detailed study of a handful of algorithms might be superior than spreading one's professional development time across all of them. It is worth noting that those that have the time and attention to learn R, which would also reward study, could learn hundreds of classifiers, and many hundreds of algorithms. The problem is that while mastering algorithms comes slowly, one lesson comes quickly; it is not about algorithms. Certainly, the career data miner needs to learn many algorithms, and Modeler's workbench style rewards the career data miner with lots of room to grow. Between the beginning and mastery, however, this process takes years. The big gains in a model's effectiveness come primarily from good data preparation, followed secondarily by carefully applying the right technique, and followed finally by tuning.

CRISP-DM describes this chapter's topic in the following way:

Modeling

"In this phase, various modeling techniques are selected and applied, and their parameters are calibrated to optimal values. Typically, there are several techniques for the same data mining problem type. Some techniques have specific requirements on the form of data. Therefore, stepping back to the data preparation phase is often needed."

- Selecting a modeling technique
- Testing
- Building a model

We begin the chapter focusing on the selection aspect, finalizing issues of whether to balance and whether to include extreme cases. Hopefully, this process began in the very beginning, but it is at this phase that one must commit to a model, or more likely try two or three variations' and let the data itself steer the way. We continue with the critical issue of data reduction. This is a potentially huge topic, deserving of an entire short course. Here, as always, we focus on the unusual and the non-obvious. We move on to topics related to a particular kind of ensembles made of multiple subsets of our data. Two recipes cover bootstrap samples and custom bagged models. Also, in one of the shorter recipes we show an easy-to-use application of KNN to not classify, but merely measure distances. Finally, we discover two ways of saving time. One recipe for saving our time, *Using auto classifier to tune models*, and one for saving our processor's time, *Next-best-offer for large data sets*.

Evaluating balancing with Auto Classifier

Two traps to avoid in data mining are that one should always balance, or that there is only one way to balance. Like most questions asked during a data mining project, the question of whether to balance or not should be answered empirically. The purpose of this recipe is to show how three common kinds of balancing can be compared easily using the Auto Classifier node. This is not to suggest that the resulting models are final models. Rather, this is an early test that can be conducted to evaluate whether or not to balance. One of the kinds of balancing suggested here is to not balance at all. Another suggestion is to double the numbers in a fully reduced balance node.

Getting ready

We will start with the `Choose Balance.str` stream.

How to do it...

To show how three common kinds of balancing can be compared easily using the Auto Classifier Node:

1. Open the starting stream.

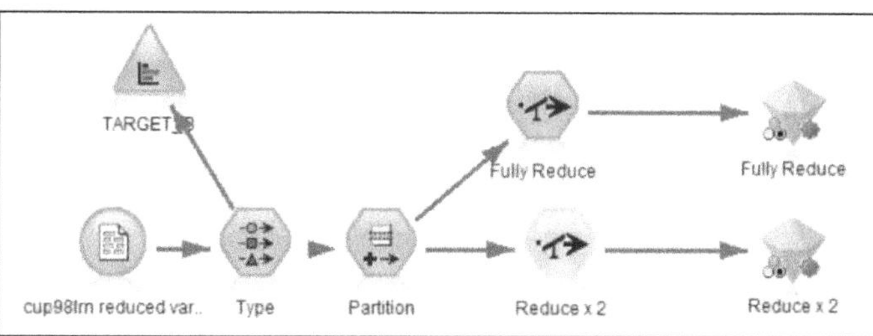

2. Edit the Balance node labeled `Fully Reduce`. This node was automatically generated by Distribution node on the stream.

Factor	Condition
0.0535	TARGET_B = 0
1.0	TARGET_B = 1

3. Edit the second Balance node. Note that this node, which was created manually, has had the numbers doubled. In effect, the donors have been slightly boosted.

Factor	Condition
0.107	TARGET_B = 0
2.0	TARGET_B = 1

4. Add an Auto Classifier node directly to the Partition node and run. Note that two existing generated models are already on the stream. The new one is the third.
5. Copy the two previous generated models and place all three in a row downstream of the Partition node and connected to an Analysis node.

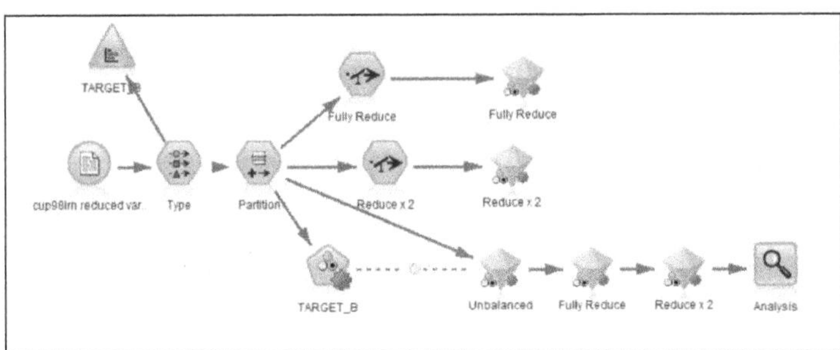

6. Run the Analysis node.

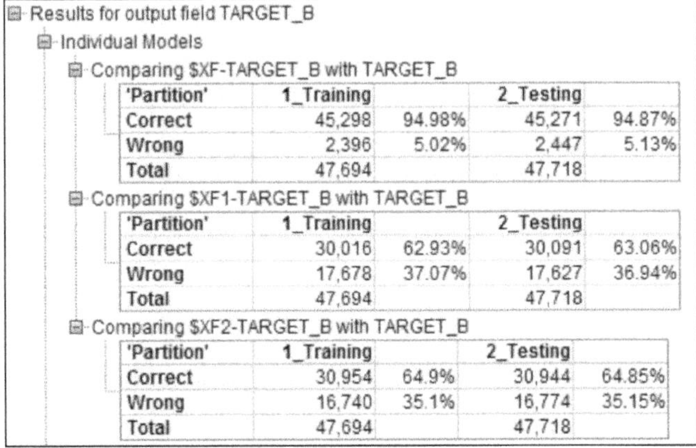

Results for output field TARGET_B

Individual Models

Comparing $XF-TARGET_B with TARGET_B

'Partition'	1_Training		2_Testing	
Correct	45,298	94.98%	45,271	94.87%
Wrong	2,396	5.02%	2,447	5.13%
Total	47,694		47,718	

Comparing $XF1-TARGET_B with TARGET_B

'Partition'	1_Training		2_Testing	
Correct	30,016	62.93%	30,091	63.06%
Wrong	17,678	37.07%	17,627	36.94%
Total	47,694		47,718	

Comparing $XF2-TARGET_B with TARGET_B

'Partition'	1_Training		2_Testing	
Correct	30,954	64.9%	30,944	64.85%
Wrong	16,740	35.1%	16,774	35.15%
Total	47,694		47,718	

How it works...

The basic idea of this recipe is simple: if you are not sure whether or not to balance then try both. The fully-reduced Balance node was made with the Generate feature of the Distribution node.

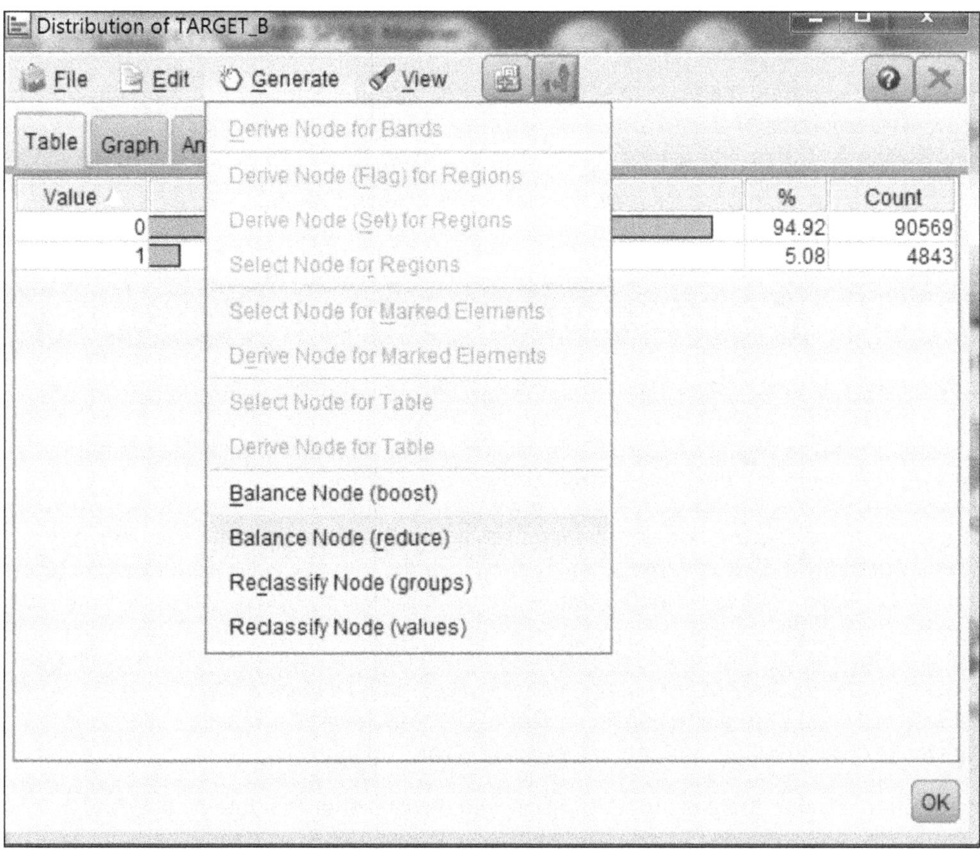

As we've seen, the second Balance node used a straightforward trick, double the numbers from the first node. This can be helpful because fully reducing discards a lot of cases. However, fully boosting, or making copies of rare cases, can be problematic. In this data set, each donor would be copied 20 times on average, some more and some less. The doubling trick is simply a compromise. It discards less data, leaving a bigger sample size, while only boosting a small amount. Finally, we try doing no balancing at all. It would be extremely useful to compare and contrast balancing to the approach in another recipe, *Correcting a confusion matrix for an imbalanced target variable by incorporating priors* recipe in *Chapter 7, Modeling – Assessment, Evaluation, Deployment, and Monitoring*.In that recipe an alternative is offered to balancing.

What do we learn from the Analysis node? As is common in these situations, the first model's 95 percent accuracy reveals that everyone has been predicted to be a non-donor. This will not be useful, so it is out of the running. Of the two other choices, the doubling trick seems to be a bit better. The data miner might then proceed to build a variety of models downstream to this Balance node to confirm their choice.

See also

- The *Evaluating the need to sample from the initial data* recipe in *Chapter 1, Data Understanding*
- The *Correcting a confusion matrix for an imbalanced target variable by incorporating priors* recipe in *Chapter 7, Modeling – Assessment, Evaluation, Deployment, and Monitoring*

Building models with and without outliers

The Anomaly Modeling node can automatically identify and remove outliers. Why not always remove outliers? Even when the data is examined closely, it can be difficult to decide whether any cases should be regarded as outliers and, if so, which. Even when the data miner feels confident about this, the internal or external client may not agree.

Some types of analysis are not affected much by outliers, for example, the calculation of a median. But many widely used modeling methods can be strongly influenced by the presence of outliers. A linear regression model can be shifted significantly by a single outlier in the data.

What are the risks? A model that is affected by an outlier may frequently predict values that are too high, or too low. The level of uncertainty in estimated values will be increased. When the predicted values are plotted against actual outcomes, viewers will likely sense that the graph looks or feels wrong, and the model does not fit.

That is not to say that there is anything wrong with the outlier or the data as a whole. On the contrary, this is a limitation of most modeling techniques: they don't handle unusual cases very well. A more common approach is to focus on the bulk of the data and simply remove the outlier before analysis. Deleting outliers before building models is very common, and the resulting models fit the data better for most cases. But this approach has its drawbacks.

Remember that the outlier is a legitimate data point. There is no universal agreement that removing outliers is an appropriate way to deal with modeling challenges, let alone on which cases should be viewed as outliers. Data miners, on the whole, are not sticklers on such issues. Like most decisions in data mining, it should be determined empirically, which is the premise of this recipe. In the recipe we will build and model with and without outliers, and then we will score and evaluate the model with and without outliers. At Deployment, the data miner always has the option of screening for outliers before scoring, leaving outliers unscored. The premise is that, by attempting a number of variations, we will attempt four, that a strategy can be determined that is based on the data and the potential accuracy of the resulting models. One must never forget that there may be business reasons to include or exclude outliers, but any choice should begin with a proper evaluation, which this approach provides.

Getting ready

We will start with the `With and Without Outliers.str` stream.

How to do it...

To build and model with and without outliers and then score and evaluate the model with and without outliers:

1. Open the stream.

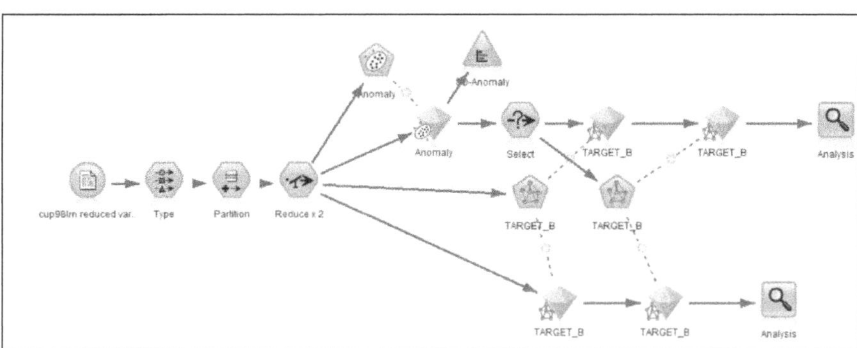

2. Edit the **Anomaly** generated model. The algorithm has identified two clusters.

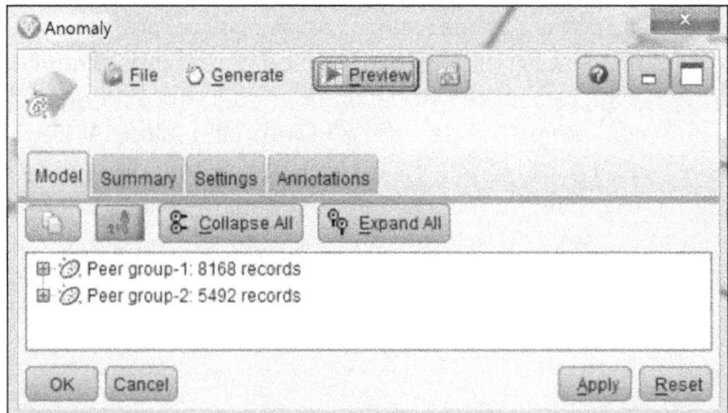

3. Run the Distribution node. Note that 435 cases are potential outliers, about 1 percent of the sample.

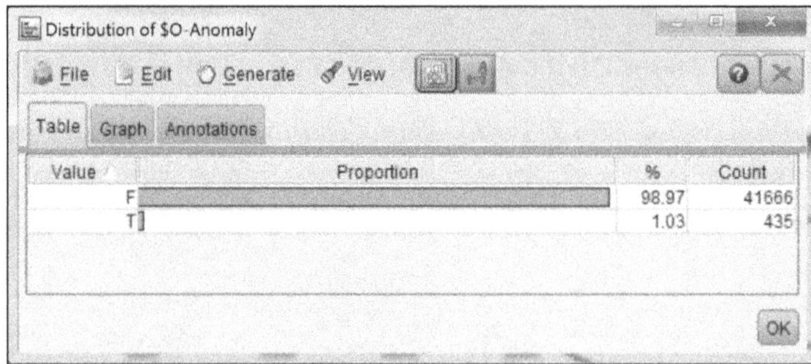

4. The four generated models represent four different outlier handling scenarios:
   - Model built on all data, but scored without outliers
   - Model built without outliers and scored without outliers

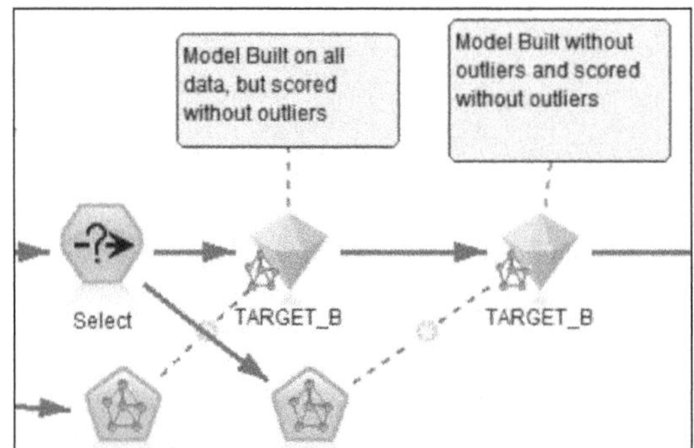

- Built and scored on all data
- Built without outliers, but scored on all data

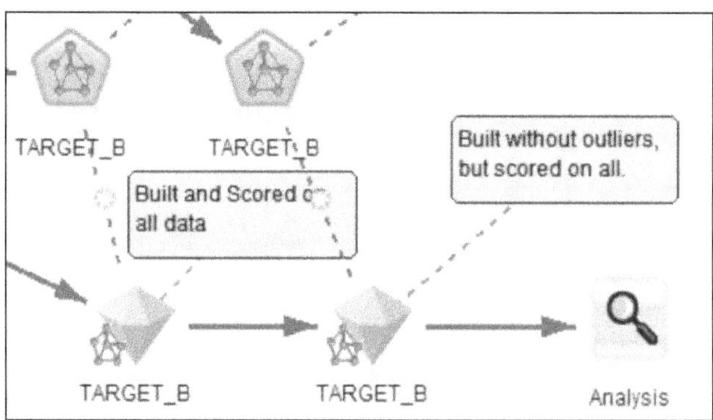

5. Edit the two Analysis nodes. The table below consolidates the four results:

Built On	Scored On	Test Accuracy
All	Without outliers	57.35 percent
Without outliers	Without outliers	60.77 percent
All	All	57.29 percent
Without outliers	All	60.92 percent

How it works...

In this recipe we empirically determine the potential accuracy of four different scenarios. Does that imply that we should always go with the most accurate? In short, we should not. It is certainly intriguing that the Neural Net built without outliers still performed the best while scoring everyone. However, the model built without outliers that did not score outliers was also a good performer in the rankings. (Note that much work would have to be done to improve these models.) Would the model variants that did not score outliers be acceptable to the person or team using the model? If the outliers were not the intended target of a campaign, the answer might be yes. If they were the most interesting customers of the lot, then the answer would certainly be no. This recipe shows Modeler's workbench strength. The results of generated models can be manipulated easily, so experiments such as the one conducted here are the best way to generate evidence to weigh the pros and cons of any model in solving the business problem.

See also

- The *Evaluating the need to sample from the initial data* recipe in *Chapter 1, Data Understanding*
- The *Correcting a confusion matrix for an imbalanced target variable by incorporating priors* recipe in *Chapter 7, Modeling – Assessment, Evaluation, Deployment, and Monitoring*

Using Neural Network for Feature Selection

When building a predictive model, there may be a large number of data fields available for use as inputs to the model. Selecting only those fields most useful to the model has a variety of advantages; it simplifies the model-building process, leading to better and simpler models, and it simplifies the resulting models, leading to more effective insight and easier Deployment.

This Feature Selection can be achieved through a variety of techniques, business and data knowledge can be applied to select the fields likely to be relevant, and univariate techniques can be used to select individual fields that have a relation to the predictive target. It is also a common practice to use other models to help select features whose relevance is more multivariate in nature. Decision trees are often used for this purpose, because building a decision tree model implicitly selects relevant variables; each variable is either used in the model, therefore indicated as relevant, or not used, in which case no relevance is indicated. Decision trees are often used to select the input variables for other models, because of the principle that combining different kinds of modeling techniques produces better models.

This recipe shows Feature Selection by modeling, but the algorithms are used the other way around from that described previously; it shows how to simplify a decision tree model by reducing the number of input variables using a Neural Network for a Feature Selection.

Getting ready

This recipe uses `cup98LRN.txt` data set and `Neural_Network_Feature_Selection.str` stream file.

How to do it...

To do a Neural Network Feature Selection:

1. Open the stream `Neural_Network_Feature_Selection.str` by navigating to **File | Open Stream**.

2. Edit the Type node; you can see the shape of the data by clicking on **Preview** in the edit dialog. The Type node specifies 324 input fields and one target field for modeling. These modeling roles specified by the Type node will be used for all model building in this stream, but in some cases the input variables will be reduced by a Filter node.
3. Run the Distribution node `Target_B`. In the raw data, the target field is mostly zeros, so a Balance node has been used to select a more balanced sample for Modeling (shown in the following screenshot). This step also fills the cache on the Balance node so that the same sample will be used for all the models.

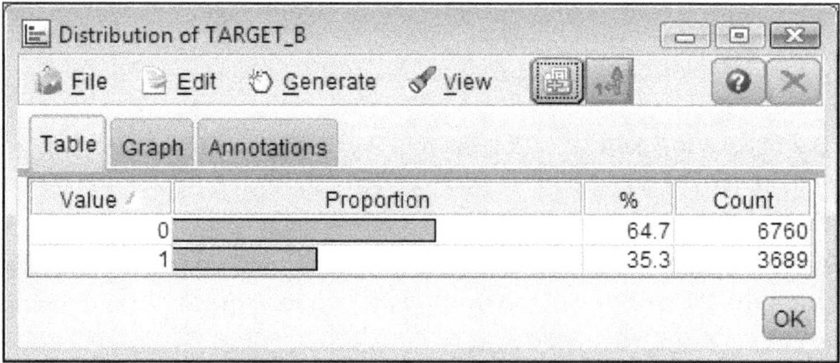

4. Browse the **CHAID** model `TARGET_B` and explore the decision tree. A graphical representation of the decision tree is shown in the following screenshot; the tree is complex:

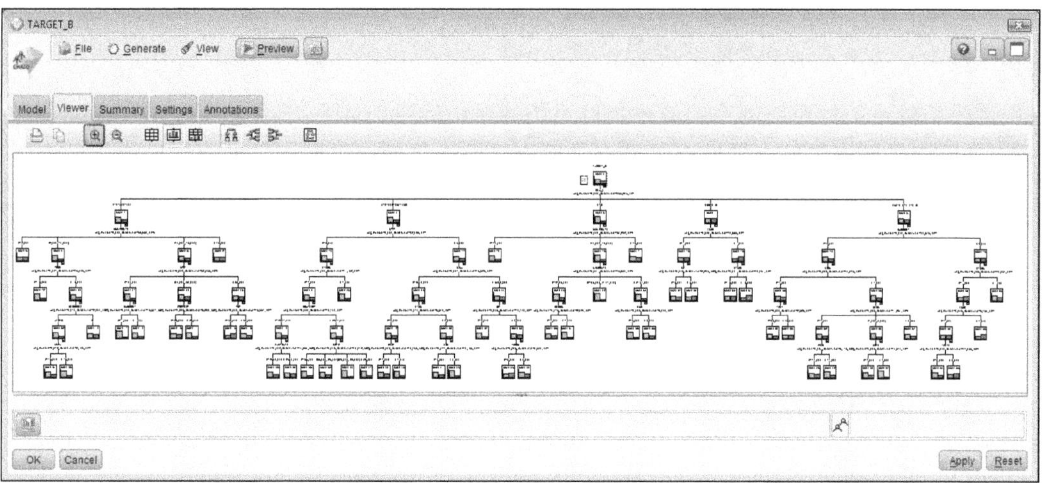

5. Browse the Neural Network model **TARGET_B**; this was built with the same fields as the initial CHAID model. From the **Generate** menu in the browser, select **Field Selection** (predictor importance); the field selection dialog is shown below. The number of fields to be selected has been set to 20 (the default is 10).

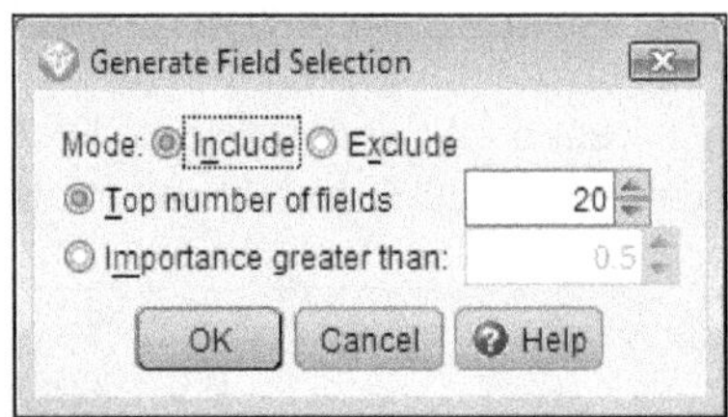

6. Edit the Filter node `TARGET_B`; it selects 21 fields from the initial 325, including the target field. (When using a Filter node generated from a Neural Network model it is necessary to switch on the target field manually.)
7. Browse the **CHAID** model **TARGET_B 2** and explore the decision tree; this model was built from the 21 fields selected by the Filter node. A graphical representation of the decision tree is shown in following screenshot; this tree is much simpler than the one shown in step 4.

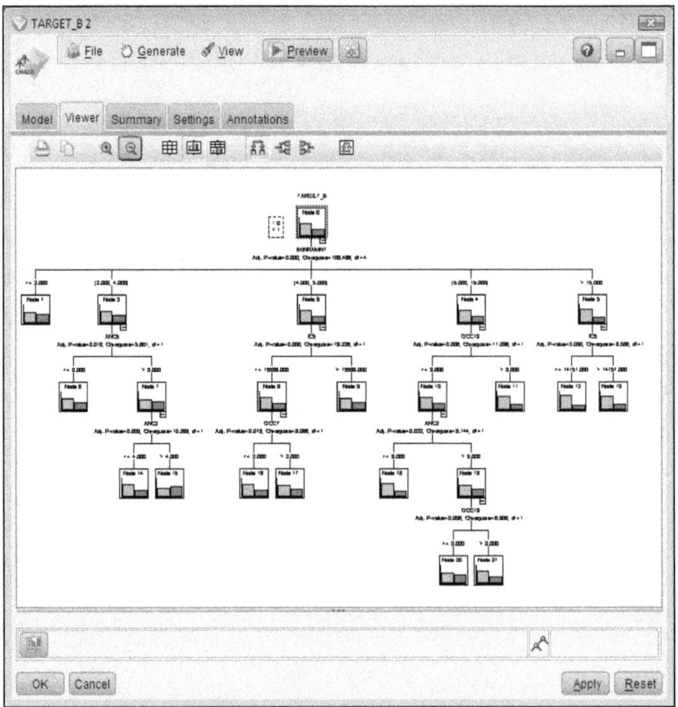

8. Run the Analysis node; each of the three models has a similar predictive accuracy to the others. In particular, the accuracy of the second CHAID model is not significantly lower than that of the first, showing that the Neural Network has done a good job of selecting relevant input variables.

How it works...

Neural Networks have several advantages as predictive models: they are powerful, so that they can find patterns that other algorithms cannot, they do not suffer ill-effects when presented with collinear input variables, and they do not suffer from the masking effects whereby a highly relevant variable eliminates a slightly less relevant variable from the model. All of these qualities make Neural Networks highly suitable for Feature Selection.

Using a Neural Network to simplify a decision tree is also appropriate because the algorithms producing the two models are very different; this means that they are likely to make mistakes in different places, or miss different patterns, so that it is beneficial to use them together.

It is normal that a decision tree built from many variables will use many variables, and will therefore be more complex than one built from fewer variables. Complex models are not always produced when many variables are available; the better the algorithm, the more it will generalize and simplify the model. However, complex decision trees are a common problem, and this recipe provides a straightforward technique to simplify them.

There's more...

Neural Networks are not the only modeling technique that can be used in this way. For example, regression models and support vector machines can also be used to select input variables for another model or algorithm. When a large number of input variables are available, it is recommended that several different Feature Selection techniques be used; sometimes it is useful to combine sets of selected features from several sources.

See also

- The *Using the Feature Selection node creatively to remove or decapitate perfect predictors* recipe in *Chapter 2, Data Preparation - Select*
- The *Selecting variables using the CHAID Modeling node* recipe in *Chapter 2, Data Preparation - Select*

Creating a bootstrap sample

A bootstrap sample is a random sample with replacement, meaning that each record has an equal chance of being selected; after it has been selected, that record has an equal chance of being selected again. Usually, when we select records for training and testing, we sample without replacement, so that each record will appear in only the training or the testing data set.

In this recipe we learn how to build bootstrap samples, a feature not included in Modeler.

Getting ready

This recipe uses the datafile `cup98lrn_reduced_vars3.sav` and the stream `Recipe - bootstrap one sample.str`.

How to do it...

To create a bootstrap sample:

1. Open the stream `Recipe - bootstrap one sample.str` by navigating to **File** | **Open Stream**.
2. Make sure the datafile points to the correct path to the datafile `cup98lrn_reduced_vars3.sav`.
3. Open the Derive node ,`recordID`. The formula for the node is just the @INDEX function that returns an integer number indicating the record number. Click on **OK**.
4. Open the supernode, **find max recID**. The steps are similar to those described in the *Using an empty aggregate to evaluate sample size* recipe in *Chapter 1, Data Understanding*. Close the supernode.
5. Open the supernode, **one bootstrap sample** and note that it contains four nodes. Open the Derive node, `_rnd` and note that it creates a random integer with values less than or equal to the `recordID_Max` created in step 4. Close the node by clicking on **OK**.

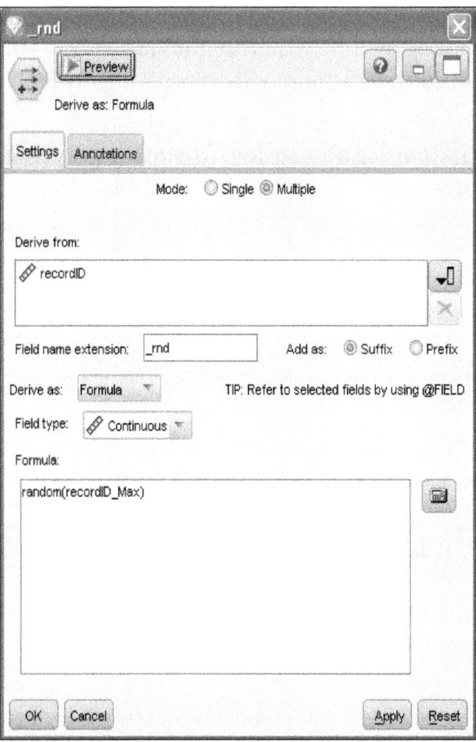

6. Open the Filter node, `rnd names`. Note that the node renames the new variable just created, `recordID_rnd`, to `recordID`, and removes the other fields. Close the node by clicking on **OK** and exit the supernode.

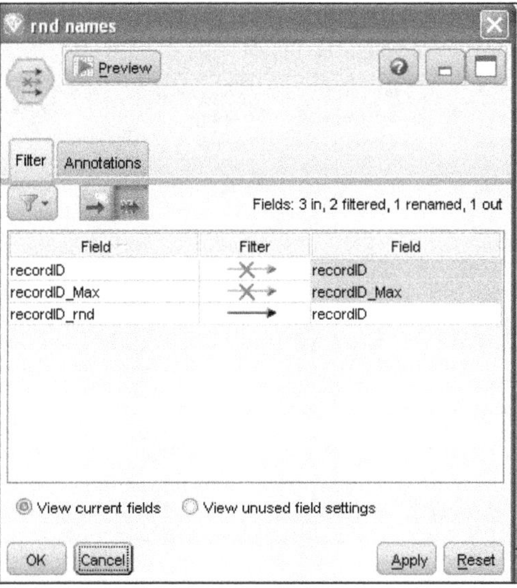

7. Open the Merge node, `Bootstrap Sample`, click on the **Merge** tab and note that the node is performing an inner join (the **Include only matching records** radio button) on key recordID. Close the node by clicking on **OK**.
8. Open the Merge node, `Bootstrap Outofsample`, click on the **Merge** tab, and note that the node is performing an Anti-Join (the **Include records in first dataset not matching any others** radio button) on key recordID.
9. Insert an Append node and place it inline with the Filter node named Training. Connect the Filter node named Training and the Filter node named Testing to the Append node.
10. Open the Append node. Check the checkbox next to **Tag records by including source dataset in feed** and change the text **Input** in the text box to `Partition`. Leave the Append node open.
11. Click on the **Inputs** tab of the Append node and click on the Tag column text box with value 1. If the Connected node value for this entry is `Testing`, change the value of the tab to `2_Testing`. If the Connected node value for this entry is `Training`, change the value to `1_Training`. Now click on the tab column text box with value 2. Replace the text with the label not used already, `1_Training` if the Connected node entry is `Training`, and `2_Testing` if the Connected node value is `Testing`. The Append node input tab should look like the next screenshot. Close the Append node by clicking OK.

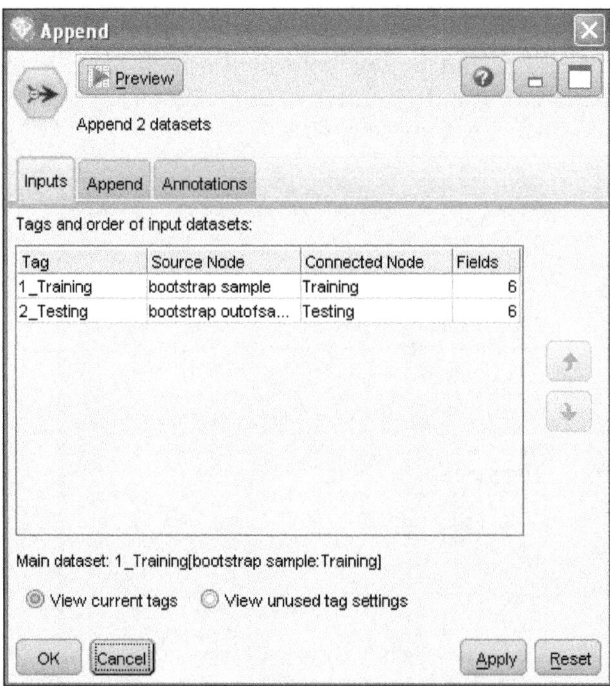

12. Insert a Type node in the stream and connect it to the Append node. Change the `Role` of the field named `Partition` to `Partition` as shown in the following screenshot. Dismiss the Type node by clicking on **OK**.

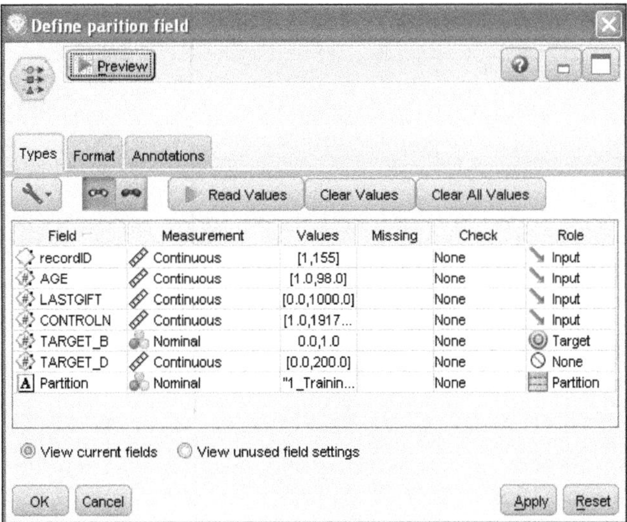

13. Turn caching on for the Type node by right-clicking on it, mouse over the **Cache** option, and select **Enable**. You will see a white piece of paper icon appear at the upper-right of the Type node.

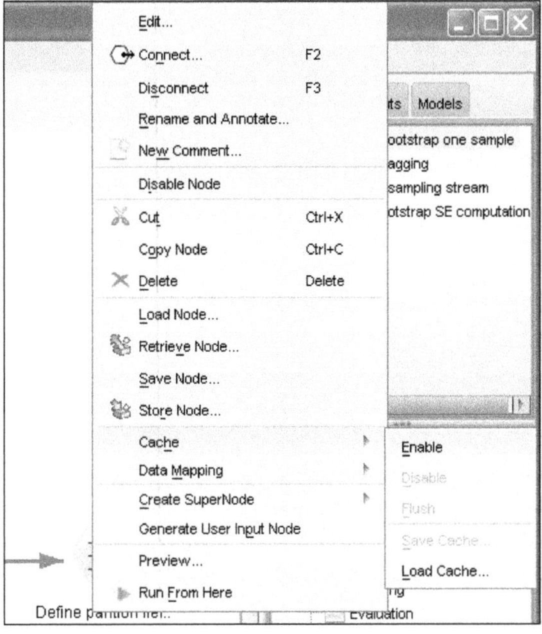

14. Rename the Type node to `Define partition field` by right-clicking on the node and this time selecting the **Rename and Annotate** option. Replace the text **Type** in the text box with `Define partition field`. Dismiss the node by clicking on **OK**.

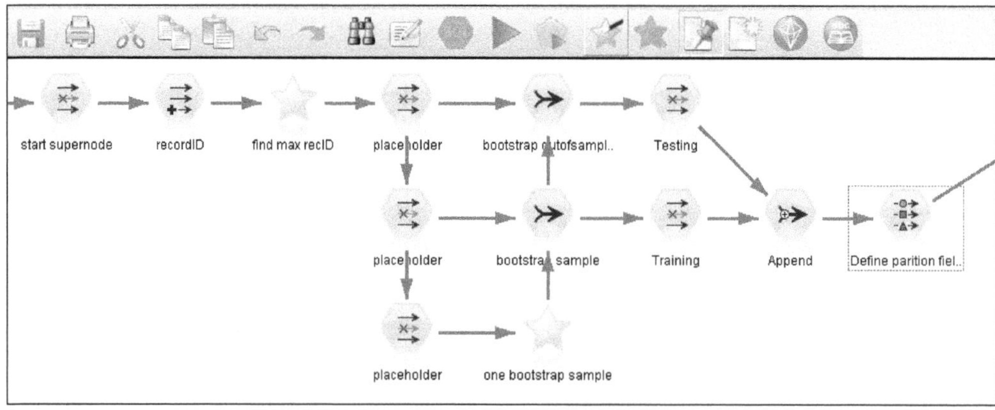

15. Select the Filter node, `start supernode`, hold the *Shift* key and click on the Type node, **Define partition field**. If all the nodes do not highlight, hold the *Ctrl* key and click on the remaining nodes, one at a time, until all the nodes shown in the previous screenshot are highlighted. Click on the toolbar icon with the star. This icon has a tooltip **Encapsulate selected nodes into a supernode**. Now all of the nodes that build the bootstrap sample will be encapsulated into a single supernode. Rename the supernode `Bootstrap Sample`.

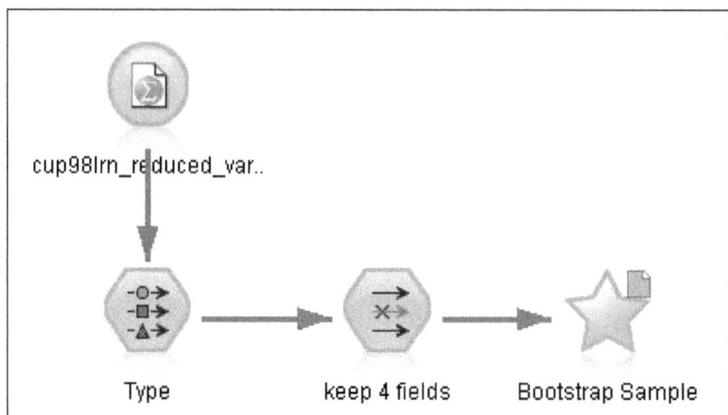

16. Connect a Distribution node and insert it into the stream, connecting it to the supernode. Open the Distribution node and select **Partition** and the field to plot. Click on **Run**. The resulting plot should show 95,412 records for Partition value 1_Training, and approximately 35,000 records for the Partition value 2_Testing. The number of records with the label 2_Testing will vary because of the random selection of records. Close the Distribution node by clicking on **OK**.

How it works...

Usually, a bootstrap sample of a data set is created to have the same size as the original data. In the KDD Cup 1998 LRN set, there are 95,412 records. Therefore, we bootstrap a sample of the data set to this size. Since this is a random sample, some of the random integers will occur more than once and some not at all. In fact, with the standard bootstrap sample, only 63 percent of the records will be included in the sample itself and 37 percent will be omitted. In other words, 37 percent of the random integers will not match a record ID. In a sample of 95,412 records, this means, of course, that many records will end up in the bootstrap sample more than once.

The procedure for bootstrap sampling outlined here uses the built-in uniform random sampling function, `random()`. The implementation of `random()` in Modeler is very well done; you can specify the maximum value of the uniform random sample. Moreover, Modeler creates the random sample of the same type as the variable argument to `random()`, real or integer. Since the variable `recordID_Max` is an integer, `random(recordID_Max)` will create a random integer value with maximum value `recordID_Max`, perfect for sampling with replacement.

The key to creating our bootstrap sample is the join operation created by the Merge node. In step 3, we created a unique, sequential integer for each record. The random integer can be repeated and often will have repeated values in the data. In fact, as shown in the following table, there are 5 records that appear 7 times in this particular bootstrap sample (the actual number of replicates and which records have replicates will vary from sample to sample). Most often, however, a record will appear only once in the bootstrap sample.

The number of replicates in the bootstrap sample is shown:

# Times in Bootstrap Sample	# Records with Count	Count of All Records	Cumulative Record Count	Count of Record Counts_pct	Cumulative Record Count_pct
7	5	95,412	5	0.0%	0.0%
6	34	95,412	39	0.0%	0.0%
5	345	95,412	384	0.4%	0.4%
4	1,460	95,412	1,844	1.5%	1.9%
3	5,804	95,412	7,648	6.1%	8.0%
2	17,603	95,412	25,251	18.4%	26.5%
1	34,990	95,412	60,241	36.7%	63.1%

There's more...

Bootstrap sampling can be used for many more purposes than just building predictive models. One example is computing measures such as 95 percent confidence intervals for coefficients or predictions for algorithms that don't provide these measures. Consider a 90 percent confidence interval for predicted accuracy from a Neural Network. One can build the Neural Network and obtain a classification accuracy measure such as **Percent Correct Classification** (**PCC**) for the test set. This gives you one value as a measurement.

However, this is only one number. To get an expected range of values, one can generate 200 bootstrap samples, run each sample through the Neural Network, compute PCC for that sample, and save the result. After testing the model on the 200 bootstrap samples, one sorts the list and identifies the value at 10th and 190th rows (the 5 percent and 95 percent percentiles, so that 90 percent of the PCC values fall within these bounds). These values form the 90 percent confidence interval.

Caching is a good idea when creating any random sample if reproducibility is desired. The `random()` function will create a different random sample each time one runs the stream, so if one would like the sample to remain the same, caching any node after the random sample will keep the same sample for subsequent processing. After exiting Modeler, that cache is flushed, however, and a new random sample will be selected the next time the stream is run. If one wants to keep that same random sample even after exiting, one must save the cache to a file and use that saved cache file in the future. One can either save the cache to a disk and load the cache the next time the stream is opened; or, since the cache files are merely SPSS Statistics `.sav` files, one can also load them with a Statistics Source node.

See also

- The *Detecting potential model instability early using the Partition node and Feature Selection node* recipe in *Chapter 1, Data Understanding*
- The *Creating bagged logistic regression models* recipe in this chapter

Creating bagged logistic regression models

Many modeling algorithms in Modeler have Bagging and Boosting options already built-in. However, some models do not, including Logistic Regression. Even for these algorithms that do not have Bagging and Boosting, these model ensembles can help predictive accuracy significantly. In this recipe we learn how to build a bagged ensemble of logistic regression models from 10 bootstrap samples.

Getting ready

This recipe uses the datafile `cup98lrn_reduced_vars3.sav` and the stream `Recipe - bootstrap ensemble.str`.

How to do it...

To create bagged logistic regression models:

1. Open the stream `Recipe - bootstrap ensemble.str` by navigating to **File** | **Open Stream**.
2. Make sure the datafile points to the correct path to `cup98lrn_reduced_vars3.sav`.
3. Locate the supernode, **Bootstrap Sample**, select it with a left-click, and copy it by using **Edit** | **Copy** or by typing the shortcut *Ctrl* + *C*.
4. Paste the supernode to the stream by using **Edit** | **Paste** or by typing the shortcut *Ctrl* + *V*. Do this eight more times so that you have a total of 10 Bootstrap Sample supernodes.
5. Connect each of these 10 Bootstrap Sample supernodes to the Type node, Classification Types. Space the supernodes out on the canvas, as shown in the following screenshot:

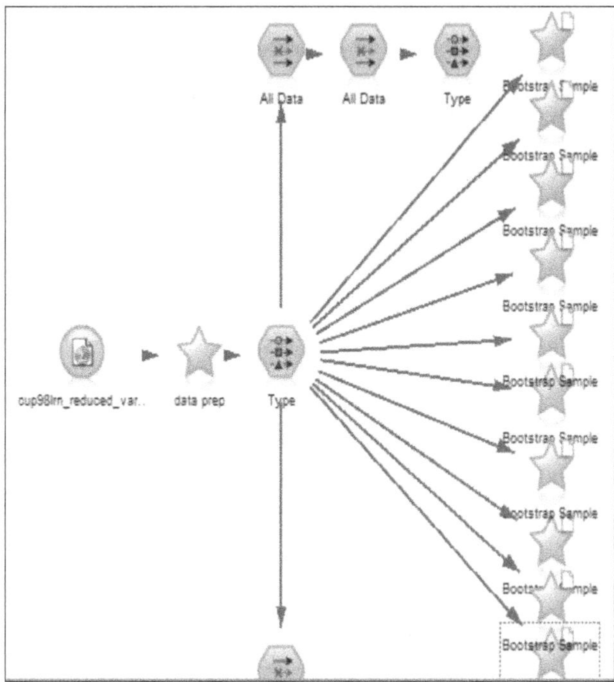

6. Insert a Type node and connect it to the Bootstrap Sample supernode. Open the Type node and make sure fields **recordID** and **CONTROLN** are set to measurement **Typeless**, field **TARGET_B** has **Role** value `Target`, and **Field** named **Partition** is set to **Role** value `Partition`. Click on **OK**.

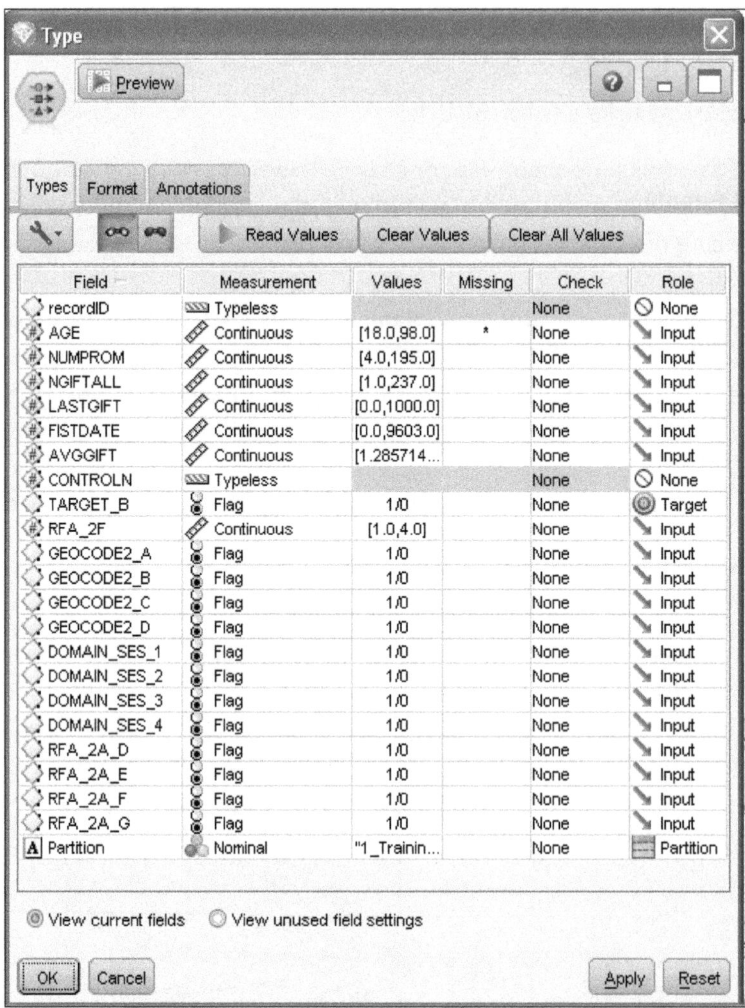

7. Insert a Logistic Regression node and connect it to the Type node set up in step 6.

8. Open the Logistic Regression node. Change the **Procedure** setting to **Binomial** and change the **Method** to **Forwards**.

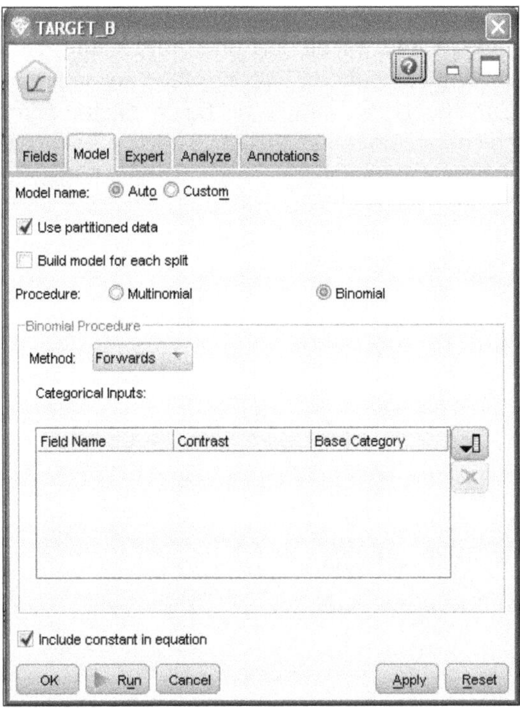

9. Highlight the Type node and Logistic Regression nodes, copy them (right-click **Edit** | **Copy**) and paste them nine times. Connect each of these nine additional Logistic Regression nodes to the remaining nine Bootstrap Sample supernodes.

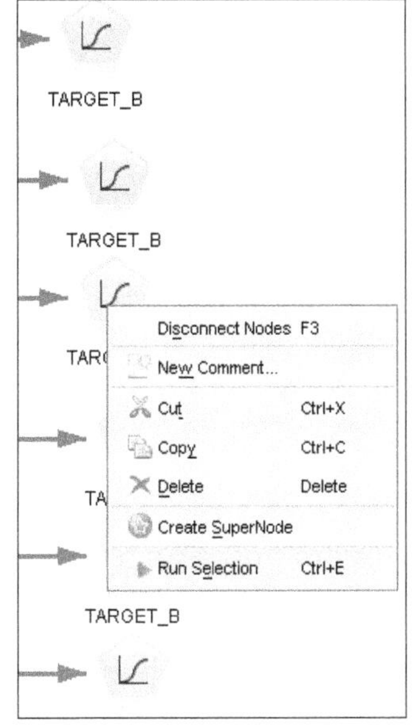

10. Highlight the ten Logistic Regression nodes, right-click, and select **Run Selection**. Ten Logistic Regression models will be built and the resulting Generated Model nodes will appear on the canvas. (Be patient. This may take several minutes, or even a half an hour or more.) Each bootstrap sample will be connected to the Type node and each Type node will be connected to its respective generated model.

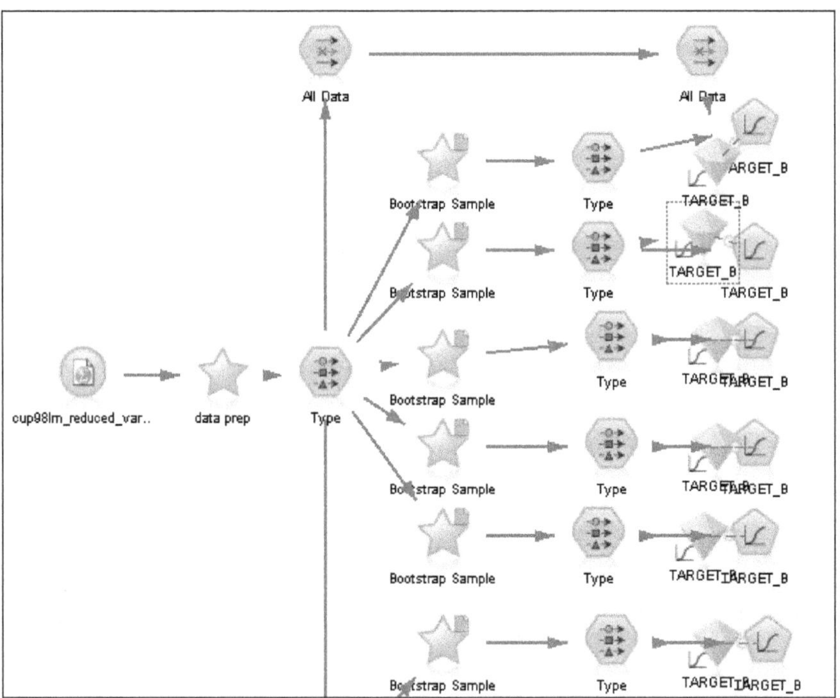

11. Connect the top-most generated model nodes to the `All Data` Filter node immediately above it. Then connect the remaining nine generated models to each other, forming a single data flow of ten consecutive models.
12. Insert an Ensemble node from the **Fields** palette and connect it to the last of the ten Logistic Regression generated nodes.

13. Open the Ensemble node. For the option **Target Field for ensemble**, pick **TARGET_B**, de-select **Filter out fields generated by ensemble models**, and change the **Ensemble method** to **Average raw propensity**. Click on **OK**.

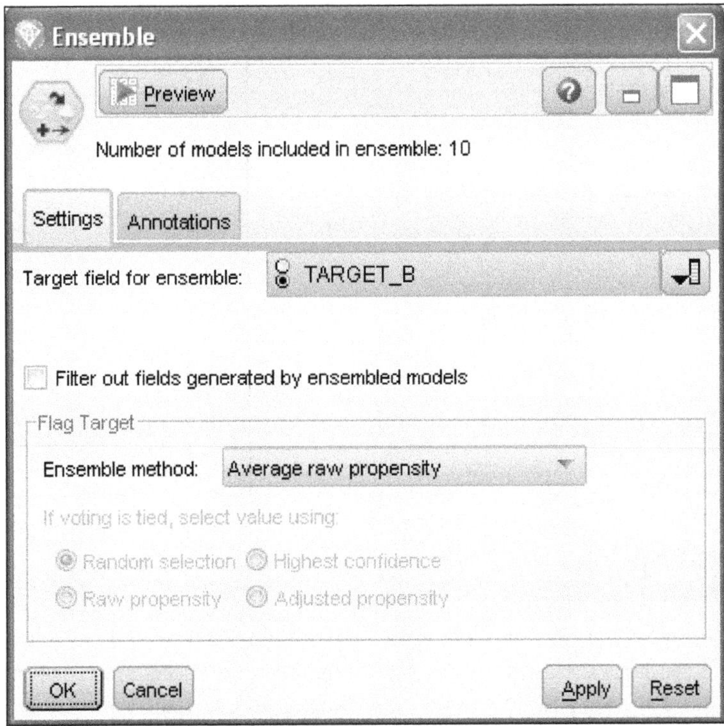

14. Insert an Evaluation node and connect it to the Ensemble node. Open the Ensemble node and select **Lift** for the **Chart type**, de-select **Cumulative Plot**, and at the bottom, for the **Plot** option, change it from **Percentiles** to **Deciles**. Click on **OK**.

After completing step 14, the stream should look like the one shown in the following screenshot:

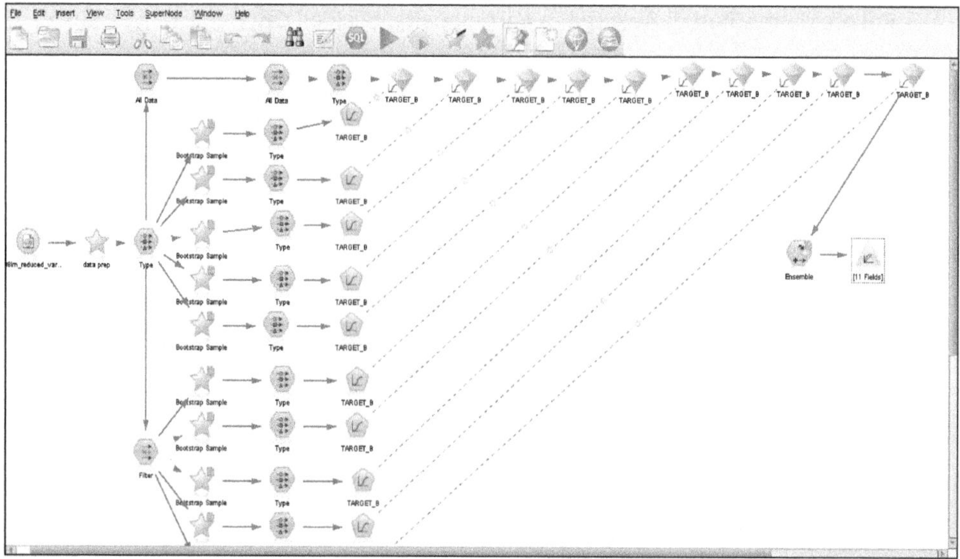

How it works...

Bagging is an acronym for bootstrap aggregating and refers to a model ensemble technique that reduces the model error variance by smoothing the predictions of several models. The Ensemble node is a very flexible node in Modeler, and provides a simple way to build ensembles from multiple models. When one connects the generated models in sequence, each model's predictions are added to the data and can be picked up by the Ensemble node to combine in a number of ways. Simple averaging is the usual aggregating method for Bagging, but any of the Ensemble node methods can be used.

In addition, rather than averaging the probabilities, one can instead vote, with the target category receiving the most votes resulting in the winning predicted category value. To avoid ties, it is best to have an odd number of models for binary classification.

This manual approach to building ensembles can be somewhat tedious the first time but, once it is built, the models can be rebuilt with different inputs without changing the modeling nodes and the Ensemble node. One way to speed up the connections of the generated models is to drag each generated model to the location desired (each one to the right of the prior one). Then, one can drag the connection arrow on top of the prior generated model. Make sure you don't drag the dotted connector (that connects the generated model to the Logistic node).

There's more...

Each model is built from a separate bootstrap sample. In the original algorithm, each model was overfit purposely so that it would have high accuracy (low error) on the training set. However, overfitting on training data usually results in worse accuracy on held-out data. The averaging step in Bagging smooths the predictions so the final ensemble model is unlikely to be overfit if enough models are included in the ensemble. Ten models is a typically low-end number of predictive models to combine, though one can combine between 10 and 50 models depending on the complexity of the data and the amount of overfit.

This recipe shows how to build ensembles from bootstrap samples, but one can also build multiple models from simple random selection as well. This can be accomplished simply by replacing the Bootstrap Sample supernode with a Partition node. Each Partition node must have a different random seed to ensure each sample will be different. Bootstrap sampling is more likely to produce greater model variety but the simple random sample using the Partition node can work as well.

Ensembles work best when they disagree. If the correlation coefficients between all pairs of models are high, greater than 0.95, combining the models has little value; they will merely reinforce each other. This will likely be the case with the default settings in this recipe. One can test for this by inserting a Statistics node and computing all pairwise correlations between model predictions.

In the Logistic Regression node advanced options, for the **Forward Selection** model, one can allow for more overfit by changing the **Entry** and **Removal** values from the default (**0.05** and **0.1**, respectively) to higher values, such as `0.1` and `0.2` respectively. To set these values go to the **Expert** tab, click on **Stepping...**, and change the values to `0.1` and `0.2`.

See also

- The *Detecting potential model instability early using the Partition node and Feature Selection node* recipes in *Chapter 1, Data Understanding*
- The *Creating a bootstrap sample* recipe in this chapter

Using KNN to match similar cases

K-Nearest Neighbors (**KNN**) is found in the **Classification** tab of the **Modeling** palette, but it is actually two different applications in one node. Methodologically they are similar, but different in their application. In addition to classification, the KNN Modeling node can be used to calculate differences and find those cases in a Deployment data set that have the smallest distances. Online dating services use this approach. Men can be scored to find women that they resemble, and women can be scored to find men that they resemble. In the case of a dating service, the answers to survey questions define similarity.

In this recipe, we will focus on patterns of purchase. The goal will be to have online sales reps assigned to assist customers via online support chat to be those reps with the most experience in those products lines that the customer has shown interest in. The whole idea of the *Cookbook* is to introduce non-obvious applications of techniques; at first glance, this seems a simple application of the technique. Two aspects of this recipe are interesting, however. Many users discover KNN only in the classification context, and miss out on the distance feature. Second, the role of a modeling data set and a deployment data set is rather different in this technique, and many new users of KNN find themselves calculating the distance of records to themselves. The results can be confusing. This recipe will show how to use two data sets - one with which to create the generated model, and another to score.

Getting ready

We will start with the `KNN.str` stream. The stream starts with the `Sales Rep Proportions` data set for Modeling, but also uses the `Customer Proportions` data set for scoring.

How to do it...

To use KNN to match similar cases:

1. Open the stream.

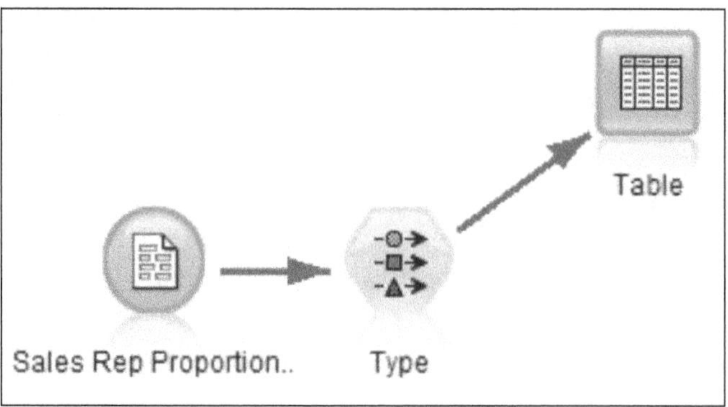

2. Add a **KNN** Modeling node and edit it.

3. Choose **Only identify the nearest neighbors**. Click on **Run**. (You may need to broaden your idea of what a generated model in Modeler is. In this case, it is really just the locations of the sales reps in the space defined by the product categories.)

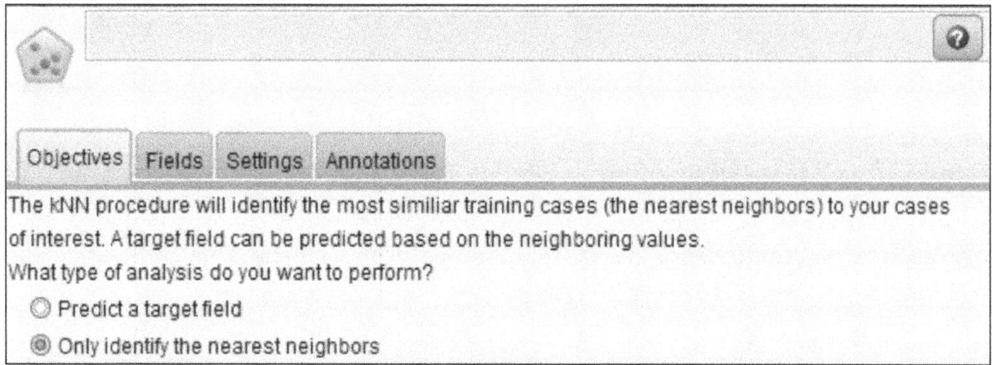

4. Add a Source node for the datafile `Customer Proportions`.
5. Set up the stream to have data from the new source flow through the generated model and to a table.

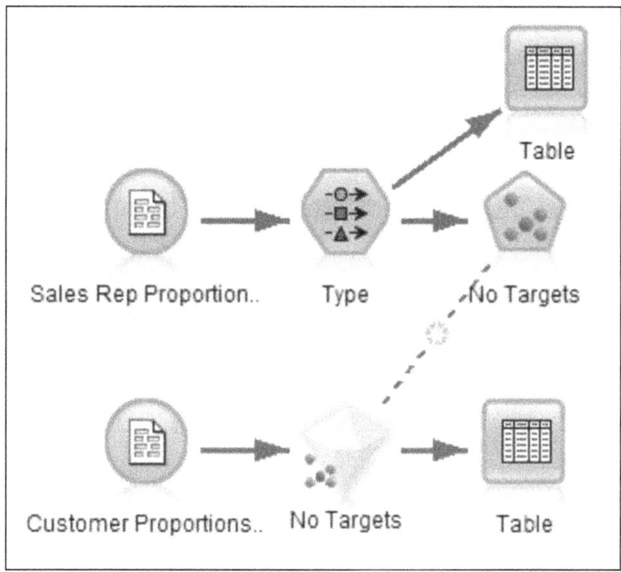

6. Run the Table node. The results for the first five customers are shown. For the first customer, the sales rep that is closest is **32**, and that rep must have an identical pattern because the distance is zero.

$KNN-neighbor-1	$KNN-distance-1
32	0.000
31	0.292
62	0.703
66	0.115
46	0.422

How it works...

Let's examine the first two customers and the sales rep that most of them resemble on the variables, their nearest neighbor. We see that the first pair are a perfect match. Their amount spent is entirely in one category, Video Games.

Customer_ID	Entertainment	Game Consoles	Hardware	Movies	Software	Streaming	Video Games
100004832	0.000	0.000	0.000	0.000	0.000	0.000	1.000

RepID	Entertainment	Game Consoles	Hardware	Movies	Software	Streaming	Video Games
32	0.000	0.000	0.000	0.000	0.000	0.000	1.000

The second customer does not have a perfect match among the reps but, perhaps, that makes the idea behind the technique even more clear. They are indeed a close match, except that the rep has a few Movies transaction, while the customer does not.

Customer_ID	Entertainment	Game Consoles	Hardware	Movies	Software	Streaming	Video Games
100004870	0.621	0.000	0.000	0.000	0.000	0.000	0.379

RepID	Entertainment	Game Consoles	Hardware	Movies	Software	Streaming	Video Games
31	0.659	0.000	0.000	0.079	0.000	0.000	0.262

The theory behind the technique is as simple as that. Distance is literally the Euclidian distance between the reps and the Customers based on these seven proportions. If you are rusty on your Euclidian distances, perhaps you would recall calculating the length of the hypotenuse of a triangle. If there were only two proportions the calculation would be identical to that, with seven proportions there is a little bit more math, but the concept is the same. Recommendation engines such as those on LinkedIn, or Facebook's next friend concept, utilize this approach, often in combination with other approaches. Here is the utility, in our imaginary company, in assigning an online chat resource that would be likely to understand the customer and the customer's past purchase history.

See also

- The *Using aggregate to write cluster centers to Excel for conditional formatting* recipe in *Chapter 7, Modeling – Assessment, Evaluation, Deployment, and Monitoring*

Using Auto Classifier to tune models

At first glance, the role of the Auto Classifier node seems to be limited to choosing an algorithm. In fact, it arguably allows one to avoid the choice of algorithm altogether in that it automatically chooses the top three and then creates an ensemble. However, model accuracy owes more to good data prep than algorithm choice. So what is one to make of Auto Classifier?

It is certainly true that, lacking the time or training for a proper modeling phase, the Auto Classifier would possibly do a better job than a data miner selecting a single method at random. It is worth noting, however, that some data mining experts have suggested that mastering a single method and its settings is often superior to attempting to use a host of algorithms without that mastery. Readers of an intermediate guide such as this one presumably have both the allocated time and the training to do a more complete job than just using the Auto Classifier on default settings. So how do we leverage this tool?

This recipe capitalizes on an extremely easy, but underutilized feature of the Auto Classifier, its ability to run dozens of models with slightly different settings. A proper modeling phase takes about one to two weeks. Also, by the time you reach the modeling phase you will certainly have exposed the data to some modeling algorithms during data exploration. We will not try to show all of the ways that this time management tool can be used during the entire project. Instead, the recipe will assume that **Support Vector Machines** (**SVMs**) has been identified as a potential algorithm, and will show how to build 40 different SVMs with varying settings. 40, in fact, is not sufficient to show all possible combinations of settings, but it will illustrate the technique and prove that the settings can make a difference. Remember, however, to be brilliant in the basics, tuning is done near the end of modeling and is a way to squeeze another half percent of accuracy out of a model. Rushing to tune a model when you have done a mediocre job on the previous phases will not save the model from poor or incomplete data preparation.

Getting ready

We will start with tuning the `Auto Classifier.str` stream. The stream uses the `TELE_CHURN_MERGED.sav` data set.

How to do it...

To use the Auto Classifier node to tune models:

1. Open the stream. Add an Auto Classifier node to the stream.

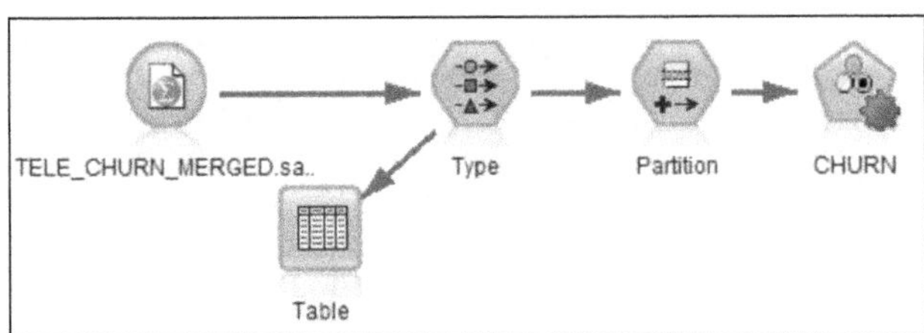

2. Edit the Auto Classifier node. Under the **Expert** tab, indicate that you want to specify model parameters:

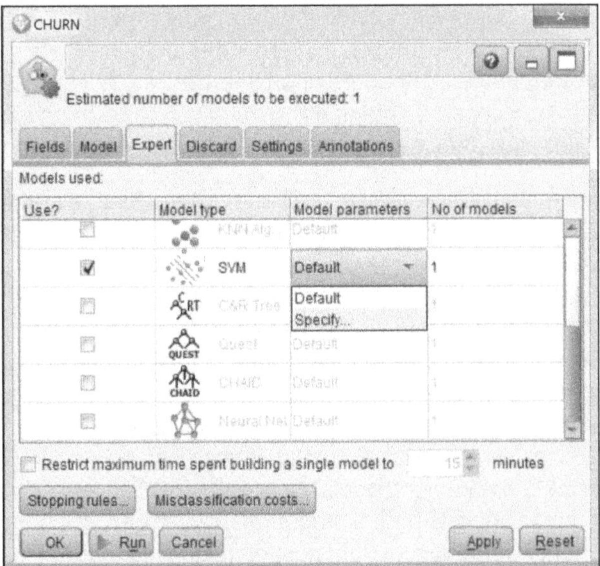

3. In the specification menu indicate **Expert** options.

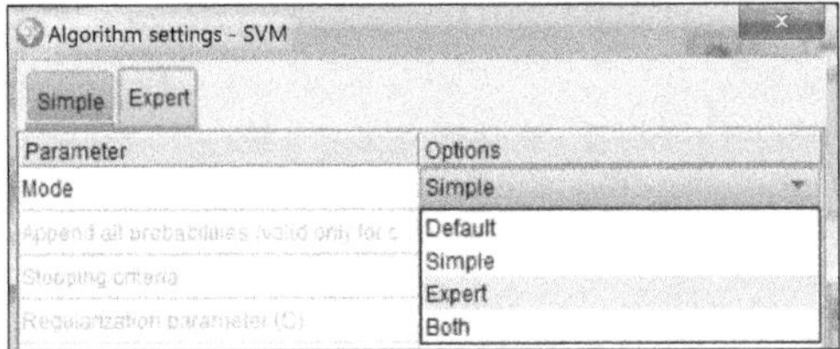

4. There are numerous technical parameters. We will choose one that often has an impact, the **Regularization Parameter**. Values ranging from 1 to 10 are recommended and we will test all of them.

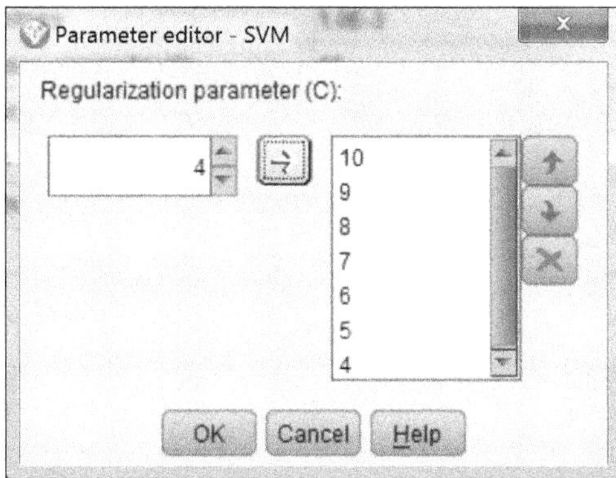

5. Of the numerous remaining parameters, we will adjust just one more. Select all four Kernel types.

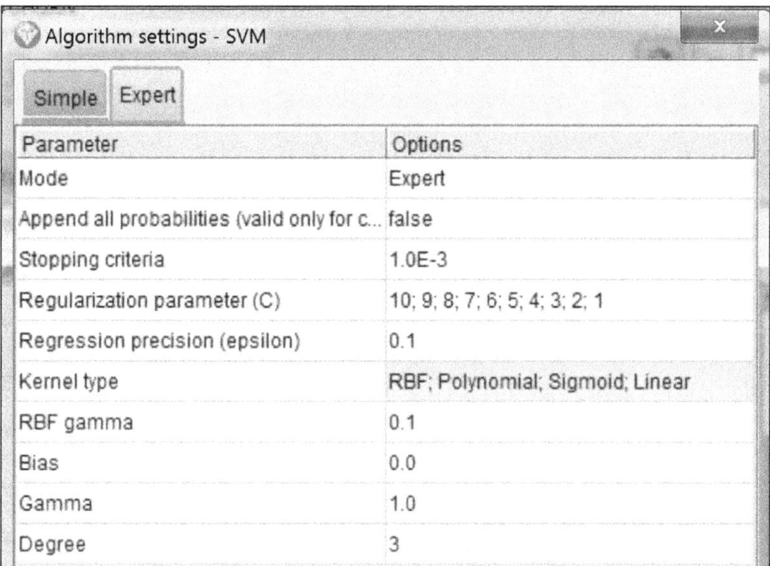

6. Run the Auto Classifier and examine the results. **SVM17** appears to be the number-one ranked model, but even with three decimal places displayed there appears to be very tough competition. Double-click on the generated model symbol in the table.

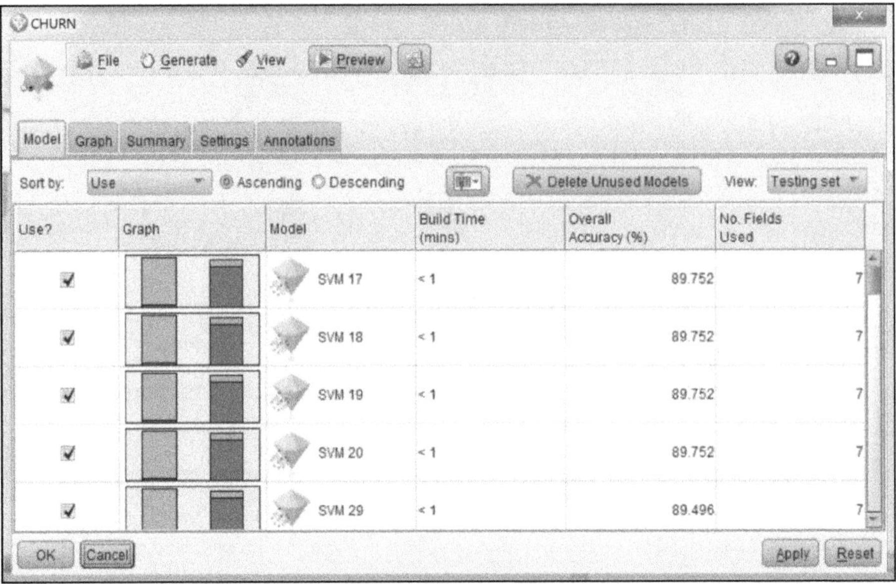

7. Using the **Generate** menu, select **Model to Palette**.

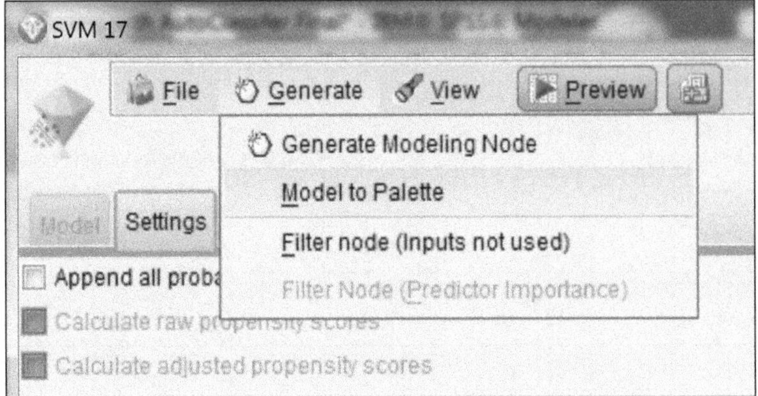

8. Attach the generated model, add an Analysis node, and click on **Run**.

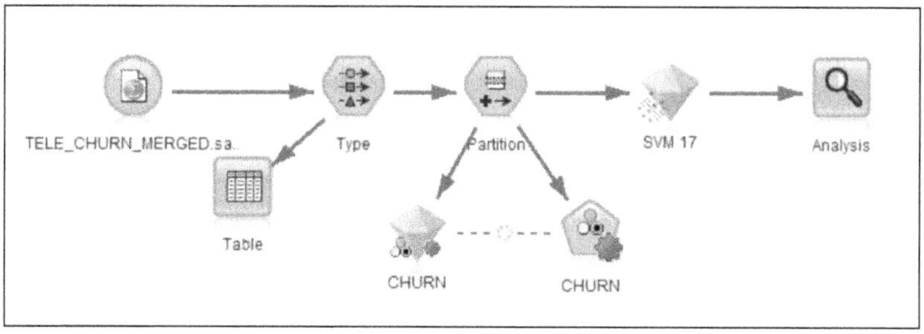

How it works...

A lot of work precedes the need for this recipe. The data has been merged and prepped. The data has been explored. New variables have likely been created. In this data set, the ratios are a great example. SVMs have been indicated as a possible solution. Perhaps an Auto Classifier was used, on the defaults, in an earlier phase and SVM showed some early promise. Perhaps, we have the time and training to consider several different algorithms at this level of details.

Having accomplished all of those prerequisite steps, we need to apply our expert knowledge of SVMs to tune the model, that is, to choose the optimal settings for this particular model. The recipe probably piques our curiosity about what C is? Although a detailed discussion is not possible here, it is a tradeoff between accuracy and generality. Even the kernel, the names of which partly reveal their nature, is addressing this issue. Do we go for accuracy and risk overfitting, or go for a more generalizable model, or a compromise in between? There are other parameters as well that were not considered to limit the number of recipe models to 40.

The Auto Classifier is perfect for this task. The recipe showed that, in just a couple of minutes of work, and a substantial bit of waiting, we could have the results of 40 models. Obviously, without knowledge of SVMs, the choosing of parameters can be difficult. However, it is easier to learn the range, and let the Auto Classifier run and then try to choose individual combinations. In effect, we have done a grid search, a systematic search of parameter combinations. It is terribly important to stay focused on the business problem and the preparation of the data set for modeling. This is critical because one is not going to see accuracy climb 5 percent or 10 percent from tuning. Tuning is for final, incremental gains, built on a strong foundation, or perhaps increases the effectiveness of two or three algorithms that have survived a weeding out process. Once a strong modeling approach is chosen, however, this recipe will allow you to get the optimal performance out of a chosen algorithm.

See also

- The *Using aggregate to write cluster centers to Excel for conditional formatting* recipe in *Chapter 7, Modeling – Assessment, Evaluation, Deployment, and Monitoring*

Next-Best-Offer for large datasets

Association models have been the basis for next-best-offer recommendation engines for a long time. Recommendation engines are widely used for presenting customers with cross-sell offers. For example, if a customer purchases a shirt, pants, and a belt; which shoes would he also likely buy? This type of analysis is often called market-basket analysis as we are trying to understand which items customers purchase in the same basket/transaction.

Recommendations must be very granular (for example, at the product level) to be usable at the check-out register, website, and so on. For example, knowing that female customers purchase a wallet 63.9 percent of the time when they buy a purse is not directly actionable. However, knowing that customers that purchase a specific purse (for example, SKU 25343) also purchase a specific wallet (for example, SKU 98343) 51.8 percent of the time, can be the basis for future recommendations.

Product level recommendations require the analysis of massive data sets (that is, millions of rows). Usually, this data is in the form of sales transactions where each line item (that is, row of data) represents a single product. The line items are tied together by a single transaction ID.

IBM SPSS Modeler association models support both tabular and transactional data. The tabular format requires each product to be represented as column. As most product level recommendations would contain thousands of products, this format is not practical. The transactional format uses the transactional data directly and requires only two inputs, the transaction ID and the product/item.

Getting ready

This example uses the file `stransactions.sav` and `scoring.csv`.

How to do it...

To recommend the next best offer for large datasets:

1. Start with a new stream by navigating to **File** | **New Stream**.
2. Go to **File** | **Stream Properties** from the IBM SPSS Modeler menu bar. On the **Options** tab change the **Maximum members for nominal fields** to `50000`. Click on **OK**.

3. Add a Statistics File source node to the upper left of the stream. Set the file field by navigating to `transactions.sav`. On the **Types** tab, change the **Product_Code field** to **Nominal** and click on the **Read Values** button. Click on **OK**.
4. Add a **CARMA** Modeling node connected to the Statistics File source node in step 3. On the **Fields** tab, click on the **Use custom settings** and check the **Use transactional format** check box. Select **Transaction_ID** as the **ID field** and **Product_Code** as the **Content field**.

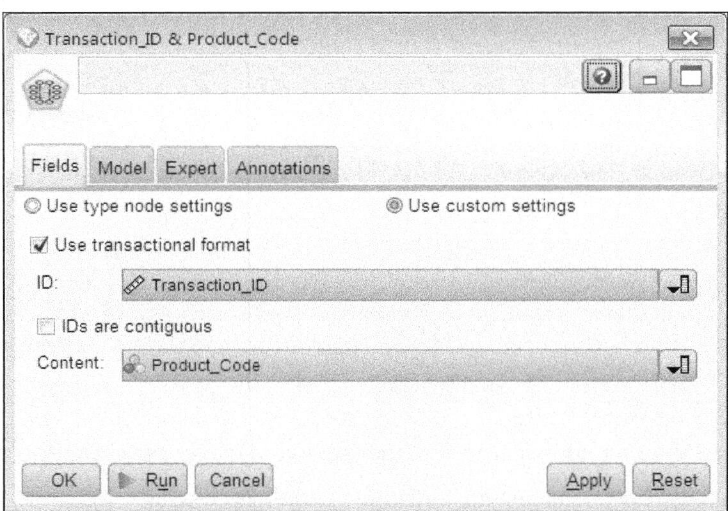

5. On the **Model tab** of the CARMA Modeling node, change the **Minimum rule support (%)** to `0.0` and the **Minimum rule confidence (%)** to `5.0`. Click on the **Run** button to build the model. Double-click the generated model to ensure that you have approximately 40,000 rules.

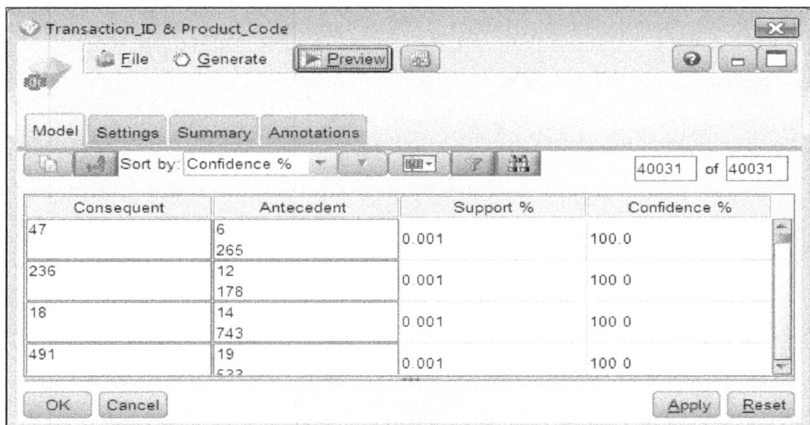

6. Add a Var File source node to the middle left of the stream. Set the file field by navigating to `scoring.csv`. On the **Types** tab, click on the **Read Values** button. Click on the **Preview** button to preview the data. Click on **OK** to dismiss all dialogs.

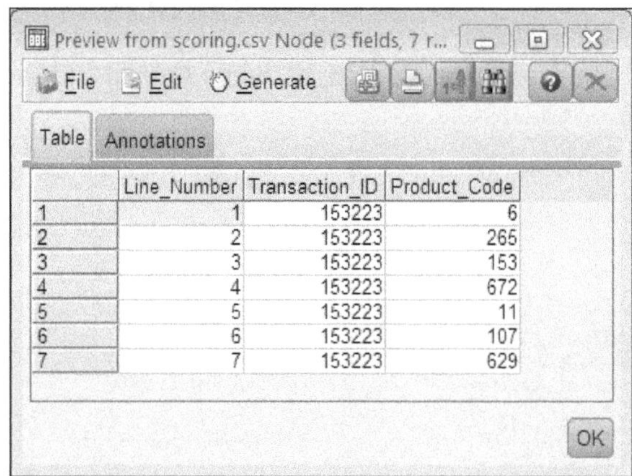

	Line_Number	Transaction_ID	Product_Code
1	1	153223	6
2	2	153223	265
3	3	153223	153
4	4	153223	672
5	5	153223	11
6	6	153223	107
7	7	153223	629

7. Add a Sort node connected to the Var File node in step 6. Choose **Transaction_ID** and **Line_Number** (with Ascending sort) by clicking the down arrow on the right of the dialog. Click on **OK**.
8. Connect the Sort node in step 7 to the generated model (replacing the current link).
9. Add an Aggregate node connected to the generated model.
10. Add a Merge node connected to the generated model. Connect the Aggregate node in step 9 to the Merge node. On the **Merge** tab, choose **Keys** as the **Merge Method,** select **Transaction_ID**, and click on the right arrow. Click on OK.
11. Add a Select node connected to the Merge node in step 10. Set the condition to `Record_Count = Line_Number`. Click on OK. At this point, the stream should look as follows:

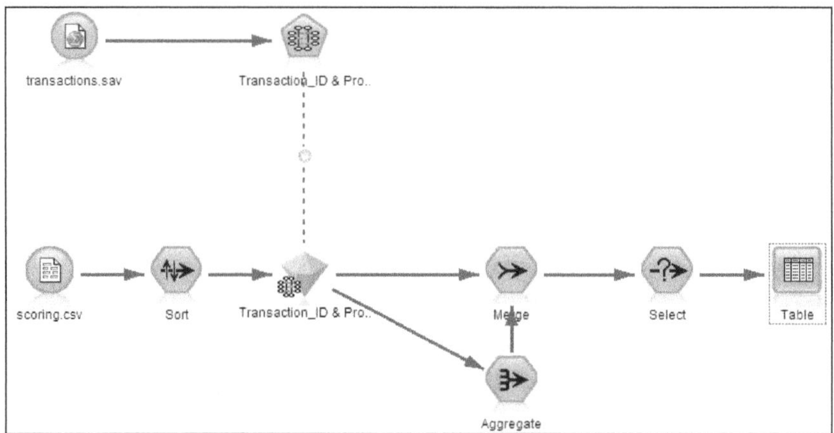

12. Add a Table node connected to the Select node in step 11. Right-click on the Table node and click on **Run** to see the next-best-offer for the input data.

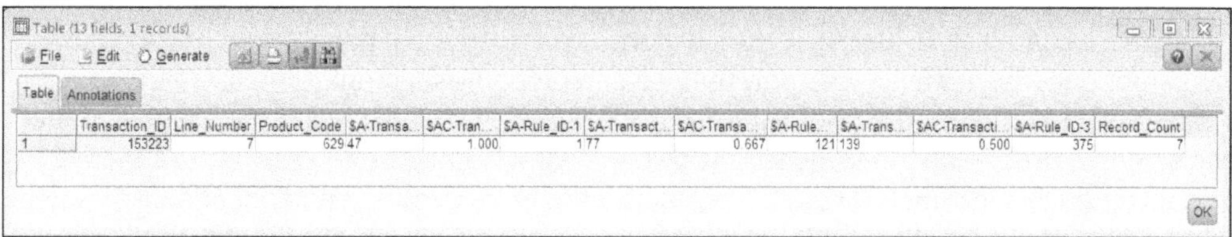

Table (13 fields, 1 records)

	Transaction_ID	Line_Number	Product_Code	$A-Transa...	$AC-Tran...	$A-Rule_ID-1	$A-Transact...	$AC-Transa...	$A-Rule...	$A-Trans...	$AC-Transacti...	$A-Rule_ID-3	Record_Count
1	153223	7	629	47	1.000	1	77	0.667	121	139	0.500	375	7

How it works...

In steps 1-5, we set up the CARMA model to use the transactional data (without needing to restructure the data). CARMA was selected over A Priori for its improved performance and stability with large data sets. For recommendation engines, the settings for the Model tab are somewhat arbitrary and are driven by the practical limitations of the number of rules generated. Lowering the thresholds for confidence and rule support generates more rules. Having more rules can have a negative impact on scoring performance but will result in more (albeit weaker) recommendations.

Rule Support	How many transactions contain the entire rule (that is, both antecedents ("if" products) and consequents ("then" products))?
Confidence	If a transaction contains all the antecedents ("if" products), what percentage of the time does it contain the consequents ("then" products)?

In step 5, when we examine the model we see the generated Association Rules with the corresponding rules support and confidences.

In the remaining steps (7-12), we score a new transaction and generate 3 next-best-offers based on the model containing the Association Rules. Since the model was built with transactional data, the scoring data must also be transactional. This means that each row is scored using the current row and the prior rows with the same transaction ID. The only row we generally care about is the last row for each transaction where all the data has been presented to the model. To accomplish this, we count the number of rows for each transaction and select the line number that equals the total row count (that is, the last row for each transaction).

Notice that the model returns 3 recommended products, each with a confidence, in order of decreasing confidence. A next-best-offer engine would present the customer with the best option first (or potentially all three options ordered by decreasing confidence). Note that, if there is no rule that applies to the transaction, nulls will be returned in some or all of the corresponding columns.

There's more...

In this recipe, you'll notice that we generate recommendations across the entire transactional data set. By using all transactions, we are creating generalized next-best-offer recommendations; however, we know that we can probably segment (that is, cluster) our customers into different behavioral groups (for example, fashion conscience, value shoppers, and so on.). Partitioning the transactions by behavioral segment and generating separate models for each segment will result in rules that are more accurate and actionable for each group. The biggest challenge with this approach is that you will have to identify the customer segment for each customer before making recommendations (that is, scoring). A unified approach would be to use the general recommendations for a customer until a customer segment can be assigned then use segmented models.

See also

- The *Using KNN to match similar cases* recipe

7

Modeling – Assessment, Evaluation, Deployment, and Monitoring

In this chapter, we will cover:

- How (and why) to validate as well as test
- Using classification trees to explore the predictions of a Neural Network
- Correcting a confusion matrix for an imbalanced target variable by incorporating priors
- Using aggregate to write cluster centers to Excel for conditional formatting
- Creating a classification tree financial summary using aggregate and an Excel Export node
- Reformatting data for reporting with a Transpose node
- Changing formatting of fields in a Table node
- Combining generated filters

Introduction

The objective of data mining is to understand and predict behavior. A retailer wants to know why people buy, and how to sell more. An educator wants to know what factors influence educational and professional success and how to help students learn and prepare for a career. A criminologist wants to understand the factors that lead to crime, and how to prevent crime.

Data miners often speak of valuable patterns in data, and powerful models. What makes a pattern valuable? It's valuable if it adds to our understanding of behavior. What makes a model useful? It's useful if it is effective at predicting behavior.

Data miners aim to identify influential factors that drive behavior. When we identify those driving factors, through exploration of patterns in the data, we can understand behavior. If we can describe, with a quantitative model, the relationship between driving factors and behavior, then we can predict behavior.

It's easy for a data miner to make a model; that takes little more than a few mouse clicks. Assuring that the model reflects the true mechanism that drives behavior requires more thought. As can be seen, particularly in the Churn example from *Chapter 4, Data Preparation - Construct*, that clever manipulation of the data is often required to allow behavior to be visible in our data.

There are many ways for data miners to test the validity of a model. Use of Test Partition data sets is one of the most common approaches. Another is field testing—collecting new data and comparing model results to actual performance. Each of these approaches provides good feedback to the data miner, helping him/her to identify which models are (and which models are not) effective for predicting behavior. In particular, a *dress rehearsal* using data that did not exist when the project began can have a powerful psychological effect on colleagues that have been watching from the sidelines. It sometimes seems a more compelling validation than a third data sample.

Why is it necessary to do these things? Why is it that one model provides accurate predictions, while another, created in much the same way, does not?

An automatically-generated model is an equation, of a specified form (the model type), that describes a particular set of data. Classical statisticians invest up-front effort considering relevant theory, selecting a model type, and investigating data for problematic patterns, to develop models that suit their intended purpose. In contrast, data miners take a much less formal approach, generating models quickly, without fussing over theory. This saves time, yet increases the risk that the model won't work well when applied to new data. So data miners must test their models.

When a model does not work well with new data, what's causing the problem? The broad term for this situation is *overfitting*, meaning that the equation is so strongly tailored to the data set for which it was created that it won't work with anything else. The computer knows nothing more about the data than the numbers in its memory; when you generate a model, it is based solely on those numbers and the model type you select. The computer does not have the human ability to reason about what variables would make sense in a model. It can only use math, and sometimes the result is a great fit to one set of data, and not another.

A common overfitting problem is instability. A model is said to be unstable when the predictor variables selected by fitting the model to one set of data are very different from those selected when the same model type is derived from another data set. The chance of creating an unstable model varies from one model type to another. The data mining practices of using many candidate predictors and sidestepping the preparation steps used by classical statisticians adds considerably to the risk of producing an unstable model. Although they appeared in earlier chapters, there are two recipes in particular that touch this theme:

- The *Detecting potential model instability early using the Partition node and Feature Selection node* recipe in *Chapter 1, Data Understanding*
- The *Removing redundant variables using correlation matrices* recipe in *Chapter 2, Data Preparation - Select*

What's the remedy for an unstable model? First, you must detect the problem. If the model does not perform well when applied to test and validation data sets, the problem may be an unstable model. Explore further by fitting the same model type, using the same set of predictors, to another sample of data, or to several others. If the model type is a neural network, you might also try using the same data sample and changing the random seed. If the resulting models have significantly different predictor variables, you have an unstable model. You may obtain better results with another model type, or by limiting the predictors that you input to a few that you have selected based on your own business knowledge.

Despite the obvious value of some accuracy, and the established importance of stability, we still don't have enough. We need more. We need business relevance and the ability to take action.

The Value Law, The Nine Laws of Data Mining, **Tom Khabaza** (`http://khabaza.codimension.net/index_files/Page346.htm`):

> *The value of data mining results is not determined by the accuracy or stability of predictive models*
>
> *"The disconnect between accuracy and value ... can be highlighted by the question "Is the model predicting the right thing, and for the right reasons?" In other words, the value of a model derives as much from of its fit to the business problem as it does from its predictive accuracy. For example, a customer attrition model might make highly accurate predictions, yet make its predictions too late for the business to act on them effectively. Alternatively an accurate customer attrition model might drive effective action to retain customers, but only for the least profitable subset of customers. A high degree of accuracy does not enhance the value of these models when they have a poor fit to the business problem.*
>
> *The same is true of model stability; although an interesting measure for predictive models, stability cannot be substituted for the ability of a model to provide business insight, or for its fit to the business problem. Neither can any other technical measure."*

In this chapter, a number of recipes attempt to broaden our evaluation beyond the Analysis node—to go beyond technical measures based on statistical criteria and into the realm of business measures. The recipes on exporting summaries of results to Excel for distribution to management are among them.

One topic that deserves much attention in one's data mining education, but is addressed in relatively few recipes, is Deployment. Deployment is a challenging subject to address in a book dedicated to one software package because Deployment almost by definition means leaving Modeler and sending the results elsewhere. Modeler is quite capable of a number of forms of Deployment, but the results must reach a member of the data miner's organization in a form that can be put immediately to use, often automatically. There is so much diversity in the needs of different organizations, and the logistics of those organizations, that Deployment truly deserves its own book. Nonetheless there are some important tricks to know. The *Combining generated filters* recipe in this chapter includes such valuable Deployment phase tricks of the trade.

How (and why) to validate as well as test

In this recipe we explore the importance of validation. The test data set sometimes carries a great burden. During the modeling phase it is not unusual to produce dozens of models. During that process, for some data miners, accuracy of the model on the test data set becomes the sole criterion for the ranking of the modeling attempts. That would certainly seem to be a violation of the Value Law quoted in the chapter introduction.

One can argue that this issue—the issue of value—and the issue of validation are not identical, but they are related. Even if one applies the recommended broader definition of value, if the actual behavior in choosing the semi-finalist models during the modeling phase is to check for stability and accuracy in the Analysis node, then one runs the risk of putting too much emphasis on a single source of information. After all, even if one wisely chooses the best model on a variety of criteria, the selection of the top 3 or top 5 might be based on test accuracy in part because that is what Modeler makes it easiest to evaluate.

If one were to choose a different test data set at random and to compare the performance of 100 models, it is a near certainty that the ranking of many of those models would change. The accuracy might move only a fraction of a point up or down, but nonetheless the ranking would be affected nearly every time. Even if we embrace what we know about the behavior of random variables, recognizing that the ranking won't change all that much, and if we choose our strong models with care, we are still making the decision of what to examine closely largely on their performance (accuracy) on the test data set and its stability (similarity of train and test performance).

It is better to make two changes when it comes time to validate:

- Validate on a third data set
- Validate on a number of business criteria and not just on the criteria available in the Analysis node

This recipe shows how to validate on a third data set. The *Creating a classification tree financial summary using aggregate and an Excel Export node* recipe explores how to incorporate other business criteria, usually more financial and less statistical in nature.

Getting ready

We will start with the `Train Test Validate.str` stream.

How to do it...

To explore the importance of validation follow these steps:

1. Edit the Partition node and examine the settings. Click on **Train and test**, and note how validation is grayed out and not available for editing.

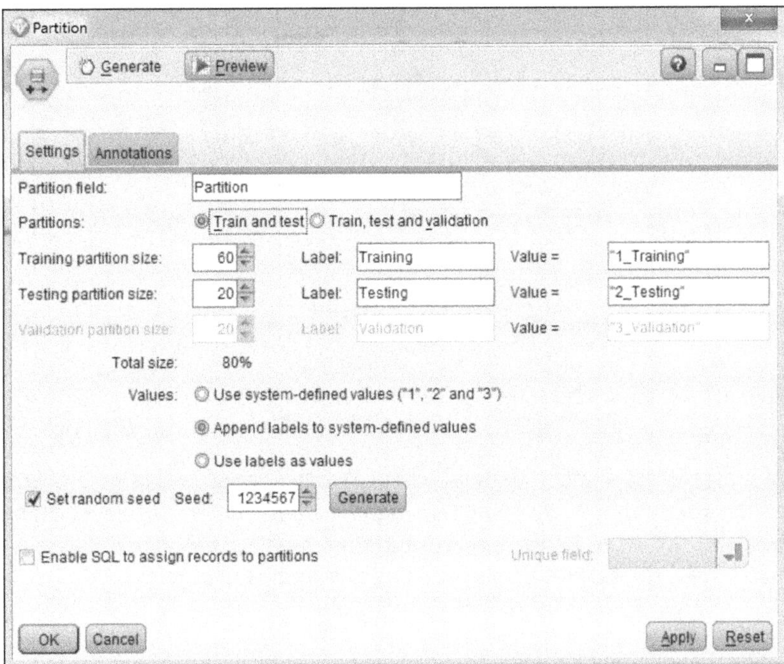

2. Zoom into the supernode named 9 models—examine some of the model features of the 9 models. They represent some of the choices that might emerge for the Modeling phase—some strong choices and some weak ones.

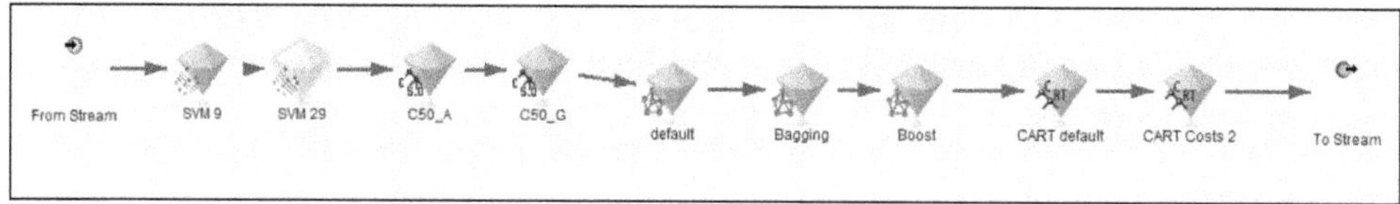

3. Run the Analysis node and note that train and test results can be easily compared. The strongest performers are the two SVMs and the C5.0 models on general settings.

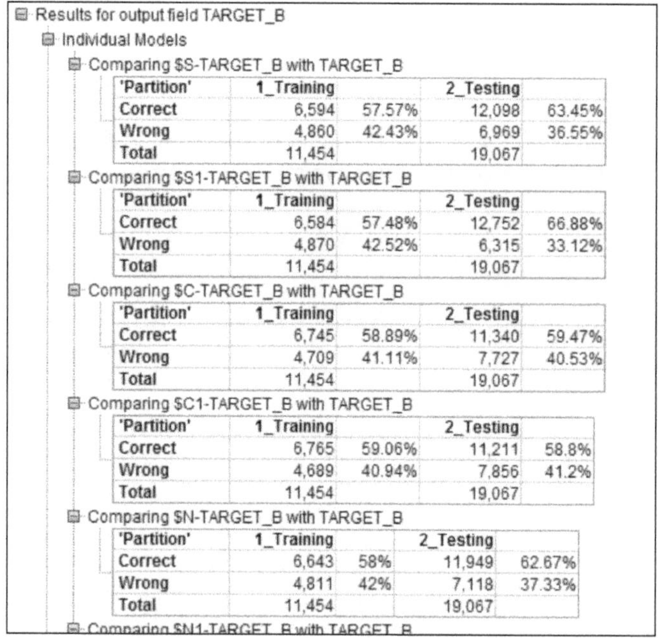

Results for output field TARGET_B

Individual Models

Comparing $S-TARGET_B with TARGET_B

'Partition'	1_Training		2_Testing	
Correct	6,594	57.57%	12,098	63.45%
Wrong	4,860	42.43%	6,969	36.55%
Total	11,454		19,067	

Comparing $S1-TARGET_B with TARGET_B

'Partition'	1_Training		2_Testing	
Correct	6,584	57.48%	12,752	66.88%
Wrong	4,870	42.52%	6,315	33.12%
Total	11,454		19,067	

Comparing $C-TARGET_B with TARGET_B

'Partition'	1_Training		2_Testing	
Correct	6,745	58.89%	11,340	59.47%
Wrong	4,709	41.11%	7,727	40.53%
Total	11,454		19,067	

Comparing $C1-TARGET_B with TARGET_B

'Partition'	1_Training		2_Testing	
Correct	6,765	59.06%	11,211	58.8%
Wrong	4,689	40.94%	7,856	41.2%
Total	11,454		19,067	

Comparing $N-TARGET_B with TARGET_B

'Partition'	1_Training		2_Testing	
Correct	6,643	58%	11,949	62.67%
Wrong	4,811	42%	7,118	37.33%
Total	11,454		19,067	

Comparing $N1-TARGET_B with TARGET_B

4. Sometimes with balanced data it is difficult to assess stability (the similarity of accuracy between the two samples). In the Partition node, deselect **balance only Train data,** rerun the Analysis node, and then reselect **balance only Train data**. All of the first five models have similar training and testing accuracy.

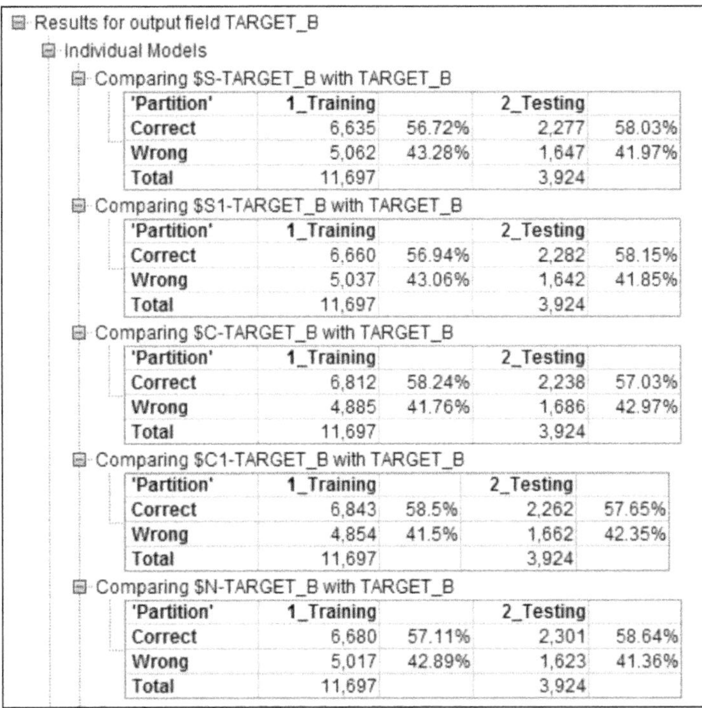

Results for output field TARGET_B

Individual Models

Comparing $S-TARGET_B with TARGET_B

'Partition'	1_Training		2_Testing	
Correct	6,635	56.72%	2,277	58.03%
Wrong	5,062	43.28%	1,647	41.97%
Total	11,697		3,924	

Comparing $S1-TARGET_B with TARGET_B

'Partition'	1_Training		2_Testing	
Correct	6,660	56.94%	2,282	58.15%
Wrong	5,037	43.06%	1,642	41.85%
Total	11,697		3,924	

Comparing $C-TARGET_B with TARGET_B

'Partition'	1_Training		2_Testing	
Correct	6,812	58.24%	2,238	57.03%
Wrong	4,885	41.76%	1,686	42.97%
Total	11,697		3,924	

Comparing $C1-TARGET_B with TARGET_B

'Partition'	1_Training		2_Testing	
Correct	6,843	58.5%	2,262	57.65%
Wrong	4,854	41.5%	1,662	42.35%
Total	11,697		3,924	

Comparing $N-TARGET_B with TARGET_B

'Partition'	1_Training		2_Testing	
Correct	6,680	57.11%	2,301	58.64%
Wrong	5,017	42.89%	1,623	41.36%
Total	11,697		3,924	

5. Make a copy of the more promising nodes and paste them onto the canvas. We will pick the two SVMs and the first C5.0.
6. Edit the Partition node and activate **Validation**.

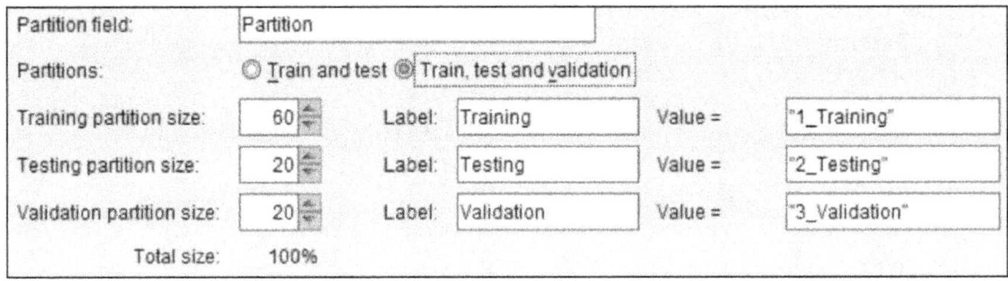

7. Add an Analysis node after the copied models and **Run**. Note that we now have Validation results in addition to our train and test results.

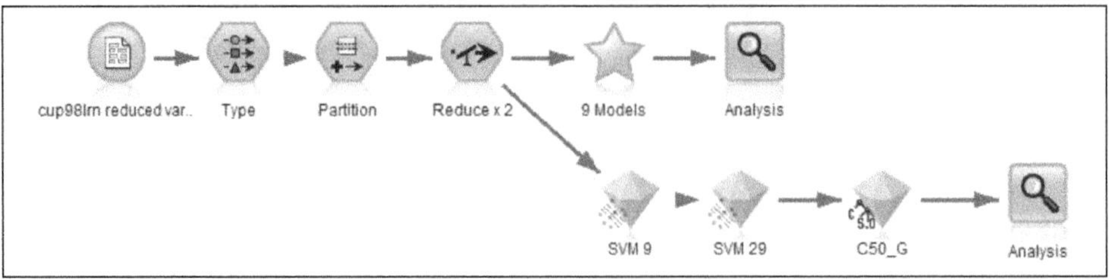

8. The validation results are quite consistent. If accuracy was the most important criterion, the more accurate of the two SVMs might be chosen, if the implications of having a less detailed description were an issue C5.0 might win the day. The weeding out process would last throughout the modeling phase. Other recipes will consider other factors such as financial variables to weigh along with accuracy and stability.

Results for output field TARGET_B

Individual Models

Comparing $S-TARGET_B with TARGET_B

'Partition'	1_Training		2_Testing		3_Validation	
Correct	6,643	56.95%	12,098	63.45%	12,115	63.73%
Wrong	5,022	43.05%	6,969	36.55%	6,895	36.27%
Total	11,665		19,067		19,010	

Comparing $S1-TARGET_B with TARGET_B

'Partition'	1_Training		2_Testing		3_Validation	
Correct	6,644	56.96%	12,752	66.88%	12,755	67.1%
Wrong	5,021	43.04%	6,315	33.12%	6,255	32.9%
Total	11,665		19,067		19,010	

Comparing $C-TARGET_B with TARGET_B

'Partition'	1_Training		2_Testing		3_Validation	
Correct	6,823	58.49%	11,211	58.8%	11,263	59.25%
Wrong	4,842	41.51%	7,856	41.2%	7,747	40.75%
Total	11,665		19,067		19,010	

Agreement between $S-TARGET_B $S1-TARGET_B $C-TARGET_B

'Partition'	1_Training		2_Testing		3_Validation	
Agree	10,078	86.4%	16,460	86.33%	16,323	85.87%
Disagree	1,587	13.6%	2,607	13.67%	2,687	14.13%
Total	11,665		19,067		19,010	

Comparing Agreement with TARGET_B

'Partition'	1_Training		2_Testing		3_Validation	
Correct	5,940	58.94%	10,678	64.87%	10,666	65.34%
Wrong	4,138	41.06%	5,782	35.13%	5,657	34.66%
Total	10,078		16,460		16,323	

How it works...

It is important to place these steps in the proper context. The train and test setting in the Partition node would stay selected for virtually the entire modeling phase, during which many, many models would be considered. The models that survive that process, and they might not all be evaluated at the same time as we have done here, would be tracked and cataloged. An Excel spreadsheet with one row per model is not a bad idea.

There is nothing magic about three models to make semifinalist status. Here, one model has the high accuracy, a second SVM actual has a higher lift (although we didn't explore output that showed that), and the third choice is a different algorithm. In particular C5.0 is not a black box; that is, it provides detailed description of the model, so it is a nice contrast to the SVMs.

See also

- The *Creating a classification tree financial summary using aggregate and an Excel Export node* recipies in this chapter

Using classification trees to explore the predictions of a Neural Network

Neural Nets have the reputation of being a black box technique; that is, that they are not highly revelatory of the reasoning behind their predictions. Compared to other techniques, information regarding what variables played the most important role in the model is fairly thin. It would be an exaggeration to say, however, that the Neural Net algorithm in Modeler provides no information; it does. Neural Nets are sometimes strong performers, and when they are the top performer they might be (and should be) a tempting option for Deployment. Is it possible to use other techniques to get a deeper insight into what the Neural Net has done behind the scenes? It is possible and one method for doing so is the subject of this recipe. We will be using CHAID to explore Neural Net predictions.

Getting ready

We will start with the `Look Inside NN.str` stream that uses the `TELE CHURN MERGED` data set.

How to do it...

To use classification trees to explore neural net predictions:

1. Open the `Look Inside NN.str` stream.

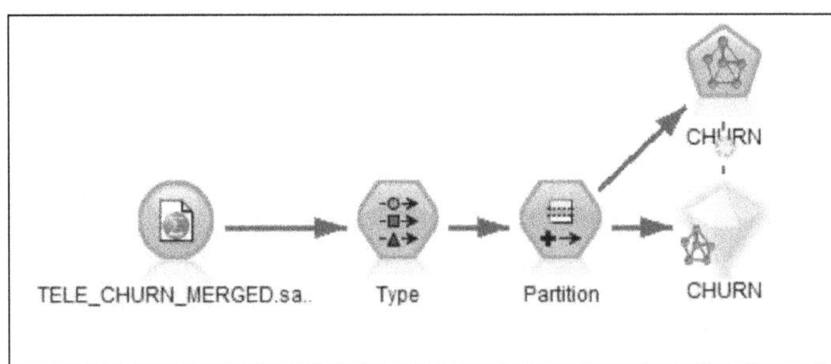

2. Edit the Neural Net's generated model. Note that, although Predictor Importance is available, there is nothing quite like the tree diagram of classification tree methods, nor a detailed statistical output as one would find in a technique such as Logistic Regression.

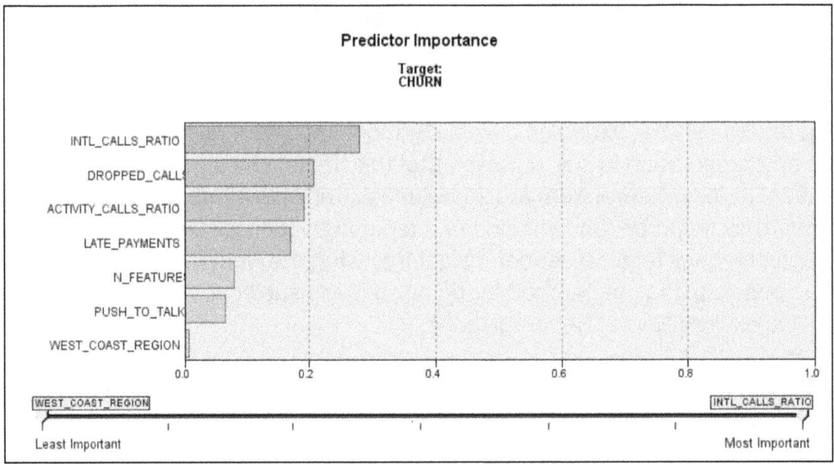

3. Add a Type node downstream of the generated model.

4. Change the **Role** of our current target to **None**. Set the role of the Neural Net's prediction to be our new target. Also, set the Neural Net's prediction confidence to **None**.

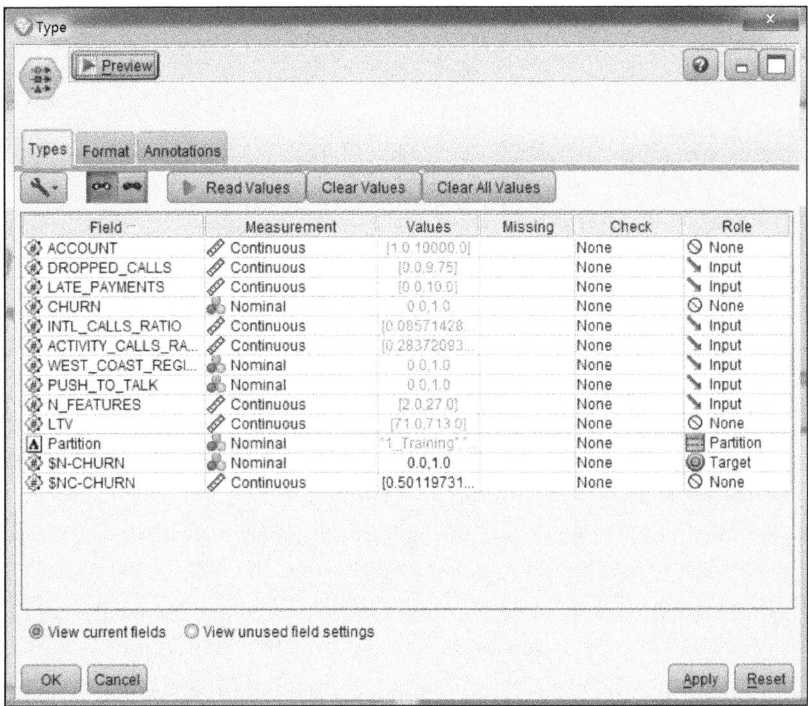

5. Connect a tree-based modeling algorithm to the Type node. We will choose CHAID. Run the CHAID node.
6. Edit the generated model and examine the top branch. (Only partially shown in the following screenshot.)

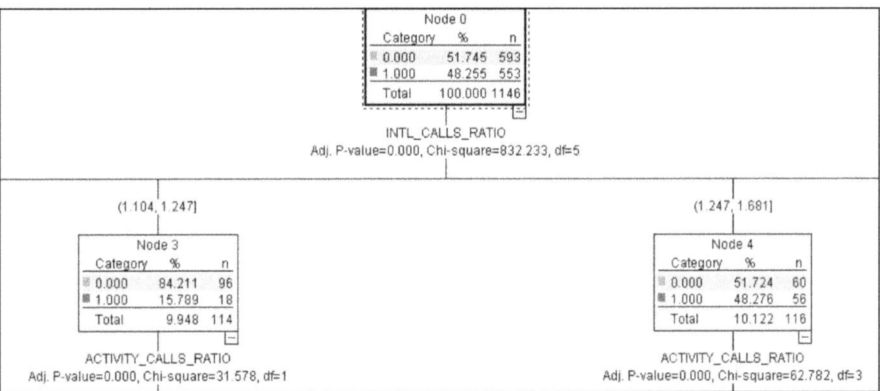

7. Further explore the results.
8. Add an Analysis node and run it. (You might, at first, be surprised by the level of accuracy because the Neural Net has removed much of the noise in the original data).

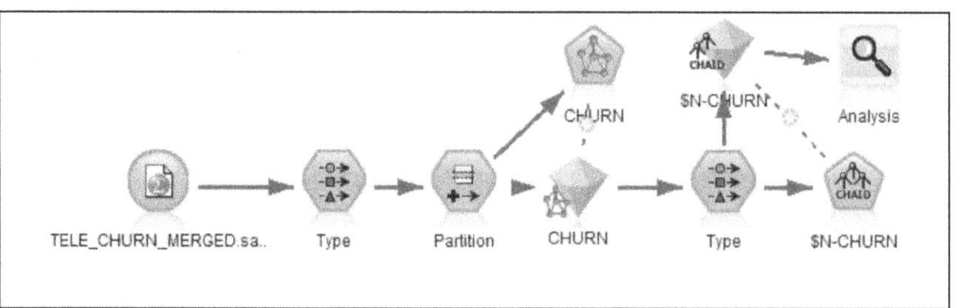

How it works...

There is a simple threefold premise to this recipe:

1. Compared to other techniques, the information that Neural Net produces regarding the inner workings of the model is a bit sparse.
2. CHAID, in contrast, is a relatively straightforward, easy to understand technique that produces a tree diagram that more readily reveals the logic of the model.
3. It is an easy matter to change our target from the actual business target to the Neural Net prediction in order to produce a CHAID style summary for a Neural Net.

It is important to note the resulting tree is only an estimate of what is going on in the Neural Net. While it is usually possible to get a highly accurate CHAID tree using this approach, it is never 100 percent accurate, as there are countless methodological differences between the two techniques that would prevent one from being a true copy of the other. However, if our goal is simply *what was important?* then this approach reveals a substantial portion of the particular Neural Net's logic.

If you are familiar with CHAID's advanced settings, you could consider adjusting them to lean towards a somewhat more accurate (less generalizable) tree. The easiest example would be either turning off the Bonferroni adjustment or setting the confidence level to a lower confidence value. The danger of doing so is minimal since you will not be deploying the CHAID tree. You will still be deploying the Neural Net, so getting a somewhat more detailed tree might be desirable. The screenshot shows the defaults, but a more aggressive tree could be built with settings of 0.10 instead of 0.05 and by removing the check box for the Bonferroni method.

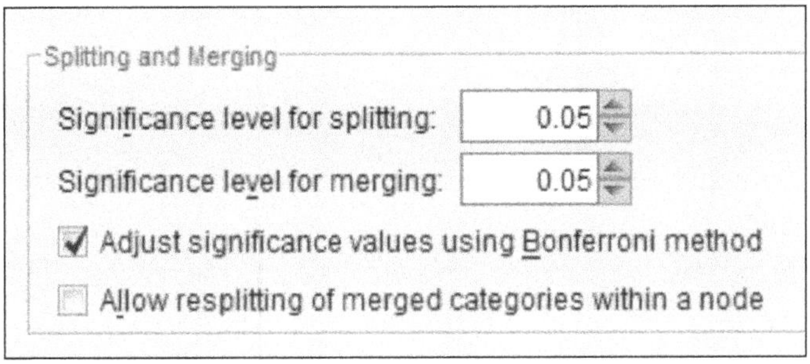

Splitting and Merging

Significance level for splitting: 0.05

Significance level for merging: 0.05

☑ Adjust significance values using Bonferroni method

☐ Allow resplitting of merged categories within a node

See also

- The *Creating a classification tree financial summary using aggregate and an Excel Export node* recipies in this chapter

Correcting a confusion matrix for an imbalanced target variable by incorporating priors

Classification models generate probabilities and a classification predicted class value. When there is a significant imbalance in the proportion of True values in the target variable, the confusion matrix as seen in the Analysis node output will show that the model has all predicted class values equal to the False value, leading an analyst to conclude the model is not effective and needs to be retrained. Most often, the conventional wisdom is to use a Balance node to balance the proportion of True and False values in the target variable, thus eliminating the problem in the confusion matrix.

However, in many cases, the classifier is working fine without the Balance node; it is the interpretation of the model that is biased. Each model generates a probability that the record belongs to the True class and the predicted class is derived from this value by applying a threshold of 0.5. Often, no record has a propensity that high, resulting in every predicted class value being assigned False.

In this recipe we learn how to adjust the predicted class for classification problems with imbalanced data by incorporating the prior probability of the target variable.

Getting ready

This recipe uses the datafile `cup98lrn_reduced_vars3.sav` and the stream `Recipe - correct with priors.str`.

How to do it...

To incorporate prior probabilities when there is an imbalanced target variable:

1. Open the stream `Recipe - correct with priors.str` by navigating to **File** | **Open Stream**.
2. Make sure the datafile points to the correct path to the datafile `cup98lrn_reduced_vars3.sav`.
3. Open the generated model **TARGET_B,** and open the **Settings** tab. Note that compute Raw Propensity is checked. Close the generated model.
4. Duplicate the generated model by copying and pasting the node in the stream. Connect the duplicated model to the original generated model.
5. Add a Type node to the stream and connect it to the generated model. Open the Type node and scroll to the bottom of the list. Note that the fields related to the two models have not yet been instantiated. Click on **Read Values** so that they are fully instantiated.

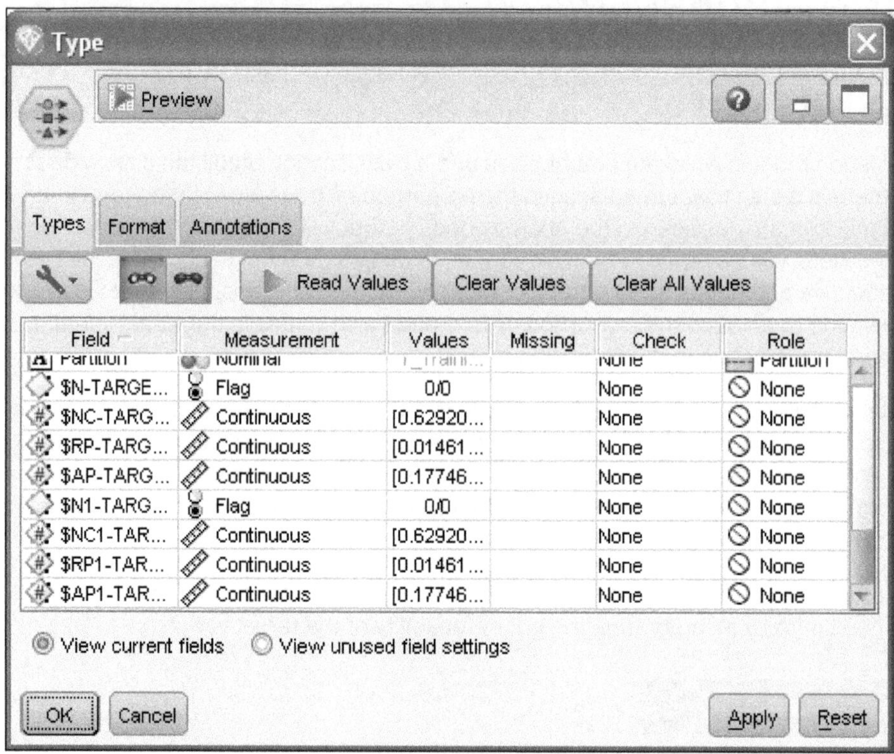

6. Insert a Filler node and connect it to the Type node.

7. Open the Filler node and, in the variable list, select `$N1-TARGET_B`. Inside the Condition section, type `$RP1-TARGET_B' >= TARGET_B_Mean`, Click on **OK** to dismiss the Filler node (after exiting the Expression Builder).

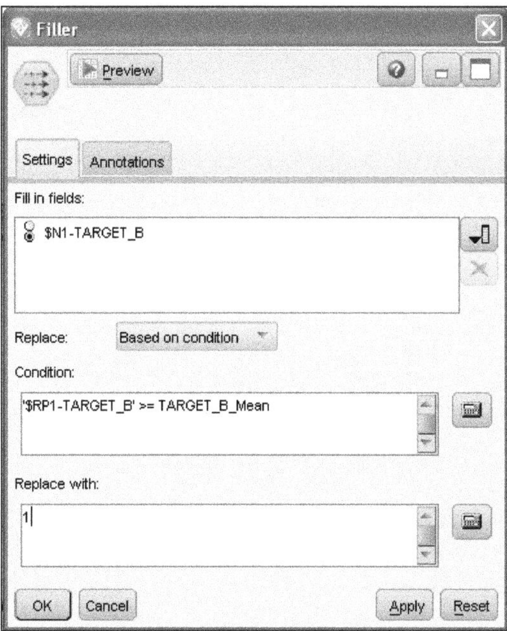

8. Insert an Analysis node to the stream. Open the Analysis node and click on the check box for **Coincidence Matrices**. Click on **OK**.

9. Run the stream to the Analysis node. Notice that the coincidence matrix (confusion matrix) for `$N-TARGET_B` has no predictions with value = 1, but the coincidence matrix for the second model, the one adjusted by step 7 (`$N1-TARGET_B`), has more than 30 percent of the records labeled as value = 1.

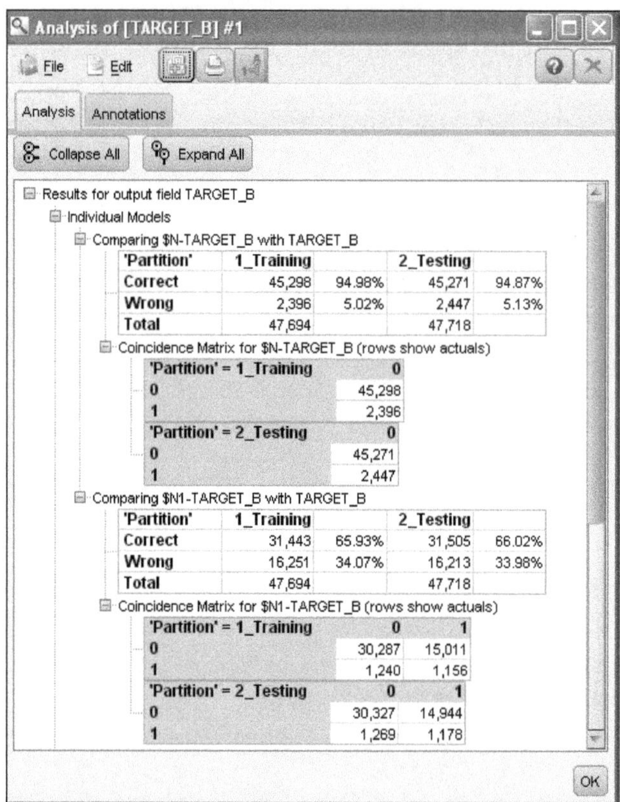

How it works...

Classification algorithms do not generate categorical predictions; they generate probabilities, likelihoods, or confidences. For this data set, the target variable, TARGET_B, has two values: 1 and 0. The classifier output from any classification algorithm will be a number between 0 and 1. To convert the probability to a 1 or 0 label, the probability is thresholded, and the default in Modeler (and all predictive analytics software) is the threshold at 0.5. This recipe changes that default threshold to the prior probability.

The proportion of TARGET_B = 1 values in the data is 5.1 percent, and therefore this is the classic imbalanced target variable problem. One solution to this problem is to resample the data so that the proportion of 1s and 0s are equal, normally achieved through use of the Balance node in Modeler. Moreover, one can create the Balance node from running a Distribution node for TARGET_B, and using the **Generate | Balance node (reduce)** option. The justification for balancing the sample is that, if one doesn't do it, all the records will be classified with value = 0.

The reason for all the classification decisions having value 0 is not because the Neural Network isn't working properly. Consider the histogram of predictions from the Neural Network shown in the following screenshot. Notice that the maximum value of the predictions is less than 0.4, but the center of density is about 0.05. The actual shape of the histogram and the maximum predicted value depend on the Neural Network; some may have maximum values slightly above 0.5.

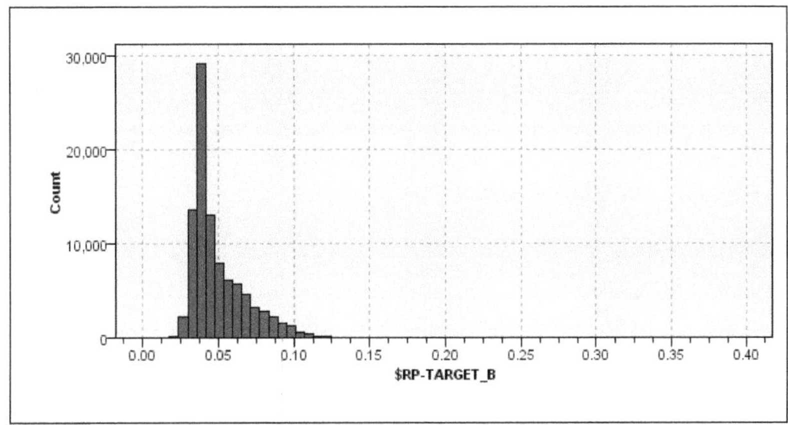

If the threshold for the classification decision is set to 0.5, since no neural network predicted confidence is greater than 0.5, all of the classification labels will be 0. However, if one sets the threshold to the TARGET_B prior probability, 0.051, many of the predictions will exceed that value and be labeled as 1. We can see the result of the new threshold by color-coding the histogram of the previous figure with the new class label, in the following screenshot.

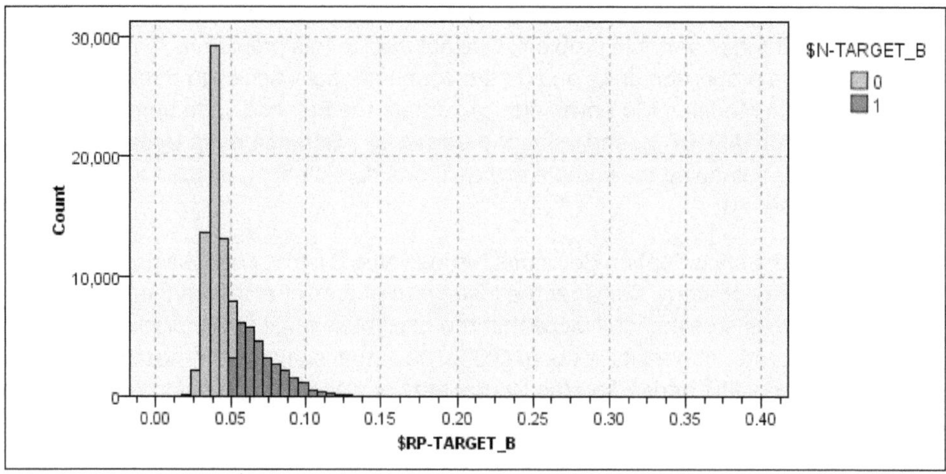

This recipe used a Filler node to modify the existing predicted target value. The categorical prediction from the Neural Network whose prediction is being changed is `$N1-TARGET_B`. The `$` variables are special field names that are used automatically in the Analysis node and Evaluation node. It's possible to construct one's own `$` fields with a Derive node, but it is safer to modify the one that's already in the data.

There's more...

This same procedure defined in this recipe works for other modeling algorithms as well, including logistic regression. Decision trees are a different matter. Consider the following screenshot. This result, stating that the C5 tree didn't split at all, is the result of the imbalanced target variable.

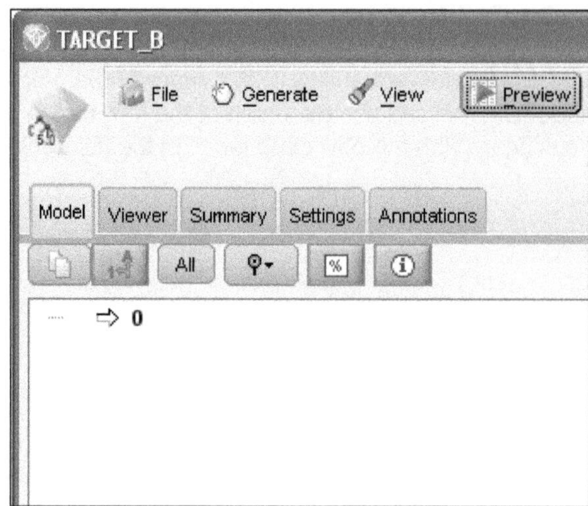

Rather than balancing the sample, there are other ways to get a tree built. For C&RT or Quest trees, go to the **Build Options**, select the **Costs & Priors** item, and select **Equal for all classes** for priors: equal priors. This option forces C&RT to treat the two classes mathematically as if their counts were equal. It is equivalent to running the Balance node to boost samples so that there are equal numbers of 0s and 1s. However, it's done without adding additional records to the data, slowing down training; equal priors is purely a mathematical reweighting.

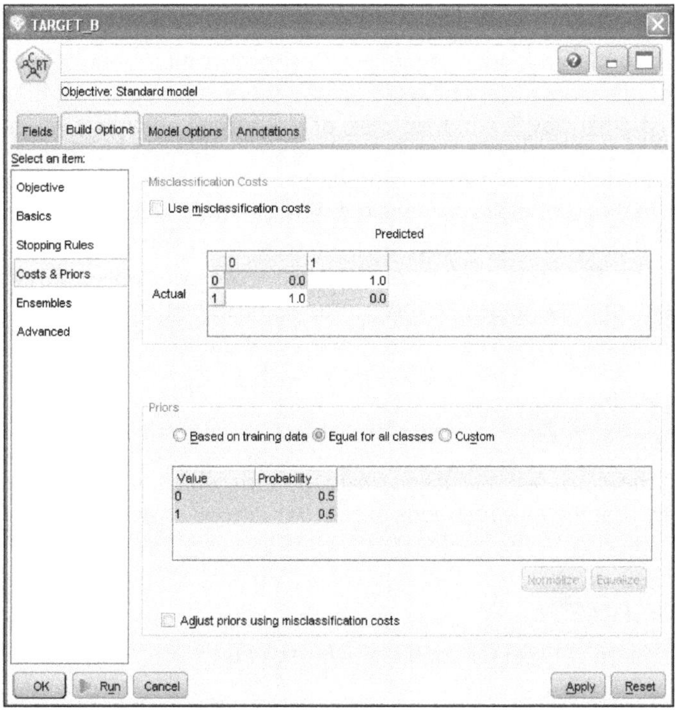

The C5 tree doesn't have the option of setting priors. An alternative, one that will work not only with C5 but also with C&RT, CHAID, and Quest trees, is to change the **Misclassification Costs** so that the cost of classifying a one as a zero is 20, approximately the ratio of the 95 percent 0s to 5 percent 1s.

See also

- The *Evaluating the need to sample from the initial data* recipe in *Chapter 1, Data Understanding*
- The *Evaluating balancing with Auto Classifier* recipe in *Chapter 6, Selecting and Building a Model*

Using aggregate to write cluster centers to Excel for conditional formatting

In nearly all organizations, the Modeler practitioners and model builders are reporting to a management team that either does not have day to day access to Modeler or is unfamiliar with the tool. Therefore, during the evaluation phase, if the analyst is to break away from the constraints of a purely technical judging of models, then he or she needs to give management the ability to join into the evaluation of models. One rarely exports raw data to Excel. The size limitation would almost always be a factor, and there is rarely any good reason to do it. However, Excel is a great way to send, discuss, and report on summary information.

In this recipe, we will take the summary information about a handful of clusters and prepare it in a form that a modeler can easily share with their colleagues. The idea of a cluster center is simple; it is the average value on a series of fields that were used when the clusters were formed. By conditionally coloring those values we can see where the clusters have high, medium, and low values. In this example, those high and low averages reflect their purchasing behavior.

Getting ready

We will start with the `Cluster to Excel.str` stream, which uses a modified subset of the retail data. The file that the stream needs is called `Cluster Data`.

How to do it...

To write cluster centers to Excel for conditional formatting:

1. Open the `Cluster to Excel.str` stream.

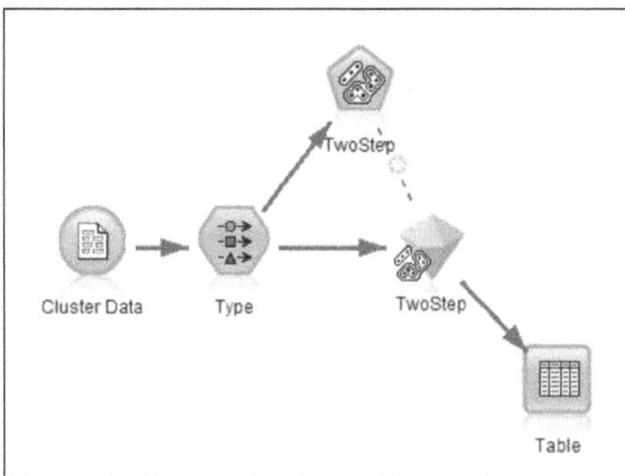

2. Edit the TwoStep generated model. Notice that seven clusters have been found.

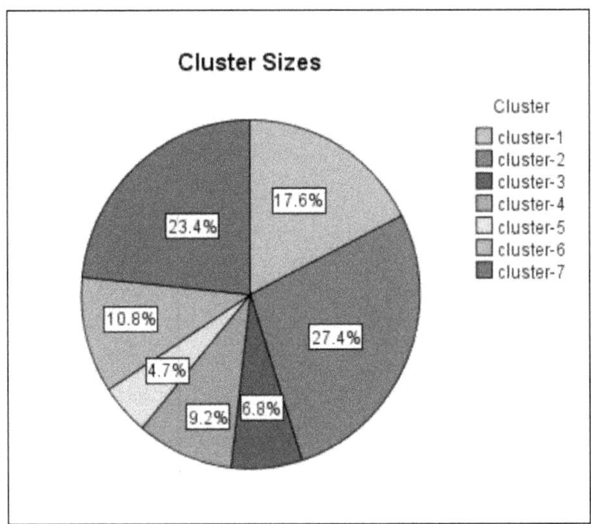

3. Run the Table node. The data is a series of proportions showing the categories within which the customer has been spending. The clusters are groups of customers with similar spending patterns. The cluster variable is at the far right.

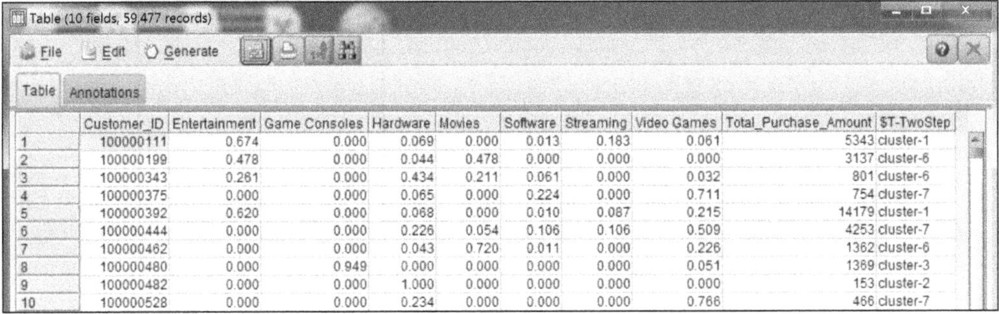

	Customer_ID	Entertainment	Game Consoles	Hardware	Movies	Software	Streaming	Video Games	Total_Purchase_Amount	$T-TwoStep
1	100000111	0.674	0.000	0.069	0.000	0.013	0.183	0.061	5343	cluster-1
2	100000199	0.478	0.000	0.044	0.478	0.000	0.000	0.000	3137	cluster-6
3	100000343	0.261	0.000	0.434	0.211	0.061	0.000	0.032	801	cluster-6
4	100000375	0.000	0.000	0.065	0.000	0.224	0.000	0.711	754	cluster-7
5	100000392	0.620	0.000	0.068	0.000	0.010	0.087	0.215	14179	cluster-1
6	100000444	0.000	0.000	0.226	0.054	0.106	0.106	0.509	4253	cluster-7
7	100000462	0.000	0.000	0.043	0.720	0.011	0.000	0.226	1362	cluster-6
8	100000480	0.000	0.949	0.000	0.000	0.000	0.000	0.051	1369	cluster-3
9	100000482	0.000	0.000	1.000	0.000	0.000	0.000	0.000	153	cluster-2
10	100000528	0.000	0.000	0.234	0.000	0.000	0.000	0.766	466	cluster-7

4. Add an Aggregate node downstream of the generated model. Make the cluster membership variable, `$T-TwoStep`, the **Key** field, and allow all of the proportions to be **Aggregate fields** with a **Mean** calculated. Finally, make **Total_Purchases** an Aggregate field with both **Sum** and **Mean** selected.

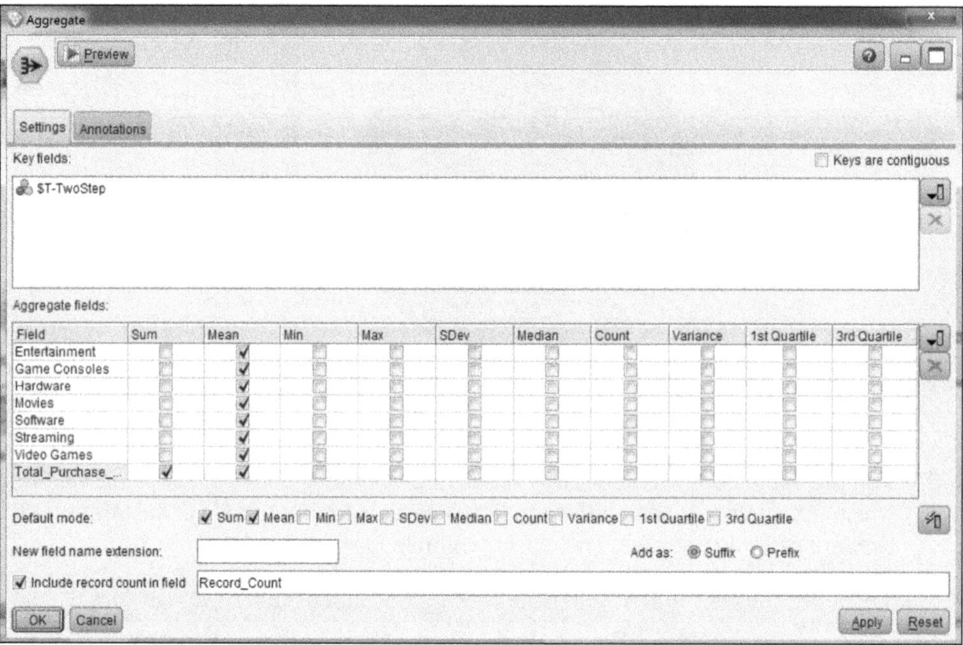

5. Add a Type node downstream of the Aggregate node. The default settings will be fine.
6. Add an Excel Export node, and give the file a path on your computer.

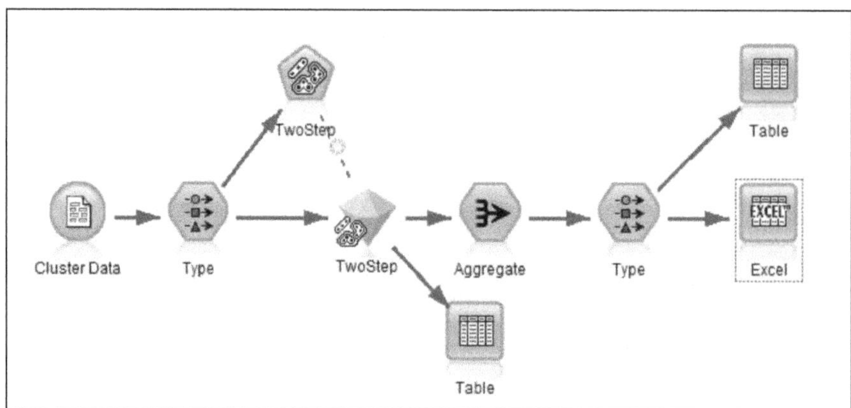

7. Open the resulting Excel file in Excel. (Some minor formatting has been applied such as currency and percentages.)
8. Highlight just the proportions and apply three-color conditional formatting in Excel.

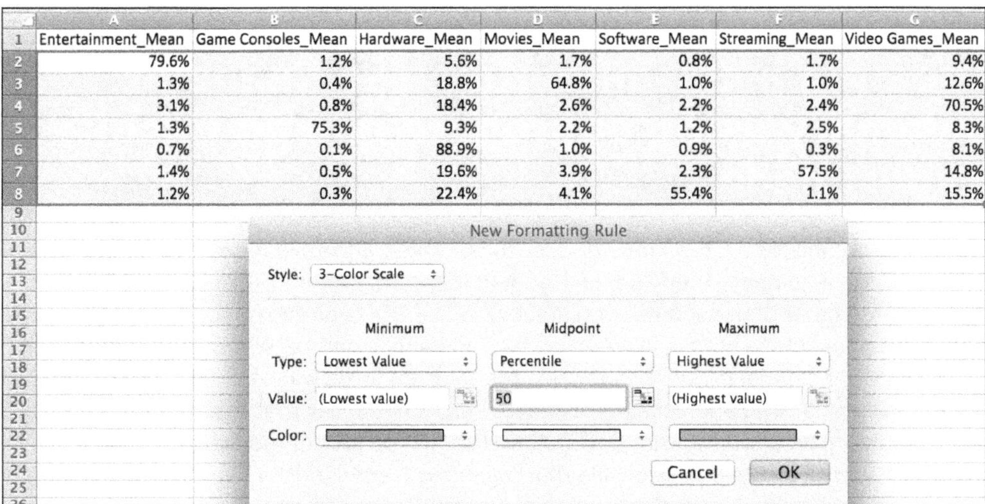

Entertainment_Mean	Game Consoles_Mean	Hardware_Mean	Movies_Mean	Software_Mean	Streaming_Mean	Video Games_Mean
79.6%	1.2%	5.6%	1.7%	0.8%	1.7%	9.4%
1.3%	0.4%	18.8%	64.8%	1.0%	1.0%	12.6%
3.1%	0.8%	18.4%	2.6%	2.2%	2.4%	70.5%
1.3%	75.3%	9.3%	2.2%	1.2%	2.5%	8.3%
0.7%	0.1%	88.9%	1.0%	0.9%	0.3%	8.1%
1.4%	0.5%	19.6%	3.9%	2.3%	57.5%	14.8%
1.2%	0.3%	22.4%	4.1%	55.4%	1.1%	15.5%

9. The final result makes it easy to see that the cluster in the first row spends a large proportion on Entertainment. Other clusters spend in other areas.

Entertainment_Mean	Game Consoles_Mean	Hardware_Mean	Movies_Mean	Software_Mean	Streaming_Mean	Video Games_Mean
79.6%	1.2%	5.6%	1.7%	0.8%	1.7%	9.4%
1.3%	0.4%	18.8%	64.8%	1.0%	1.0%	12.6%
3.1%	0.8%	18.4%	2.6%	2.2%	2.4%	70.5%
1.3%	75.3%	9.3%	2.2%	1.2%	2.5%	8.3%
0.7%	0.1%	88.9%	1.0%	0.9%	0.3%	8.1%
1.4%	0.5%	19.6%	3.9%	2.3%	57.5%	14.8%
1.2%	0.3%	22.4%	4.1%	55.4%	1.1%	15.5%

How it works...

The results directly out of the cluster analysis are not as helpful to colleagues because it has a row for each customer. The generated model offers lots of interesting analyses, some of which might make for good PowerPoint slides, but colleagues without Modeler need some way of examining the cluster results in more detail.

By making the cluster membership a Key Field in an Aggregate node, all of the important information is summarized. The conditional formatting makes it even easier to read, and colleagues can not only see, but also manipulate the result.

See also

Creating a classification tree financial summary using aggregate and an Excel Export node recipe in this chapter

Creating a classification tree financial summary using aggregate and an Excel Export node

In nearly all organizations, the Modeler user collaborates with colleagues that do not have Modeler. If one is to honor the *Value Law* quoted in the chapter introduction, criteria must be considered other than accuracy and stability. Since ROI is on the mind of the data miner, those additional criteria always include some of a financial nature. Whether it be potential cost savings or potential revenue increases, the relevant fields will be ones that management will be very familiar with and very interested in. This is not to say that these variables must be model inputs—quite often they are not—but they should be part of the evaluation process. In this recipe, we will process an Excel file that organizes these kinds of variables in the context of a tree segmentation. It combines variables exported from the tree model, including Rule Identifier and the Model's prediction, with financial variables in summary, from the data set.

Getting ready

We will start with `CHAID Financial Summary.str` stream.

How to do it...

To process an Excel file that organizes these kinds of variables in the context of a tree segmentation:

1. Open the `CHAID Financial Summary.str` stream.

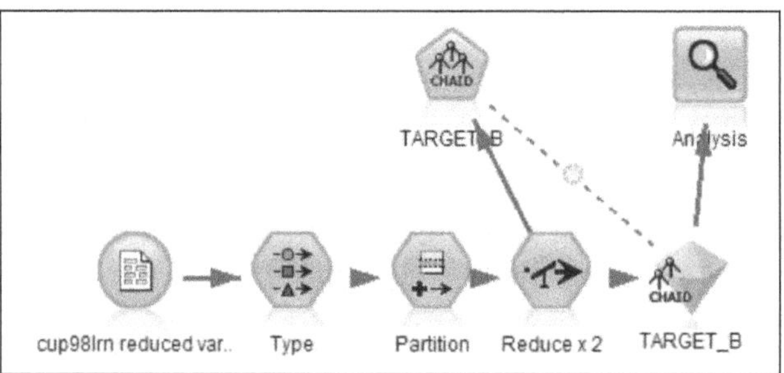

2. Edit the CHAID's generated model. In Settings, verify that **Rule identifier** is selected.

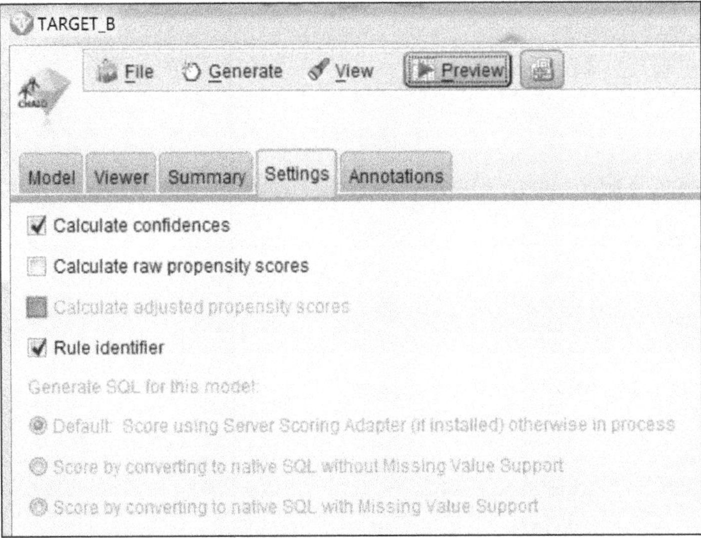

3. Add a Select node selecting only **Validate Partition**. (Basing ROI estimates and other business decisions on Validation data is a very conservative and appropriate move. Sometimes the data that we will use to validate will be brand new data that didn't exist when the project began.)
4. Add an Aggregate node. The **Rule Identifier** will be our **Key** Field. **NGIFTALL** and **AVEGIFT** will have a **Sum** and a **Mean**. **LASTGIFT** and **TARGET_B** will have a **Mean** only.

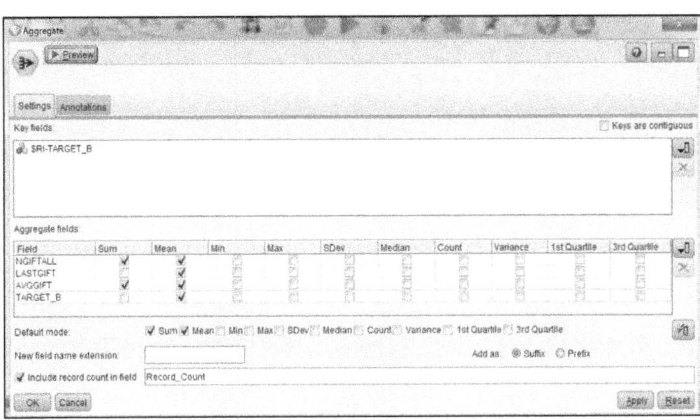

5. Add a Sort node and select **Sort in Descending order** for the variable **TARGET_B_ mean**. The mean of a 0/1 variable is the same as the percentage of 1. In this case, this trick allows us to put the most responsive segments in the top row and the least responsive in the bottom row.

6. Add a Table node and click on **Run**.
7. Add a Type node and an Excel Export node. Click on **Run.**

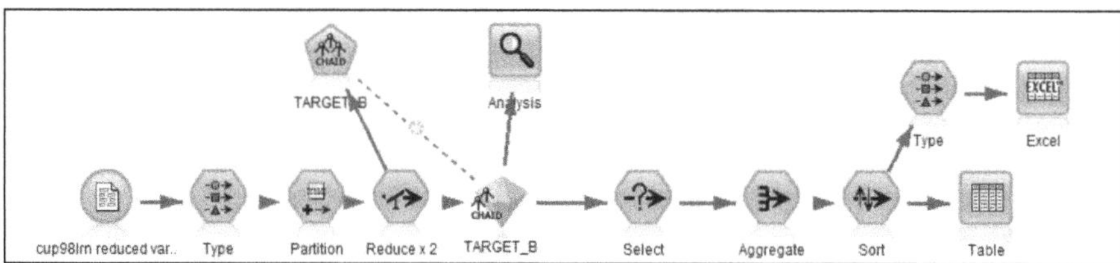

The provided file has had some light editing to add currency and percentage labeling where appropriate.

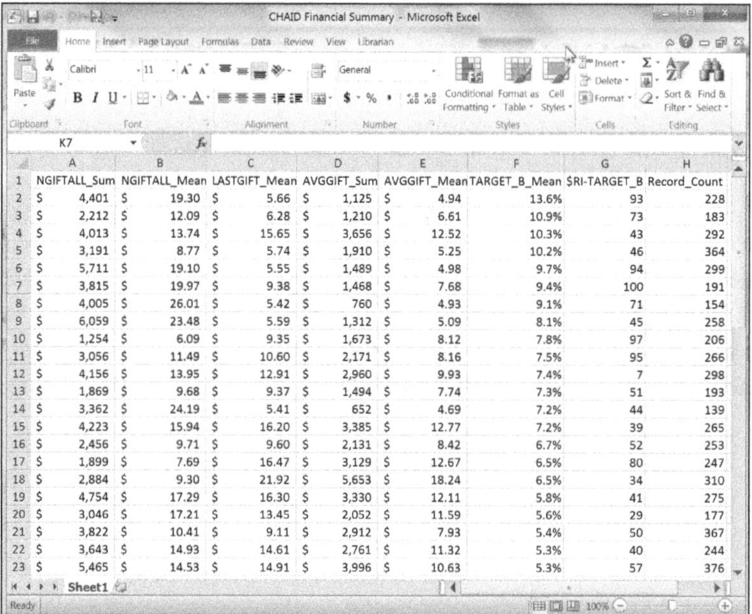

	NGIFTALL_Sum	NGIFTALL_Mean	LASTGIFT_Mean	AVGGIFT_Sum	AVGGIFT_Mean	TARGET_B_Mean	$RI-TARGET_B	Record_Count
2	$ 4,401	$ 19.30	$ 5.66	$ 1,125	$ 4.94	13.6%	93	228
3	$ 2,212	$ 12.09	$ 6.28	$ 1,210	$ 6.61	10.9%	73	183
4	$ 4,013	$ 13.74	$ 15.65	$ 3,656	$ 12.52	10.3%	43	292
5	$ 3,191	$ 8.77	$ 5.74	$ 1,910	$ 5.25	10.2%	46	364
6	$ 5,711	$ 19.10	$ 5.55	$ 1,489	$ 4.98	9.7%	94	299
7	$ 3,815	$ 19.97	$ 9.38	$ 1,468	$ 7.68	9.4%	100	191
8	$ 4,005	$ 26.01	$ 5.42	$ 760	$ 4.93	9.1%	71	154
9	$ 6,059	$ 23.48	$ 5.59	$ 1,312	$ 5.09	8.1%	45	258
10	$ 1,254	$ 6.09	$ 9.35	$ 1,673	$ 8.12	7.8%	97	206
11	$ 3,056	$ 11.49	$ 10.60	$ 2,171	$ 8.16	7.5%	95	266
12	$ 4,156	$ 13.95	$ 12.91	$ 2,960	$ 9.93	7.4%	7	298
13	$ 1,869	$ 9.68	$ 9.37	$ 1,494	$ 7.74	7.3%	51	193
14	$ 3,362	$ 24.19	$ 5.41	$ 652	$ 4.69	7.2%	44	139
15	$ 4,223	$ 15.94	$ 16.20	$ 3,385	$ 12.77	7.2%	39	265
16	$ 2,456	$ 9.71	$ 9.60	$ 2,131	$ 8.42	6.7%	52	253
17	$ 1,899	$ 7.69	$ 16.47	$ 3,129	$ 12.67	6.5%	80	247
18	$ 2,884	$ 9.30	$ 21.92	$ 5,653	$ 18.24	6.5%	34	310
19	$ 4,754	$ 17.29	$ 16.30	$ 3,330	$ 12.11	5.8%	41	275
20	$ 3,046	$ 17.21	$ 13.45	$ 2,052	$ 11.59	5.6%	29	177
21	$ 3,822	$ 10.41	$ 9.11	$ 2,912	$ 7.93	5.4%	50	367
22	$ 3,643	$ 14.93	$ 14.61	$ 2,761	$ 11.32	5.3%	40	244
23	$ 5,465	$ 14.53	$ 14.91	$ 3,996	$ 10.63	5.3%	57	376

How it works...

The whole idea behind this recipe is that on any project you have many colleagues that have access to Excel, but not to Modeler. By writing out the tree, not as a tree diagram but with the financial characteristics of the tree segments, you are giving your colleagues something that they can study, but that they can also manipulate. They can help decide how many segments to market to in a more detailed way than they could with only a picture or slides. They can use their Excel skills to dig deeper. You might decide to offer up the original data in a second tab if it does not exceed the file size limitations.

The mechanics of the recipe are quite simple. The key is to request the Rule Identifier. This feature is not available for every technique. Both C&RT and CHAID have it, for instance. C5.0 does not. Also, a technique such as Neural Net or SVMs will not have it because they do not produce segments.

See also

- The *Using aggregate to write cluster centers to Excel for conditional formatting* recipe in this chapter

Reformatting data for reporting with a Transpose node

The Transpose node is very useful for restructuring data. One way it can be particularly helpful is with reporting of results, especially when the data has many more columns than rows.

Getting ready

This recipe uses the datafile `cup98lrn_reduced_vars3.sav` and the stream `Recipe - report with transpose.str`.

How to do it...

To reformat data with a Transpose node:

1. Open the stream `Recipe - report with transpose.str` by navigating to **File | Open Stream**.
2. Make sure the datafile points to the correct path to `cup98lrn_reduced_vars3.sav`.
3. Insert an Aggregate node and connect it to the Type node.

4. Open the Aggregate node and in the **Key fields:** area, select **TARGET_B** as the field to aggregate. In the **Default Mode:** options, deselect **Sum** so only **Mean** is checked. Click on the **Apply default operations** button at the right-end of the **Default Mode:** options. In the **Aggregate fields** region, select all of the continuous fields (except **CONTROLN**) and all of the flag fields. Only the **Mean** should be checked. If **Sum** is still checked, uncheck **Sum** for all fields. Click on **OK**.

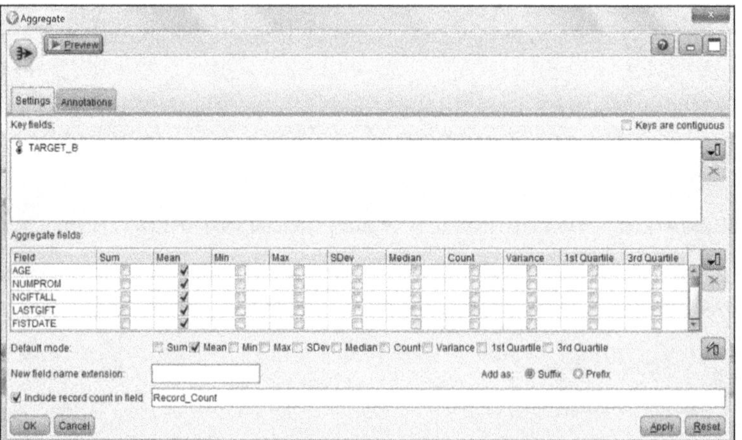

5. Insert a Transpose node and connect it to the Aggregate node.
6. Open the Transpose node. Click on the **Read from field** radio button and select **TARGET_B** from the drop-down menu. Click on the **Read Values** button. You should see the values **0** and **1** listed. Click on **OK**.

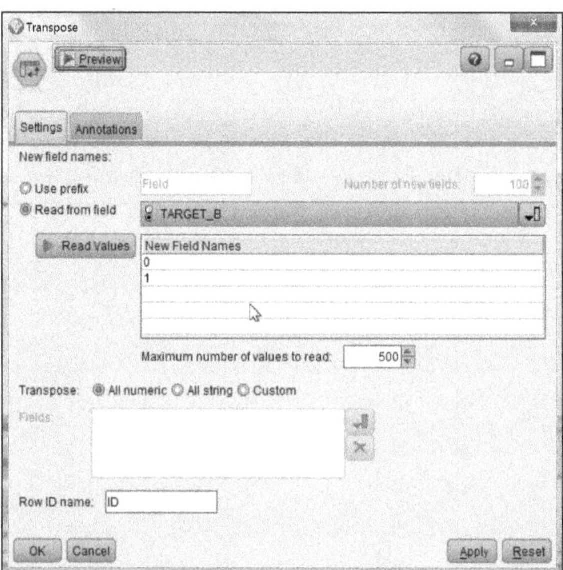

7. Insert a Table node and connect it to the Transpose node. Run the Table node to see the report.

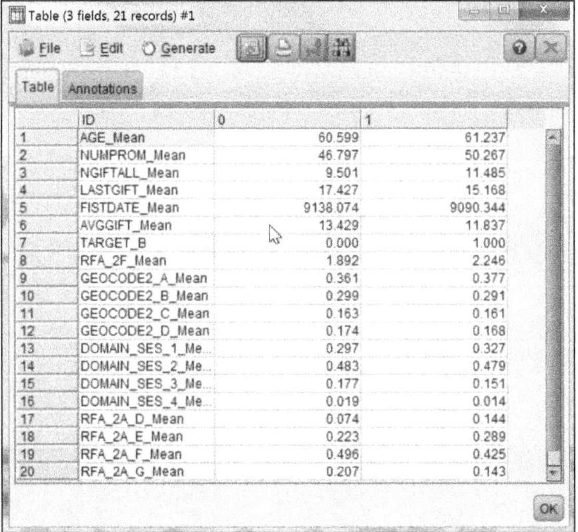

	ID	0	1
1	AGE_Mean	60.599	61.237
2	NUMPROM_Mean	46.797	50.267
3	NGIFTALL_Mean	9.501	11.485
4	LASTGIFT_Mean	17.427	15.168
5	FISTDATE_Mean	9138.074	9090.344
6	AVGGIFT_Mean	13.429	11.837
7	TARGET_B	0.000	1.000
8	RFA_2F_Mean	1.892	2.246
9	GEOCODE2_A_Mean	0.361	0.377
10	GEOCODE2_B_Mean	0.299	0.291
11	GEOCODE2_C_Mean	0.163	0.161
12	GEOCODE2_D_Mean	0.174	0.168
13	DOMAIN_SES_1_Me...	0.297	0.327
14	DOMAIN_SES_2_Me...	0.483	0.479
15	DOMAIN_SES_3_Me...	0.177	0.151
16	DOMAIN_SES_4_Me...	0.019	0.014
17	RFA_2A_D_Mean	0.074	0.144
18	RFA_2A_E_Mean	0.223	0.289
19	RFA_2A_F_Mean	0.496	0.425
20	RFA_2A_G_Mean	0.207	0.143

How it works...

The Transpose node simply rotates the data so the columns in the data are shown in rows, and the rows in the data are shown in columns. For reporting, when there are only a few rows but there could be several, dozens, or even hundreds of columns, transposing the summary output makes it easier to read.

There's more...

The Transpose node output is easier to copy and paste into Excel or Word for reporting.

Another example of a report that can be improved using a Transpose node is with clustering. After running a K-means clustering model, each record now has a cluster label.

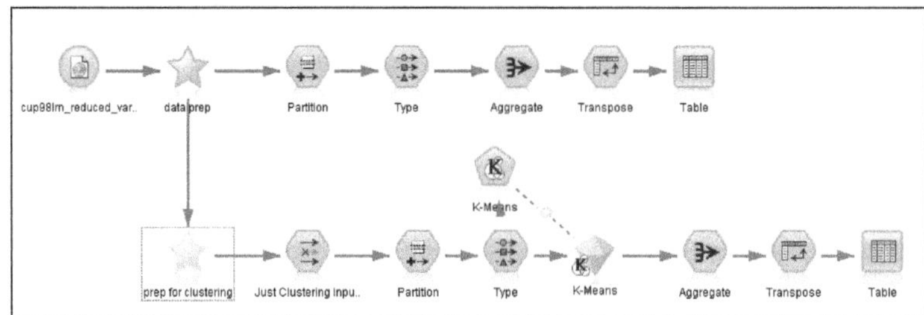

One can use the same procedure described in this recipe to aggregate key fields by cluster number, transpose the results, and generate a report where the field mean values are in the rows and cluster IDs are in the columns.

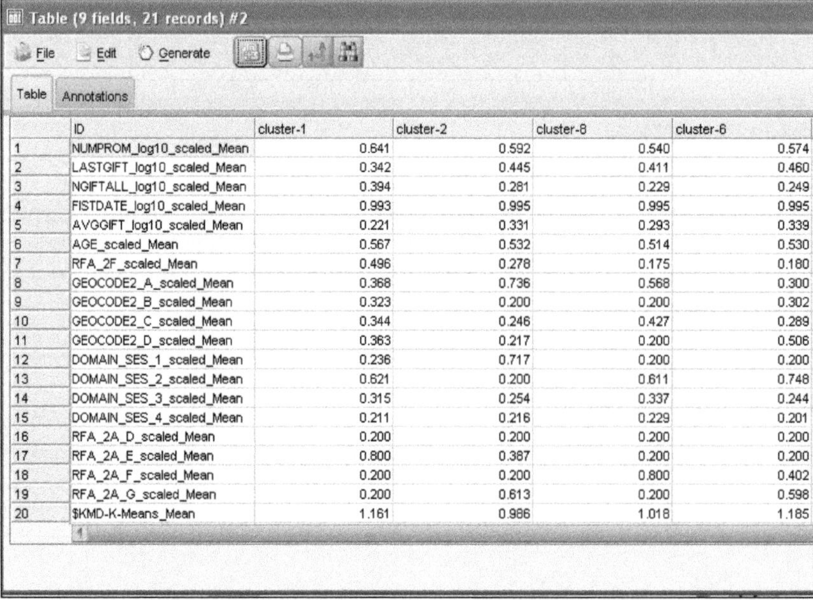

	ID	cluster-1	cluster-2	cluster-8	cluster-6
1	NUMPROM_log10_scaled_Mean	0.641	0.592	0.540	0.574
2	LASTGIFT_log10_scaled_Mean	0.342	0.445	0.411	0.460
3	NGIFTALL_log10_scaled_Mean	0.394	0.281	0.229	0.249
4	FISTDATE_log10_scaled_Mean	0.993	0.995	0.995	0.995
5	AVGGIFT_log10_scaled_Mean	0.221	0.331	0.293	0.339
6	AGE_scaled_Mean	0.567	0.532	0.514	0.530
7	RFA_2F_scaled_Mean	0.496	0.278	0.175	0.180
8	GEOCODE2_A_scaled_Mean	0.368	0.736	0.568	0.300
9	GEOCODE2_B_scaled_Mean	0.323	0.200	0.200	0.302
10	GEOCODE2_C_scaled_Mean	0.344	0.246	0.427	0.289
11	GEOCODE2_D_scaled_Mean	0.363	0.217	0.200	0.506
12	DOMAIN_SES_1_scaled_Mean	0.236	0.717	0.200	0.200
13	DOMAIN_SES_2_scaled_Mean	0.621	0.200	0.611	0.748
14	DOMAIN_SES_3_scaled_Mean	0.315	0.254	0.337	0.244
15	DOMAIN_SES_4_scaled_Mean	0.211	0.216	0.229	0.201
16	RFA_2A_D_scaled_Mean	0.200	0.200	0.200	0.200
17	RFA_2A_E_scaled_Mean	0.800	0.387	0.200	0.200
18	RFA_2A_F_scaled_Mean	0.200	0.200	0.800	0.402
19	RFA_2A_G_scaled_Mean	0.200	0.613	0.200	0.598
20	$KMD-K-Means_Mean	1.161	0.986	1.018	1.185

But one can do even more for clustering models and reporting. Rather than aggregating by cluster value to compute average values, one can generate the prototype record for each cluster, which is the record that is closest to the center of each cluster.

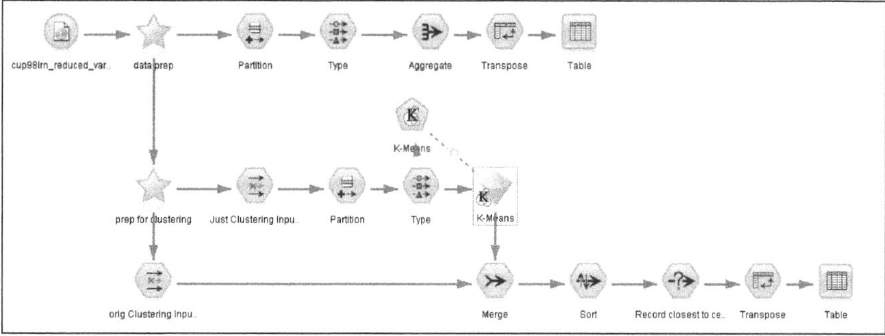

To create this report, one first sorts the records by cluster ID (`$KM-K-Means`) and then by the distance the record is from the cluster center (`$KMD-K-Means`), ascending. Then one selects the first-occurring record for each cluster with a Select node (@INDEX = 1 or @OFFSET($KM-K-Means, 1) /= $KM-K-Means). The @OFFSET portion of the Select node condition identifies when the cluster label for the current record differs from the cluster label of the previous record—the record with the smallest distance from the cluster center. Then the Transpose node is used to generate the report. In this report, `CONTROLN` (customer ID) 110971 is the closest to the center of cluster-1.

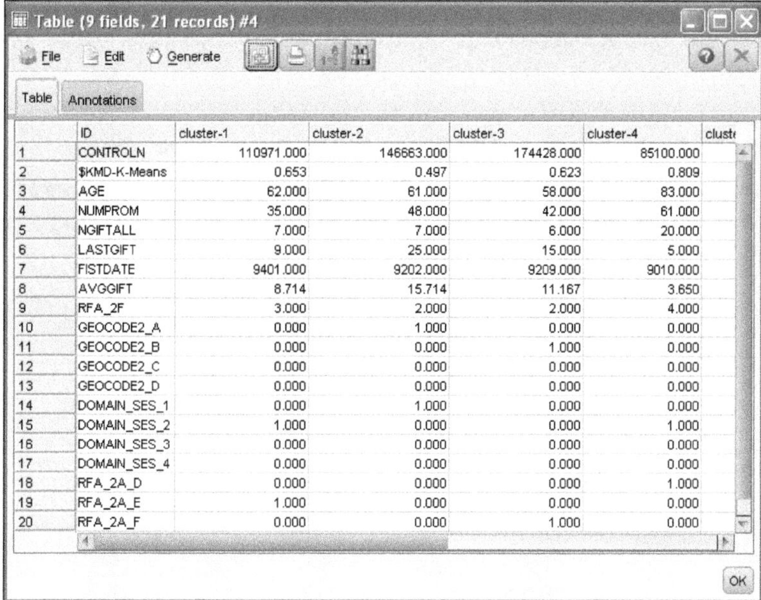

Table (9 fields, 21 records) #4

File Edit Generate

Table Annotations

	ID	cluster-1	cluster-2	cluster-3	cluster-4	clust
1	CONTROLN	110971.000	146663.000	174428.000	85100.000	
2	$KMD-K-Means	0.653	0.497	0.623	0.809	
3	AGE	62.000	61.000	58.000	83.000	
4	NUMPROM	35.000	48.000	42.000	61.000	
5	NGIFTALL	7.000	7.000	6.000	20.000	
6	LASTGIFT	9.000	25.000	15.000	5.000	
7	FISTDATE	9401.000	9202.000	9209.000	9010.000	
8	AVGGIFT	8.714	15.714	11.167	3.650	
9	RFA_2F	3.000	2.000	2.000	4.000	
10	GEOCODE2_A	0.000	1.000	0.000	0.000	
11	GEOCODE2_B	0.000	0.000	1.000	0.000	
12	GEOCODE2_C	0.000	0.000	0.000	0.000	
13	GEOCODE2_D	0.000	0.000	0.000	0.000	
14	DOMAIN_SES_1	0.000	1.000	0.000	0.000	
15	DOMAIN_SES_2	1.000	0.000	0.000	1.000	
16	DOMAIN_SES_3	0.000	0.000	0.000	0.000	
17	DOMAIN_SES_4	0.000	0.000	0.000	0.000	
18	RFA_2A_D	0.000	0.000	0.000	1.000	
19	RFA_2A_E	1.000	0.000	0.000	0.000	
20	RFA_2A_F	0.000	0.000	1.000	0.000	

OK

See also

- The *Changing formatting of fields in a Table node* recipe in this chapter

Changing formatting of fields in a Table node

Table nodes are typically used as they are without any customization. In this recipe, we will modify the settings so that some fields that are really integers are displayed without any decimals and other fields are displayed with additional digits of precision.

Getting ready

This recipe uses the datafile `cup98lrn_reduced_vars3.sav` and the stream `Recipe - modify table.str`.

How to do it...

To change formatting of fields in a Table node:

1. Open the stream `Recipe - modify table.str` by navigating to **File** | **Open Stream**. This is the stream you completed in the recipe *Reformatting data for reporting with a Transpose node*.
2. Make sure the datafile points to the correct path to `cup98lrn_reduced_vars3.sav`.
3. Insert a Table node and attach it to the Type node. Open the Table node. Right-click on the node and select the **Edit** option and then the **Format tab**.
4. Double-click on the **AGE** row, select **Field Format** (that appears as **####.###**). In the row that has **Standard decimal places:**, click on the **Specify:** radio button and change the digits of precision from **3** to **0**. Click on OK.

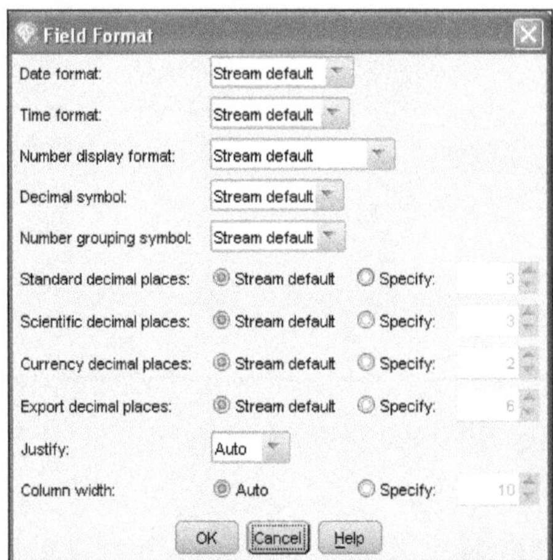

5. Next, for **AGE**, in the **Justify** column, click on **Auto** and select **Center**.
6. Repeat Steps 4 and 5 for variables **LASTGIFT**, **FISTDATE**, **CONTROLN**, and **RFA_2F**.
7. For the field **AVGGIFT_STATEMean**, change the **Format field** from **3** digits of precision to **6** by following the step 4 process, but change the Specify field to **6**.
8. Change the **Justify** column to **Center** for all of the remaining fields that are not yet centered.
9. Run the Table node.

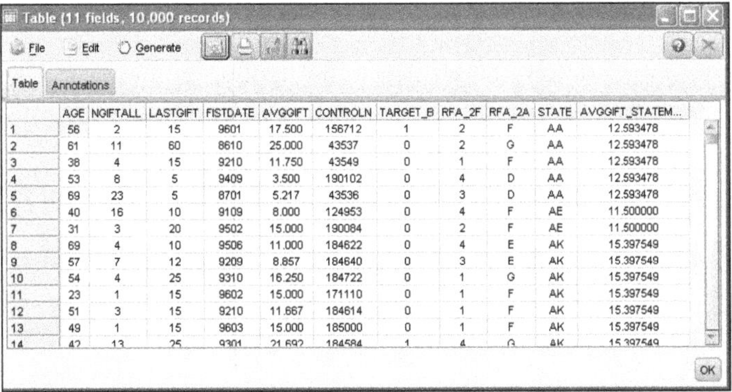

How it works...

Usually, the default settings for the Table node are sufficient for seeing the values in the data. However, sometimes changing the format improves the visual appeal of the table layout. In this data, changing all of the numerical data that are integers to have no decimal places cleans the look of the table considerably. The default Table node output, without the modifications in this recipe, would result in the output shown in the following screenshot:

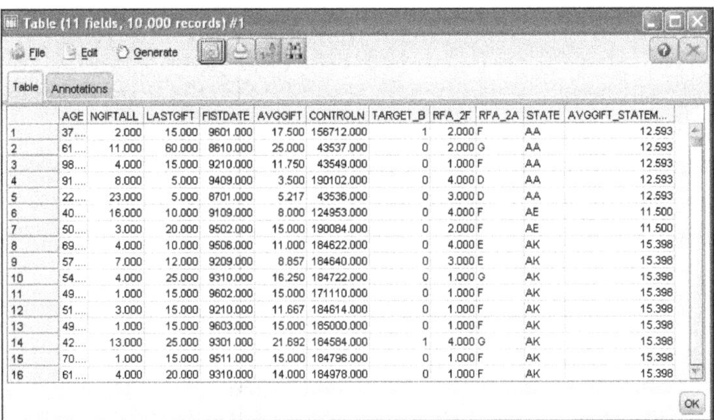

There's more...

The Table Format options also controls the column width. This is particularly useful when the field name is long, which makes the column width big. Changing this from auto to a smaller number such as 10 or 20 will restrain that default width.

If one changes Table node Format settings often for a particular stream, one can make a global change to the formats (digits of precision, not justification). Navigate to **Tools** | **Stream Properties** | **Options** where one finds a screen such as the one shown in the following screenshot.

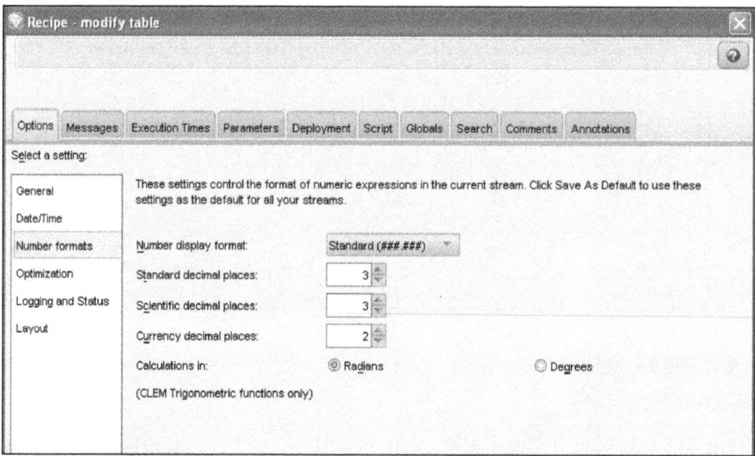

See also

- The *Reformatting data for reporting with a Transpose node* recipe in this chapter

Combining generated filters

When building a predictive model, if many data fields are available to use as inputs to the model, then reducing the number of inputs can lead to better, simpler and easier-to-use models. Fields or features can be selected in a number of ways: by using business and data knowledge, by analysis to select individual fields that have a relation to the predictive target, and by using other models to select features whose relevance is more multivariate in nature.

In a Modeler stream, selections of fields are usually represented by Filter nodes. If multiple selections from the same set of fields have been produced, for example by generating Filter nodes from different models, then it is useful to combine these filters. Filters can be combined in different ways; for example, if we wish to select only the fields that were selected by both models, then the filters are placed in sequence. If we wish to select all the fields that were selected by either model, then a different technique is required.

This recipe shows how to combine two Filters nodes, in this example each generated from a different model, to produce a new filter that selects all the fields that were selected in either of the original filters.

Getting ready

This recipe uses the datafile, `cup98LRN.txt` and the stream file, `Combining_Generated_Filters.str`.

How to do it...

To combine generated filters:

1. Open the stream `Combining_Generated_Filters.str` by navigating to **File** | **Open Stream**.
2. Edit the Type node; you can see the shape of the data by clicking on **Preview** in the edit dialogue. The Type node specifies 324 input fields and one target field for modeling. These modeling roles specified by the Type node will be used for all model building in this stream, and the models will be used to generate filter nodes.
3. Run the Distribution node `Target_B`. In the raw data, the target field is mostly zeros, so a Balance node has been used to select a more balanced sample for modeling (shown in the following screenshot). This step also fills the cache on the Balance node so that the same sample will be used for all the models.

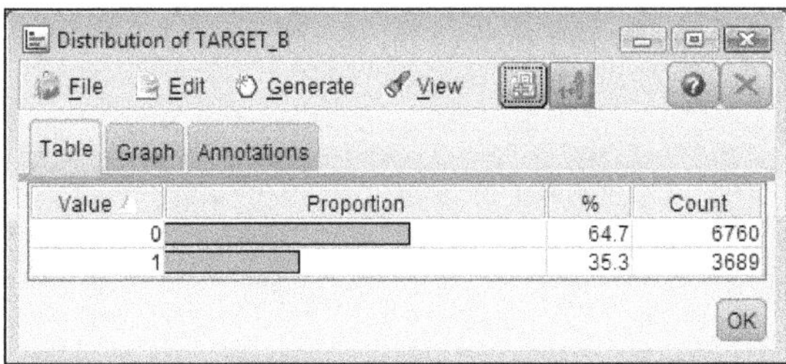

Note that random selection by the Balance node means that the stream will not do exactly the same thing when run again; the models and therefore the generated filters may be slightly different, but the principles remain the same.

4. Edit the Filter node `TARGET_B T` to the left of the stream. This Filter node was generated from the CHAID decision tree **TARGET_B**; as shown in the following screenshot, the filter selects 34 out of the available 325 fields, including the target variable.

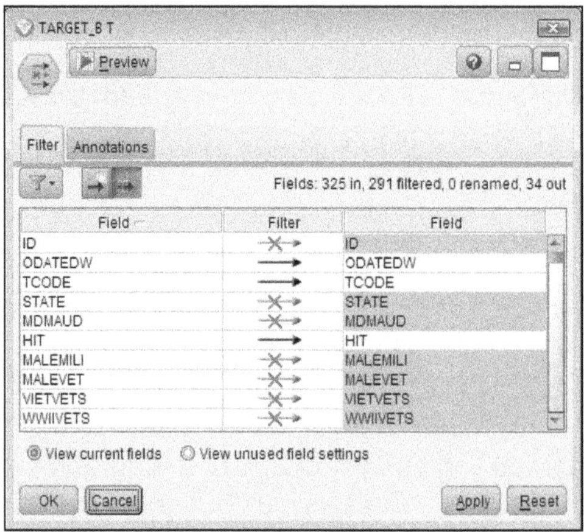

5. Edit the Filter node `TARGET_B N` to the left of the stream. This Filter node was generated from the Neural Network model **TARGET_B**; as shown in the following screenshot, the filter selects 21 out of the available 325 fields, including the target variable and the top 20 fields used by the Neural Network.

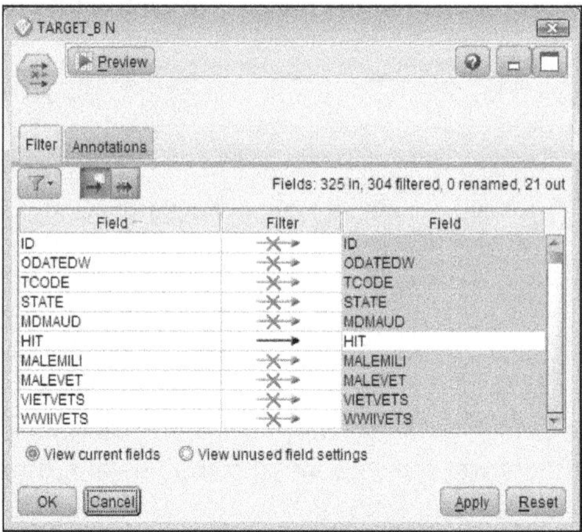

6. Edit the Filter node `TARGET_B T` toggled in the branch with 3 Filter nodes to the right of the stream. This is a copy of the Filter node TARGET_B T in which all fields have been toggled; that is, fields that were on are switched off, and those that were off are switched on. It is important that this is done using the **Filter options menu** and the option **Toggle All Fields**. The Filter node dialogue is shown in the following screenshot; note that it is the inverse of the filter shown in the screenshot in step 4: instead of 34 fields output, 34 fields are filtered.

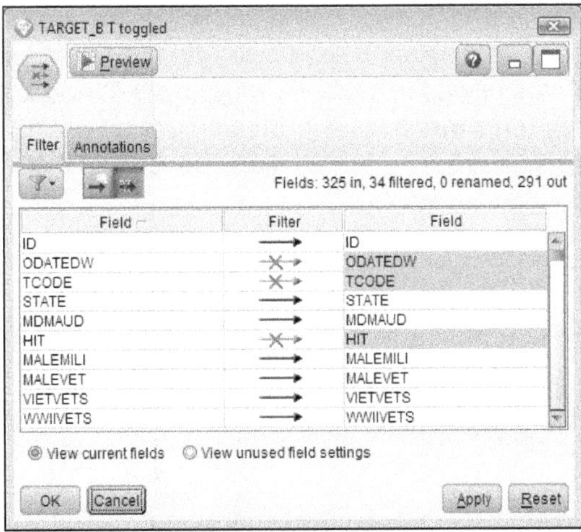

7. Edit the Filter node `TARGET_B N` toggled in the branch with 3 Filter nodes to the right of the stream. This is a copy of the Filter node TARGET_B N that has been connected in sequence with TARGET_B T toggled and all fields have been toggled, as in step 6. Again it is important that this was done using the **Filter options menu** and the option **Toggle All Fields**. The Filter node dialogue is shown in the following screenshot. Again this is the inverse of the filter shown in the screenshot in step 5 but with a slightly less obvious relationship; it filters 18 fields instead of 21 because some of the relevant fields have already been filtered out by the previous node.

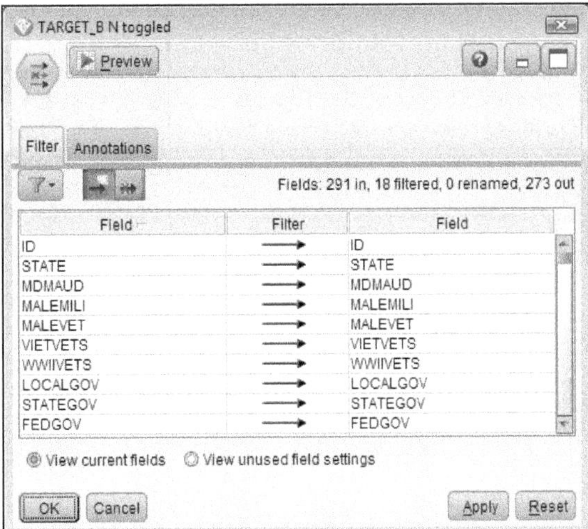

8. Edit the Filter node `New Filter` on the far right of the stream. This is a new Filter node that has been connected in sequence with the two toggled Filter nodes and then has itself been toggled in the same way; again it is important that this is done using the **Filter options menu**. All the remaining fields are filtered out, but because it is a new Filter node, it holds no information about fields that were filtered out by the previous filters in the sequence.

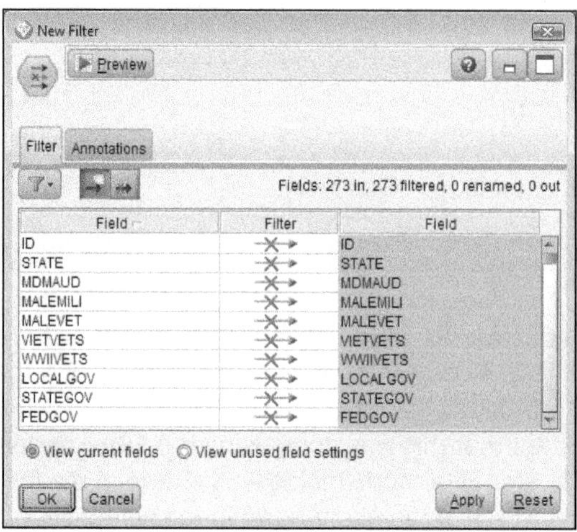

9. Edit the Filter node `New Filter` at the lowest edge of the stream; this is a copy of the New Filter node examined in step 8, but reconnected to the original set of fields. Viewed in this context, this node now makes sense, it outputs 52 fields, all of those output by the two generated filters. It does not output 55 fields (34 plus 21) because there is a slight overlap between the two generated filters.

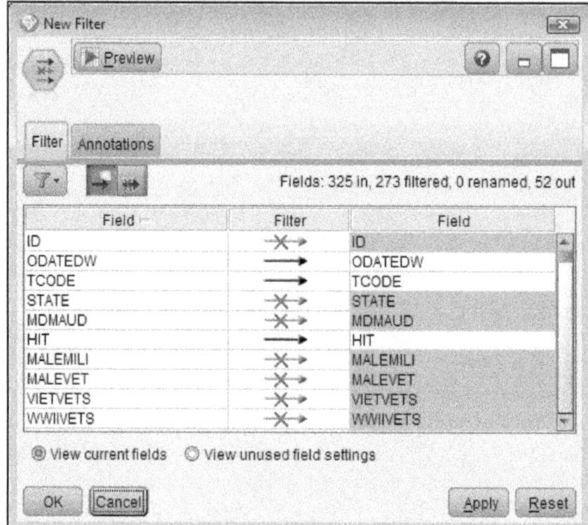

How it works...

This technique can be viewed as performing Boolean logic on arrays or vectors of Boolean values represented by Filter nodes. Under this view, placing filters in sequence acts like a Boolean conjunction (AND), allowing a field to pass through (switched on or true) only if it is switched on in both of the original filters. Toggling a filter provides the equivalent of a Boolean negation or NOT. We want to construct a Boolean disjunction (OR), which will allow a field to pass through if it was true in either of the original filters. We use the equivalence:

p OR q = NOT(NOT(p) AND NOT(q))

First we negate (toggle) each of the filters, then we conjoin (sequence) them, then we negate (toggle) the result in a new filter, producing the equivalent disjunction in the new filter.

This recipe has emphasized the importance of using the option to **Toggle All Fields** from the **Filter options menu**. This is important because there is another, more obviously accessible operation in the Filter node dialogue, the button whose tooltip is **Remove fields by default**. Using this button appears to have the same effect as toggling, but the semantics of the operation are different; this has the undesired effect that the final Filter node does not output any fields, even when reconnected to the original set of fields.

There's more...

This technique could be used to combine more than two filters in exactly the same way, only using a longer sequence of toggled filters. In all cases, the result is produced by adding a new filter at the end of the sequence and toggling it.

The technique could also be generalized to situations where other Boolean operations are required. For example, we might use it to test whether one filter is a superset of another by treating this as a Boolean implication.

This technique was developed for a project in which a large number of fields represented topological features in organic molecules. Because the number of fields was too large to manipulate individual field selections by hand, it was necessary to find semi-automated ways to manipulate filter nodes in order to control field selection **en masse**.

See also

- The *Using the Feature Selection node creatively to remove or decapitate perfect predictors* recipe in *Chapter 2, Data Preparation – Select*

8
CLEM Scripting

In this chapter, we will cover:

- Building iterative Neural Network forecasts
- Quantifying variable importance with Monte Carlo simulation
- Implementing champion/challenger model management
- Detecting outliers with the jackknife method
- Optimizing K-means cluster solutions
- Automating time series forecasts
- Automating HTML reports and graphs
- Rolling your own modeling algorithm – Weibull analysis

Introduction

IBM SPSS Modeler is the core product in an incredibly powerful and scalable predictive analytics platform. The visual, point-n-click Modeler interface makes it almost immediately accessible to business analysts or anyone with a quantitative background. However, having a tool that is easy to use but cannot be automated severely limits the usefulness and scalability of that tool. That's why CLEM scripting was added to the Modeler platform.

CLEM scripting is an important pillar of the Modeler platform scalability. It serves a number of functions that cover data preparation, modeling, evaluation, and deployment. First, scripting allows tedious, repetitive processes within data preparation to be automated. ETL and other data preparation processes can involve many disconnected steps. Scripting can connect these processes into a single connected workflow. Second, model building often involves much experimentation with variable combinations, row samples, time windows, and so on. With scripting, advanced techniques such as Monte Carlo simulation and jackknifing can be implemented easily and invoked with a single mouse click. Lastly, scripting is the mechanism to deliver automation within the deployment environment. Repetitive tasks such as batch scoring, ETL processes, and champion/challenger model management all require scripting. All the automation features of the **IBM SPSS Collaboration and Deployment Services** depend on automation through CLEM scripting.

CLEM scripting best practices

IBM does not publish any official best practices for CLEM scripting; however, they are implied in the documentation. Also, anyone who has been a software developer will recognize many of these recommendations as best practices across the industry. Some of them are listed as follows:

1. Pick a variable-naming convention and stick to it. In this book, all variables are lower case with underscores between words (for example, `sales_data`, `first_name`, and so on.). Having spaces in variable names and node names is possible, but it makes code difficult to read because of the need for quotes (for example, 'Sales Data').
2. Give variables descriptive names such as `iteration_number` and not short names such as `i`.
3. When local variables are referenced, precede them with a circumflex (for example, `^sales_data`). If you omit the circumflex, the script will often fail intermittently.
4. Name all your Modeler nodes with unique names (across the entire stream). This makes it possible to uniquely identify a node by name in the CLEM script.
5. Perform as much configuration as possible in your stream using the point-n-click interface. The CLEM script should be as concise as possible.

CLEM scripting shortcomings

CLEM script is incredibly easy to learn because of its simple English style syntax. However, CLEM script is not as full-featured as most other scripting languages (for example, JavaScript). Hence, there is no way to handle exceptions in CLEM script. If an error occurs, the script simply fails. You must be diligent in checking for error conditions and preventing them. Also, CLEM script does not allow you to access every Modeler node attribute or function. The following examples show some unique workarounds to these limitations.

Even with CLEM scripting's shortcomings, it is incredibly powerful, and mastering it will reap many rewards, saving you time, enabling new functionality, and providing increased scalability.

Building iterative Neural Network forecasts

Artificial Neural Networks (**ANN**) models provide a robust method of generating forecasts. ANN can be built using nearly any input types including categorical, flag, and continuous inputs. ANN models are relatively insensitive to outliers and are capable of capturing subtle interactions between input variables. All of these benefits have made ANN models increasingly popular for many applications such as forecasting product sales, energy demand, spot market prices, and so on.

Even though ANN forecast models are generally superior to traditional forecasting techniques such as **ARIMA**, they do have a few drawbacks. The first drawback of ANN forecast models is that they are not autoregressive (as compared to ARIMA). The model builder must choose the appropriate lags for the input variables. For example, do we look at the price one day ago, one week ago, or one month ago when predicting the current price? The second drawback is that the ANN models predict a single point in the future. ARIMA models can easily generate *N* predictions into the future with a single invocation. ANN models require iteration to generate multiple, successive future predictions (that is, a forecast).

Calling an ANN model iteratively can be a tedious undertaking. For large data sets, a manual approach is completely impractical. CLEM scripting is the solution. CLEM scripts can iteratively read the input data, score a single row, and write the results to disk (or database) as the input to the next iteration. When all rows are scored, the process stops.

Getting ready

This example depends on the files `power_demand.csv`, `power_demand_score.csv`, and `clem_script_interactive_ann_forecast.txt`. This example writes temporary files to `C:\temp`. Please ensure that this directory or a substitute directory exists.

To disable warning dialogs that require you to click on **OK** repetitively, go to **Tools** | **Options** | **User Options** and deselect the **Warn when a node overwrites a file** and **Warn when a node overwrites a database table** options.

How to do it...

The steps for building iterative Neural Network forecasts are as follows:

1. Start with a new stream by clicking on **File** | **New Stream**.

2. Add a file source node to the upper-left of the stream. Set the file field by navigating to the `power_demand.csv` file using the ellipsis button. Name the node `historical_data` by clicking on the **Annotations** tab and setting a custom name. Click on the **Data** tab to override the **Cal Date** input format to **MM/DD/YYYY**.

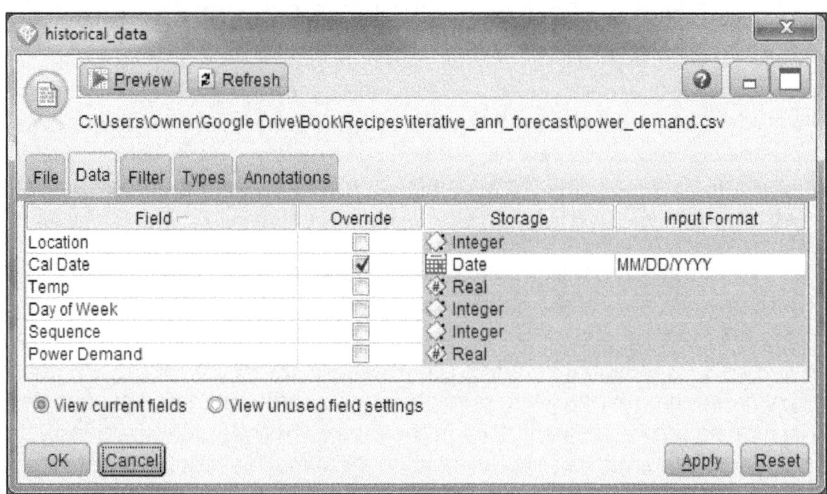

3. Add a Sort node connected to the VAR file in step 2. Choose the **Cal Date** field by clicking the button on the far-right of the dialog box. Leave the sort direction as ascending.
4. Add six Derive nodes connected in a line after the Sort node in step 3. Use the following settings for each node:

Name	Derive As	Formula
`power_lag_1`	Formula	`@OFFSET('Power Demand',1)`
`power_lag_7`	Formula	`@OFFSET('Power Demand',7)`
`power_avg_3`	Formula	`@MEAN('Power Demand',3)`
`temp_lag_1`	Formula	`@OFFSET(Temp,1)`
`temp_lag_7`	Formula	`@OFFSET(Temp,7)`
`temp_avg_3`	Formula	`@MEAN(Temp,3)`

5. Select all six Derive nodes in step 4. Click on the Encapsulate and Selected nodes into the supernode button on the **Modeler** toolbar. Name the `create_lags` supernode by clicking on the **Annotations** tab and setting a custom name.

6. Add a Type node connected to the supernode in step 5. Click on the **Read Values** button to instantiate the Type node. Set the roles for each field as follows:

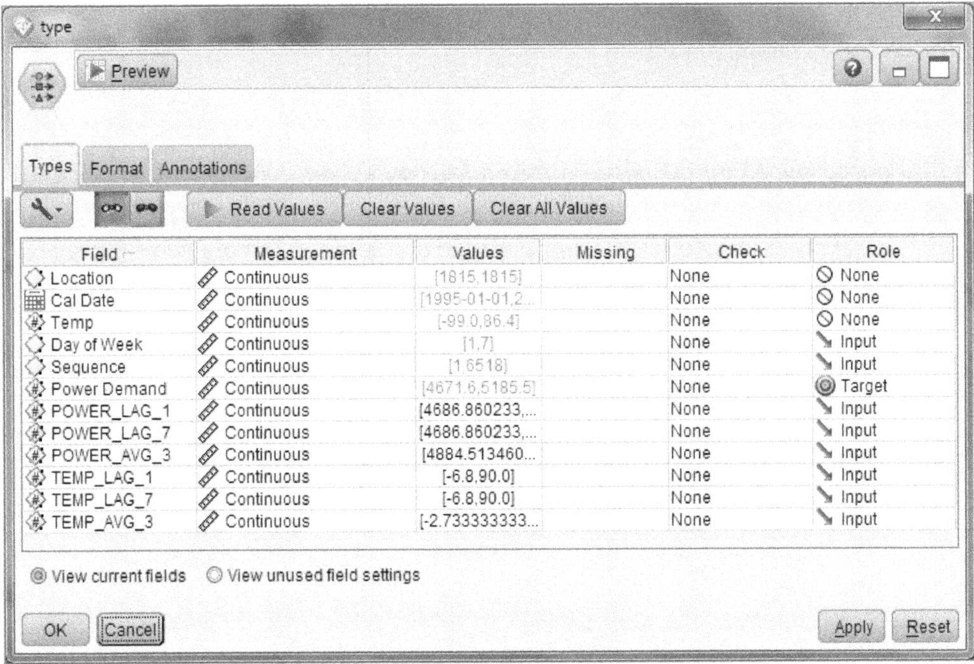

7. Add a Partition node connected to the Type node in step 6. Name the Partition node `partition` by clicking on the **Annotations** tab and setting a custom name.

8. Add a Neural Network node to the Partition node in step 7. Name the Neural Network node `ann_forecast` by clicking on the **Annotations** tab and setting a custom name. Set a custom model name of `ann_forecast_model` by clicking on the **Model Options** tab and setting the model name.

9. Right-click on the Neural Network node and select **Run**. Right-click on the generated model and choose **Disconnect**. At this point, the stream should look as follows:

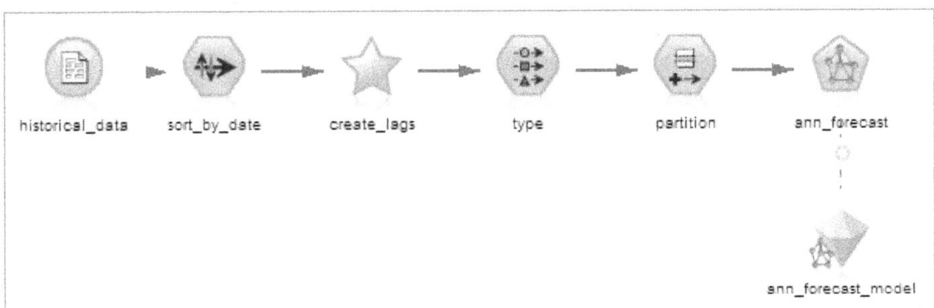

10. Add a new VAR file Source node below the `historical_data` node (not connected). Set the **File** field by navigating to the `power_demand_score.csv` file using the ellipsis button. Name the node `forecast_data` by clicking on the **Annotations** tab and setting a custom name. Click on the **Data** tab to override the **Cal Date** input format to **MM/DD/YYYY**.
11. Copy the `sort_by_date` and `create_lags` nodes above and connect them to the VAR file node in step 10.
12. Connect the `ann_forecast_model` to the new `create_lags` node in step 11.
13. Add a Filler node connected to the `ann_forecast_model` node. Name the node `filler` by clicking on the **Annotations** tab and setting a custom name. Finish configuring the node as follows:

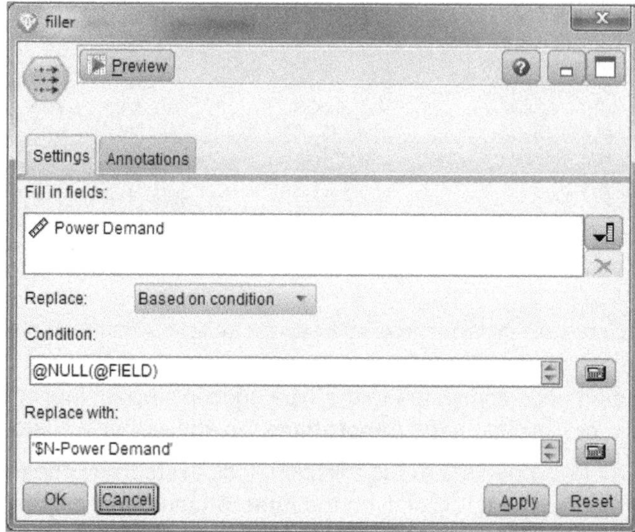

14. Add a Filter node connected to the Filler node in step 13. Filter out the last seven fields (those after Power Demand) by clicking on the Filter column.
15. Add a Flat File node connected to the Filter node in step 14. Set the File field by navigating to the `power_demand_score.csv` file using the ellipsis button. Click on the **Overwrite** option. Name the node `forecast_data_overwrite` by clicking on the **Annotations** tab and setting a custom name.
16. Add a Select node connected to the `forecast_data` node. Set the condition field to `@NULL('Power Demand')`. Name the node `select_forecast_recs` by clicking on the **Annotations** tab and setting a custom name.
17. Add an Aggregate node connected to the Select node in step 16. Set the **Include record count field** to `N`. Name the node `N` by clicking on the **Annotations** tab and setting a custom name.

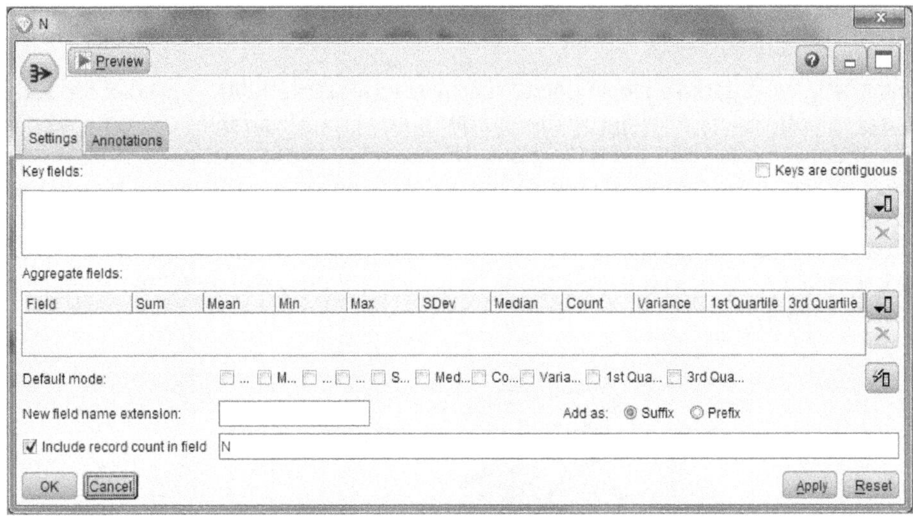

18. Add a Table node connected to the Aggregate node in step 17. Name the node `rec_count_table` by clicking on the **Annotations** tab and setting a custom name. The finished stream should look as follows:

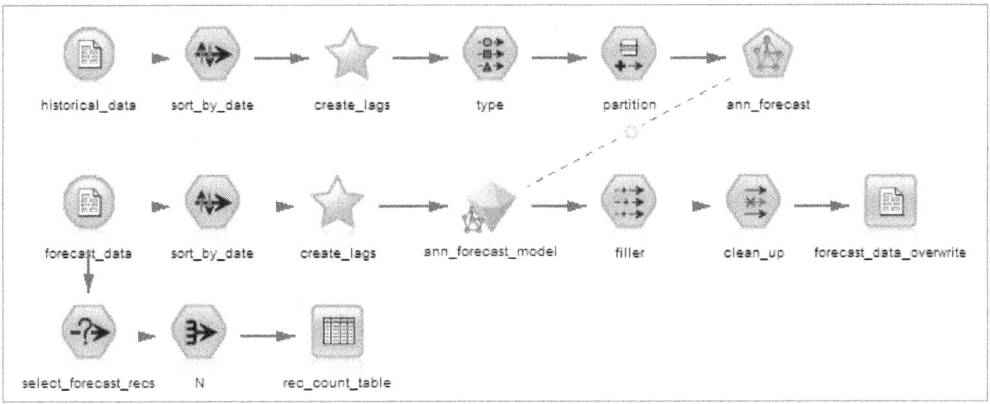

19. Go to **Tools** | **Stream Properties** and select the **Script** tab. Click on the first icon in the toolbar (suitcase) and navigate to the `clem_script_interactive_ann_forecast.txt` file. This will load the script into the top textbox. At the bottom of the dialog choose the **Run this Script** option for On Stream Execution. Click on **OK**.
20. You can now execute the script by clicking on the large green arrow on the main toolbar.

How it works...

In steps 1 to 9, we created a single point Artificial Neural Network (ANN) prediction model using lagged data inputs. The lagged [temperature and power] variables are generated using a series of derive nodes with the @ functions (for example, @MEAN, @OFFSET). The Power Demand variable is the target with the lagged variables as inputs. The model tries to predict the power demand using only lagged inputs. The ANN model has an accuracy of greater than 94 percent. The ANN model shows that power and temperature are the top predictors with strong interactions between the inputs (that is, where neurons have more than one dark line attached to them).

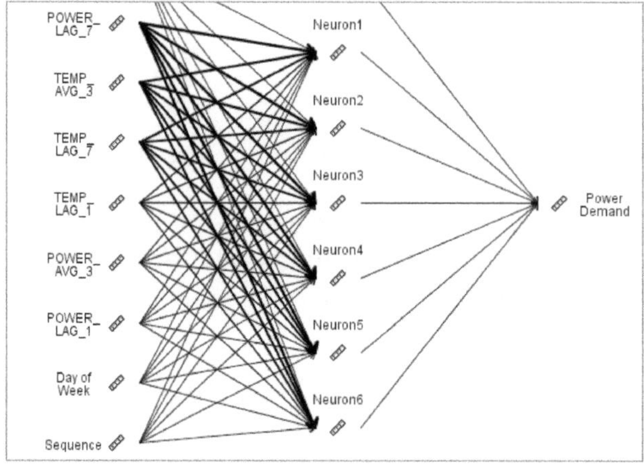

The remaining steps involve scoring the ANN model. The scoring data in step 10 provides all the input variables including a weather forecast. There are seven days we would like to forecast.

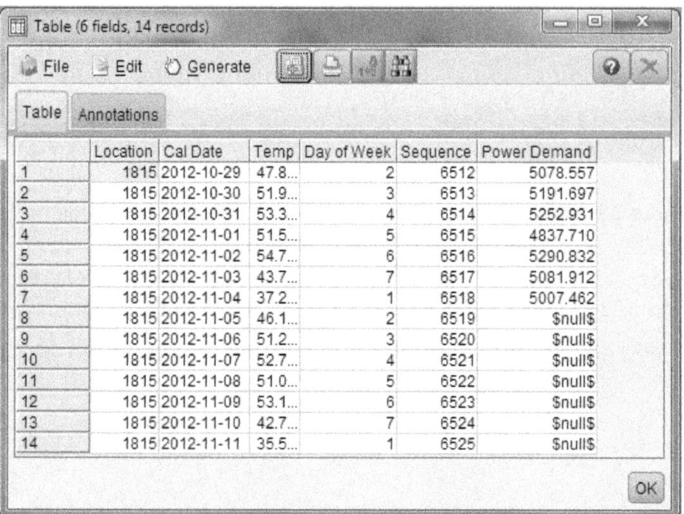

	Location	Cal Date	Temp	Day of Week	Sequence	Power Demand
1	1815	2012-10-29	47.8...	2	6512	5078.557
2	1815	2012-10-30	51.9...	3	6513	5191.697
3	1815	2012-10-31	53.3...	4	6514	5252.931
4	1815	2012-11-01	51.5...	5	6515	4837.710
5	1815	2012-11-02	54.7...	6	6516	5290.832
6	1815	2012-11-03	43.7...	7	6517	5081.912
7	1815	2012-11-04	37.2...	1	6518	5007.462
8	1815	2012-11-05	46.1...	2	6519	$null$
9	1815	2012-11-06	51.2...	3	6520	$null$
10	1815	2012-11-07	52.7...	4	6521	$null$
11	1815	2012-11-08	51.0...	5	6522	$null$
12	1815	2012-11-09	53.1...	6	6523	$null$
13	1815	2012-11-10	42.7...	7	6524	$null$
14	1815	2012-11-11	35.5...	1	6525	$null$

Initially, only a single row (row 8) can be scored. Row 9 cannot be scored yet because the lagged power demand cannot be determined until we score row 8.

Script section 1

The screenshot of the script section 1 is as follows:

```
1   var num_recs
2
3   execute rec_count_table
4
5   # count the number of records to be forecast
6   set num_recs = value rec_count_table.output at 1 1
7
8   for idx from 1 to num_recs
9       # generate forecast one record at a time
10      execute forecast_data_overwrite
11  endfor
```

This script is simple but powerful. In lines 3 to 7, we determine the number of rows to be forecast and read it into a local variable (that is, `num_recs`). In lines 8 to 11, we iteratively score the ANN model a single row at a time. Each successive scoring run allows a new set of lagged variables to be generated and in turn a new row to be scored. The end result is that we have a 7-day forecast using a robust ANN model.

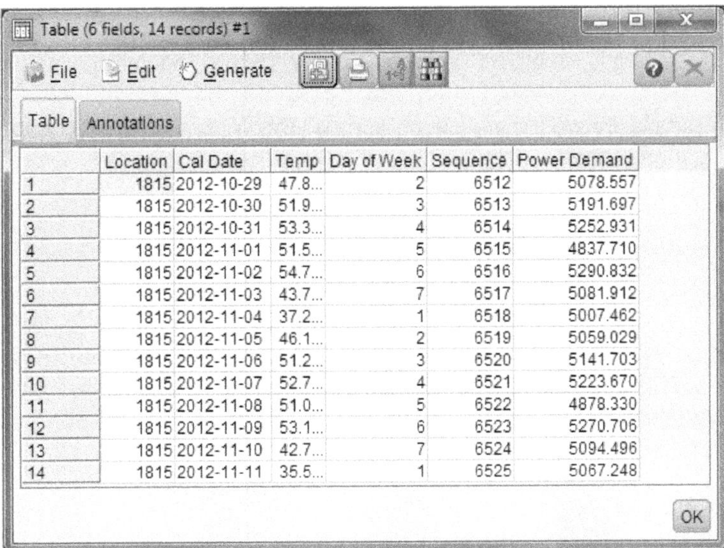

	Location	Cal Date	Temp	Day of Week	Sequence	Power Demand
1	1815	2012-10-29	47.8...	2	6512	5078.557
2	1815	2012-10-30	51.9...	3	6513	5191.697
3	1815	2012-10-31	53.3...	4	6514	5252.931
4	1815	2012-11-01	51.5...	5	6515	4837.710
5	1815	2012-11-02	54.7...	6	6516	5290.832
6	1815	2012-11-03	43.7...	7	6517	5081.912
7	1815	2012-11-04	37.2...	1	6518	5007.462
8	1815	2012-11-05	46.1...	2	6519	5059.029
9	1815	2012-11-06	51.2...	3	6520	5141.703
10	1815	2012-11-07	52.7...	4	6521	5223.670
11	1815	2012-11-08	51.0...	5	6522	4878.330
12	1815	2012-11-09	53.1...	6	6523	5270.706
13	1815	2012-11-10	42.7...	7	6524	5094.496
14	1815	2012-11-11	35.5...	1	6525	5067.248

There's more...

In this recipe, we didn't address the need to determine the optimal time lags for the model building process. The next recipe *Quantifying variable importance with Monte Carlo simulation* gives a robust method for variable selection.

Quantifying variable importance with Monte Carlo simulation

Finding the smallest subset of all possible input variables that result in an accurate model (that is, a parsimonious solution) is often the biggest challenge for many data mining projects. It's common for data sets to contain 10s to 100s of input variables. Models that are over-trained or simply fail to build are both possible with so called "wide" data sets. Removing unimportant variables to find the sweet spot between model accuracy and stability is where experienced data miners can deliver significant value.

The primary method of variable selection in Modeler is Feature Selection. The Feature Selection process identifies the significance of each variable individually. Statistically insignificant variables below a specified p-value are dropped. While this technique works well with simple data sets and "main effects" models such as regression, it completely ignores the interaction between variables. As often happens, the interaction of two weak (or statistically insignificant variables) can have a significant effect on the target variable. The interaction between variables may be significant for all observations or a smaller subset of observations. Models such as decision trees and artificial Neural networks (ANN) are capable of incorporating the effects of these subtle variable interactions.

The following recipe builds multiple C5 models using different random row samples (that is, the Monte Carlo method). The variable importance results from each trial are averaged to minimize the variability between single scoring runs. The Winnow attributes setting on the C5 node also allows a (potentially) large number of input variables to be "winnowed" down to a more manageable number.

The data set for this recipe was generated using the following equation:

$$output = 0.4a + 0.2b - 0.2c + 0.15d - 0.05e + \varepsilon$$

where *a*, *b*, *c*, *d*, and *e* are input variables; *output* is the target variable, and ε is a random error term. The coefficients [*0.4*, *0.2*, *-0.2*, *0.15*, *-0.05*] are the variable importance coefficients. The data set also includes three random variables as "sanity checks". These variables are included to gauge the "floor" for variable importance.

Getting ready

This example depends on the files `input_data.sav`, `inputs.csv`, and `clem_script_variable_selection.txt`. This example writes temporary files to `C:\temp`. Please ensure that this directory or a substitute directory exists.

To disable warning dialogs, that require you to click on **OK** repetitively, go to **Tools** | **Options** | **User Options** and deselect the **Warn when a node overwrites a file** and **Warn when a node overwrites a database table** options.

How to do it...

The steps for quantifying variable importance with Monte Carlo simulation are as follows:

1. Start with a new stream by clicking on **New Stream** in **File**.
2. Click on **Stream Properties** in the **File** menu and choose the **Parameters** tab. Set up the following parameter (exactly as shown in the screenshot):

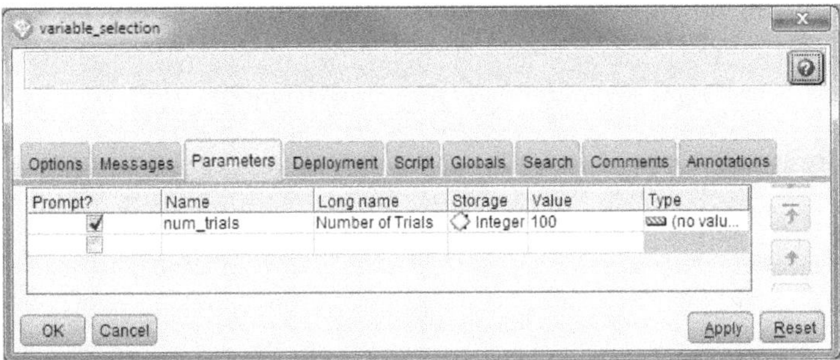

3. Add a Statistics File Source node to the upper-left of the stream. Set the **Input File** field by navigating to the `input_data.sav` file using the ellipsis button. Name the `input_data` node by clicking on the **Annotations** tab and setting a custom name. Right-click on the node and select **Cache** | **Enable**.
4. Add a Binning node connected to the Statistics File node in step 3. Add the **OUTPUT** field to the list of bin fields by clicking the button on the far right of the dialog box. Choose the **Decile (10)** option. Name the Binning node by clicking on the **Annotations** tab and setting a custom name.
5. Add a Type node to the Binning node in step 4. Click on the **Read Values** button on the **Types** tab to instantiate the Type node. Set the roles of each field as follows:

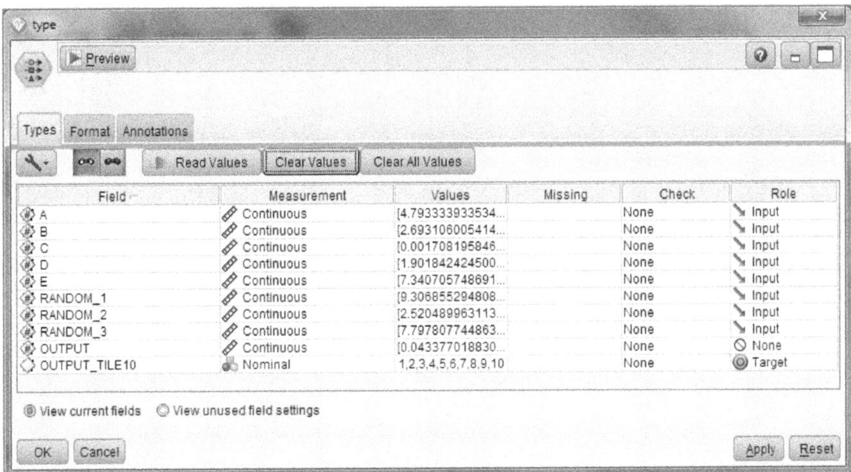

Name the node type by clicking on the **Annotations** tab and setting a custom name:

6. Add a Partition node connected to the Type node in step 5. Set the training partition to 70 and the test partition to 30. Deselect the **Set Random Seed** option. Name the node `partition` by clicking on the **Annotations** tab and setting a custom name.
7. Add a C5.0 node to the Partition node in step 6. Set the **Mode** option to **Expert** on the **Model** tab. Select the **Winnow attributes** option. Name the generated model `c5_model` by clicking on the **Model** tab and setting a custom name. Name the node `c5` by clicking on the **Annotations** tab and setting a custom name.

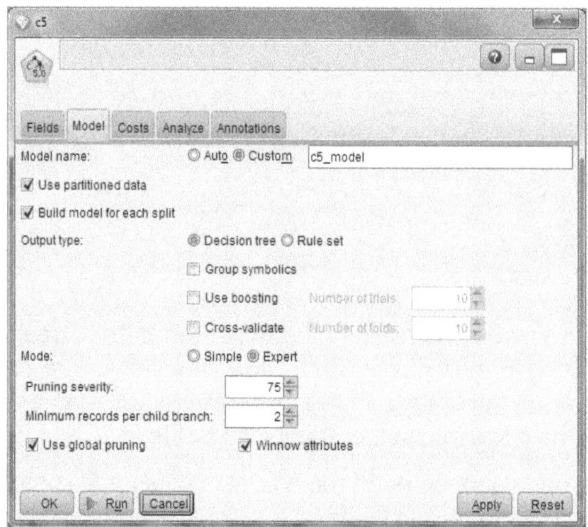

8. Right-click on the c5 model node in step 7 and select **Run** to generate a model nugget named c5_model.
9. Right-click on the c5_model nugget in the Models tab. Choose **Export PMML** and save the file to `C:\temp\c5_model.xml`. At this point the stream should look as follows:

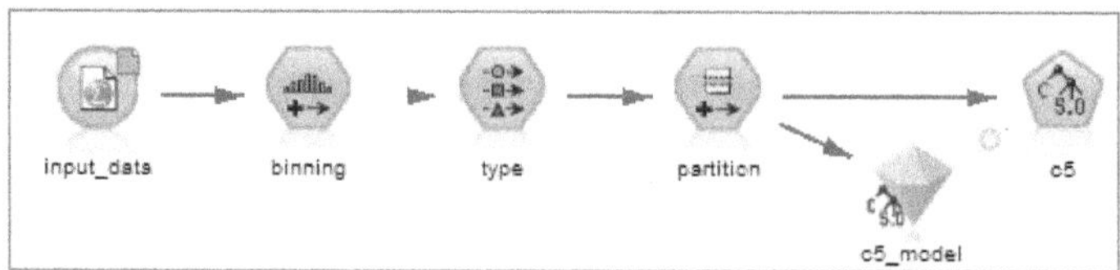

10. Add an XML source node below the Statistics File node in step 3. Set the XML data source field to `C:\temp\c5_model.xml`. Navigate the PMML tree to `/PMML/TreeModel/MiningSchema/MiningField` and then click on the right arrow to set the **Records** field.

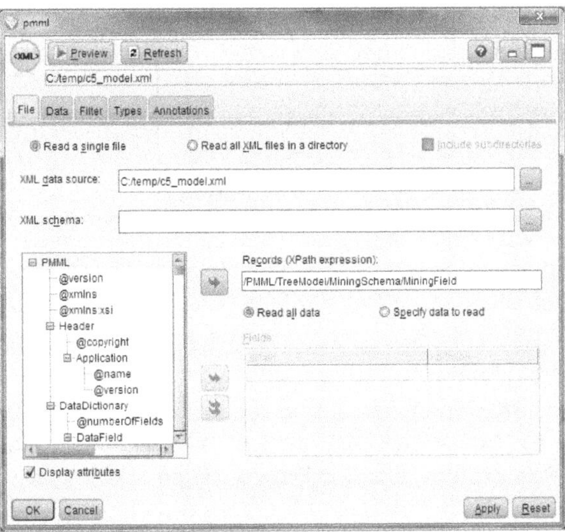

Name the node PMML by clicking on the **Annotations** tab and setting a custom name.

11. Add a Var. File node below the XML source node in step 10. Set the File field by navigating to the `inputs.csv` file using the ellipses button. Click on the **Read Values** button on the **Type** tab to instantiate the Type node. Name the node `inputs` by clicking on the **Annotations** tab and setting a custom name.
12. Connect the nodes in step 10 and 11 to a new Merge node. Select keys as the method of performing the join. Choose name as the Key to join the data on. Choose the partial outer join option. Click on the **Select** button and click the check box next to the inputs. Name the node `Merge` by clicking on the **Annotations** tab and setting a custom name.
13. Add a Filler node connected to the Merge node in step 12. Select importance as the **Fill in** field. Choose **Always** as the replace option. Set the **Replace with formula** field to `to_real(@FIELD)`. Name the node `filler` by clicking on the **Annotations** tab and setting a custom name.
14. Add another Filler node connected to the Filler node in step 12. Select importance as the **Fill in** field. Choose **Based on Condition** as the replace option. Set the **Condition** field to `@NULL(@FIELD)`. Set the **Replace with formula** to: `0.0`. Name the node `Filler` by clicking on the **Annotations** tab and setting a custom name.
15. Add a Sort node connected to the Filler node in step 14. Select the name field with the ascending sort option. Name the node `Sort` by clicking on the **Annotations** tab and setting a custom name.
16. Add a Transpose node connected to the Sort node in step 15. Set the **Read from** field option to `name`. Click on the **Read Values** button. Name the node `transpose` by clicking on the **Annotations** tab and setting a custom name.

17. Add a Filter node connected to the Transpose node in step 16. Filter out the **ID** field by clicking the Filter column next to the field. Name the node `filter` by clicking on the **Annotations** tab and setting a custom name.
18. Add a Flat File export node to the Filter node in step 17. Set the **Export file** option to `C:\temp\trials.txt`. Choose **Tab** as the field separator. Name the node `trials_output` by clicking on the **Annotations** tab and setting a custom name.
19. Add a Var. File node below the Var. File source node in step 11. Set the **File** field by navigating to the `C:\temp\trials.txt` file using the ellipses button. Select **Tab** as the delimiter. Click on the **Read Values** button on the **Type** tab to instantiate the Type node. Name the node `trials_inputs` by clicking on the **Annotations** tab and setting a custom name.
20. Add a Statistics node connected to the Var. File node in step 19. Select the fields **A**, **B**, **C**, **D**, **E**, **RANDOM1**, **RANDOM2**, and **RANDOM3** in the **Examine** field. Select the **Min**, **Max**, **Mean**, **Std Dev**, and **Std Error** of **Mean** options. The final stream should look as follows:

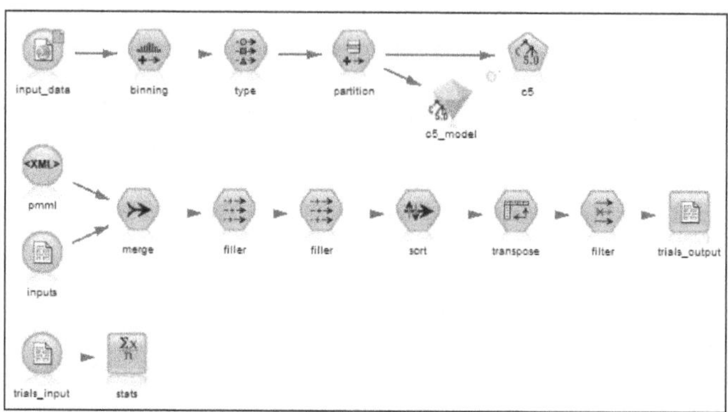

21. Click on **Stream Properties** in the **Tools** menu and select the **Script** tab. Click the first icon in the toolbar (suitcase) and navigate to the `clem_script_variable_selection.txt` file. This will load the script into the top textbox. At the bottom of the dialog choose the **Run this Script** option for On Stream Execution. Click on **OK**.
22. You can now execute the script by clicking the large green arrow on the main toolbar.

How it works...

In this stream, we are generating multiple C5 tree models against random row samples (that is, the Monte Carlo simulation). CLEM scripting does not allow direct access to the variable importance results so we have to use a generated PMML model (an XML file) as a method of reading them into the stream. The results of each Monte Carlo trial are written to text file for the final analysis.

In steps 1 to 7, we are building a standard C5 model building stream with a few twists. First, we had to bin the target variable into deciles because the C5 model does not support continuous targets. Second, in the Partition node we turned off the random seed. This ensures that every time the data flows through the node a new random row sample is generated. Finally, when configuring the C5 node we chose the export option and selected **Winnow attributes**. This critical last step allows us to dramatically reduce the number of [final] input variables so that we can support models with 10s to 100s of input variables.

In steps 8 to 17, we are exporting each C5 mode to PMML, reading the variable importance results and writing the final results to a CSV file. The PMML source node allows us to extract values from the PMML XML file using XPath statements. Navigating the XML tree in the node automatically generates the appropriate XPath statement for us. The `inputs.csv` file contains all the variable names. The list of all input variables is outer-joined to the PMML node results. The outer join ensures that we have all possible variables in the final output even if they have no significance. The C5 model may have "winnowed out" some of the variables. The remaining steps restructure the data from columns to rows and replace nulls with 0.0.

The final steps 18 to 21 allow us to review the results. The Statistics node shows us the range of each variable importance trial. Of particular interest are the Mean and Std Error of Mean fields. These metrics give us the final variable importance and a measure of how confident we are in the result respectively.

Script section 1

The screenshot of the script section 1 is as follows:

```
1   var num_trials
2   var temp_dir
3   var idx
4   var tmp_node
5   var current_field
6   var pmml_file
7
8   # read parameters into local variables
9   set num_trials = '$P-num_trials'
10
11  # delete all existing models
12  for tmp_node in ^stream.nodes
13      if ^tmp_node.node_type = applyc5node then
14          delete ^tmp_node
15      endif
16  endfor
17
18  set trials output.write mode = Overwrite
```

In lines 1 to 18 of the script, we read the total number of trials into a local variable. The user sets this value when the stream is executed. Next we remove any lingering C5 models.

Script section 2

The screenshot of the script section 2 is as follows:

```
20  for idx from 1 to num_trials
21      if (idx = 2) then
22          set trials_output.write_mode = Append
23      endif
24
25      # build model
26      clear generated palette
27      execute c5
28
29      # export pmml
30      set pmml_file = "C:/temp/c5_model_" >< to_string(random(100000)) >< ".xml"
31      export model c5_model as ^pmml_file
32
33      # source pmml and write to CSV
34      set pmml.full_filename = ^pmml_file
35      execute trials_output
36  endfor
37
38  # show final stats for each variable importance
39  execute stats
```

In lines 20 to 39, we execute the C5 model through multiple trials. Next the script exports the C5 model to a PMML file using a random file name. If the script overwrites the same file, it will fail randomly due to a race condition. Finally we execute the Statistics node to view the results. After 100 trials the results are as shown in the following table:

Variable	Actual	C5 Mean (Std Error)	C5 Mean Range
A	0.4	0.408 (0.019)	0.0 - 0.768
B	0.2	0.154 (0.015)	0.0 - 0.625
C	0.2	0.149 (0.018)	0.0 - 0.959
D	0.15	0.074 (0.010)	0.0 - 0.482
E	0.05	0.020 (0.004)	0.0 - 0.209
RANDOM_1	0.0	0.048 (0.011)	0.0 - 1.000
RANDOM_2	0.0	0.090 (0.013)	0.0 - 1.000
RANDOM_3	0.0	0.056 (0.011)	0.0 - 0.738

The results (mean of multiple trials) are in good overall agreement with the known values; however, we see that individual runs vary widely. Using Monte Carlo simulation with random row samples allows us to prevent overtraining (with partitioning) but gives us the benefit of multiple trials that cover the entire data set and smooth the variability inherent in a single model building trial.

There's more...

In this script, we treat each trail (that is, model) as being equivalent; however, some of the models are more accurate than others. To improve this script, the accuracy of each model could be calculated and used to weight the resultant variable importance values. In that way, more accurate models would have greater weight in determining the importance of overall variable.

Implementing champion/challenger model management

In most real-world predictive analytics applications, models must change over time. This need for change is often due to evolving customer behavior, new offerings/promotions, and/or changes in data availability. Regardless of the reason necessitating change, it's often advantageous to automate the process of building updated models. Frequency of the model refresh process depends on the nature of the business. In some rapidly changing businesses, the refresh process is sub-hourly and automation is an absolute necessity.

With the champion/challenger technique, the currently deployed model is called the champion model. New models built by training on the latest data are called the challenger models. Challenger models can replace the champion model if the challenger is more effective than the champion model. Model effectiveness can be defined many ways including, but not limited to, **mean absolution percent error** (**MAPE**) for continuous targets and overall accuracy, or lift for categorical targets. Which metric is chosen is driven by business need.

In this example, we simulate changes in data surrounding a sales promotion. The champion/challenger process is implemented to keep the response model relevant and up-to-date with changes in customer preferences.

Getting ready

This example depends on the `promotion_response.sav` and `clem_script_champion_challenger.txt` files.

To disable warning dialogs that require you to click on **OK** repetitively, go to **Tools** | **Options** | **User Options** and deselect the **Warn when a node overwrites a file** and **Warn when a node overwrites a database table** options.

How to do it...

The steps for implementing champion/challenger model are as follows:

1. Start with a new stream by clicking on **New Stream** in the **File** menu.

2. Click on **Stream Properties** in **File** and choose the **Parameters** tab. Set up the following parameter (exactly as shown):

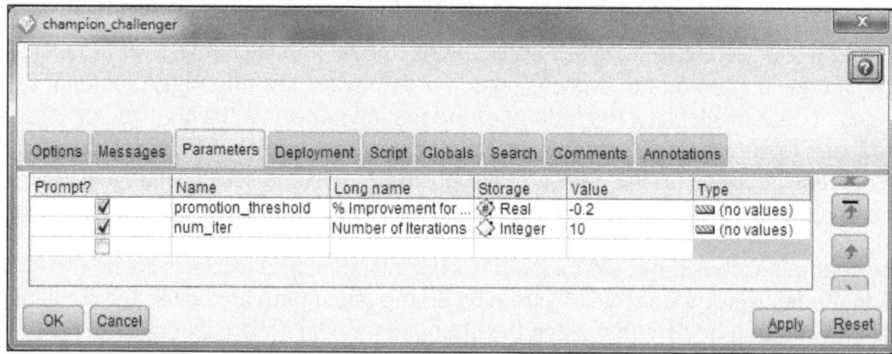

3. Add a Statistics File source node to the upper-left of the stream. Set the input file field by navigating to the `promotion_response.sav` file using the ellipsis button. Name the node `promotion_data` by clicking on the **Annotations** tab and setting a custom name. Right-click on the node and select **Cache | Enable**.
4. Add a Partition node to the Statistics File source node in step 1. Set the training partition size to 10 and the testing partition to 90. Deselect the **Set random seed** option. Name the node `partition` by clicking on the **Annotations** tab and setting a custom name.
5. Add a CHAID node to the Partition node in step 4. Name the generated model `chaid_model` by clicking on the **Model** tab and setting a custom name. Name the node CHAID by clicking on the **Annotations** tab and setting a custom name. Right-click on the CHAID node and select **Run** to build the model nugget.
6. Add a Select node connected to the CHAID node in step 5. Set the condition to `Partition = "2_Testing"`. Name the node `select_test_partition` by clicking on the **Annotations** tab and setting a custom name.
7. Add a Derive node connected to the Select node in step 6. Configure the node as follows:

Name the node correct by clicking on the **Annotations** tab and setting a custom name.

8. Add an Aggregate node connected to the Derive node in step 7. Select **Correct** as the aggregate field and choose the **Sum** option. Select the **Include record count in field** option and enter N as the field value.

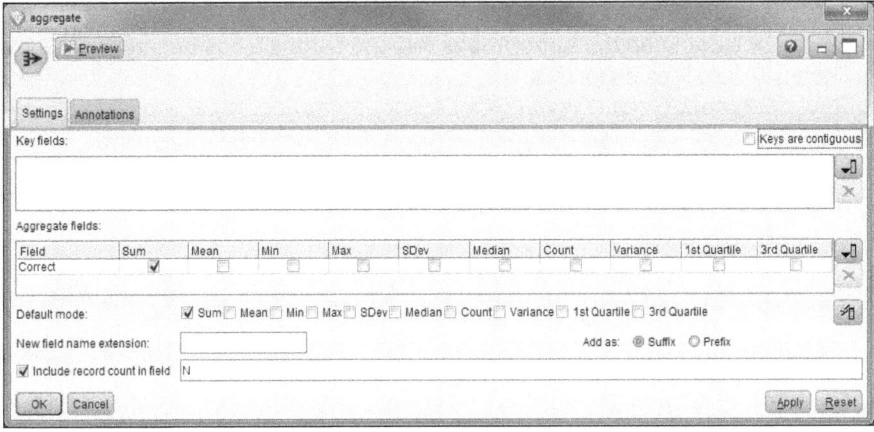

Name the node aggregate by clicking on the Annotations tab and setting a custom name.

9. Add a Derive node connected to the Aggregate node in step 8. Set the **Derive field** value to `Percent Correct`. Choose **Formula** in the **Derive as** field. Set the Formula field to `Correct_Sum/N`. Name the node `select_test` by clicking on the **Annotations** tab and setting a custom name.

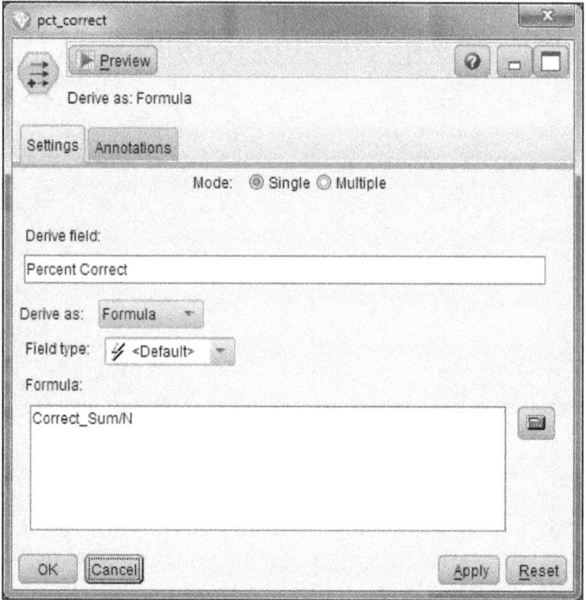

10. Add a Table node connected to the Derive node in step 9. Name the node `eval_table` by clicking on the **Annotations** tab and setting a custom name. The final stream should look as follows:

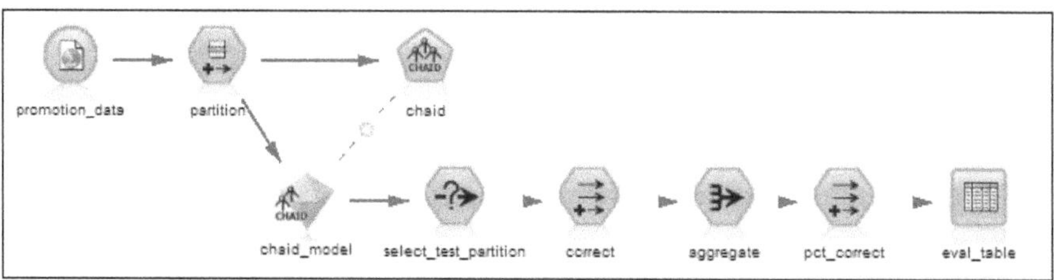

11. Go to **Tools** | **Stream Properties** and select the **Script** tab. Click on the first icon in the toolbar (suitcase) and navigate to the `clem_script_champion_challenger.txt` file. This will load the script into the top textbox. At the bottom of the dialog, choose the **Run this Script** option for on-stream execution. Click on **OK**.
12. You can now execute the script by clicking the large green arrow on the main toolbar.

How it works...

In this example, we simulate new data by drawing randomly from a large data set. In a real-world implementation, this stream would perform time-windowing on historical data, pulling the most recent window of data for building the Challenger models. The performance metric used here is simply the accuracy (number of correct predictions/ total number of predictions).

In steps 1 to 5, we build a CHAID model against a random 10 percent row sample. In steps 6 to 12, we evaluate the model by calculating the overall accuracy of the predictions on the training data set.

The stream is incredibly simple because the majority of the logic is delivered via the script.

Script section 1

The screenshot of the script section 1 is as follows:

```
1   var iteration
2   var challenger_accuracy
3   var champion_accuracy
4   var num_iter
5   var promotion_threshold
6   var tmp_node
7
8   # read parameters into local variables
9   set num_iter = '$P-num_iter'
10  set promotion_threshold = '$P-promotion_threshold'
11
12  # delete all existing models
13  for tmp_node in ^stream.nodes
14      if ^tmp_node.node_type = applychaidnode then
15          delete ^tmp_node
16      endif
17  endfor
```

In lines 1 to 17, the script reads the user supplied parameters into local variables. The `promotion_threshold` is the minimum change in accuracy that results in a promotion from challenger to champion (for example, a -0.2 value means the accuracy must improve by 0.2 percent to crown a new champion model). The script also deletes any existing CHAID models.

Script section 2

The screenshot of the script section 2 is as follows:

```
19  for iteration from 1 to ^num_iter
20      # build a CHAID model using a subset of data
21      execute chaid
22      insert model chaid_model connected between partition and select_test_partition
23      clear generated palette
24      execute eval_table
25
26      set challenger_accuracy = value eval_table.output at 1 3
27      clear outputs
28
29      # if this is the first iteration, then the champion model is set to the current model
30      if (iteration = 1) then
31          set champion_accuracy = ^challenger_accuracy
32          disconnect chaid_model
33          duplicate chaid_model as champion_chaid_model
34          position champion_chaid_model at 200 200
35      else
36          # if new (challenger) model is more accurate, make it the new champion
37          if ((^challenger_accuracy - ^champion_accuracy) <= ^promotion_threshold) then
38              delete champion_chaid_model
39              set champion_accuracy = ^challenger_accuracy
40              disconnect chaid_model
41              duplicate chaid_model as champion_chaid_model
42              position champion_chaid_model at 200 200
43          endif
44      endif
45
46      # remove the challenger
47      delete chaid_model
48  endfor
49
50  # place the champion challenger back into the stream
51  position champion_chaid_model connected between partition and select_test_partition
```

In lines 21 to 51, we start by building an initial model and calculating the overall accuracy of that model. If this is the first iteration, we promote this model to the champion. Normally, this model would already exist from prior work and this step would not be necessary. On subsequent iterations, if the gain in accuracy is greater than the user-specified threshold, we promote the model generated on line 21 and promote it to champion. Finally, we remove the challenger model and if the iterations are complete we place the champion model back into the stream to be used for future scoring.

There's more...

This example simulates new data by generating random samples. A true production implementation would use a moving time window. For example, the challenger would be built with data from the past 90 days.

Detecting outliers with the jackknife method

Outlier observations can have a dramatic (often negative) impact on the accuracy of many predictive models. Identifying Outlier observations and handling them appropriately is an important step in the data preparation phase of the CRISP-DM process. Outliers are often defined as observations with extreme values. This is a very limited criterion for defining an outlier. A more robust definition of outlier is an observation that contains a value that is significantly different from what would be predicted by a model built using the other observations in the sample. This definition is more robust as it allows observations to have extreme values if the model predicts an extreme value.

Extreme values can represent normal/predictable outcomes especially in cases of strong variable interaction.

The jackknife method is based on a Monte Carlo simulation where individual data points are held out of the training and testing partition. The overall accuracy of this step is then compared to a model where the same data point is included in the training partition but not the testing partition. Stated differently, we test the effect of a single observation on the accuracy of the model across the entire data set (minus that data point). The jackknife approach answers the question: "Is the model significantly more accurate by excluding a single data point?" If excluding the observation is significantly beneficial to the overall model accuracy, the observation is labeled an outlier. In the absence of the ability to easily define statistical significance in Modeler, the script substitutes a simple arbitrary metric to define significance: percent change in the absolute error for all observations.

The linear model in this example predicts customer value (that is, annual customer spend). The goal of the script is to identify Outlier customers. Outlier customers will exhibit actual annual spends that vary significantly from their predicted annual spend as predicted by a model built from the remaining customers. The final result of this Monte Carlo simulation is a list of customers ordered by percent change of absolute model error. The customers at the top of the list are the most likely outliers.

Getting ready

This example depends on the file `customer_spend.sav`. This example writes temporary files to `C:\temp`. Please ensure this directory or a substitute directory exists.

To disable warning dialogs that require you to click on **OK** repetitively, go to **Tools** | **Options** | **User Options** and deselect the **Warn when a node overwrites a file** and **Warn when a node overwrites a database table** options.

How to do it...

The steps for detecting outliers with the jackknife method are as follows:

1. Start with a new stream by clicking on **File** | **New Stream**.
2. Add a Statistics File source node to the upper-left of the stream. Set the input file field by navigating to the `customer_spend.sav` file using the ellipsis button. Name the node `spend_data` by clicking on the **Annotations** tab and setting a custom name. Right-click on the node and select **Cache** | **Enable**.
3. Add a Select node connected to the Statistics File in step 2. Choose the **Discard** option. Set the **Condition** to: `CUSTOMER_ID = -1`. Name the node `deselect_cust` by clicking on the **Annotations** tab and setting a custom name.

4. Add a Linear model node connected to the Select node in Step 3. Name the generated model `linear_model` by clicking on the **Model** tab and setting a custom name. Name the node linear by clicking on the **Annotations** tab and setting a custom name. Right-click on the Liner node and select **Run** to build the model nugget.
5. Add a Derive node connected to the Linear node in step 4. Name the new field by setting the **Derive field** to error. Choose Formula for the Derive as field. Set the **Formula** to `abs('$L-ANNUAL_SPEND' - ANNUAL_SPEND)`. Name the node error by clicking on the **Annotations** tab and setting a custom name.

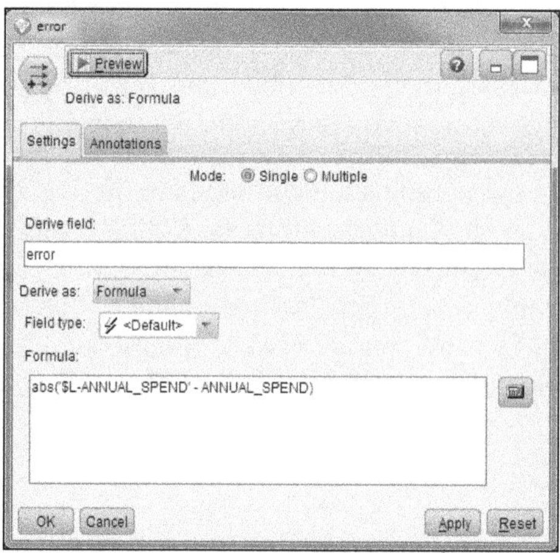

6. Add an Aggregate node connected to the Derive field in step 5. Select the **error** field as an **Aggregate fields** and choose the **Sum** option. Deselect the **Include record count in field** option. Name the node `sum_abs_error` by clicking on the **Annotations** tab and setting a custom name.

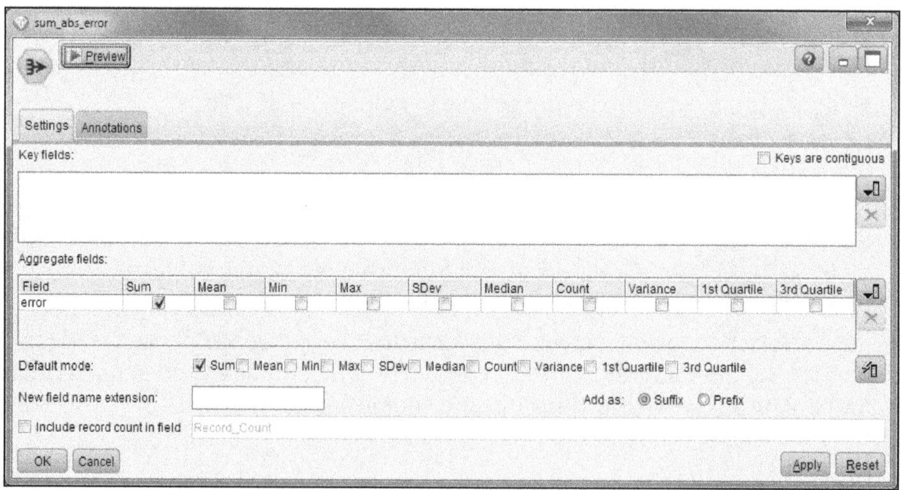

7. Add a Table node connected to the Aggregate node in step 6. Name the node `sum_abs_error_output` by clicking on the **Annotations** tab and setting a custom name.
8. Add a Table node connected below the Statistics File node in step 2. Name the node `cust_id_output` by clicking on the **Annotations** tab and setting a custom name.
9. Using Notepad or another text editor, create a text file `C:\temp\output.csv` with the contents:

   ```
   CUSTOMER_ID,FULL_MODEL_ERROR,JACK_KNIFE_ERROR,PCT_DIFF
   ```

10. Add a Var. File node below the Table node in step 8. Set the file field by navigating to the `C:\temp\output.csv` file using the ellipsis button. Name the node `output_data` by clicking on the **Annotations** tab and setting a custom name.
11. Add a Sort node connected to the Var. File node in step 10. Select the **PCT_DIFF** field in the Sort by field. Name the node `sort_by_diff` by clicking on the **Annotations** tab and setting a custom name.
12. Add a Table node connected below the Sort node in step 11. Name the node `output_table` by clicking on the **Annotations** tab and setting a custom name. The final stream should look as follows:

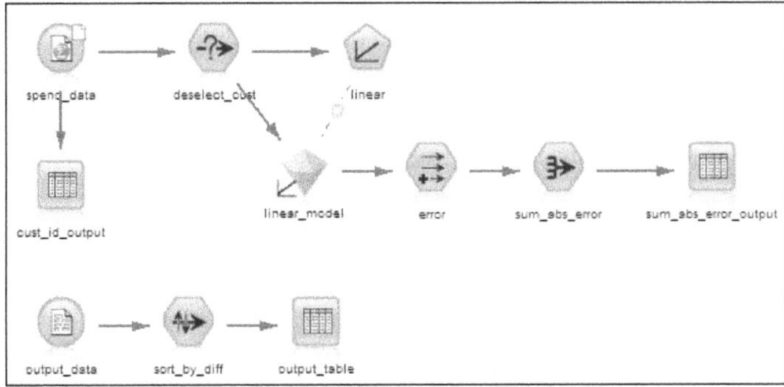

How it works...

The stream is quite simple. The stream is set up to build a linear regression model and calculate the total absolute error across all observations. The jackknife algorithm is implemented via the CLEM script. The script manipulates the filter condition in the `deselect_cust` field while iterating over all the customer records. The results of each iteration are written to a CSV file. The results include the customer ID and the change in total model error by excluding the customer. Finally, the customer records are sorted by the error metric with the most likely Outlier customers at the top of the list.

Script section 1

The screenshot of the script section 1 is as follows:

```
1  var temp_dir
2  var idx
3  var full_error
4  var jack_error
5  var pct_diff
6  var csv_output
7  var tmp_node
8  var num_cust
9  var customer_id
10
11 # delete all existing models
12 for tmp_node in ^stream.nodes
13     if ^tmp_node.node_type = applylinearnode then
14         delete ^tmp_node
15     endif
16 endfor
17
18 # open output CSV file
19 set csv_output = open create "c:/temp/output.csv"
20 writeln csv_output "CUSTOMER_ID,FULL_MODEL_ERROR,JACK_KNIFE_ERROR,PCT_DIFF"
21
22 execute cust_id_output
23 set num_cust = cust_id_output.output.row_count
```

In lines 1 to 23, the script first cleans up any lingering linear models. Next the script opens a text file (that is, a CSV file) and writes a header row to the file.

Script section 2

The screenshot of the script section 2 is as follows:

```
25 for idx from 1 to ^num_cust
26     set customer_id = value cust_id_output.output at ^idx 1
27
28     # select all customers by excluding a bogus customer id
29     set deselect_cust.condition = "CUSTOMER_ID = -1"
30
31     # build full model (all customers)
32     execute linear
33     insert model linear_model connected between deselect_cust and error
34
35     # evaluate full model (minus this customer)
36     set deselect_cust.condition = "CUSTOMER_ID = " >< customer_id
37     execute sum_abs_error_output
38     set full_error = value sum_abs_error_output.output at 1 1
39
40     # build jack-knife model (minus this customer)
41     delete linear_model
42     execute linear
43     insert model linear_model connected between deselect_cust and error
44
45     # evaluate jack-knife model (minus this customer)
46     execute sum_abs_error_output
47     set jack_error = value sum_abs_error_output.output at 1 1
48     set pct_diff = (jack_error - full_error)/full_error
49
50     # write CSV row
51     writeln csv_output customer_id >< "," >< full_error >< "," >< jack_error >< "," >< pct_diff
52
53     delete linear_model
54     clear outputs
55 endfor
```

In lines 25 to 55, the jackknife algorithm is implemented. The script iterates through all customers by reading the customer IDs from the spend data. On line 29, the script excludes a bogus customer (that is, -1) to build a full model. Next, the script excludes the actual customer and calculates the total error. One line 42, a model based on all customers minus the current customer is built. Next, the script calculates the total model error with this new jackknife model. On line 48, the difference in model error is calculated by excluding this customer. Finally, a new row is added to the output CSV file.

Script section 3

The screenshot of the script section 3 is as follows:

```

# view results
set output_data.fule_filename = file_name
execute output_table

```

Finally, the results for all customers are shown in table format by reading the CSV results file.

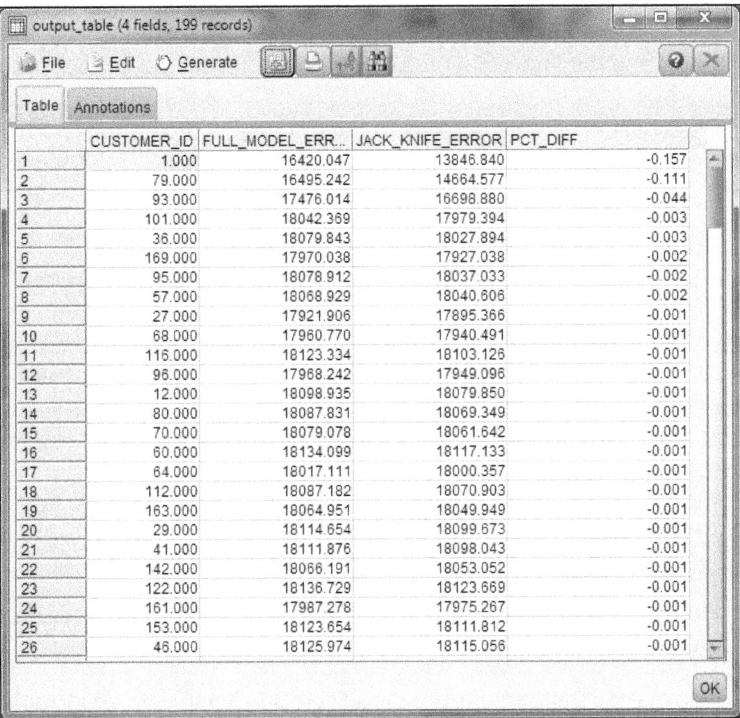

output_table (4 fields, 199 records)

	CUSTOMER_ID	FULL_MODEL_ERR...	JACK_KNIFE_ERROR	PCT_DIFF
1	1.000	16420.047	13846.840	-0.157
2	79.000	16495.242	14664.577	-0.111
3	93.000	17476.014	16698.880	-0.044
4	101.000	18042.369	17979.394	-0.003
5	36.000	18079.843	18027.894	-0.003
6	169.000	17970.038	17927.038	-0.002
7	95.000	18078.912	18037.033	-0.002
8	57.000	18068.929	18040.606	-0.002
9	27.000	17921.906	17895.366	-0.001
10	68.000	17960.770	17940.491	-0.001
11	116.000	18123.334	18103.126	-0.001
12	96.000	17968.242	17949.096	-0.001
13	12.000	18098.935	18079.850	-0.001
14	80.000	18087.831	18069.349	-0.001
15	70.000	18079.078	18061.642	-0.001
16	60.000	18134.099	18117.133	-0.001
17	64.000	18017.111	18000.357	-0.001
18	112.000	18087.182	18070.903	-0.001
19	163.000	18064.951	18049.949	-0.001
20	29.000	18114.654	18099.673	-0.001
21	41.000	18111.876	18098.043	-0.001
22	142.000	18066.191	18053.052	-0.001
23	122.000	18136.729	18123.669	-0.001
24	161.000	17987.278	17975.267	-0.001
25	153.000	18123.654	18111.812	-0.001
26	46.000	18125.974	18115.056	-0.001

There appears to be a sharp drop-off in the error differences after the first three customers. These customers probably merit further investigation (see next).

There's more...

Now that we can identify likely Outlier customers, we can use a C5 model to help us identify the common characteristics of the outliers. First, we would add a flag variable `IS_OUTLIER` to the original spend data set. `IS_OUTLIER` would have a value of 1 for the top three outliers; otherwise 0. `IS_OUTLIER` would then become the target of a C5 model with all the other fields as inputs. A generated C5 rule may then be able to identify the common attributes of the outliers.

Optimizing K-means cluster solutions

K-means clustering is a well-established technique for grouping entities together based on overall similarity. It has many applications including customer segmentation, anomaly detection (finding records that don't fit into existing clusters), and variable reduction (converting many input variables into fewer composite variables).

For all its power and popularity, the K-means algorithm does have a number of known limitations. First, the K-means algorithm is iterative and can arrive at many possible solutions based on the data and the initial algorithm parameters. Some solutions may be better than other solutions and the final solution generally depends on the choice for the location of the initial cluster centers. In most implementations of K-means (including the Modeler implementation), the initial centers depend on the ordering of the data. Thus the quality of the clusters depends on the order of the data during modeling. Second, the K-means algorithm does not determine the optimal number of clusters. Practitioners must have some a prior knowledge or constraints that helps determine how many clusters to use.

In this example, we use scripting to automate the process of finding the optimal number of clusters and initial cluster centers. The example involves clustering (or segmenting) retail store locations based on the demographics of the store trade area. These cluster assignments (or segments) can be used directly by marketing or operations or in further modeling (potentially as an input to split on, resulting in a separate model for each segment). As you will see, this tedious process, that might take a few hours for a practitioner, is reduced to a few minutes and a single click with scripting.

Getting ready

This example depends on the files `customer_location_demographics.sav` and `clem_script_scripting_k_means.txt`.

To disable warning dialogs that require you to click on **OK** repetitively, go to **Tools** | **Options** | **User Options** and deselect the **Warn when a node overwrites a file** and **Warn when a node overwrites a database table** options.

How to do it...

The steps for optimizing K-means cluster solutions are:

1. Start with a new stream by clicking **File** | **New Stream**.

2. Click on **File** | **Stream Properties** and choose the **Parameters** tab. Set up the following parameters (exactly as shown):

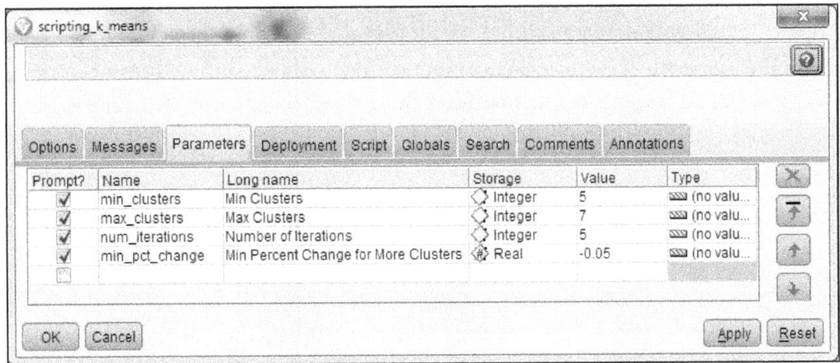

3. Add a Statistics File source node to the upper-left of the stream. Set the import file field by navigating to the `customer_location_demographics.sav` file using the ellipsis button. Select the **Types** tab and click on the **Read Values** button. Name the node `store_demographics` by clicking on the **Annotations** tab and setting a custom name. Click on **OK** to exit to the stream overview. Right-click the node and chose **Cache** | **Enable**.
4. Add a Derive node to the canvas connected to the Statistics Node in step 3. Name the node `random_number` by clicking on the **Annotations** tab and setting a custom name. Choose the **Settings** tab and create a formula field shown as follows:

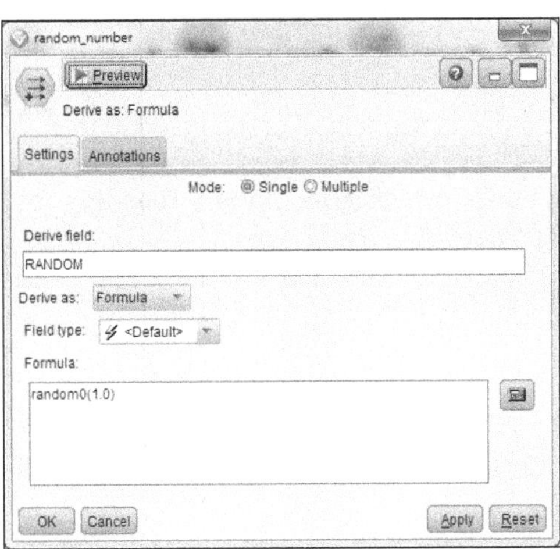

5. Add a Sort node connected to the Derive node in step 4. Name the node `sort_by_rand_num` by clicking on the **Annotations** tab and setting a custom name. Choose the **RANDOM** field by clicking on the button on the far right of the dialog. It doesn't matter which sort direction you choose.

6. Add a Filter node connected to the Sort node in step 4. Name the node `filter_rand_num` by clicking on the **Annotations** tab and setting a custom name. Choose the **Filter** tab and click on the arrow next to the **RANDOM** field (to filter it out). It should display a red x when it is filtered out.
7. Add a K-Means modeling node connected to the Filter node. Name the node `k_means` by clicking on the **Annotations** tab and setting a custom name. Choose the Model tab and set the following options (including the custom Model name field).

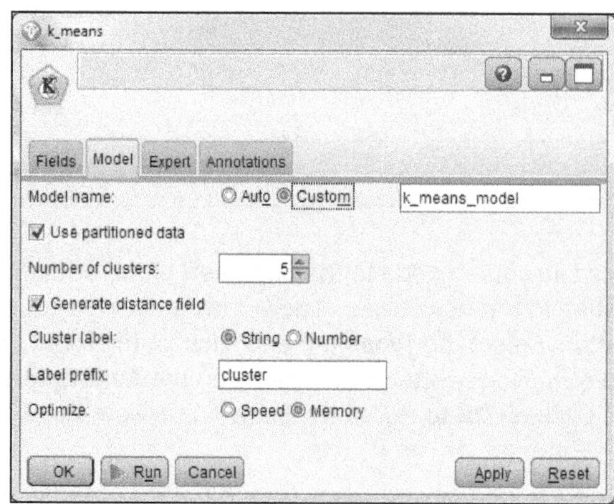

8. Create a temporary K-Means model node by right-clicking on the K-means node in step 7 and choosing **Run**. When the parameters dialog appears, click on **OK**. A gold model nugget named `k_means_model` should be generated, connected to the K-means node.
9. Create an Aggregate node connected to the gold model nugget created in step 8. Name the node `sum_euclid_dist` by clicking on the **Annotations** tab and setting a custom name. Choose the **$KMD-k_means_model** in the **Aggregate** fields section. Ensure that only the sum option is checked.

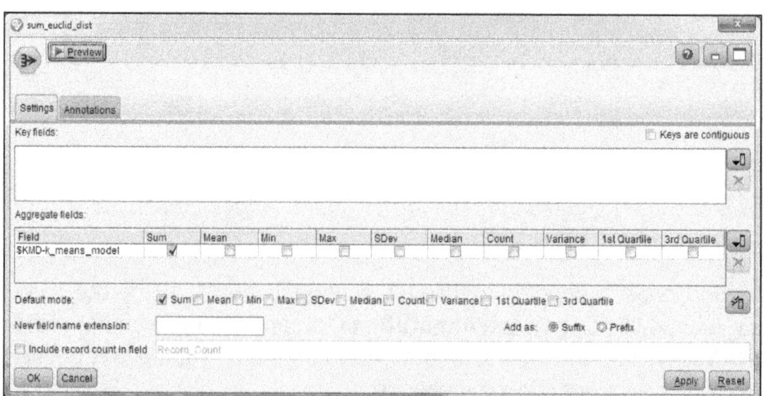

10. Create a Table node connected to the Aggregate node. Name the node `eval_table` by clicking on the **Annotations** tab and setting a custom name. At this point your stream should look like the following:

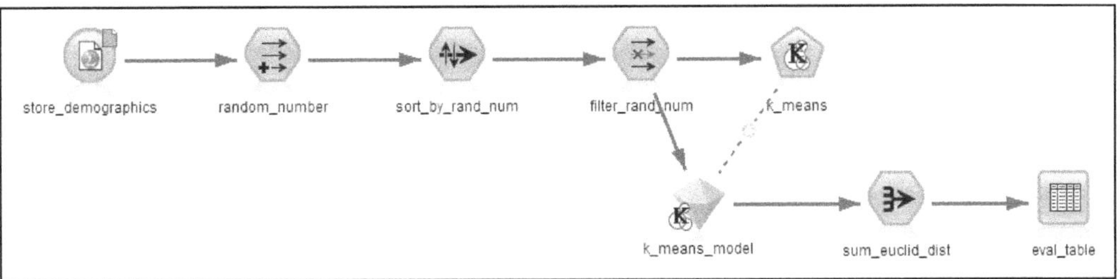

11. Go to **Tools** | **Stream Properties** and select the Script tab. Click on the first icon in the toolbar (suitcase) and navigate to the `clem_script_scripting_k_means.txt` file. This will load the script into the top textbox. At the bottom of the dialog choose the **Run this Script** option for On Stream Execution. Click on **OK**.
12. You can now execute the script by clicking the large green arrow on the main toolbar.

How it works...

Let's look at how the stream functions without the script. First, it loads and caches the store demographic records. Second, it generates a random number field and appends it to the store demographic records. Third, we sort the records using this random number. In effect, we are randomizing the order of the data. Fourth, we cluster the randomized records by generating a K-means model. Fifth, we calculate the Euclidian distance between each record and its closest cluster center. Finally, this distance field is then summed in the aggregation step. The result is a single measure of the effectiveness of the chosen clusters. A smaller number equates to tighter clusters. Note that adding more clusters will generally decrease the total Euclidean distance. In fact, if you have as many clusters as data points the total Euclidean distance can be zero. However, the reality is that at some point we reach a diminishing return. Adding more clusters becomes impractical as the improvement is marginal.

The script attempts to find the optimal (in this case practical) number of clusters that minimizes the total Euclidean distance and also to run multiple trials so that optimal initial cluster centers can be located. Running the script prompts you to enter some parameters that are used within the script.

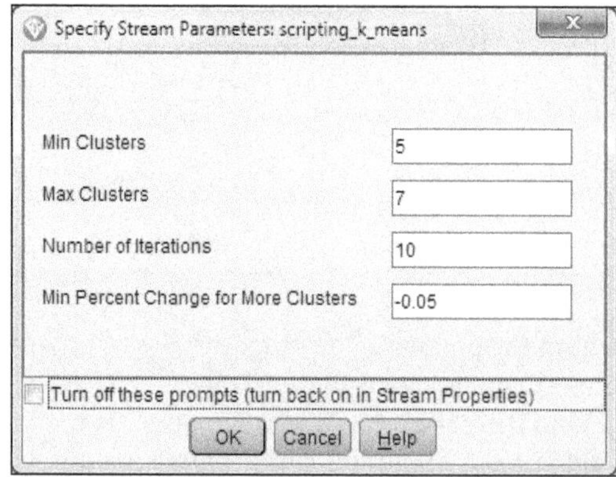

Min Clusters is the minimum number of clusters to use. **Max Clusters** is the maximum number of clusters to be considered. The **Number of Iterations** is the number of models to be built (with randomly ordered data) for each cluster size. **Min Percent Change for More Clusters** determines if we move to a model with more clusters. In this case, if adding one more cluster decreases the total Euclidean distance by more than 5 percent then the script promotes the model to the new champion model. Without the check, we would almost always have the maximum number of clusters (even if they didn't add much value).

Script section 1

The screenshot of the script section 1 is as follows:

```
var min_clusters
var max_clusters
var num_iterations
var cluster_size
var iteration
var champion_distance
var challenger_distance
var pct_change
var min_pct_change
var tmp_node

# read parameters into local variables
set min_clusters = '$P-min_clusters'
set max_clusters = '$P-max_clusters'
set num_iterations = '$P-num_iterations'
set min_pct_change = '$P-min_pct_change'
```

In section 1, we define some script-level variables, and set their initial values to the user-entered values from the parameters dialog.

Script section 2

The screenshot of the script section 2 is as follows:

```
# delete all existing models
for tmp_node in ^stream.nodes
    if ^tmp_node.node_type = applykmeansnode then
        delete ^tmp_node
    endif
endfor
```

In section 2, we loop through all the stream nodes and check for K-means models. If they exist, we delete them. This code allows the script to be re-run even if we have an error.

Script section 3

The screenshot of the script section 3 is as follows:

```
for cluster_size from ^min_clusters to ^max_clusters
    set k_means.num_clusters = ^cluster_size

    for iteration from 1 to ^num_iterations
        # build a challenger model
        execute k_means
        insert model k_means_model connected between filter_rand_num and sum_euclid_dist
        clear generated palette
        execute eval_table
        set challenger_distance = value eval_table.output at 1 1
        clear outputs

        # if this is the first iteration, then the champion model is set to the current model
        if (^cluster_size = ^min_clusters and iteration = 1) then
            set champion_distance = ^challenger_distance
            disconnect k_means_model
            duplicate k_means_model as champion_k_means_model
            position champion_k_means_model at 200 200
        endif

        # check for a better model (smaller euclidian distance)
        # if model is better then promote it to champion
        set pct_change = (^challenger_distance - ^champion_distance)/^champion_distance
        if ((^cluster_size = ^min_clusters and ^challenger_distance < ^champion_distance) or (^pct_change < ^min_pct_change)) then
            delete champion_k_means_model
            set champion_distance = ^challenger_distance
            disconnect k_means_model
            duplicate k_means_model as champion_k_means_model
            position champion_k_means_model at 200 200
        endif

        # remove the challenger
        delete k_means_model
    endfor
endfor
```

In section 3, we implement the loop that gradually increases the cluster size and runs the trials for each cluster size. Within each trial, we implement a champion/challenger approach to finding the best model. The change in total Euclidean distance is the metric by which we compare models.

Script section 4

The screenshot of the script section 4 is as follows:

```
# place the champion back into the stream in its place of honor
position champion_k_means_model connected between filter_rand_num and sum_euclid_dist
```

Finally a winning model is declared and placed back into the stream.

There's more...

Another shortcoming of the K-means algorithm is that K-means can be very sensitive to the Outlier records (records with extreme values). Just a few Outlier records can dominate the final solution as they can have a big impact on the total Euclidean distance forcing an "Outlier cluster".

This stream/script could easily be modified to identify the Outlier records, and exclude them from the model building phase. Identification could be achieved by looking at the Euclidean distance of individual records after building the model, and exclude the records that fall outside the three standard deviations of the mean. The model could then be rebuilt with the new data set. Alternatively, you could use the Anomaly node to identify and filter out the Outlier records.

Automating time series forecasts

The Expert Modeler functionality in Modeler greatly simplifies **time series forecasting**. The Time Series node will automatically determine which model type is most appropriate for your data: ARIMA, exponential smoothing, seasonal model, and so on. However, in practice, a time series model nugget can only generate forecast models for a single time series. It is possible to generate multiple time series forecasts using the Time Series node but it is largely impractical. First, you must pivot the data such that each series is a column. Second, defining input variable roles can become convoluted due to each field having only a single role (for example, a field cannot be an input for one series but none for another input). Finally, you must reverse-pivot the forecast data back to the original format to make use of it. This reverse pivot requires you to have a fixed set of input names to pivot. With all of these limitations, the Time Series node does not scale to large data sets without CLEM scripting.

Scripting time series models is simple and straightforward. Data sets with 10 to 100k separate time series can be modeled and forecasted by invoking a simple script. Each time series is individually modeled and the inclusion of input variables does not present any complication.

Examples of large time series data sets are wide-spread. In finance, it's common to forecast financial performance across regions, divisions, warehouse, factory, store level, and so on. The following example is taken from retail. In this example, we forecast the sales performance for individual SKUs (that is, the individual products) at different store locations. CLEM scripting makes this process simple and scalable. Without scripting, the forecast process would be a tedious and time-consuming process.

Getting ready

This example depends on the `weekly_sales.sav` and `clem_script_time_series_forecasting.txt` files. This example writes temporary files to `C:\temp`. Please ensure that this directory or a substitute directory exists.

To disable warning dialogs that require you to click OK repetitively, go to **Tools** | **Options** | **User Options** and deselect the **Warn when a node overwrites a file** and **Warn when a node overwrites a database table** options.

How to do it...

The steps for automating time series forecasts are as follows:

1. Start with a new stream by clicking on the **New Stream** option in the **File** menu.
2. Add a Statistics File source node to the upper-left of the stream. Set the input file field by navigating to the `weekly_sales.sav` file using the ellipsis button. Review the preset roles for each input variable by clicking on the **Types** tab.

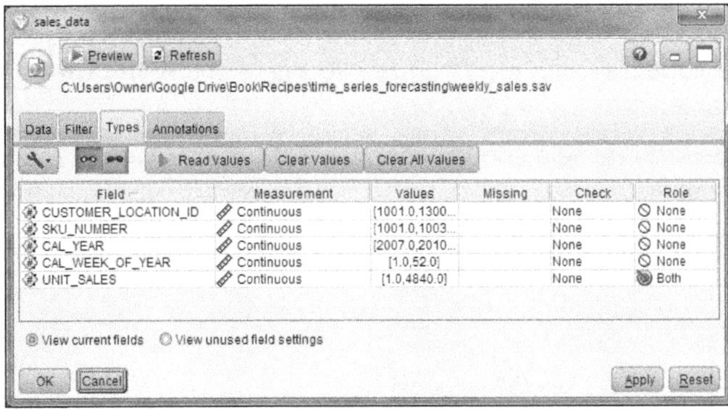

   Name the node `sales_data` by clicking on the **Annotations** tab and setting a custom name.

3. Add a Sort node connected to the Statistics File node in step 2. Select the Sort by field: `CUSTOMER_LOCATION_ID`, `SKU_NUMBER`, `CAL_YEAR`, and `CAL_WEEK_OF_YEAR` ascending.

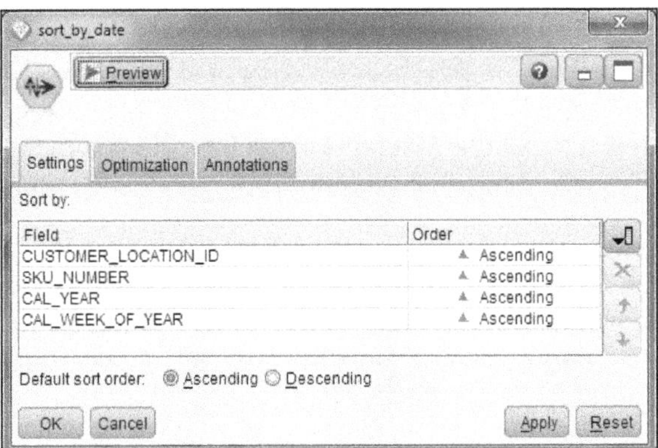

Name the node sort_by_date by clicking on the **Annotations** tab and setting a custom name. Right-click on the node and go to **Cache** | **Enable**.

4. Add a Distinct node connected to the Sort node in step 3. Choose **CUSTOMER_LOCATION_ID** and **SKU_NUMBER** as the key fields for grouping. Name the node distinct by clicking on the **Annotations** tab and setting a custom name.
5. Add a Filter node connected to the Distinct node in step 4. Filter out the last three fields: CAL_YEAR, CAL_WEEK_OF_YEAR, and UNIT_SALES by clicking the Filter column next to each field. Name the node filter by clicking on the **Annotations** tab and setting a custom name.
6. Add a Table node connected to the Filter node in step 5. Name the node sku_loc_table by clicking on the **Annotations** tab and setting a custom name.
7. Add a Select node connected below the sort_by_date node in step 3. Set the **Condition** field to: CUSTOMER_LOCATION_ID = 1001 and SKU_NUMBER = 1001. Name the node select_sku_loc by clicking on the **Annotations** tab and setting a custom name.
8. Add a **Time Interval** field connected to the Select node in step 7. Configure the **Intervals** tab as follows:

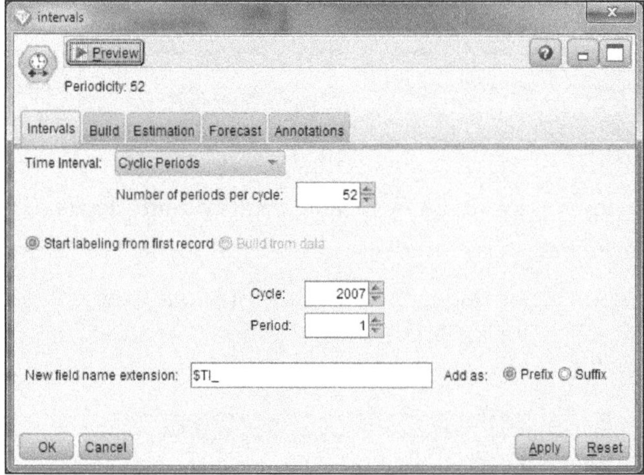

On the **Forecast** tab, set the **Extend records into the future** field to 4. Name the node intervals by clicking on the **Annotations** tab and setting a custom name.

9. Add a Time Series node connected to the Time Intervals node in step 8. Name the generated model time_series_model by clicking on the **Model** tab and setting a custom name. Name the node time_series by clicking on the **Annotations** tab and setting a custom name. Right-click on the node and select **Run** to build the model nugget.

10. Add a Filler node connected to the model nugget generated in step 9. Configure the node to replace null values with the last non-null value as follows:

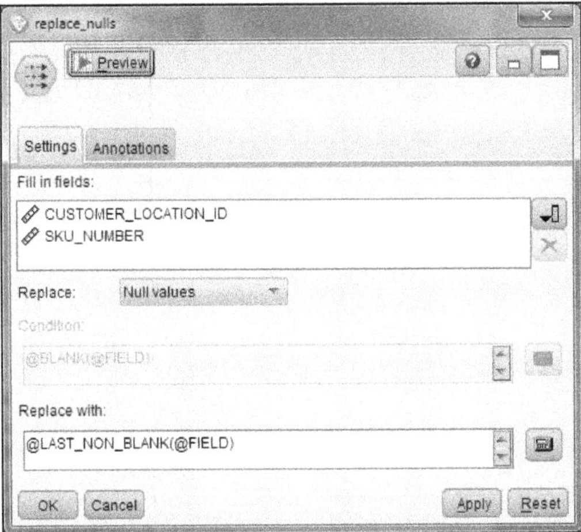

Name the node `replace_nulls` by clicking on the **Annotations** tab and setting a custom name.

11. Add a Derive node connected to the Filler node in step 10. Set the Derive field to: `TIME_LABEL`. Choose `Formula` for the **Derive as** field. Set the formula to: `"W" >< '$TI_Period' >< "-" >< '$TI_Cycle'`. Name the node `time_label` by clicking on the **Annotations** tab and setting a custom name.

12. Add a Filter node connected to the Derive node in step 11. Configure the **Filter** tab as follows (note the renamed fields):

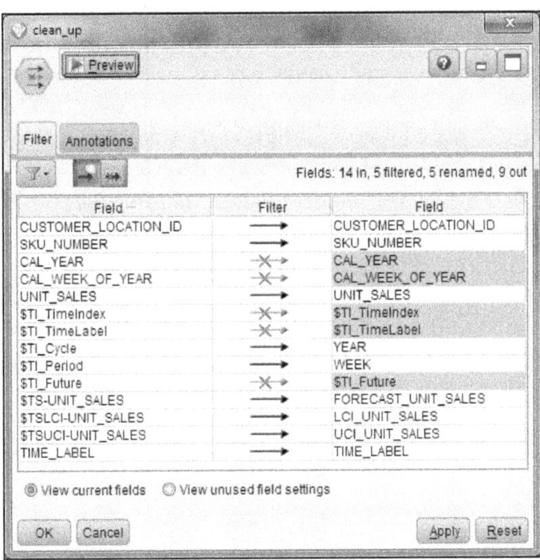

Field	Filter	Field
CUSTOMER_LOCATION_ID	→	CUSTOMER_LOCATION_ID
SKU_NUMBER	→	SKU_NUMBER
CAL_YEAR	✕	CAL_YEAR
CAL_WEEK_OF_YEAR	✕	CAL_WEEK_OF_YEAR
UNIT_SALES	→	UNIT_SALES
$TI_TimeIndex	✕	$TI_TimeIndex
$TI_TimeLabel	✕	$TI_TimeLabel
$TI_Cycle	→	YEAR
$TI_Period	→	WEEK
$TI_Future	✕	$TI_Future
$TS-UNIT_SALES	→	FORECAST_UNIT_SALES
$TSLCI-UNIT_SALES	→	LCI_UNIT_SALES
$TSUCI-UNIT_SALES	→	UCI_UNIT_SALES
TIME_LABEL	→	TIME_LABEL

Name the node `clean_up` by clicking on the **Annotations** tab and setting a custom name.

13. Add a Flat File output node connected to the Filter node in step 12. Set the **Export file** field to `C:\temp\time_series_forecast_output.csv`. Name the node `forecast_output` by clicking on the **Annotations** tab and setting a custom name. The final stream should look as follows:

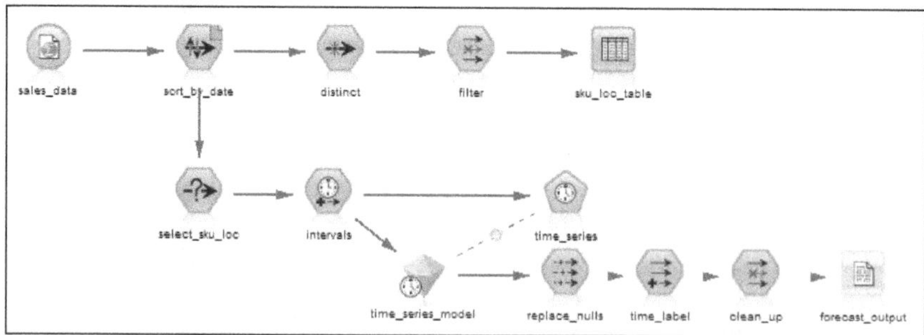

14. Click on the **Stream Properties** option from the **Tools** menu and select the **Script** tab. Click on the first icon in the toolbar (suitcase) and navigate to the `clem_script_time_series_forecasting.txt` file. This will load the script into the top textbox. At the bottom of the dialog choose the **Run this Script** option for On Stream Execution. Click on **OK**.
15. You can now execute the script by clicking on the large green arrow on the main toolbar.

How it works...

In steps 1 to 6, we sort and cache the time series data by location, SKU number, and date. Next, we determine the distinct location/SKU combinations so that we can iterate over all combinations to generate the time series forecasts.

In steps 7 to 9, we define the specific time series to model/forecast (that is, location and SKU combination). Next we define the time series interval to be cyclic weeks. We also specify a four-week forecast interval. Finally, we use the Expert Modeler within the Time Series node to generate an initial forecast model nugget.

In step 8 to 13, we clean up the final forecast data and write it to a CSV text file. This file will be used in the next *Automating HTML reports and graphs* recipe. The `replace_nulls` Filler node uses an interesting function `@LAST_NON_BLANK(@FIELD)`. The `@LAST_NON_BLANK` field is useful with time series forecasts because the non-target fields are null for the forecasted rows. This function allows us to replicate the last non-null value into fields such as the location and SKU.

Script section 1

The screenshot of the script section 1 is as follows:

```
1   var num_sku_loc
2   var customer_location
3   var sku_number
4   var idx
5   var tmp_node
6
7   # delete all existing models
8   for tmp_node in ^stream.nodes
9       if ^tmp_node.node_type = applytimeseriesnode then
10          delete ^tmp_node
11      endif
12  endfor
13
14  # create distinct list of SKUs and locations
15  execute sku_loc_table
16
17  set num_sku_loc = sku_loc_table.output.row_count
18
```

In script lines 1 to 17, we delete any lingering time series models. Next, we populate the table with all the location/SKU combinations to iterate over.

Script section 2

The screenshot of the script section 2 is as follows:

```
14  # create distinct list of SKUs and locations
15  execute sku_loc_table
16
17  set num_sku_loc = sku_loc_table.output.row_count
18
19  for idx from 1 to num_sku_loc
20      set sku_number = value sku_loc_table.output at ^idx 2
21      set customer_location = value sku_loc_table.output at ^idx 1
22
23      # update select statement with new location and SKU
24      set select_sku_loc.condition = "CUSTOMER_LOCATION_ID = " >< ^customer_location >< " and SKU_NUMBER = " >< ^sku_number
25
26      if idx = 1 then
27          set forecast_output.write_mode = Overwrite
28      else
29          set forecast_output.write_mode = Append
30      endif
31
32      # build model
33      execute time_series
34      insert model time_series_model connected between intervals and replace_nulls
35
36      # generate forecast
37      execute forecast_output
38
39      # delete time series model
40      delete time_series_model
41      clear outputs
42  endfor
```

In lines 17 to 42, we iterate over all the possible location/SKU combinations. Setting the Select node condition, we can pull each location/SKU time series, build a unique model, and generate a four-week forecast. The results are written to a CSV text file for further processing.

There's more...

This script allows a repetitive task of model building and forecasting to be fully automated, but does not necessarily scale well. A 100k location/SKU forecast data set may take more than 8 hours to complete using a single instance of Modeler running this script. A possible solution to this single-threaded model would be to have this script running in parallel across several instances of Modeler. This can be accomplished by:

1. Running multiple instances of the Modeler client on one or more computers.
2. Using **IBM SPSS Modeler Batch** with command-line scheduling.
3. Deployment to **IBM SPSS Collaboration and Deployment Services**.

No matter which method is employed, the script would need to handle concurrent access to the same data. It would not make sense for more than one script to execute the same forecast. The easiest approach to concurrency would be to somehow divide the input data set by location or SKU set. A select node that filtered the input data by a range of locations or SKUs would allow each Modeler script instance to have a unique input data set. The final solution would need to consolidate the resultant CSV file (or simply modify the stream to write to a shared database table).

Automating HTML reports and graphs

Generating reports from predictive models is not very exciting but it is one of the most common applications of scripting. The main benefit of scripting is the ability to generate large amounts of graphics and make them easy to navigate through an HTML interface. It's certainly possible and often advisable to use a **BI** (**Business Intelligence**) platform to deliver these graphics; however there are a few cases when the BI solution is not possible and we must use scripting:

- A BI solution is not available
- The visualization (for example, web plot, chloropleth, and so on) is not available in the BI platform
- The data to generate the BI visualization is not persisted to the database

The following example generates plots for the sales forecasts in the previous example.

Getting ready

This example depends on the `sales_forecasts.sav` file. Choose a local directory where this script can write the HTML report file and JPEG images.

To disable warning dialogs that require you to click on **OK** repetitively, go to **Tools** | **Options** | **User Options** and deselect the **Warn when a node overwrites a file** and **Warn when a node overwrites a database table** options.

How to do it...

The steps for automating the HTML reports and graphs are as follows:

1. Start with a new stream by clicking on the **New Stream** option in the **File** menu.
2. Click on the Stream Properties option in the **File** menu and choose the **Parameters** tab. Set up the following parameters (exactly as shown):

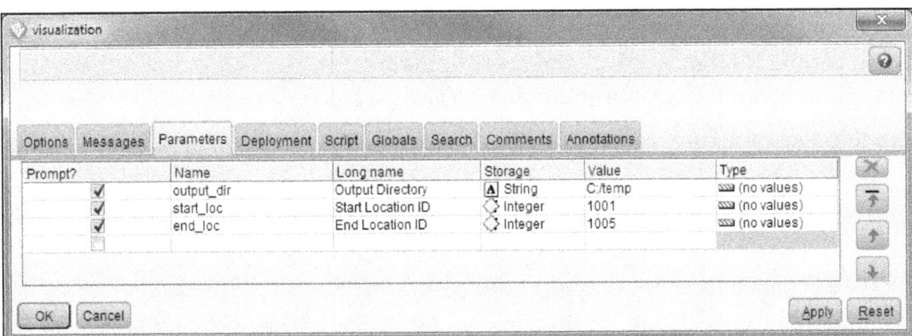

3. Add a Statistics File source node to the upper-left of the stream. Set the input file field by navigating to the `sales_forecast.sav` file using the ellipsis button. Name the node `forecast_data` by clicking on the **Annotations** tab and setting a custom name.
4. Add a Sort node connected to the Statistics File node in step 3. Select the Sort by fields: `CUSTOMER_LOCATION_ID`, `SKU_NUMBER`, `YEAR`, and `WEEK` ascending.

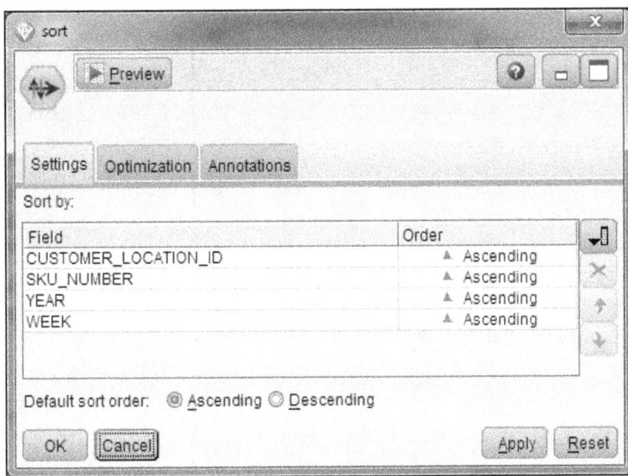

Name the node `sort` by clicking on the **Annotations** tab and setting a custom name. Right-click on the node and go to **Cache** | **Enable**.

5. Add a Select node connected to the Sort node in step 4. Set the **condition** to `CUSTOMER_LOCATION_ID = 1001` and `SKU_NUMBER = 1001`. Name the node `choose_sku_loc` by clicking on the **Annotations** tab and setting a custom name.
6. Add a Derive node to the Select node in step 5. Set the **Derive** field to `Week_Num`. Choose `Formula` for the **Derive as** field. Enter the Formula `@INDEX`. Name the node `forecast_data` by clicking on the **Annotations** tab and setting a custom name.
7. Add a Multiplot graph node connected to the Derive node in step 6. Choose `Week_Num` as the **X field**. Choose `UNIT_SALES`, `FORECAST_UNIT_SALES`, `LCI_UNIT_SALES`, and `UCI_UNIT_SALES` as the **Y fields** on the **Plot** tab. On the **Appearance** tab set the **X label** to `Week` and the **Y label** to `Unit Sales`. Name the node `graph` by clicking on the **Annotations** tab and setting a custom name.
8. Add a Select node connected below the Statistic File node in step 3. Set the condition to `CUSTOMER_LOCATION_ID >= '$P-start_loc'` and `CUSTOMER_LOCATION_ID <= '$P-end_loc'` on the **Settings** tab. Name the node `loc_range` by clicking on the **Annotations** tab and setting a custom name.
9. Add a Distinct node connected to the Select node in step 8. Select `CUSTOMER_LOCATION_ID` and `SKU_NUMBER` as the key fields for grouping. Name the node `distinct` by clicking on the **Annotations** tab and setting a custom name.
10. Add a Sort node connected to the Distinct node in step 9. Choose `CUSTOMER_LOCATION_ID` and `SKU_NUMBER` with the **Ascending** option in the **Sort by** field. Name the node `sort` by clicking on the **Annotations** tab and setting a custom name.
11. Add a Table node connected to the Sort node in step 10. Name the node `sku_loc_table` by clicking on the **Annotations** tab and setting a custom name. The final stream should look as follows:

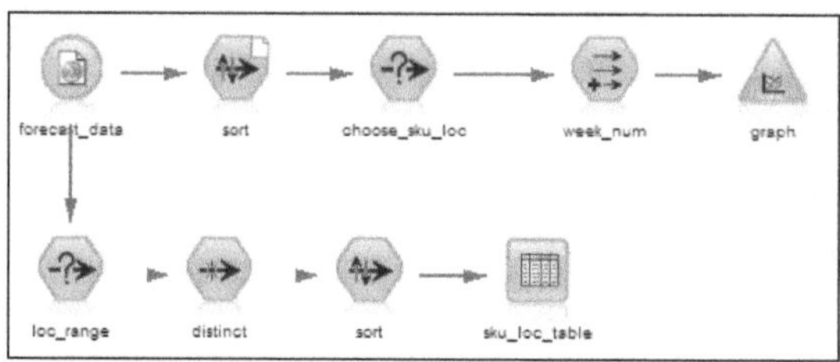

12. Click on the **Stream Properties** option on the **Tools** menu and select the **Script** tab. Click the first icon in the toolbar (suitcase) and navigate to the `clem_script_visualization.txt` file. This will load the script into the top textbox. At the bottom of the dialog choose the **Run this Script** option for On Stream Execution. Click on **OK**.
13. You can now execute the script by clicking on the large green arrow on the main toolbar.

How it works...

This script generates a series for forecast graphs by iterating through a distinct list of locations and SKUs. The output of the graph node is redirected to disk as a JPEG file using a standard naming convention (using location and SKU number). The HTML report file references these graphs using an IMG (image) and A (anchor) tag. The HTML report file is created by writing a HTML syntax directly to a text (HTML) file. The final result is a report where each graph is shown in preview. Clicking on the smaller image preview causes the full graph image to be shown (by following a hyperlink to the JPEG file).

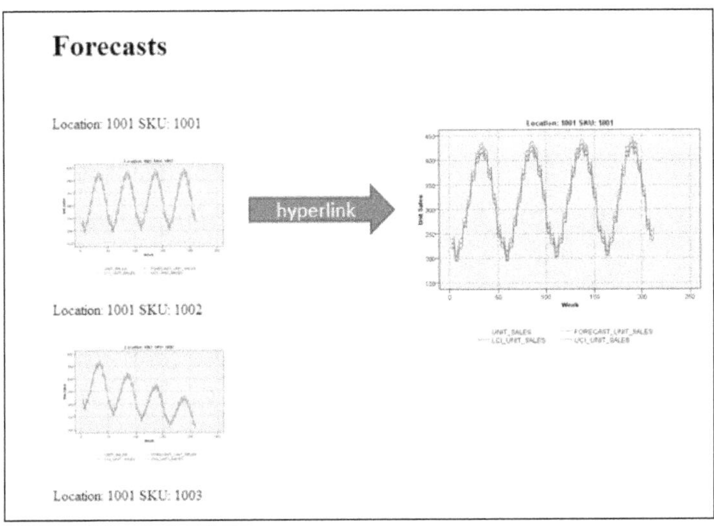

Script section 1

The screenshot of the script section 1 is as follows:

```
1  var output_dir
2  var idx
3  var num_sku_loc
4  var file_name
5  var title
6  var html_out
7  var report_file_name
8  var customer_location
9  var sku_number
10 var start_loc
11 var end_loc
12
13 # read parameters into local variables
14 set output_dir = '$P-output_dir'
15
16 # determine which customer locations will be charted
17 execute sku_loc_table
18 set num_sku_loc = sku_loc_table.output.row_count
```

In lines 1 to 18, we read the user-specified output directory into a local variable. Next, we create a table of distinct location and SKU combinations.

Script section 2

The screenshot of the script section 2 is as follows:

```
19
20  # setup the HTML output file
21  set report_file_name = ^output_dir >< "/sku_loc_forecasts.html"
22  set html_out = open create ^report_file_name
23  writeln html_out "<html><head><title>SKU-Loc Forecasts</title></head></html><body><h1>Forecasts</h1><br/>"
24
```

In lines 19 to 24, we create an HTML report file, write the HEAD section, and add an overall header for the report.

Script section 3

The screenshot of the script section 3 is as follows:

```
24
25  for idx from 1 to num_sku_loc
26      set customer_location = value sku_loc_table.output at ^idx 1
27      set sku_number = value sku_loc_table.output at ^idx 2
28
29      # update select statement with new location and SKU
30      set choose_sku_loc.condition = "CUSTOMER_LOCATION_ID = " >< ^customer_location >< " and SKU_NUMBER = " >< ^sku_number
31
32      # customize and generate graph
33      set title = "Location: " >< to_integer(^customer_location) >< " SKU: " >< to_integer(^sku_number)
34      set file_name = to_integer(^customer_location) >< "_" >< to_integer(^sku_number) >< ".jpg"
35      set graph.full_filename = ^output_dir >< "\\" >< ^file_name
36      set graph.title = ^title
37      execute graph
38
39      write html_out "<p>" >< title >< "</p><a href=\"" >< ^file_name >< "\"><img width=200 height=150 src=\"" >< ^file_name >< "\"/></a></br>"
40  endfor
41
42  write html_out "</body></html>"
43  close html_out
```

In lines 25 to 43, we iterate over all the location/SKU combinations and generate the time series graphs. The graphs are redirected to JPEG files on disk using a standard naming convention. After each JPEG is generated an IMG (image) and surrounding A (anchor) tag are created to show the preview and hyperlink to the full image. Finally, we close the HTML output and close the file.

There's more...

This example generates a very basic report. A more realistic implementation would provide a mechanism for grouping the forecasts and provide more detail on the four-week forecast. A Table node or Flat File node could generate a CSV file that contains the entire forecast. The HTML report could link to each CSV file for users that wanted to pull the forecast tools such as Microsoft Excel.

Rolling your own modeling algorithm – Weibull analysis

Weibull analysis is a well-known technique for understanding the reliability of physical assets over time and is not directly supported in Modeler. The analysis is based on understanding the failure distribution of physical assets such as bearing, switches, electrical components, pipes (think corrosion), and so on. The only inputs to the model are the times to failure. A Weibull failure distribution is fit to the empirical failure distribution. In the two-parameter Weibull model, there are Alpha and Beta parameters. The parameters give insights into the failures:

- Beta < 1 indicates **infant mortality**
- Beta = 1 indicates **random failures**
- Beta > 1 indicates **wear-out**

Alpha is the number of cycles where approximately 68 percent of circuit boards would have failed (and can also be used to calculate the **MTTF** (**mean time to failure**). Lastly, the **CDF** (**cumulative distribution function**), which can be calculated directly from the Weibull parameters, can be used to predict the reliability of an asset at any point in its lifetime.

In this example, we play the role of a manufacturer testing circuit boards. All boards are run to failure and the number of cycles at the time of failure is the input to the Weibull analysis. If there were circuit boards that had not failed yet (so called **censored observations**), this method of calculating the parameter estimates would be biased and we would need to use a slightly different approach.

Getting ready

This example depends on the `circuit_board_failures.csv` and `clem_script_visualization.txt` files.

To disable warning dialogs that require you to click on **OK** repetitively, go to **Tools** | **Options** | **User Options** and deselect the **Warn when a node overwrites a file** and **Warn when a node overwrites a database table** options.

How to do it...

The steps for rolling your own modeling algorithm (Weibull analysis) are as follows:

1. Start with a new stream by navigating to **File** | **New Stream**.
2. Add a Var. File source node to the upper-left of the stream. Set the file field by navigating to the `circuit_board_failures.csv` file using the ellipsis button. Name the node `circuit_board_failures` by clicking on the **Annotations** tab and setting a custom name.

3. Add a Sort node connected to the Var. File in step 2. Choose **Cycles** in the Sort by field. Name the node `sort` by clicking on the **Annotations** tab and setting a custom name.
4. Add a Derive node connected to the Sort node in step 3. Set the Derive Field to RANK. Choose `Formula` for the **Derive as** field. Set the **Formula** to `@INDEX`. Name the node `rank` by clicking on the **Annotations** tab and setting a custom name.
5. Add an Aggregate node connected below the Derive node in step 4. Select the **Include record count in field** option and specify `N` in the name field. Name the node `calc_n` by clicking on the **Annotations** tab and setting a custom name.
6. Add a Merge node connected to both the Derive and Aggregate nodes in steps 4 to 5. Choose `Keys` as the **Merge Method**. There will be no possible keys. Choose the **Include matching and selected non-matching records (partial outer join)** option. Click on the **Select** button. Select the **Outer Join** option for the first row.

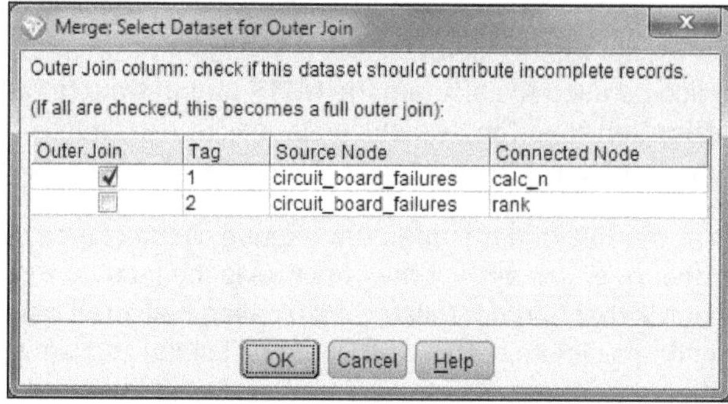

Name the node `merge` by clicking on the **Annotations** tab and setting a custom name.

7. Add three Derive nodes connected in succession to the Merge node in step 6. Configure the nodes, in order, using the following table:

Name	**Derive Field**	**Formula**
median_rank	MEDIAN_RANK	((RANK-0.3)/(N+0.4))
trans_median_rank	LN_MEDIAN_RANKS	log(log(1/(1-MEDIAN_RANK)))
ln_cycles	LN_CYCLES	log('Cycles'

8. Select the nodes from **sort** to **ln_cycles** and enclose them in a supernode by clicking on the first star icon in the main toolbar. Name the supernode `weibull_calculations` by clicking on the **Annotations** tab and setting a custom name. The supernode contents should look as follows:

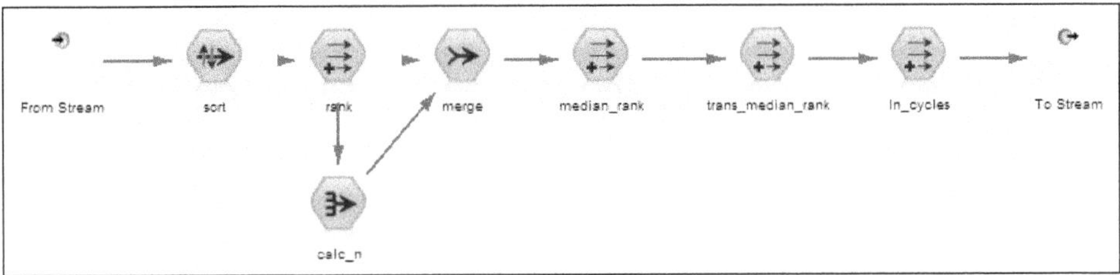

9. Connect a Plot graph node to the supernode in step 8. Choose `LN_CYCLES` as the **X field** and `LN_MEDIANK_RANKS` as the **Y field**. Name the node `weibull_plot` by clicking on the **Annotations** tab and setting a custom name.
10. Add a Type node connected below the supernode in step 8. Click on the **Read Values** button on the **Types** tab to instantiate the Type node. Set the role for **LN_MEDIAN_RANKS** to `Target` and **LN_CYCLES** to `Input`. All other inputs should be set to `None`. Name the node `type` by clicking on the **Annotations** tab and setting a custom name.

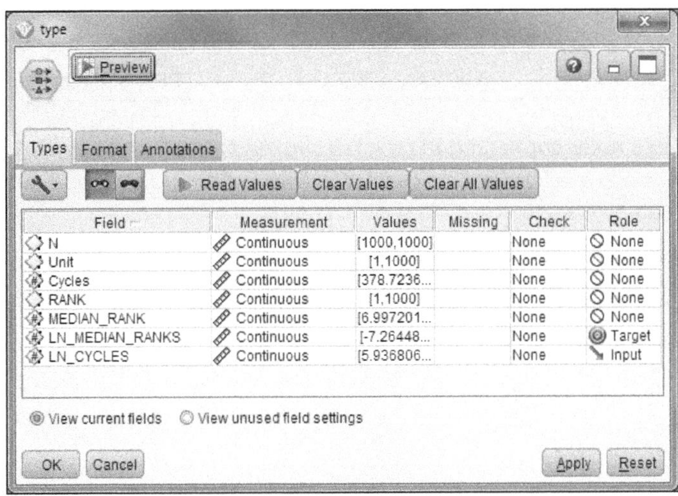

11. Add a Linear model node connected to the Type node in Step 10. Name the generated model `linear_model` by clicking on the **Model** tab and setting a custom name. Name the node `linear` by clicking on the **Annotations** tab and setting a custom name. Right-click on the Liner node and select **Run** to build the model nugget.
12. Right-click on the `linear_model` nugget on the **Model** tab and choose **Export PMML**. Save the PMML file to `C:\temp\linear_model.xml`.

13. Add an XML source node below the Statistics File node in step 3. Set the XML data source field to `C:\temp\lineaer_model.xml`. Navigate PMML tree to: `/PMML/GeneralRegressionModel/ParamMatrix/PCell` and then click the right arrow to set the **Records** field. Name the node `pmml` by clicking on the **Annotations** tab and setting a custom name. Right-click on the Liner node and select **Run** to build the model nugget.
14. Add a Transpose node connected to the XML source node in step 12. Choose the **Read from** field option and click on the **Read Values** button. Name the node `transpose` by clicking on the **Annotations** tab and setting a custom name.
15. Add a Select node to the Transpose node in step 14. Set the condition to `ID = 'beta'`. Name the node `select_model_params` by clicking on the **Annotations** tab and setting a custom name.
16. Add a Filter node connected to the Select node in step 15. Deselect the ID variable by clicking on the **Filter** column. Name the node `clean_up` by clicking on the **Annotations** tab and setting a custom name.
17. Add three Derive nodes connected in succession to the Filter node in step 6. Configure the nodes, in order, using the following table:

Name	Derive Field	Formula
beta	BETA	to_number(SLOPE)
alpha	ALPHA	exp(-INTERCEPT/SLOPE)
median_life	MEDIAN_LIFE	ALPHA * log(2)**(1/BETA)

18. Add a Table node connected to the `median_life` node in step 17. Name the node `output_table` by clicking on the **Annotations** tab and setting a custom name. The final stream should look as follows:

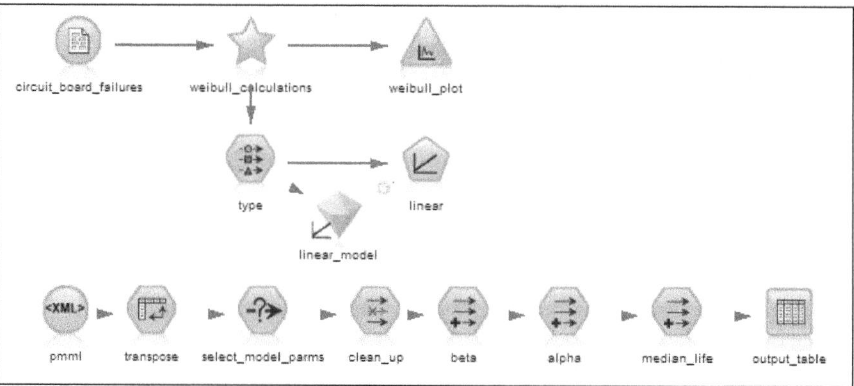

19. Go to **Tools** | **Stream Properties** and select the Script tab. Click on the first icon in the toolbar (suitcase) and navigate to the `clem_script_weibull.txt` file. This will load the script into the top textbox. At the bottom of the dialog choose the **Run this Script** option for On Stream Execution. Click on **OK**.
20. You can now execute the script by clicking on the large green arrow on the main toolbar.

How it works...

This script and corresponding stream determine the best estimates for the Weibull distribution parameters (that fit a set of failure data) using the regression method. The `weibull_calculations` supernode contains a data preparation routine that calculates the median ranks for the failure data. The results of the data preparation are plotted in the `weibull_plot`. A straight line on this plot implies a single failure node (and ultimately that the data came from a single failure distribution). The linear node creates a linear regression model that is used to calculate the Weibull parameter estimates. Exporting the linear model to PMML (XML file) allows the slope and intercept to be read into the parameter calculations (that is, a series of derive nodes). The final results are parameter estimates for a best-fit Weibull distribution to the failure data.

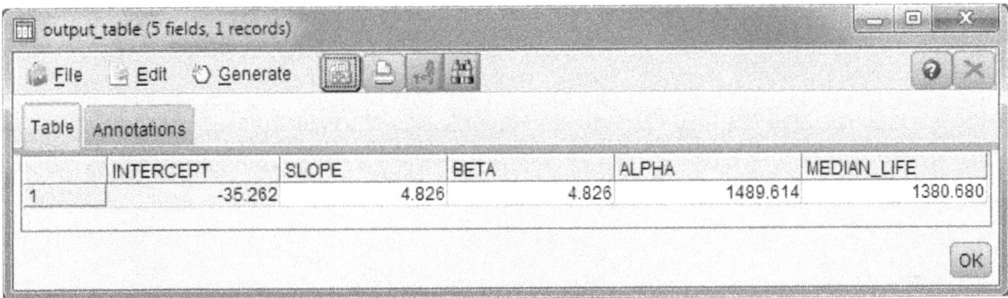

	INTERCEPT	SLOPE	BETA	ALPHA	MEDIAN_LIFE
1	-35.262	4.826	4.826	1489.614	1380.680

The large beta (>1) implies that the failure is due to wear-out (not infant mortality or random failure). The median life is an (average) estimate of how many cycles a circuit board will experience before failure. Using the ALPHA and BETA estimates we can also determine the probability of a failure at any cycle count (for example, the probability of failure between time `t` and `t+n` is the difference in the Weibull CDF at times `t` and `t+n`). The Weibull CDF is the cumulative density function and can be calculated directly from ALPHA and BETA.

Script section 1

The screenshot of the script section 1 is as follows:

```
var tmp_node

# delete all existing models
for tmp_node in ^stream.nodes
    if ^tmp_node.node_type = applylinearnode then
        delete ^tmp_node
    endif
endfor

# create linear model and export PMML
execute linear
export model linear_model as "c:/temp/linear_model.xml"

execute output_table
```

The script starts by removing lingering linear models. Next, it generates a linear model using the input failure data. The PMML model is exported to disk, read into memory, and the Weibull parameters are calculated and displayed.

There's more...

This example does not use the final Weibull model for predictions. It would be a simple modification to calculate the CDF for various time windows and calculate the probability of failure (also known as "reliability") of circuit boards that are currently in service.

Business Understanding

This chapter consists of four essays on the critical first phase of CRISP-DM:

- Defining business objectives by Tom Khabaza
- Assessing the situation by Meta Brown
- Translating your business objective into a data mining objective by Dean Abbott
- Producing a project plan ensuring a realistic timeline by Keith McCormick

Introduction

This is a special chapter because it does not consist of recipes but four essays through which it addresses the subtasks within the opening phase of any data mining project—the business understanding phase:

> *"Understanding the project objectives and requirements from a business perspective, then converting this knowledge into a data mining problem definition".*

Business understanding is about problem definition. It should involve management. It should involve stakeholders. It should involve key players who will benefit from it or will be involved in the deployed model; if deployment has not been discussed, that oversight needs to be addressed during this phase as well. "Why are we doing this?" is the question of this phase. It is about restating lofty goals, and turning vaguely-defined needs into a soluble problem. It is about making better decisions, decisions informed by data.

What decisions are you trying to make using data?

The business understanding phase should be scheduled to occur over quite a few days. They might not be, and often are not, for days. Business understanding is all about meetings, and therefore it suffers from the same delays that plague anything involving calendars and meeting rooms. It is more important to get the right people than to rush through it. Deadlines are important, but it is even more important to get it right. It is probably about a week's work but is often spread out over two to three weeks. It is hard work, but you will know when you have done it well. You will either feel a sense of consensus or you won't. If you have sold the importance of it to your own self, you will find your way.

Define business objectives by Tom Khabaza

Business objectives are the origin of every data mining solution. This may seem obvious for how can there be a solution without an objective? Yet this statement defines the field of data mining; everything we do in data mining is informed by, and oriented towards, an objective in the business or domain in which we are operating. For this reason, defining the business objectives for a data mining project is the first key step from which everything else follows.

The importance of business objectives in data mining

It is possible to describe data mining or other analytical activities without reference to business context but to do so is to omit a crucial component. It's because business knowledge is central to every step of the data mining process. There are two reasons for this:

- Data necessarily provides a narrow or limited view of the world—the real world is always much richer than the data we collect about it—business knowledge is therefore always required in order to interpret this data and relate it back to reality
- Data mining and all forms of data analysis perform a function such as perception; therefore, like perception, they are determined by knowledge and directed towards goals

Defining the business objectives of a data mining project

Defining the business objectives of a data mining project can be broken down into four steps:

1. Understanding the overall goals of the business
2. Understanding the objectives of your client
3. Connecting these objectives to analytical results
4. Linking these results to data mining goals

Understanding the goals of the business

The first step in defining the business objective is to understand the overall goals of the business or the domain in which data mining is undertaken. These vary considerably depending on the business context, but even supposedly simple goals such as commercial ones can have surprising subtleties, for example:

- **Commercial goals**: In a commercial situation, it might be expected that the primary goal will always be to increase profit or revenue. However, most companies are considerably more sophisticated than this and focus on customer relationships, quality, and the market position of their products; they often include broader concerns such as ethical or social motives.
- **Service goals**: For many organizations and government organizations in particular, business objectives focus on the service they provide, although they may also have revenue goals.
- **Scientific goals**: Scientific organizations, and scientific departments within commercial or government organizations, often formulate their goals in terms of the development of knowledge.

Therefore, at the start of every data mining project, make sure that you understand the nature of the business and its goals.

Understanding the objectives of your client

Within a given business, different individuals or departments have their own objectives; these may be stated in writing or may be implicit in a job title or job description. Often these objectives are embodied in one or more **KPIs** (**key performance indicators**) that are used to measure success in or progress towards these objectives. When formulating business objectives for a data mining project, it is helpful to relate these to the objectives and KPIs of the client who commissions the analysis; this allows a direct understanding of the benefits that the project will bring in relation to the objectives of the client. For example, in a project for a client with customer management objectives, the business objectives may be expressed in terms of KPIs such as churn rate or cost of acquisition per customer.

Connecting specific objectives to analytical results

Once you have understood the overall goals of the organization and the objectives of your client, the next step is to select analytical results or targets that will have benefits from these objectives or KPIs.

This requires a combination of business understanding and analytical knowledge, and these results can be very varied; however, for data mining, they always fall into two categories:

- **Insight or new knowledge**: An analysis may reveal a new fact, for example, a relationship between customer attrition and the length of service or products held, or a complex relationship such as combinations of factors influencing customer retention. The key property of insight is that it is knowledge in the head; insight is usually delivered as a presentation or a report providing information, which will then be used by the business.
- **Predictive models**: Data mining also has the option to deliver results in the form of predictive models, that is, knowledge in an artificial form. Different kinds of predictive models (such as classification, regression, clustering, or association models) vary in how they are used, but they all have one thing in common: they can improve the information available about a specific example (such as a customer). They do this by adding information that has been derived by generalizing over a range of examples—this is the function of data mining algorithms.

In order to select analytical results that will contribute to a specific objective or KPI, consider how newly acquired knowledge or predictions of models will be used to further these objectives; the use of analytical results should always be at the front of a data miner's thoughts. One guideline is that management or strategic objectives are often served by insight, whereas operational decision making is often aided by predictive models. However, predictive models of more readable kinds such as decision trees and rule sets (and also analyses of the behavior of less-readable models) can be interpreted to deliver insight for management or strategic purposes.

Specifying your data mining goals

When defining business objectives for a data mining project, the data miner must simultaneously consider the likely data mining goals that these objectives will generate, such as segmenting the customer base in a particular way or predicting the likelihood of a specific customer behavior. This is necessary because the likely consequent data mining goals, considered in the light of what is technically possible, may lead to adjustments or refinements of the business objectives. The specification of data mining goals will be described in more detail in the *Translating your Business Objective into a Data Mining Objective by Dean Abbott* essay, later in this Appendix.

Assessing the situation by Meta Brown

Modern computers and software make it easy to dive into data and explore, so why delay the action with assessment and planning? Why not get right down to business and see what develops? Your organization, be it business, a government agency, or nonprofit, has a mission. Your role as a data miner is to provide relevant information in support of that mission. Assessment and planning early in the data mining process aligns your efforts with management goals and maximizes your chances of developing information that is actionable, rather than merely interesting.

Time is your most precious resource, so ensure that you use it to meet the expectations set out for you. There's a simple survival motivation—if you don't deliver what your manager requires, and on time, it won't be good for you. Yet you want more than mere survival. It feels good to uncover really useful information, to find something that was not obvious to others, or to give factual support to what was once just a hunch. Perhaps you have some personal theories you'd like to explore; you will be able to do that if you get the requirements covered first.

Does any project go so smoothly that no roadblocks are encountered along the way? Perhaps you will face unexpected resistance to access the data you require. The tech support contact that has always been so helpful may be replaced by someone who is less cooperative. The subject matter expert whose help you require may not consider your project a high priority. Early preparation readies you to effectively address problems such as these so you can get on with your work.

As you go through the assessment and planning steps, understand that you are about to do much more than thinking and chatting. Each item must be documented in writing. Sponsoring managers should review these documents and revise them if necessary. Documents must be easily available to the data miners as the project progresses. These documents provide guidance as you go about your everyday work, support when challenges arise, and verify that the information you deliver is consistent with the goals set at the start.

Taking inventory of resources

Gather all the documents that mention the resources to be used in your project. Think broadly when considering resources; these may include intangibles such as executive sponsorship and approvals as well as direct resources such as people participating in the project, budgets, and hardware. Any informal notes and verbal or informal understandings should now be properly documented.

Some documents may contain private or sensitive information that is not appropriate to include in the project file. For each document of this type, create a simple document outlining the nature of the resource mentioned and the information that data miners working on the project will require. In some instances, these replacement documents may be as simple as the originals with sensitive information such as passwords omitted and replaced with the name of the person who has access and knows the password. While the original document contains a lot of sensitive or irrelevant information, the replacement document may be a summary of any sections relevant to data mining project resources, again with reference to the original source document and appropriate contacts.

Create an outline listing the major resource types for your project. These will include items such as the project description, personnel, data sources, and other relevant categories. Using the information in the documents that you have saved, prepare a summary for each heading in your outline. For example, under personnel, list the names and roles (data miners assigned to the project, a business expert or subject matter expert, and so on) of each person, information about skills and experience, and other details. Data should include explanations of the general purpose of the data source, how it may be accessed, data dictionaries (detailed descriptions of fields and coding within the data source), and so on. The project description may be the most difficult section to complete. In most instances, you will find that there are gaps in either your level of understanding or in project resources, or in documentation.

Take action now to obtain additional documentation for any areas where your understanding about resources is still informal. In some instances, this may require only an e-mail to confirm that a certain resource is at your disposal. Other items may be far more challenging, requiring meetings and considerable discussion. Tackle these now. Most important are the elements of the project description itself.

By establishing a clear, documented explanation of the work to be done and the resources available, you will save time and other resources while the work is underway. Revise and complete your summaries of each resource type in the outline. Circulate the document to project participants for final review and make any necessary corrections.

Doubts or disagreements about the direction of your project can be resolved by reviewing the project description and its evaluation criteria. Resistance from data gatekeepers can be addressed by referring to the original correspondence assuring access. In most instances, you will be able to resolve questions and conflicts without requiring further involvement of the management, and when it is required, your preparation will smooth the path.

Reviewing requirements, assumptions, and constraints

Prepare summaries for your understanding of project requirements, assumptions, and constraints. The more thoroughly you determine business objectives, the easier it will be to prepare these summaries. In most instances, though, you will discover some gaps in your understanding. The requirements section should refer to the project description and also include information regarding executive sponsorship and success criteria. You must establish a clear understanding of expectations, especially of how results will be evaluated. Assumptions may be verifiable (such as the distribution of a particular variable in the dataset) or not (such as the future level of growth in GDP). State whether each assumption is verifiable and if so, how. Constraints may include deadlines, resources and technological limitations, boundaries related to privacy and legal obligations, and others.

A well-defined understanding of management expectations is the most valuable thing a data miner can have. Establishing this from the start maximizes the chances of producing results that will motivate an executive to take action. Remedy any obvious gap in information through additional research and discussions to complete the summary of requirements, assumptions, and constraints.

When your project is completed, you will be making a report to the management on the results in writing, as a presentation, or both. By introducing your report with a reminder of the goals and success criteria set by the management for you at the start, you will establish that the results you are about to show are exactly what was requested. It means that they must be evaluated based on the criteria that were set from the start, and that if the results meet those criteria, the executive must follow through with the next steps.

Identifying risks and defining contingencies

Using the documents that you have saved, including dark and creative thinking, list all the risks that could delay or halt your work; organize these in categories. For example, your work depends on computing resources. What could threaten your access to computing resources? Hardware failure, network failure, and competing demands for use of equipment are among the possibilities. For each of these, create a contingency plan with one or more alternatives. Each contingency plan should first include preventive measures. Often, a bit of maintenance or negotiation now avoids aggravation and delays later. If you encounter any risks for which a satisfactory contingency is not available, address this concern with the management. An influential advocate may be able to open up alternatives or assure a greater level of security. If any of the contingencies that you have planned require the assistance of others or access to resources not normally under your control, contact the parties involved and verify that the contingency is realistic.

When your project is threatened, you will be able to respond quickly and effectively if you have a clear contingency planned in advance. No executive is sympathetic to excuses about project delays, no matter how valid they are. Stand out from the crowd by making productive use of all your time, even when conditions make that difficult, and completing your work on time, even when others do not.

Defining terminology

Review the documents that you have created and saved earlier. Cull these, creating a list of abbreviations, acronyms, and terminology that may not be immediately understood by all the stakeholders. As you review materials, imagine that it will be read long after the project is completed by someone who has a good understanding of business in general, does not work in your organization, is not very familiar with your field, and is not a data miner. What terms would be less than clear if the reader were an outside consultant, a new employee, or a manager coming from a different department or industry?

Organize the terms into three categories: general business terms—those that are used in many organizations—organization-specific terms, and data mining terms. Pay particular attention to organization-specific terms, as these are often problematic for outsiders or for those reviewing older projects after internal changes have caused terminology to change. If you have not documented those terms, important points in your work may become incomprehensible over time. Define all the terms, making an effort to explain how these are used within your organization. Illustrate your definitions with examples that are relevant to the project.

A glossary of terminology is a resource that helps all the stakeholders to clearly understand one another.

As you proceed with your work, refer to the glossary occasionally and make an effort to add additional terms as they arise and improve on the definitions you have created. You may choose to refer to specific steps and results in the data mining project.

Never consider the glossary as completely finished; treat it as a living document.

When the time comes to prepare your final report, the glossary will remind you of what terms to use that can be clearly understood by the management as well as refining your own understanding of those terms. You may choose to include the glossary as an appendix to written reports. In any event, be sure that the glossary is archived with other project resources. It is an important resource, even for your own use, when reviewing projects at a later time.

Evaluating costs and benefits

Review the material that you have prepared earlier in the project assessment, particularly materials relating to project requirements and their success criteria. Extract goals and success metrics. If these are not already stated in monetary terms, they must be converted. For example, perhaps the success metric is the conversion rate for a marketing campaign, and the success criteria calls for action if the conversion rate improves by 5 percent for a particular intervention.

How much money will that bring in for the company? You may have to assemble several facts to determine the answer. If the current campaign results in 100,000 sales at an average of 50 dollars, meeting the success criteria implies an additional 100,000 sales, which means it need to be 5 percent of 50 dollars per sale, or at least 250,000 dollars in increased revenue. In the same manner, identify any costs associated with the alternatives you will investigate. Include these in your summary side-by-side with benefits.

The cost/benefit analysis is a reality check for both the data miner and the business. Data miners must be reminded of the difference between an interesting model and solid return for the business; business managers cannot dismiss analytics when the financial impact is made clear.

Keep in mind that you are a data miner and not an accountant, so keep the analysis simple. It must be reasonable but not perfect. If your project absolutely demands a sophisticated cost/benefit analysis, it may be worthwhile to enlist the aid of an appropriate expert in finance.

No part of your final report will be more important or compelling than the information that is expressed in terms of cold, hard dollars. Indeed, this varies little even in organizations that are not profit-making businesses. If you have performed a cost/benefit analysis at the start of your project, you have a good motivator for everyone involved. You can be certain that your effort is worthwhile and that executives will understand the significance of your findings, not in the statistical sense but in terms of financial impact to the organization.

Translating your business objective into a data mining objective by Dean Abbott

The business objectives use business language to describe the purpose of the data mining project. However, business objectives are not sufficiently specific to build predictive models; business objectives must be translated into data mining goals. These data mining objectives should be expressed in the language of data mining or data mining software so that the objectives are clear and reproducible.

For example, let's assume the federal government is trying to crack down on government-contracting invoice fraud. A broad business objective may be to identify fraudulent invoices more effectively from the millions of invoices submitted annually. A more specific business objective may be to develop predictive models to identify 100 invoices per month for investigators to examine that are highly likely to be fraudulent.

For the former, the business objective can be to create a data mining objective such as building classification models to predict the likelihood of an invoice being fraudulent. Note that this definition not only defines what type of model will be built (classification) but also the level of analysis to be used (each record is an invoice, rather than an invoice payee).

One could be more specific in the data mining definition to clarify the nature of the prediction. Rather than a single binary outcome of fraudulent versus nonfraudulent as the label for each invoice, if we hypothesize that models can be built more accurately and that the specific type of fraud should be predicted, our data mining objective can be rephrased as building classification models to predict the likelihood of an invoice belonging to each of the four types of invoice fraud.

One other aspect to consider in creating the data mining objective is that data mining projects require data miners with particular skill sets. The tuning of the business objective should keep in mind who will be performing the analysis so that there is sufficient matching of the skill set with the analyst.

The key to the translation – specifying target variables

As we have seen, the data mining objective(s) is a translation of the business objective, worded in the language of data mining. *Latent* in the data mining objective is perhaps the most critical part of the data mining objective definition: specification of one or more target variables. The very process of creating one or more columns in the data that are the target variables requires clarity and specificity in ways that can be finessed when only words are used in describing the data mining objective.

In the invoice fraud example, the very definition of *fraud* is key to the data mining modeling process. Two definitions are often considered in fraud detection. The first definition is the strict one, labeling an invoice as fraudulent if and only if the case has been prosecuted and the payee of the invoice has been convicted of fraud. The second definition is that of a looser, labeling an invoice as fraudulent if the invoice has been identified as being worthy of investigating further by one or more managers or agents. In the second definition, the invoice has failed the "smell test" but there is no proof yet that the invoice is fraudulent. Many more potential target variable definitions exist, but these two are each reasonable definitions for our consideration here.

Note that there are advantages and disadvantages of each option. The primary advantage of the first definition is clarity; all of those labeled 1 are clearly fraudulent. However, there are also several disadvantages. First, some invoices may have been fraudulent, but they did not meet the standard for a successful prosecution. Some may have been dismissed based on technicalities. Others may have had potential but were too complex to prosecute efficiently. Still others may have shown potential, but the agency did not have sufficient resources to pursue the case. The result is that many 0 values really have potential but are labeled the same as those cases that have no potential at all. In fact, there may be more of these ambiguous nonfraudulent invoices than there are fraudulent invoices in the data.

On the other hand, if we use the second definition, many cases labeled 1 may not be fraudulent after all, even if they appear suspicious upon first glance. In other words, some "fraudulent" labels are done prematurely; If we had waited long enough for the case to proceed, it would have been clear that the invoice was not fraudulent after all. Relaxed definitions of fraud can increase the number of invoices labeled as fraudulent in the data by a factor of 10 or more.

There is no perfect definition of a target variable. The definition should be formulated to match the business objective as completely as possible and to meet the core business objectives of the organization. It may be the case that the best match of a target variable definition with the business doesn't exist, and a compromised target variable must instead be selected. It is often the case that these compromises, while not desirable, enable the organization to build models that improve upon already established practices, and thus are still valuable.

Data mining success criteria – measuring how good the models actually are

The determination of what is considered as a good model is project-dependent and depends on the business success criterion or criteria. If the purpose of the model is to provide highly accurate predictions or decisions to be used by the business, measures of accuracy will be used. If interpretation of the business is what is of most interest, accuracy measures will not be used; instead, subjective measures of what provides maximum insight may be most desirable. Some projects may use a combination of both so that the most accurate model is not selected if a less accurate but more transparent model with nearly the same accuracy is available.

Success criteria for classification

For classification problems, the most frequent metrics for model selection in data mining include **Percent Correct Classification** (**PCC**); confusion matrix metrics such as precision and recall, sensitivity and specificity, Type I and Type II errors, and false alarms and false dismissals; and rank-ordered metrics such as Lift, Gain, ROC, and **Area Under the Curve** (**AUC**). AUC can be computed from any of the rank-ordered metrics.

PCC and the confusion matrix metrics are good when an entire population must be scored and acted on. Medical diagnoses are an example of this. If one will treat only a subset of the population, rank-ordering the population and acting on only a portion of those in that "select" group can be accomplished through metrics such as Lift, Gain, ROC, and AUC.

Also, any number of customized cost functions can be created from the quadrants of a confusion matrix. Most commonly, practitioners will weigh the quadrants to emphasize some errors over others as being particularly unwelcome. If one would like to reduce false alarms, for example, one could weigh these twice as much as false dismissals and create a single score base on the custom formula.

Success criteria for estimation

For continuous-valued estimation problems, metrics often used for assessing models are R^2, average error, **Mean Squared Error** (**MSE**), median error, average absolute error, and median absolute error. In each of these metrics, one first computes the error of an estimate, which is the actual value minus the predicted estimate. The metrics then sum errors over all the records in the data.

Average errors can be useful in determining whether the models are biased toward positive or negative errors. Average absolute errors are useful in estimating the magnitude of the errors (whether positive or negative). Analysts most often examine not only the overall value of the success criterion, but also examine the entire range of predicted values by considering scatter plots of actual versus predicted values or actual versus residuals (errors).

In principal, one can also include rank-ordered metrics such as AUC and Gain as candidates to estimate the success criteria, though they often are not included in data mining software for estimation problems. In these instances, one needs to create a customized success criterion.

Other customized success criteria

Sometimes none of the typical success criteria are sufficient to evaluate predictive models because they do not match the business objective. Consider the invoice fraud example described earlier. Let's assume that the purpose of the model is to identify 100 invoices per month to investigate from the hundreds of thousands of invoices submitted. If one builds a classification model and selects a model that maximizes PCC, we can be fooled into thinking that the best model as assessed by PCC is good, even though none of the top 100 invoices are good candidates for investigation. How is this possible? If there are 100,000 invoices submitted in a month, we are selecting only 0.1 percent of them for investigation. The model could be perfect for 99.9 percent of the population and miss what we care about the most, the top 100.

In situations such as this one, when there are very specific needs for the organization, it is best to consider customized cost functions. In this instance, we want to identify a population of 100 invoices such that it maximizes the chances of these 100 invoices being true alerts (not false alarms). What metric does this? No metric addresses this directly, though ROC curves are close to the idea. Instead, the best way to rank the models is the direct method, that is, pick the model that maximizes the true fraud alert rate in the top 100 invoices of the scored population, ignoring the rest of the population. Data miners should adjust their algorithm settings appropriately to focus the attention of the classifiers on accuracy at the top of the predicted probabilities, such as weighting the cost of false alarms higher than the errors estimating true alerts.

Another candidate for customized scoring functions include **Return On Investment** (**ROI**) or profit, where there is a fixed or variable cost associated with the treatment of a customer or transaction (a record in the data), and a fixed or variable return or benefit if the customer responds favorably. For example, if one is building a customer acquisition model, the cost is typically a fixed cost associated with mailing or calling the individual; the return is the estimated value of acquiring a new customer. For fraud detection, there is a cost associated with investigating the invoice or claim, and a gain associated with the successful recovery of the fraudulent dollar amount.

Note that for many customized success criteria, the actual predicted values are not nearly as important as the rank order of the predicted values. If one computes the cumulative net revenue as a customized cost function associated with a model, the predicted probability may never enter into the final report, except as a means to threshold the population into the "select" group (that is to be treated) and the "nonselect" group.

Produce a project plan – ensuring a realistic timeline by Keith McCormick

Since data mining is closely affiliated with other approaches, new practitioners of data mining often surprise their colleagues when they suggest that the data mining project will take many weeks. If one is confusing it with running ad hoc reports on an already identified problem area, the timeline discussed in this section may seem surprising. On one's very first data mining project, the new data miner may not feel fully prepared themselves. This section will explore each of the CRISP-DM phases and examine some considerations for estimating how long each phase will take. In general, something in the order of 8 to 20 weeks is probably a good rule of thumb.

Business understanding

There is a general agreement among veteran data miners that novice data miners do not spend enough time on business understanding. One of the challenges during business understanding is that it involves many voices throughout the enterprise. The junior analyst might not frequently attend meetings with C-level executives, but during this phase, it is always a good idea to work their way up the hierarchical chart until one reaches the decision maker who will be approving the actual deployed results of the data mining project. If the internal beneficiary of the project is not in attendance for at least one planning meeting, the project will probably be deployed via a slide presentation. One hopes that it is a slide presentation leavened with considerable insight, but it will still be just a slide presentation. If the project's ambition aims higher, it is critical to involve key decision making in the actual activity of business understanding, or at the very least, signing off on the conclusions of business understanding before the project begins in earnest.

As a result of having many players, business understanding cannot be rushed. This is not a phase where the data miner can burn the midnight oil and push forward on their own. It is good practice to assume the eight hours of progress each day may not be possible in this phase. Real progress can only be made in a group setting, and meetings can be hard to schedule. Although it may only require two to five days of solid work, it is a good idea to allow two weeks on the calendar to accomplish it. Finally, always remember to allow time to write the conclusions of each phase and to communicate those results to others. This is not to say that CRISP-DM phases come to an abrupt halt before the next phase can begin. This is not true. CRISP-DM tends to be highly iterative. Nonetheless, writing a business understanding report before moving on is being wise.

Phase	**About the phase**	**Duration**
Business understanding	2 to 5 days of solid work, but it is difficult to schedule. Give yourself plenty of "calendar time".	1 to 2 weeks
Data understanding	It helps in understanding whether: ▸ Analysts have direct access to the data ▸ Analysts have ready access to IT support ▸ There are delays in getting data	2 to 8 weeks

Phase	About the phase	Duration
Data preparation	Famously estimated to be 70 to 90 percent of the actual work hours of the data mining lead. "Clean" data doesn't eliminate this need, although it helps. Tread carefully ... data preparation can explode your timeline.	3 to 10 weeks*
Modeling	No model is ever optimal but diminishing returns kick in pretty early. An experienced modeler can make tremendous progress in a week as long as there is no residual data preparation.	1 to 2 weeks
Evaluation	Evaluation is usually not very time-consuming, but the following two factors can change that: ▸ Whether management needs a walk-through ▸ Whether you want to conduct a "dress rehearsal" on the current data	1 week*
Deployment	This phase will answer the following questions: ▸ What form will deployment take? ▸ Will deployment involve changes to the data warehouse? ▸ Will deployment be complex in real time?	1 to 6 weeks

Data understanding

Reasonable veterans of the process might quibble on this distinction, but a general tendency is for data understanding to be largely a group activity whereas data preparation is often a largely solitary one. Why? When the data miner is an outsider (either of the department or of the entire organization), he/she has to seek out allies who know some aspect of the organization's data that they do not. Even when a data miner and a subject matter expert are sitting side by side throughout the process, the most compelling data mining projects always involve some integration of data that has not been attempted before, leaving even the subject matter experts seeking help from others. When one only searches in standard tables that pre-exist the project, there is a considerable risk that what will be discovered has already been baked into a cake, that is, your discoveries might be limited to problems that have been at least partially addressed.

As a result, data understanding will tend to expand to the amount of time that you can allocate to it. One attempts to get access to as much relevant data as one can while still staying on schedule. One approach is to identify a true expert within each major department, getting an audience with them along with one's lead SME in attendance, and asking them what they have to offer. How long will this take? How many departments are there, and how many SMEs do you have to interview? A key step in the process is to mark the calendar with the arrival date of each piece of data—the contribution of each department. If this is not a factor in your project, the phase will go quicker. If you have direct access to all the data and do not rely on third parties to help you get it, the phase will go quicker.

Once the data is available in its raw form, you will have to explore it. Naturally, 50 variables tend be quicker than 1,200. While in statistics, one usually attempts all the univariates and bivariates, this is often impossible in data mining as the number of variables scale up. Still, some effort must be made to look at the individual pieces before data cleaning, data augmentation, and data integration can begin (during data preparation).

Don't forget to leave time for:

- A round of questioning with SMEs during and after data exploration
- Delays waiting for data to arrive a second time (if problems are found)
- Documenting what you have found
- Revisiting business understanding if you conclude that certain data is not available after all (or not available on schedule)

Data preparation

Where does all the time go? If the old adage that 70 to 90 percent of the project hours may be spent in activities associated with data understanding and this phrase is true, where are all of those hours being spent? The origin of this estimate is mysterious, and its source cannot be easily nailed down; however, even though most of them have acknowledged that there is no hard evidence to back it up, most agree that its percentage should be high. If your organization has super clean data stored in the latest data warehousing technology, will your experience be different, better? Does Big Data complicate, slow down data preparation?

The trick in understanding where the time goes is that data preparation comes in more than one flavor, and no data warehouse will eliminate all of it. CRISP-DM lists five: select, clean, construct, integrate, and format. Data in a data warehouse is there to support routine reporting and operating the business.

A really solid data warehouse may help with clean and format but will not likely help with select, construct, or integrate. Why? Let's investigate each in turn.

- **Select**: Data will be usually selected for reasons that are driven by the goals of the project and as such will not have been anticipated by the teams that are in charge with long term storage of data. Most data miners agree that sampling is a critical component of data mining. It is not a technology issue, nor is it a question of the increasingly vast amounts of data, and not all of it is relevant. Good modeling often requires balancing and always requires partitioning (training and test partitions). In short, the size of your data warehouse since its inception is not a good indicator of the size of your training data set. Assessing this and choosing the right data to model takes time, and that time must be allocated.
- **Clean**: If you have done a good job of building your data warehouse, this step is simplified. The less messy, the less time it would take; however, ensure that you make no mistake. Few data miners will ever encounter truly clean data in their careers. And even when it is clean, a null in the data warehouse might need to be a zero in the model of vice versa. Nonetheless, if the data has been thoroughly cleaned, this particular generic task might take less than a week. If it is not clean, there is almost no limit to the potential delays. One might even conclude that the data mining project must wait until the situation is addressed, first addressing the overall problem and only then cleaning for the purpose of a particular data mining project.
- **Construct**: At the risk of generalizing too much, this is the phase that gets data miners in trouble; the time consumer that they don't see coming, the destroyer of time lines, the endangerer of model quality. Quite simply, the best variables in one's model probably don't exist at the start of the project. A variable such as previous month spend/rolling 12 months spend is a good example. No variable such as this is stored in one's data warehouse but can be terribly useful in predicting changes in behavior. Their relevance has to be slowly ferreted out, their formulas have to be crafted often with much trial and error, and their efficacy must be shown. Then they have to be paraded in front of the algorithms along with dozens or hundreds of their siblings, awaiting the conclusion of dozens of modeling attempts. When you're done with the modeling, you will notice that it is often these kind of variables that are populating the top 10 list.
- **Integrate**: Most data miners anticipate this—the combining of data tables. In Modeler, this takes the form of merging, appending, and aggregating. However, one might assume that the queries that one needs already exist. Probably not. The data miner frequently has to go all the way back to the billing detail to calculate something that was lost in the aggregating done for reporting. In other words, it often has to be done all over again since the needs of reporting and the needs of the data miner are almost always different. Doing this over again takes time, usually a couple of weeks.

- **Format**: How compatible are the formatting decisions you have already made with the needs of your data mining software? Did you anticipate all the variable declarations, data formatting, file formatting, naming conventions, and so on as they apply to the modeler? Frankly, it's unlikely. There are always little, and not so little conflicts, that pop up between the way departments store data or how data is parsed in Modeler. Modeler is a powerful software, but it is not immune to little formatting conflicts. Few data miners define this task as fun, but it is usually present at least to a degree. If the data warehouse is in good shape and your infrastructure is fairly current, this task might be no more than a bump in the road, taking relatively less amount of time. Data mining as a discipline has matured, and as Modeler has matured as well; this task is less and less of an issue. One might get away with only a data or so. An experienced user of Modeler spots these issues early and might avoid most of them before they happen. As many as 20 or 30 years ago, business users dreaded trying to install a new printer, but formatting compatibility becomes less of an issue with each new release of analytics software.

Modeling

Modeling is the phase that gets all the attention. Many books are dedicated to it. You would think that you need to allocate the vast majority of time to this phase. Not quite!

8th Law of Data Mining, by *Tom Khabaza,* the **Value Law**, states:

> *"The value of data mining results is not determined by the accuracy or stability of predictive models".*

In the clever article of *Dorian Pyle* about *rules not to follow*, the fifth rule is **Find the best algorithms** in which he urges the reader to spend all of their available time on modeling.

The blog post written by *Will Dwinell* take on this, quoted later, is a third data miner's voice in the chorus. Certainly all the authors of this cookbook would join in saying that poor workmanship in the earlier phases will not be compensated for spending extra time on modeling. So how do you know how much time to spend? One to two weeks. There you go—a rare direct recommendation. If you have more time to spend than that, consider spending the time in another phase, particularly in data understanding and data preparation.

How should the time be spent? Expect to build several dozen models such as different algorithms, difference settings, balanced and not balanced, and variations on the target variable. The details could, and have, make a book, but you will hit economies of scale in that one- to two-week time frame, and often in just the first week. By then, you will be fighting for that last 1 percent of increase in accuracy. In time, with experience, the modeling phase may even start to feel like a valediction of sorts, eventually arriving at this phase with a sense of relief that the toughest part is over.

Evaluation

Will Dwinell wrote a blog post on this subject entitled *Data Mining and Predictive Analytics*:

> *Within the time allotted for any empirical modeling project, the analyst must decide how to allocate time for various aspects of the process. As is the case with any finite resource, more time spent on this means less time spent on that. I suspect that many modelers enjoy the actual modeling part of the job most. It is easy to try "one more" algorithm: Already tried logistic regression and a neural network? Try CART next.*
>
> *Of course, more time spent on the modeling part of this means less time spent on other things. An important consideration for optimizing model performance, then, is: Which tasks deserve more time, and which less?*
>
> *Experimenting with modeling algorithms at the end of a project will no doubt produce some improvements, and it is not argued here that such efforts be dropped. However, work done earlier in the project establishes an upper limit on model performance. I suggest emphasizing data clean-up (especially missing value imputation) and creative design of new features (ratios of raw features, etc.) as being much more likely to make the model's job easier and produce better performance.*

A fair question is, what is the difference between the assessment task of modeling and the evaluation phase? Revisiting the *8th Law of Data Mining* is in order. Tools such as Lift, AUC, overall accuracy, and so on, are just those tools. They help us sort through dozens of model variations that due diligence requires us to examine during the modeling phase. When we get to the evaluation phase, however, we must remind ourselves that companies don't earn ROI on Lift (well, certainly not directly, they don't). What was the purpose of the data mining model in the first place? Reduce marketing expense—well, how much does the model help us reduce marketing expense. In other words, in this phase, we must translate the data mining question back into the language of the business question and evaluate the efficacy in business terms.

Time to get that internal customer back into the meeting room. Only with the help of management can we choose from the semifinalists the models that emerged from the modeling phase showing promise on the technical criteria. It is fine to choose those models on the basis of a criterion that is one generation removed from the business criteria because evaluation can be time-consuming and might require the analyst to collaborate with members of the marketing team, or the finance team, or the operations team to get their numbers straight. One does not do that analysis on 50 or 100 models. But the number of promising models is narrowed down to the range of three to eight; it is time for the actual beneficiaries of the model with the business to help chose the final models. Although, it is possible for this to take just a week or so, it is also possible that it might take several weeks. Often evaluation takes the form of a "dress rehearsal"—that is for a month or more, running the business on two parallel tracks. The first track is the way it has always been done, and the second track is in a way informed by the chosen model.

Perhaps it is in an experimental region or for a randomly chosen group of customers, but it is the ultimate test. Deciding how to complete work on this phase depends on the nature of the stakes and the project's budget, but naturally the duration can vary wildly as a result of it. Most internal customers, however, will recognize that when you have entered this phase, the potential for saving or for revenue gain has already arrived, and that often the analysis team can breathe a sigh of relief at this point, surrendering part of the responsibility to other parties. If you are working in an organization that has access to IBM **Collaboration and Deployment Services** (**C and DS**) or IBM Decision Management, the role of those packages will wax as the role of modeler will begin to wane.

Deployment

Deployment truly deserves its own book, perhaps even its own cookbook. It is even more difficult to generalize about this phase than the others, because for other phases, we can assume that as a reader of this book you are using Modeler for data preparation and modeling. We cannot assume very much at all about how you plan to deploy. Will you deploy in real time or in batch? Will you have the IBM deployment resources mentioned at the end of the *Evaluation* section. If you are deploying directly to a modeler client, a week is probably realistic.

What is involved? In theory, all you are doing is changing the source data and running the exact same stream on the current data; however, in practice you will not want to do that. You will want to revisit your Modeler streams and ensure that only transformations (and there will be lots of them) that are necessary at deployment are present. In other words, remove derived nodes that represent inputs that were considered but rejected. You might also discover some efficiencies that escaped your attention during modeling when speed was not as important as accuracy. Now on to deployment where accuracy has been established but speed needs to be maximized.

You may have to call a meeting to discuss topics that might not sound like they are in the analyst's bailiwick such as interface design or executive dashboards. This is all for the good, frankly, because it ensures that the model will be utilized. Isn't that the goal? If more elaborate forms of deployment are considered such as real-time deployment, the deployment phase can be equal in time and scope to the other phases combined. All of the estimates of data preparation being 70 to 90 percent of the scope did not envision the intricacies of real-time deployment. It is almost like a second project but can absolutely be worth it because the possibilities for ROI are compelling.

Deployment is a good candidate for the second prize next to business understanding in the phase that far too many data miners invest too little in. No project can really achieve anything without either. Without business understanding, you run the real risk of *solving* the wrong problem. In the final phase, an impressive model that never rises above the status of a slide deck is always inferior to a competent model that is actually deployed.

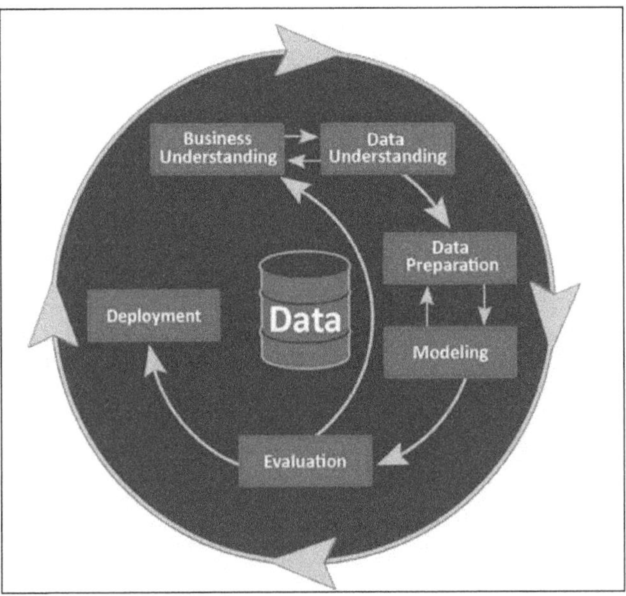

Index

Symbols

A

B

C

D

E

F

N

O

P

Q

R

S

T

U

W

Thank you for buying
IBM SPSS Modeler Cookbook

About Packt Publishing

Packt, pronounced 'packed', published its first book "*Mastering phpMyAdmin for Effective MySQL Management*" in April 2004 and subsequently continued to specialize in publishing highly focused books on specific technologies and solutions.

Our books and publications share the experiences of your fellow IT professionals in adapting and customizing today's systems, applications, and frameworks. Our solution-based books give you the knowledge and power to customize the software and technologies you're using to get the job done. Packt books are more specific and less general than the IT books you have seen in the past. Our unique business model allows us to bring you more focused information, giving you more of what you need to know, and less of what you don't.

Packt is a modern, yet unique publishing company, which focuses on producing quality, cutting-edge books for communities of developers, administrators, and newbies alike. For more information, please visit our website: `www.PacktPub.com`.

About Packt Enterprise

In 2010, Packt launched two new brands, Packt Enterprise and Packt Open Source, in order to continue its focus on specialization. This book is part of the Packt Enterprise brand, home to books published on enterprise software - software created by major vendors, including (but not limited to) IBM, Microsoft and Oracle, often for use in other corporations. Its titles will offer information relevant to a range of users of this software, including administrators, developers, architects, and end users.

Writing for Packt

We welcome all inquiries from people who are interested in authoring. Book proposals should be sent to `author@packtpub.com`. If your book idea is still at an early stage and you would like to discuss it first before writing a formal book proposal, contact us; one of our commissioning editors will get in touch with you.

We're not just looking for published authors; if you have strong technical skills but no writing experience, our experienced editors can help you develop a writing career, or simply get some additional reward for your expertise.

IBM Cognos Business Intelligence 10.1 Dashboarding Cookbook

Working with dashboards in IBM Cognos BI 10.1: Design, distribute, and collaborate

IBM Cognos Business Intelligence 10.1 Dashboarding Cookbook

ISBN: 978-1-84968-582-5 Paperback: 206 pages

Working with dashboards in IBM Cognos BI 10.1: Design, distribute, and collaborate

1. Exploring and interacting with IBM Cognos Business Insight and Business Insight Advanced
2. Creating dashboards in IBM Cognos Business Insight and Business Insight Advanced
3. Sharing and Collaborating on Dashboards using portlets
4. Best practices related to Dashboards in Cognos 10.1

IBM DB2 9.7 Advanced Administration Cookbook

Over 100 recipes focused on advanced administration tasks to build and configure powerful databases with IBM DB2

Adrian Neagu Robert Pelletier [PACKT] enterprise

IBM DB2 9.7 Advanced Administration Cookbook

ISBN: 978-1-84968-332-6 Paperback: 480 pages

Over 100 recipes focused on advanced administration tasks to build and configure powerful databases with IBM DB2

1. Master all the important aspects of administration from instances to IBM's newest High Availability technology pureScale with this book and e-book
2. Learn to implement key security features to harden your database's security against hackers and intruders
3. Empower your databases by building efficient data configuration using MDC and clustered tables

Please check **www.PacktPub.com** for information on our titles

IBM Cognos Business Intelligence

Discover the practical approach to BI with IBM Cognos Business Intelligence

Foreword by Gene Villeneuve, Director Product Management Interactive Analytics & BI, Business Analytics, IBM

Dustin Adkison 

IBM Cognos Business Intelligence

ISBN: 978-1-84968-356-2 Paperback: 318 pages

Discover the practical approach to BI with IBM Cognos Business Intelligence

1. Learn how to better administer your IBM Cognos 10 environment in order to improve productivity and efficiency
2. Empower your business with the latest Business Intelligence (BI) tools
3. Discover advanced tools and knowledge that can greatly improve daily tasks and analysis.
4. Explore the new interfaces of IBM Cognos 10

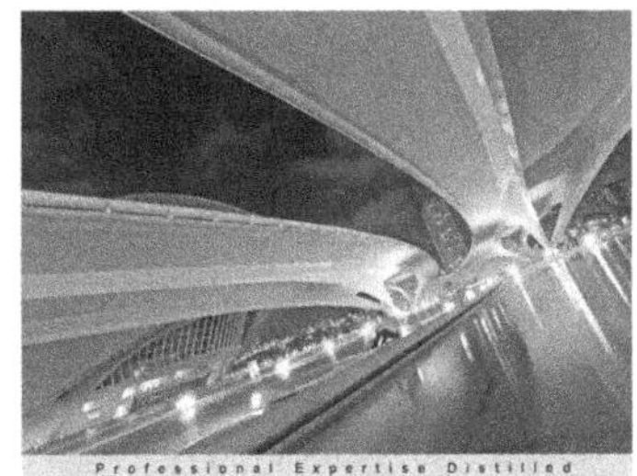

Professional Expertise Distilled

IBM Cognos TM1 Developer's Certification Guide

Fast track your way to COG-310 certification

IBM Cognos TM1 Developer's Certification guide

ISBN: 978-1-84968-490-3 Paperback: 240 pages

Fast track your way to COG-310 certification!

1. Successfully clear COG-310 certification
2. Master the major components that make up Cognos TM1 and learn the function of each
3. Understand the advantages of using Rules versus Turbo Integrator
4. This book provides a perfect study outline and self-test for each exam topic

Please check **www.PacktPub.com** for information on our titles

CPSIA information can be obtained
at www.ICGtesting.com
Printed in the USA
FFHW011929261219
57166034-62717FF